Lone Star Politics

Theories, Concepts, and Political Activity in Texas

Written and edited by Darrell Lovell

Lone Star College University Park

cognella® | ACADEMIC PUBLISHING

Bassim Hamadeh, CEO and Publisher

Kassie Graves, Director of Acquisitions and Sales

Jamie Giganti, Senior Managing Editor

Miguel Macias, Senior Graphic Designer

Bob Farrell, Acquisitions Editor

Gem Rabanera, Project Editor

Alexa Lucido, Licensing Specialist

Abbey Hastings, Associate Production Editor

Don Kesner, Interior Designer

ISBN: 978-1-5165-2477-8 (pbk) / 978-1-5165-2478-5 (br)

Lone Star Politics

Theories, Concepts, and Political Activity in Texas

Contents

Chapter 1: Texas and the Political Culture It Has Created 2

Political Culture: Relationship between a Government and its People 3

    Political Culture 4

Reading 1.1: *Political Culture* by Edward Weisband and Courtney I.P. Thomas 5

    Where Does Texas Fall? 12

One-Party Dominance 12

    Social and Economic Conservatism 13

    Low Voter Turnout 13

    Provincialism 14

Demographics of Texas: People, Places, and Money 15

    People in Texas 15

    Anglos 15

    Hispanics 17

    African Americans 18

Cultural Diversity and Changes in Political Culture 19

    Economy 19

    Agriculture 20

    Oil 20

    Technology 21

    Transition from Rural to Urban 22

Summary 23

    Can That Change? 24

References 24

Chapter 2: The Evolution and Impact of the Texas Constitution 26

The Role of a State Constitution 27

    Positive vs. Negative Rights 29

The Texas Constitution over the Years 30

    Constitution of 1827: Mexican Rule and the State of Coahulia y Tejas 31

    Constitution of 1836: The Republic of Texas 31

      Constitution of 1845: Joining the United States..33

      Constitution of 1861: Joining the Confederacy 34

      Constitutions of 1866 and 1869: Back to the Union and Reconstruction 35

      Constitution of 1876: Response to Reconstruction...36

   The Texas Constitution Today...37

      Role of the Bill of Rights...38

   The Power and Structure of Government..39

      Education 40

      Local Governments 41

      Article XVI: The Catch-All...41

   The Amendment Process: Changing the Constitution and the Reasons for Change 42

   Are Voters Overwhelmed?...43

   The US or Texas Model: Which Constitution Fits Best? 45

   Summary..46

   References 46

Chapter 3: Federalism and Texas 48

   US Federalism and Basic Governing Systems..49

      Systems of Federalism 50

   The Role of the States..51

   Use of the Necessary and Proper Clause and the Commerce 52

   Clause to Develop Informal Power

   Delegated Powers: Federal vs. State...54

      Federal Delegated Powers 54

      State Powers: Constitutional Guarantees..55

      State Limitations..57

   The Rise of Coercive Federalism..58

   The Effects of Federalism...60

      Devolution 60

      Laboratory Effect 62

   Summary..63

   References 63

Chapter 4: The Role of Local Governments in Texas 65

   Types of Government...66

      Municipalities (Cities)..67

      General Law vs. Home Rule 68

      Counties 71

      Special Districts 75

   Council of Governments...78

Summary..78

References 79

Chapter 5: The Role of the Executive Branch in Texas: Weak Lead Officials and the Administration They Function Within....... 80

Reading 5.1: *Governors Turn Pro: Separation of Powers and the*..............................81
Institutionalization of the American Governorship by Ann O'M Bowman et al.

Qualifications for the Office of Governor...87

Examining Formal and Informal Powers...88

Reading 5.2: *Do Governors Matter? Budgeting Rules and the Politics* 88
of State Policymaking by Charles Barrilleaux and Michael Berkman

Formal Powers of the Texas Governor 92

   Military Power...92

   Executive Power: Executive Orders, Administration, and Appointments....................93

   Legislative Powers: Messages and Special Sessions..94

   Veto Power: Control over Budget and Policy...94

Reading 5.3: *Why Do Governors Issue Vetoes? The Impact of*....................................95
Individual and Institutional Influences by Carl E. Klamer and Andrew Karch

Informal Powers of the Governor..103

Applying Theory to Texas Administration: Max Weber and Georg Hegel.........................104

Reading 5.4: *The Governor and the Executive Branch* by Cal Jilson........................106

Summary: How Powerful Should the Governor Be? 116

References 117

Chapter 6: Texas's Republican Legislature and the Impact it Has on the State 118

Understanding Legislator Behavior...119

   What Is a Legislator's "Home Style"? 119

   Trustee vs. Delegate 121

Structure of the Texas Legislature...122

   Bicameral Structure and Makeup of Elected Officials 122

Chamber Leadership...125

   Lieutenant Governor 126

   Speaker of the House 127

Logjam: The Effects of a Biennial Session? 128

Policy-Making Process 130

Introduction of Bills...131

Committee Discourse 132

Calendars 135

Floor Debate 136

The Home of the Filibuster 137

Conference Committee Effect 138

Influence of the Governor...139

Potential Reform...139

Summary...140

References 141

Chapter 7: The Texas Judiciary by Methias Plank.....................142

The Cultural Underpinnings of the Texas Judiciary 142

Structure of the Texas Courts...143

Types of Courts...144

The Legal Framework..146

Judicial Selection 148

Issues Related to Texas Judicial Politics...152

Crime and Punishment in Texas..153

The Death Penalty..153

Juvenile Crime 154

Rehabilitation...155

Summary...156

References 157

Chapter 8: Views on Public and Social Policy in a Conservative Texas..158

Understanding Policy: A Look at the Policy Process Framework.............159

Social and Public Policy in Texas: Major Debates 161

Education 161

Reading 8.1: Vestigial Parts by Erica Grieder 163

Healthcare 171

Moral Policies...173

Reading 8.2: The Coming Crack-Up by Erica Grieder 175

Environmental Policy..179

Summary...181

References 182

Chapter 9: Economics and the State of Texas 183

Reading 9.1: The Texas Model by Erica Grieder 184

Monetary Versus Fiscal Policy 191

Income Tax in Texas 192

    Current Texas Taxes...193

State Funds and Spending...196

The Budget Process...198

Budget and Economic Policy Debates & Crisis 201

    Education Funding...201

Summary...203

References 203

Chapter 10: Opinion, Ideology, and Voting in Texas 205

Reading 10.1: *Political Ideology* by Darrell Lovell...206

History of Voting in Texas...211

    Tradition of Exclusion 212

    White Primaries and White-Only Political Parties...212

    Poll Taxes..213

    Response and the Lead-up to Major Change with the Voting Rights Act of 1965 214

Reading 10.2: *The Return of Immigrant Voting: Demographic Change
and Political Mobilization* by Ron Hayduk..215

    Voter Requirements 230

Reading 10.3: *Texas House District* by John Klemanski and David Dulio.....................230

Summary: Why Has Voting Waned?...236

References 237

Chapter 11: The Structure and Process of Elections and
Successful—and Sometimes Harmful—Campaigns 239

Governing the Elections...240

Types of Elections...242

    Primaries 242

    General Elections...244

    Special Elections..244

Indicators of Success: Incumbency, Running Unopposed, and Redistricting.....................245

Campaign Finance in Texas: The Real Wild West 248

Reading 11.1: *Money, Politics, and Policy: Campaign Finance* 249
Before and After Citizens United by R. Sam Garrett

Campaigning Beyond Money 258

Texas and the 2016 Election..261

Measured Backing of Trump...262

Dollars Equal Votes 267

Incumbents Reign Supreme 270

Counties Changing Colors 271

What's it All Mean? 272

Summary...273

References 273

Chapter 12: Parties and Their Role in the Political Evolution of Texas..........................275

Basics of Political Parties..276

    Function of a Political Party...276

Political Party Theories 277

Issue Identification in Texas..278

Reading 12.1: *Democratic Texas* by Erica Grieder 280

Reading 12.2: *The Rise of the Right* by Erica Grieder 288

The Major Player and the Foil: Republicans and Democrats Today ...293

Party Organization in Texas 295

    Temporary Structure..296

    Permanent Structure 296

Third Parties 298

    Examples of Third Parties in Texas...299

References 300

Chapter 13: Outside Advocates: The Role of Interest Groups in Texas's Political System................301

Why We Join Interest Groups 302

Types of Interest Groups and those Operating in Texas..................303

Reading 13.1: *Interest Groups in Texas* by Cal Jillson.....................304

The Role of Interest Groups 313

Reading 13.2: *Theory of Emergent and Changing Interest Group Tactics*.............314

by Michael M. Franz

Interest Group Tactics 318

Reading 13.3: *Interests and Interest Groups* by Thomas Holyoke...........319

    Outsider Tactics: Gaining Attention through Mobilization................322

Summary...323

References 324

CHAPTER 1

Texas and the Political Culture It Has Created

June 26, 2015 will long be remembered in American history. On that day, the US Supreme Court, citing the Fourteenth Amendment of the US Constitution, made a ruling allowing same-sex couples to marry nationwide. In this landmark decision, the court ruled that same-sex couples living in the United States have the same rights as opposite-sex couples, in particular the right to financial interdependence and to enter into a binding union of marriage.

The court's 5–4 decision settled a debate that had raged for two decades during which states and plaintiffs had battled regarding access to marriage. The underlying argument was how much power a state had to limit, or make decisions regarding, its citizens' ability to do what they deemed requisite in pursuit of their lives, liberty, and/or pursuit of happiness. Thirty-seven states of the Union had already passed legislation allowing same-sex marriage. Thirteen states had yet to change their existing laws.

Texas was one of those thirteen. The state, long considered a conservative stronghold, had struck down attempts within the state to allow same-sex couples to even apply for, much less obtain, a marriage certificate and to enjoy the same financial benefits as opposite-sex couples.

Immediately after the decision was handed down, Texas jumped to the forefront of the debate. Governor Greg Abbott denounced the decision on his Twitter feed, stating that the government of Texas would stand up for what it and its base believed. State Attorney General Ken Paxton cautioned county clerks not to issue marriage certificates to same-sex couples, owing to the process of working through the legislation on the administrative side.

On the surface, the advice was reasonable. Applying for a certificate that the bureaucracy would later void or demand to be submitted in a different form would seem like an exercise in futility. But the actions were not taken that way.

Texas's reputation precedes itself. Members of the state's brass had taken a stance in their political campaigns against issues like same-sex marriage, abortion, and other moral matters that conflicted with the views of their overwhelmingly conservative base. Although the state's actions were not out of the ordinary and could have been construed as reasonable, the state was the lead "villain" in the fight against the ruling.

That outspoken bravado has been a hallmark of Texas politics. From day one, the state has taken its stances seriously and built itself and its government on the issues and beliefs that the majority of its citizens identify with in their own personal politics.

Any examination of Texas and its government must start at this point.

Texas prides itself on what its people are and believe as much as on how they act. Texas provides a classic case of a state that has built an identity and resists, for better or worse, anything that forces a change. As Governor Abbott and his lead legal counsel showed in their response to the nationwide approval of same-sex marriage, Texas politicians—and their constituents, by extension—rarely shy away from the spotlight in favor of conceding.

In the initial chapter of this book, we'll discuss the origins of that nature and how it has embedded itself in the culture of Texas. This chapter also looks at how basic forms of democracy have manifested themselves in Texas and how the state has accommodated itself to those theories. Last, although the state has an identity, how have Texas's citizens throughout the state progressed and evolved?

Political Culture: Relationship between a Government and its People

At any level of government, the first basic question to be analyzed is: What type of relationship does it have with its people? This question drives the most basic forms of government and determines how the relationship will be carried forward. Will the government be proactive? What are the issues or responsibilities on which the government performs or acts? What access do people have to their decision makers? These are all questions that surround the relationship between the government and its people and how it carries out its basic functions.

In truth, no one factor or group of factors will provide a full view of the scope of this relationship. The variables and degrees of opinions and issues included in this equation are immense, but there is a way to pare it down and understand it from an aggregate level. To do this, we can use political culture.

Political Culture

Daniel Elazar (1972) provided context to political culture with his study of how various segments of the country viewed the role of their government. By evaluating the attitudes, beliefs, common practices, and values of people in the community, Elazar was able to start to group these cultures together. He defined political culture as "the particular pattern of orientation to political action in which each political system is imbedded." Dissecting that definition, we find that political culture falls in line with the idea that the people define the role of their government.

Elazar outlines three types of cultures that dominate the landscape in the United States. First is individualistic culture, or the practice of imploring a government to take a negative view of administrative and political activity. By "negative," I do not mean that it should take negative action; that would be solely up to the individual to decide. In an individualistic political culture, the government takes limited actions in areas defined by the will of the people. The main goal of the government is to facilitate the advancement of its citizens, not through activity but by making sure that there are avenues for attaining the types of success they seek.

Individualistic political culture is most friendly to private activity. Instead of taking action to provide or shape a good society with a heavy hand, the government under this culture type would advocate for private incentives. That could be private incentives for individuals or for outside systems—the corporate or business system, for example. Making the state amenable to business would be an act of individualistic political culture.

Operating in the political realm under individualistic circumstances often breeds the backroom or "dirty" politics that we associate with the modern political system. With the emphasis on individual attainment, there is more room for professional politics, where "pork-barreling" and "logrolling" are accepted practices. The Ohio River Valley is the primary home of the individualistic culture.

Elazar places moralistic culture at the other end of the spectrum. Instead of viewing the term "moralistic," which can be a hot-button one, in the literal sense, Elazar uses the tag to indicate a culture of government that is positive in ensuring a "good" society. Under these stipulations, the government would be endowed with the power to take actions and make decisions with the intent of creating a society that is best for the whole instead of primarily for individual attainment.

A moralistic political culture mandates that governments take on issues and make decisions that have broad, sweeping effects. The goal under these circumstances would be to make decisions based on the greater good: what is in the best interest of all, not necessarily what will promote individual achievement. In doing so, the government is seen as a positive force. In this case, it is tasked with providing services or systems that ensure the implementation of various activities instead of leaving them in the hands of individuals. The approach is holistic in nature and enables the government to act under the commonwealth concept, which states that the good of the public is the main goal and may come, in many cases, at the sacrifice of individual activity. Moralistic culture is dominant in states such as Oregon, Michigan, and Wisconsin as well as the New England states.

Finally, there is traditionalistic culture. Under the previous two cultures, government is proactive in a sense: whether in a negative or positive way, government has a specific role to play in how individuals go about their daily lives. The government looks to move society forward. In a traditionalistic culture, the main goal of the government is to preserve the tried and true. Instead of being positive or negative, the government is tasked with maintaining the status quo.

Traditionalistic political culture is likely the most debated of the three and poses an interesting question: To remain traditionalistic, how much advancement is too much? Governments and societies advance regardless of terminology. Thus, it is impossible to truly preserve the status quo. What this term really means is advancing society while retaining the roots of a culture, which can include views on issues, the role of government, or social matters and activities that are acceptable and protected within a state or region.

Reading 1.1

Political Culture
From *Political Culture and the Making of Modern Nation-States*
Edward Weisband and Courtney I. P. Thomas[1]

Key Concepts

Political Culture

Political culture refers to the ideas, beliefs, values, traditions, and practices that provide the foundation for a political system. All culture is **constructed** rather than the product of **nature** or **predestination**. It is the product of history, contingency, environment, and other variables that interact to frame social, political, and economic attachments. For this reason, every country or **state** in the international system has its own unique political culture. States vary widely in terms of leadership, representation, civil and human rights, taxation, entitlements, and rule of law. Even countries in the same region will often have dramatically different political structures and values. For example, democratic ideals developed differently in England, where a strong nobility limited the powers of the monarch, from how they did in France, where the absolute monarch was overthrown by a middle-class revolution.

---

1   Edward Weisband and Courtney I. P. Thomas, "Political Culture," *Political Culture and the Making of Modern Nation-States*, pp. 5-6, 13-16, 274. Copyright © 2014 by Taylor & Francis Group. Reprinted with permission.

However, over the past three hundred years the international system has developed its own political culture, one that is defined by **states**, **nations**, **sovereignty**, **nonintervention**, **legitimacy**, **citizenship**, and **self-determination**. These constructions emerged in Europe in the aftermath of the Second Agricultural Revolution and were refined over centuries of revolution, warfare, and diplomacy. They were then exported globally through colonialism, first to the New World and then to Africa and Asia. Today, they are the foundational institutions of international relations. However, as we will see, the imposition of these modern values on cultures beholden to traditional communal values has created challenges for international order that have often resulted in political oppression, instability, and violence.

In recent decades multiculturalism has become an important political value in the international system. As a nation of immigrants, the United States has struggled to create a multicultural society throughout its history. It has tackled slavery, ethnic cleansing, structural discrimination, class bias, as well as gender and income inequality. Various forms of inequality persist in contemporary American society. Many European countries are today confronting multicultural pressures in unique ways. Great Britain, for example, has experienced a large influx of Indian and Pakistani immigrants in recent decades. These immigrant populations have brought ethnic, religious, and linguistic diversity to British society as well as political challenges associated with assimilation and coexistence. Similarly, French society has experienced large-scale immigration from its former colonies in North Africa consisting predominantly of Muslim and Arabic-speaking persons, and thus it has struggled to accommodate cultural and religious differences. In 2010, for example, France passed a law that banned face-covering headwear in public areas. This prohibition extended to traditional Muslim veils such as the niqab and burqa. This has been a controversial policy as it appears to limit religious expression among devout Muslim women in France. But its legal validity was confirmed by the European Court of Human Rights in 2014 on the grounds that a person's complete social presence constituted a human right that would be violated if females were to cover their full face in society. European societies thus struggle to define appropriate balances between their own cultural ways of life and immigrant traditions and values as they attempt to incorporate increasingly diverse populations into historically homogenous societies. As a result, they are challenged to create new political cultures that emphasize multicultural toleration, acceptance, and support alongside national cohesion.

ETHNOCENTRISM AND CULTURAL RELATIVISM

When confronted with new or different cultural traditions, values, or behaviors we may fall into one of two traps: ethnocentrism or cultural relativism. **Ethnocentrism** inheres in a set of beliefs or attitudes that assert that one's own culture is superior while all other cultures are, by extension, inferior. Persons gripped by ethnocentric views or opinions tend to judge, sometimes to condemn, different cultures or alternative cultural values through the lens of their own. In this, they perceive traditions, values, and practices other than their own against standards and sometimes prejudices set by their own value systems. In doing so, they risk falling into the traps of prejudgment and, thus, even prejudice. A sign of this is the assertion that other cultures are "primitive" or "backward." This reflects a failure to frame other cultural practices without understanding their motivations, intentions, or purposes.

Unlike ethnocentrism, **cultural relativism** adheres to the belief that cultural practices and traditions can never be judged critically. Cultural relativism is readily associated with **moral relativism**, a set of attitudes dismissive of any universal moral or ethical standard. This assumes that all cultural practices and values, regardless of their substance, are equally valid and thus defensible simply because they are justified within a culture. The problem with this kind of cultural relativism is that it can promote indifference to human suffering in the face of cruelty or oppression. The inferior role and status imposed on women in many cultures represent a set of issues in which relativism veers toward toleration of human subjugation, that is, toward acceptance of forms of brutality that must never be tolerated. Thus, it is one thing to attempt to understand a culture within the frames of its own meanings, but it is another to turn away from social injustices perpetrated by those who validate social practices on the basis of their own cultural values or traditions. As we shall see, many cultural practices—such as female genital mutilation, honor killings, discrimination, racism, sexism, nationalism, and ethnic cleansing—appear to be culturally acceptable but are morally and ethically deplorable. Relativism does not make them morally right. In our efforts to better understand different cultures and to avoid the dangerous tendencies associated with ethnocentrism, it is essential that we also guard against the moral ambiguities that can attend attitudes of cultural relativism.

CULTURE, ANXIETY, AND THE DENIAL OF DEATH

We receive culture much as we receive life: from our bond with nurturing others. The oneness between child and nurturer begins in the womb and continues throughout infancy. Infants do not know how to distinguish between the self and the nurturing other. On the contrary, the self and the world are indistinguishable to the infant consciousness; the infant and the nurturer are one from the infant's perspective. Eventually children develop the capacity for an understanding of themselves as autonomous subjects among others in the world. Separation from the nurturing other becomes an essential project in the development of person hood, a critical moment in the enculturation process. The separation of the self from the nurturing other is inevitable. It is through this process of separation that human beings emerge as independent persons. Infants gradually become aware of a distinction between themselves and their nurturers. As they become aware of the boundary between themselves and others, they begin to develop a pervasive sense of vulnerability. Infants and the very young cannot survive independent of others. And yet, no matter how closely persons intertwine their lives with others, all human beings face life and death in their own skins, that is, as beings separate or distinct from others. One author has observed, for example, that for each of us "loneliness" is a way of life. This points toward a primal anxiety universal to the human condition. As Joan Riviere writes, "helplessness is the deepest source of anxiety in human beings."[1] Rollo May elaborates, "anxiety is the experience of the threat of imminent non-being. … Anxiety is not something we 'have' but something we 'are.'"[2] In that sense, "anxiety strikes at the center core of [our] self-esteem and [our] sense of value as a self. … Anxiety overwhelms the person's awareness of existence, blots out the sense of time, dulls the memory of the past, and erases the future."[3] Anxiety is who we are; it stands as a definitive and fundamental characteristic of the human condition from which no one can escape and with which we must struggle throughout our lives. It cannot be eliminated. As Paul Tillich writes, "it belongs to existence itself."[4] Culture responds to primal anxiety. Anxiety derives from the sense of nothingness, of loneliness in the human condition, of mortality. Culture lends life meaning and embeds individuals within communities, even to the point that it foments a sense of immortality by means of cultural continuity. Through culture persons can deepen their senses of metaphysical meaning, transcendence, or uniqueness. As Ernest Becker writes, "each child grounds himself in some power that transcends him. Usually it is a combination of his parents, his social group, and the symbols of his society and nation. This is the unthinking web of support which allows him to believe in himself."[5] In this sense, "mankind has reacted [to anxiety] by trying to secure human meanings from beyond. Man's best efforts seem utterly fallible without appeal to something higher for justification, some conceptual support for the meaning of one's life from a transcendental dimension of some kind."[6]

This transcendental dimension lends cultural support for belief in values that vary from benign and benevolent to those that promote violence and various forms of malevolent behaviors especially toward those considered members of outside groups. The aspect of culture that compels ideological conviction adheres to this sense that it is possible to pursue a life that becomes "larger than life." Such cultural illusions appear to foment the personal delusions associated with certain radical forms of violence that are often religiously or ideologically inspired. These dynamics are complex and are often simplistically referred to in terms of "fundamentalism." But, broadly speaking, culture facilitates a sense of personal significance relative to the ways people identify themselves relative to the groups with which they identify. Culture, Becker teaches, conveys a sense of meaningfulness. He writes, "what man really fears is not so much extinction, but extinction *with insignificance.* Man wants to know that his life has somehow counted, if not for himself, then at least in a larger scheme of things, that he has left a trace, a trace that has meaning. ... It is culture itself that embodies the transcendence of death. ... It is the 'religion' that assures in some way the perpetuation of its members. ... All [cultures] have in the end the same goal: to raise men above nature, to assure them that in some ways their lives count in the universe more than merely physical things count."[7] Therefore, although we "can never banish anxiety," writes Becker, "what [we] can do instead is to use anxiety as an eternal spring for growth into new dimensions of thought and trust."[8] He concludes, "the child meets the terror of life and aloneness ... by using [culture] as the vehicle for his immortality."[9] Culture is immediate and concrete, but it is also the instrumentality by and through which we create symbols in ways that provide the sense of a possibility to become aligned with the eternal and everlasting. In the power of its immediacy and in the power of its invitation to symbolic transcendence, culture represents the ultimate set of values that guides desire. In so doing it is able to relieve human anxiety. This is especially true of political culture that grounds collective belonging, governance, and authority. This grounding often entails the symbols and rituals of power and glory.

NOTES

1 Joan Riviere, "On the Genesis of Psychical Conflict in Earliest Infancy," in Melanie Klein et al., eds., *Developments in Psychoanalysis*, London: Karnac Books, 2002, 43.

2 Rollo May, "Contributions of Existential Psychotherapy," in Rollo May, Ernest Angel, and Henri F. Ellenberger, eds., *Existence: A New Dimension in Psychiatry and Psychology*, New York: Basic Books, 1958, 50.

3 Ibid., 51.

4 Paul Tillich, *The Courage to Be*, New Haven, CT: Yale University Press, 1952, 39.

5 Ernest Becker, *Denial of Death*, New York: Free Press, 1973, 89.

6 Ibid., 120.

7 Ernest Becker, *Escape from Evil*, New York: Free Press, 1975, 4.

8 Becker, *Denial of Death*, 92.

9 Ibid., 120.

Under this culture, governments are run in terms of a social or hierarchal order. No, there are no monarchies; there are, however, certain fixed notions about the types of individuals who can be elected to office and manage politics. That is, governments set up to carry out the traditionalistic mandate are tasked with maintaining that order by any means necessary.

Traditionalistic attitudes, whether good or bad, seem to be associated most closely with the Deep South; therefore, it is no coincidence that Elazar places their roots with those of the Confederate rebel flag. States such as Mississippi, Georgia, South Carolina, and Louisiana are traditionally run according to the unwritten rules of "good-ol' boy" politics. Participants are born and friended into the system as much as they are elected. With this comes a powerful sense of connection to state or regional pride that takes precedence over government activity.

It may seem that these basic definitions offer only three choices for describing the culture of a state. However, like most things (including government), states and regions rarely fall into neat boxes. States have varying degrees of influence and can have varying cultures. Most states fall into this "mixed" category to some degree.

Are these fixed rules? No. Elazar's work was done nearly fifty years ago, and governments and their people change. However, the theories and standards set by Elazar still provide a measure with which to study Texas's political culture, to understand how the state functions, and to help define the relationship between the state's government and its people.

Breakout from Political Culture

Texas Democracy: How Different Is the State from the Nation?

The system of democracy can take several forms. How is it carried out at the state level in Texas? Of course, Texas has its basic tenets: citizens have the right to vote; they have a level of protection from an unjust government; and they possess natural rights. Those things are universal when it comes to states and how they treat their citizens. But how does Texas carry out that brand of democracy?

When talking about the relationship between a government and its people, we must look at the way power is used and how decision makers are installed in order to understand that relationship fully. The US form of democracy is largely founded upon four basic theories.

Elitist theory is a theory of democracy that gives decision-making power and major influence to a ruling class. Under this theory, a small group of individuals is given the power to control government. Whether it is direct control or not is irrelevant; the power of an elitist class comes from its ability to influence. If a country has a specific group of people or entities with the power to control decision making and deliberations regarding policy, its system falls under this theory. The important thing here is how the elite class is determined. Like other things in life that are identified with the concept of "elite," a democracy that falls under elitist theory has an influential class that meets a certain set of criteria. Bloodline, education, public acceptance, or wealth—there is some criteria that makes the group inclusive and provides it with power.

Group theory is the idea that government and its decisions are led by mass-population groups that have wide-ranging agendas. Power under group theory is derived from sheer numbers; a small number of large groups provides opinions (on a wide range of issues) in an agenda that the masses can connect with. This usually means creating an agenda that attracts attention, regardless of how limited, to many different issues. These groups use their "people power" to influence citizens and become the predominant decision makers in the democratic system.

Closely aligned with group theory is pluralist theory. The tenets of the group dynamic and using numbers to derive power are the same. In fact, under pluralist theory, numbers are even more important because the number of groups jockeying for position is greater. The reason for this is that pluralist theory relies on a larger number of smaller groups that have restricted or singular focuses to take control of the government. In this scenario, groups align based on specific issues and fight for control of the political landscape by advocating for their specific issue or small set of issues. These groups most closely align with the special or restricted social interest groups that we see today.

Last, we have rational choice theory. This is the most self-explanatory of the bunch because it relies on the idea that decision makers are selected, and their activity is driven, by rationality or logic. Decision makers are tasked with deciding what is best for the group or population based on logic or rationality. In turn, they are selected by their constituents based on the same criteria.

Deciding which of these theories applies most closely to the US government is difficult. There is a case to be made that legislators and executive officials have become elite. Their rates of interaction with constituents fluctuates, and the criteria for and makeup of their group has become increasingly specific with regard to age, race, education, and financial backing. There is also the idea that the United States is a "group theory" system. Two predominant political parties that practice the "big tent" model [...] provide a clear connection to this idea. It is significant that one or two predominant parties have parlayed a broad spectrum of issues into influence and focused that power, especially when you look at the makeup of the legislature and executive officials as well as the lack of third-party representation. The United States is likely a hybrid democracy when it comes to these theories and interacts with its constituents from one of these two basic partisan points of view.

Texas diverges on this latter point while still having a connection to the tenets of elitism. Ready access is given to business professionals, both as direct contact with legislators and through lobbying activities. Texas's business culture and the high level of outside influence on legislators lend credence to the elitist theory. There are also roots here in pluralist theory. Texas's legislative and executive officials are readily accessible to outside influence, as the low pay and part-time nature of government service opens them up to persuasion. Mostly we associate this with financial influence, but there is also an avenue for political access. Unlike federal politicians, who can be isolated in Washington or on duty elsewhere, state officials are rooted in the community, making them accessible to smaller groups.

Where do you feel Texas falls within these theories? Does it have to be static? Can Texas change as the population and government change? Are new influences driving Texas's brand of democracy in different directions?

Where Does Texas Fall?

Texas is one of the most unique states in the country when it comes to political culture. A state as prideful as any, Texas mixes a blend of at least two of these political cultures: traditionalistic and individualistic.

When talking with residents of Texas, one finds that many identify with their state before anything else. When Lance Armstrong won his first Tour de France, most people in the United States celebrated the fact that an American had claimed the crown, but in the Lone Star State, people were prouder that a Texan had claimed the title. Texans are known for connecting with their heritage, regardless of what that is. Politics at the state level are done in a fashion that connects back to the Constitution of 1876 (which has been added to, rather than reshaped, despite its 490 amendments). The Texas government pays considerable attention to the state's background and its traditions.

The state's politics, in many ways, center on corporate viability. From state budgeting to tax practices, Texas has made itself one of the most attractive states for businesses to operate in, which in turn creates many opportunities for its citizens to obtain wealth or a higher social standing. The state resists federal aid and has built one of the largest surpluses in the nation. It also shuns social projects that require government activity, favoring private enterprise and responsibility instead.

One-Party Dominance

In keeping with Texas's individualistic nature, the state's long history of one-party dominance in its politics rivals few others. For nearly a century after Reconstruction, Texas was dominated by Democrats who focused on agriculture and had a singular vision of how the state should be run. Since then, the dominance of one party has remained, but the color has changed from blue to red. Until the 1960s, the Republican presence in the Texas legislature was minimal. Today, Democrats have fallen well behind, making up less than 34.6 percent[2] of the legislative body, and all executive branch positions are filled by Republicans.

Politicians are business oriented or professional in nature. Many of the traditions in the legislature—low pay, part-time work—dictate this, and the constituencies overwhelmingly choose their decision makers from professional backgrounds. The idea of political elites, combined with the influence of business professionals in the state, supports an individualistic culture.

Social and Economic Conservatism

That one-party concept permeates the conservative nature of politics and policy in Texas. Legislative activity, especially in the past twenty-five years, has skewed toward economic matters, leaving social issues as truly secondary topics. Legislation has centered on making the state a welcoming place for potential business and helping businesses maximize their profit margins. The tax system is a good example. Texas has a regressive tax system (which will be explained later in this book): businesses pay taxes on profits only, and employees don't pay income tax. These practices make it easy for corporations to move to Texas and sell their employees on the state as a viable option.

As economic policy has moved to the forefront of politics, social policies and programs have taken a back seat. As the state has become focused on economics, it has taken the predictable role of resisting the advent social programs in the state and resisting the expenditures that would come with them. Texas has resisted the healthcare programs of the Affordable Care Act and has been a frontrunner in resisting social change promoted by the federal government.

Low Voter Turnout

Voter turnout is an easy and tangible way to measure political participation. As the individualistic and traditionalistic cultures persist in the state, part of that mandate is to have a restricted influence on government. Under Elazar's concept, government influence is derived from a group of elites. Some of the above activities lead into that idea, but the restricted level of access granted to individuals is a key indicator of these cultures.

2　"Member Statistics," Legislative Reference Library of Texas website, http://www.lrl.state.tx.us/legeLeaders/members/memberStatistics.cfm.

Texas politics is inherently business-based. The economic nature of policy and the coziness of insiders (with both one another and business interests) can cause state government to look very much like a closed system that restricts outside voices. Part of that inhibition translates into a lack of voter turnout. As we will see in our chapters on public opinion, Texas's voter participation rate lags behind the national average in a number of key demographics, including low-income voters and young people.[3] Those groups are two of the major drivers of change at the legislative and cultural levels in other states, but they tend to be nonparticipants in Texas.

There is also a tie to the one-party nature of the state. Democrats in Texas have a tough choice: sacrifice time and resources to cast a vote that will be drowned out or simply choose not to participate? The state's closed political system restricts access for Democrats and has created a gulf in voter participation.

All this has led to the maintenance of the status quo when it comes to political ideology, the way the state conducts business, and the preservation of current political practices.

Provincialism

There is no lack of a personal connection to the state of Texas among the state's residents. A large part of the traditionalistic nature of Texas comes from its citizens' connection to their heritage. Texans take pride in both the idea that they are the only state to start as a nation and in the battles their ancestors fought to gain independence. Their pride in the Lone Star flag, the Alamo, what many believe to be a self-sustaining economy, and their way of life drives that nearly egotistical nature.

Texas's political culture is a clear basis for the state's resistance to change. Unlike other states, which may be influenced by their neighbors' activities, Texas remains insulated from the influence of national politics. Even the transformation from Democrat to Republican signifies that traditionalistic nature. That change was driven by southern Democrats who left the party because they perceived a desire to deviate from the state's traditional conservative ways. Instead of blending into their century-old party, they chose the party that would fit their standards and traditional viewpoints. Their shift marked a choice to stick to the status quo, which revolved around what they felt were Texans' roots. The reluctance to rewrite the state's constitution is another example. The state's governing document has some 490 amendments, making it confusing and often contradictory. Instead of streamlining this document or writing a new one, Texans have kept it intact and simply added to it rather than lose the connection to their past and past decisions that they feel helped to shape the state.

---

3   Texas voter turnout is well below the national average. In the midterm elections of 2014, voter turnout was 28 percent in Texas, while the national average was 36 percent (http://www.electproject.org/2014g). In the 2012 presidential election, the national average was 59 percent, while Texas turned out 49 percent.

Demographics of Texas: People, Places, and Money

As we evaluate Texas's political culture, we find certain demographic factors that constitute key elements of that discussion. The state quite possibly represents the truest definition of the melting pot that the United States is today. Its population is a hodgepodge of races and cultures and, owing to proximity and culture, has become a leading case study in the patterns and effects of immigration, especially among the Hispanic community.

This information can help us to understand, from a political culture standpoint, where Texas has been as well as to predict where it is going. Understanding trends and views of race, economics, geography, and social issues offers insight into important questions that are tackled later in this book.

People in Texas

Texas has seen a steady growth in population since it entered the Union. It has ballooned from a rural state of 213,000 people to a packed 27,469,114 in the year 2015.[4] As we look into this increase, we note several important things. Immigration, the economy, the attraction to urban population centers, and the increasingly lopsided ratio between death and birth have contributed to this growth. All of these factors support the political culture we see in Texas today.

As previously stated, Texas has enjoyed a rich history of political culture that has revolved mainly around what Elazar would consider the traditionalistic and individualistic viewpoints. As the state has become more diverse and richer in the way it conducts business and attracts new investment, the state's political culture has been defined and slightly redefined over the years. These changes, however, have come more slowly than the population's changes would suggest.

Anglos

The ethnic makeup of Texas, especially in the urban areas, has been predominantly Anglo-American. Since being granted settlements when the Spanish controlled the territory, Anglos from the United States have seen Texas as a bastion of immigration and economic prosperity. Anglos were the predominant ethnicity in the state until the mid-twentieth century. In 1900,

---

4   US Census Bureau, "U.S. Census Data." Last modified July 1, 2016. http://www.census.gov/quickfacts/table/PST045215/48.

Anglos made up 80 percent of the 3,048,710[5] people living in the state. In 2010, that number had dwindled to 45 percent.[6] Although Anglo is still the predominant ethnicity in Texas, the population is shifting toward greater diversity as the state matures.

Anglos were granted governorship over land by the Spanish and, later, Mexican governments to help populate areas further away from the Mexican border. The purpose of granting ownership to leaders such as Moses Austin and Stephen F. Austin was to attract other US immigrants to the state. As Anglos moved into Texas, they brought with them much of their political culture. Although the Mexican way of life was moralistic in nature, those immigrating into Texas brought with them a belief in capitalism. They sought inexpensive land and looked for more business-friendly policies that lent themselves both to a more individualistic culture and a view of democracy and governing that aligned with the US style of democracy nationally. This was the impetus behind the Texas revolution, which took place as the state's affluent leadership attempted to break free from Mexico.

After Texas gained its independence, a flood of new immigrants came to the state. Most of them came from the Deep South, thus introducing the state to slavery. As farmers from these regions came into the state, they brought with them a part of their tradition, which included the use of slave labor. By the time the southern states seceded from the Union in 1861, Texas's political makeup was dominated by politicians and decision makers who shared the same ideology and political culture. Slavery, however, was not rampant. Most Texas farmers could not afford to own slaves, but the political climate certainly supported the practice of slavery and encouraged Texans to adopt the South's values in this regard. This held true past the Civil War, the Emancipation Proclamation, and Reconstruction. In short, Texas remained at the forefront of struggles over civil rights and the status of minorities throughout and beyond the next hundred years.

Although for much of the Texas's history Anglos were mainly farmers, the latest wave of immigrants has included people with a different political culture. Instead of being involved in agriculture, Anglos moving to the state are now following newer trends. Natural immigration involves the concept of people coming into the state from other parts of the Union, as opposed to other countries. Today, however, illegal or international immigration has come to be seen as the major mode of movement into the state. Although farmers are still moving into rural areas of Texas, the economic and population booms of the urban centers have larger numbers of Anglos. There has also been an influx of Roman Catholic Anglos as well as people who would classify themselves as liberal or loyal to the Democratic Party.

5   Texas state library, "United States and Texas Populaitons 1850–2016." Last modified February 8, 2017. https://www.tsl.texas.gov/ref/abouttx/census.html.

6   US Census Bureau, "American Fact Finder." http://factfinder.census.gov/faces/tableservices/jsf/pages/productview.xhtml?src=CF.

Hispanics

Although Anglos have historically led the state in immigration, Hispanics are currently the fastest-growing community within the state and in the nation. Hispanics were considered an insignificant factor in Texas's political culture and population until as recently as the 1990s. A boom of immigration, both legal and illegal, has changed this. With both second- and third-generation immigrants now living in the state, the size of Texas's Hispanic population has become significant, having risen to 37 percent[7] in the year 2010. Hispanics are projected to overtake Anglos as the majority ethnicity in Texas by the year 2040.

Hispanics in Texas are predominantly of Mexican descent. Because of the state's proximity to Mexico, this is not surprising, but there is also another reason for this. As Texas moved from being a Spanish or Mexican territory to a part of the United States, it became a refuge for those fleeing from a neighboring country that was politically and economically unstable. As Spanish and Mexican people sought a new path, they took advantage of an easy border crossing to a region that was underdeveloped.

Although this population growth was first centered in border towns, economic and labor opportunities soon drew the new immigrants to northern and western parts of Texas. As the cotton industry grew in the panhandle and West Texas, the Hispanic communities in these regions also grew. After World War II, Hispanic immigrants tended to move from agricultural areas of the state to more urban communities offering greater opportunities for economic growth. However, their participation in politics remained measured.

Along with their African American counterparts, Hispanics were prevented and often discouraged from taking part in the political process. White-only primaries and political parties limited their opportunities, and the group's less affluent members were discouraged from voting. During the 1950s, there was a growth in Hispanic advocacy, as politicians such as Henry Gonzalez took office, exemplifying political prosperity and seeking to provide representation for the state's Hispanic population. Interest groups formed, including the now-national Raza Unida Party, which battled discrimination and fought for civil rights in Texas as well educational equality in the American South. As of 2014, a total of 6,084[8] Hispanics were serving in public office nationally, with over two thousand in Texas. There are six Hispanic representatives currently serving in the US House of Representatives and another thirty-eight in the Texas Legislature. Senator Ted Cruz currently occupies one of the state's US senator spots.

---

7   US Census Bureau, "American Fact Finder." http://factfinder.census.gov/faces/tableservices/jsf/pages/product-view.xhtml?src=CF.

8   NALEO Educational Fund, 2014 National Directory of Latino Elected Officials.

African Americans

Most Texans of African descent have a history of slavery. Although some early African explorers entered the region, most African Americans came to Texas as slaves, despite the antislavery sentiments of the Spanish and Mexican governments. That ended with Texas's independence, after which the number of slaves increased, hitting a peak in 1850, with 58,000[9] enslaved individuals believed to reside in the state. That is, a history in slavery has marked African Americans living in Texas. It took over one hundred years to shake that stigma and to moderate the effects of that history on Texans' views of minorities. After the Emancipation Proclamation, Texas enacted several laws, categorized as the Black Codes, that restricted the rights of former slaves. During Reconstruction, African Americans supported the radical Republican Party and tried to push legislative and constitutional change as the state sought to return to the Union. Those changes were short-lived. As the Texas Democratic Party reclaimed power during the period after Reconstruction, many of those steps were undone, and African Americans continued to fight an uphill battle for civil rights and political involvement. Poll taxes, white-only primaries and political parties, and literacy tests all played a role in keeping African Americans out of the voting booths during the early twentieth century. As these laws and practices persisted, segregation became increasingly entrenched. Lynchings and police brutality became part of the history of Texas as well as of the entire South—a history against which African Americans were forced to fight a constant battle.

Tension increased into the middle of the twentieth century, while civil rights and liberties movements began to swell. It was only in the 1940s that landmark Supreme Court cases and decisions began to gradually correct the abusive treatment of African Americans. *Smith v. Allwright* (1944) disallowed the practice of white-only primaries, and *Sweatt v. Painter* (1950) opened graduate admission at colleges and universities to African Americans. The desegregation of schools was advanced by *Brown v. Board of Education* (1954). All these cases represented progress, and the Voting Rights Act of 1965 pushed even further, restricting Texas's ability to restrict political participation; this decision placed the state under the watchful eye of the federal government.

African American politicians today have become significant figures in local, state, and federal politics. Many of these leaders have come from population centers in eastern and Gulf Coast Texas. Dallas and Houston have had African American mayors as well as US congressional representatives.

---

9   US Census Bureau, "U.S. Census Data." Last modified July 1, 2016. http://www.census.gov/quickfacts/table/PST045215/48.

Cultural Diversity and Changes in Political Culture

Along with Texas's shifts in ethnicity, could there be a change in its political culture? Much of the state's political culture revolves around the traditional outlook of Texan Anglos. As the population is transformed, those influences will change, but will they do so in the ways that many expect?

Hispanics and African Americans are traditionally seen to be liberal or a part of the Democratic Party. Those communities have traditionally pushed for social change and reform. As the twenty-first century takes hold, many changes are likely to take place. Although Texas is individualistic and traditionalistic in practice, younger people are gaining greater influence, and some of them may rise to positions of power. With that in mind, there is room for eventual change as the prevailing political cultures change. Along those same lines, it is difficult to predict how culture may change along with changes in the population. In fact, as Hispanics and African Americans work their way into the Texas political landscape, it could be that we will see current cultures influence *their* activities rather than the other way around. Ted Cruz, who ran for the presidency in 2015, is a Republican Hispanic who could represent a trend and augur change among that population group, which falls in line with the state's current traditional and individualistic political culture.

How such change and influence will take charge will be one aspect of political and government activity to keep an eye on as the state continues to evolve. Age is also a component that could play a role. Texas is a young state, with nearly a quarter of its population under the age of eighteen. Youth populations, like minority communities, are traditionally progressive and liberal. That, plus an evolving ethnic population, could affect Texas's political trajectory.

Economy

Texas has been in constant change. The state's economy has been at the forefront of that change, and its progress has been generally positive. Texas has successfully transformed itself from a primarily rural state to one that has become amenable to evolving technology. Much of this comes from the individualistic culture of Texas, which advocates for policy that establishes paths to individual and, in Texas's case, corporate prosperity. As Texas has progressed, the "Texas Model" of low taxes and low expenditures on social programs has made for the smooth development of the state's economy. We'll talk more about the Texas Model later, but it's good to keep the policy-making theory in mind as we recount the economic history of Texas.

A part of both this individualistic culture and the Texas Model has been the advent of the concept of creative destruction. Within this concept, capitalism is seen to be a system that undergoes change that is prompted by entrepreneurs and innovation, most recently in the area of technology. As innovation in technology grows and expands, the characteristics of the economy also change and shift. With change, however, comes destruction, as new economic practices replace and destroy old ones. As the nation grew smaller and more accessible through the development of railroads and ports, local markets and products succumbed to the nationalized economic engine. While technology and oil has progressed in rural areas, farming has fallen by the wayside.

Agriculture

As has been pointed out, Texas has deep roots in agriculture, namely cotton and cattle. The mid-nineteenth century saw a boom in the agriculture industry in Texas. As railroads and transportation channels developed, it became easier for farmers to export their crops and goods for sale. The number of farms continued to grow, and by the early twentieth century, the state had more than five hundred thousand operating farms. The sheer number of farms and an eclectic climate put the state's agriculture business near the top of production among US states. That continues today. Although there have been other economic influences and policy has shifted toward other areas, farming in Texas is still a top industry. As of 2010, the state ranked second in the nation in the agriculture industry (generating $22 billion) and is a main exporter of goods.

Although the industry is thriving in terms of the bottom line, there has been a turn away from agriculture in general. The total number of farms in 2010 dropped to 250,000 as jobs moved into more professional and service-oriented fields and education pushed younger people toward other lines of work. Today farms are rarely the sole source of income for couples, as many farmers have spouses who work outside the business. Droughts, lower farm counts, the corporatization of the business, and higher costs have brought hardship to the industry in recent decades. Texas has responded with assistance and business promotion programs that have attempted to revitalize the farming industry.

Oil

Farming was the ultimate community creator. Towns and cities formed as farmers looked to come together, connect, and expand their businesses. Oil had the opposite effect. Oil has been a major player in Texas since the turn of the nineteenth century, when major oil discoveries in East Texas and the Gulf Coast sparked a boom in the industry. The ability to find oil and make it a source of wealth attracted new entrepreneurs to rural areas. The boom-or-bust nature of the business made things volatile. Areas struggled to cope with the influx of new people after the first discovery of oil in 1901 at Spindletop; within the next year, three major oil fields cropped up within a hundred-mile radius.

Refining and transporting oil then became a major business in Texas. Corporations started to move in and towns were overtaken, especially in East Texas, where many areas were greatly affected by the influx of refineries and oil fields. Ironically, a boom in the oil business could mean a struggling economy, since, as more oil fields and refineries cropped up, the market could be diluted, making it tougher for towns to survive. The oil business has become a business of relocation; it follows the oil and offers short-term work for local service workers and laborers.

State and federal policy also affected the oil industry in Texas. The Texas Railroad Commission was created to oversee transportation, specifically for carrying and transporting oil safely throughout the state. The commission was given control over oil in 1917; it then proceeded to try to stabilize the industry by enacting rules such as those that monitored and capped the production of oil from individual wells in 1930. As the commission continued to grow and gain power, taxes became a big boon to the state's economy. Texas has, since the early twentieth century, collected a tax on oil production; revenue from this tax reached a peak of $2 billion in 2012. This sum was allocated to the state's budget.

Today, several major oil and energy companies make their homes in Texas. ExxonMobil, Valero, and ConocoPhillips are among them. These corporations were attracted to the state because of its rich oil reserves and business-friendly governmental policies. These corporations have used their plants in Texas as hubs for their business. As the railroad and highway system has expanded throughout the United States, distribution from the Gulf Coast and other parts of Texas has been made much easier. Texas has always been at the forefront of oil industry policy. Fracking (the use of hydraulics and chemicals to release natural gas from underground) has been a major source of debate, drawing concern from the US Environmental Protection Agency (EPA). Unsurprisingly, Texas was at the forefront. Per the EPA, the practice could contaminate local water supplies and potentially induce earthquakes. The state took measures to monitor the practice in 2011, when the legislature passed a law that went against its political culture. The law requires the publication of information about chemicals used in the process, making Texas the first state to take policy action regarding fracking.

Technology

Although the oil industry is still a major producer within the economy, high-technology jobs involving the computer and manufacturing industries have fueled Texas's economy more recently. Over the past thirty years, technology companies have flocked to the state, mainly to the more populated or urban areas. Looking for soft landing spots and desirable locations for current and potential employees, areas such as Austin, Houston, Dallas, and San Antonio have been targets for tech expansion. These cities offer quality family areas, highly rated educational options, and a fertile ground for hiring from within the community. Corporations such as Dell, Hewlett Packard, and Texas Instruments have made Texas home and pumped fuel into its economy, with higher-salaried employees working in professionally oriented fields. Texas is second to California in the number of tech jobs it offers within its borders.

Texas has leaned into the tech expansion in some ways but has resisted it in others. In 2005 the state commissioned the Emerging Technology Fund, allocating $200 million to an effort to promote and attract technology-based businesses while stimulating programs at the community-college and four-year-university levels to advance education in these areas. This fund has met with success and has continued to produce employees trained in tech fields, thus helping to develop a built-in employee base. Other policies, including profit-based taxes in Texas's regressive tax structure, have made sustaining tech business less than a sure thing. Corporations are looking for alternative locations outside the state as well as outside the nation, mainly to lower costs. However, the lack of a labor income tax and the government's commitment to the tech industry allows it to support a tech field that is growing, if not at the previous rate.

Transition from Rural to Urban

By the mid-1800s, Texas's rural roots were deeply established. Since the creation of the state as a Mexican province, most of Texas had been centered in rural areas. The economy was rural in nature, with cotton and cattle driving the state; the best areas to prosper in business were in the rural setup. The lack of urban options played into this ratio as well: in 1900, only 17 percent[10] of the 3,048,710 people in Texas lived in urban centers. The remaining 83 percent made their homes outside of these centers, with loose, widespread settlements connecting ranch and cattle land.

This trend has turned, slowly but surely. As of 2010, some 88 percent of the twenty-five million[11] people who live in Texas reside in urban areas. This has even spawned a suburban movement, which we will discuss later. What sparked the change from looser local cities connecting ranches and farmland? Early moves to the urban setup came because the Spanish tried to expand their influence northward into Texas's Plains region. They set up urban population centers around garrisons, missions/churches, and population-driven towns. Thereafter, as the population began to become self-sustaining, the Spanish continued to colonize the state. In 1820, San Antonio was the largest such settlement, with 2,500[12] people. This trend would

---

10 U.S. Census Bureau, "Urban and Rural Population: 1900–1990." Last modified October, 1995. https://www.census.gov/population/censusdata/urpop0090.txt.

11 US Census Bureau, "American Fact Finder." http://factfinder.census.gov/faces/tableservices/jsf/pages/productview.xhtml?src=CF.

12 US Census Bureau, "American Fact Finder." http://factfinder.census.gov/faces/tableservices/jsf/pages/productview.xhtml?src=CF.

continue, with increasing numbers of Anglos moving into the state. The Spanish granted these settlers land so as to encourage immigration from the US side of the border and to help populate the northern parts of the state, further away from the Mexican border. With these settlers came a new culture that included slavery, a new language, Protestantism, and a view of democracy that diverged from the Spanish style of rule.

Aiding in this new trend was the expansion of technology and the economy. Texas's economic growth took place along the Gulf Coast first, where, as international trade traffic began to expand at the ports, areas such as Houston and Galveston became population centers. In the late nineteenth century, the coming of the railroads also led to urban expansion as station towns grew up in areas of Texas that had been previously remote. Moving through the twentieth and into the twenty-first century, the trend has grown as technology, oil and gas, and transportation have joined big businesses in making Texas a center of economic growth. Because corporations have seen Texas as a consumer-driven state with policies that favor business, the movement of workers into the state's urban areas has ballooned over time.

In addition to the changes already outlined, there has been a new movement—that of suburbanization. As corporations have moved into cities like Austin, San Antonio, Dallas, Fort Worth, and Houston, ways of accommodating this growth had to be found. As a result, a suburban movement evolved, whereby affluent families and workers moved into communities, seeking consolidated areas of living that were away from the more densely populated areas that were thought to have high crime rates. These areas are farther away from the urban business centers. Millennials have recently made moving back to the urban areas a trend, both because they battle rising gas prices and they are concerned about environmental impacts.

Summary

Evaluating Texas's political culture can be as easy or as hard as we make it. Many believe that the state is as easy to read as flipping through the pages of this book. Going back to Daniel Elazar's research, Texas has been pegged as a state that's resistant to change and focused on serving the best interests of its citizens from a mainly financial point of view.

As we have discussed, several important factors lead to that distinction. Texas's one-party predominance certainly protects the status quo and keeps the state aligned with an individualistic viewpoint. A legislature and government that is mainly focused on economic policy as a path to ensuring individual success breeds a culture that is focused much more on the individual or a group of individuals rather than on creating policies that would be perceived as focusing on the system as a whole. The connections that are ingrained generation to generation in the state also serve as a strong tie to this ideology and culture. That ideology has driven the idea that Texas fits neatly into a hybrid box of individualistic and traditionalistic cultures.

Can That Change?

In talking about political culture, there are several variables that factor into the equation. As Texas continues to grow and push the boundaries in several areas, the state could finally be seeing the supportive environment for change that other states have experienced in recent decades.

A population that is becoming more diverse with focuses in many different areas could lead to the reshaping of the status quo. The influence of diverse communities and young professionals could make Texas's political culture take a turn. There are also federal trends, such as the decision by the Supreme Court to grant the right of marriage to same-sex couples nationwide. This decision will force change in Texas's way of life. Texas has been a state that resists any change that does not fit its point of view. But how will a battle on key social issues affect the state moving forward?

Texas is at a point where its political culture—a culture that may be questioned for the first time in many years—is an important subject of discussion. Moving forward, this understanding will be important as we discuss the basic components of Texas government, the key factors in how it works today, and how it could work in the future.

References

Bezdek, Robert R., David M. Billeaux, and Juan Carlos Huerta. "Latinos, At-Large Elections, and Political Change: Evidence from the 'Transition Zone.'" *Social Science Quarterly* (2000): 207–225.

Brown v. Board of Education of Topeka, 347 U.S. 483 (1954).

Burner, D. *The Politics of Provincialism: The Democratic Party in Transition, 1918–1932*. New York: Knopf, 1968.

Burtenshaw, C. J. "The Political Theory of Pluralist Democracy." *The Western Political Quarterly* 21, no. 4 (1968), 577–587.

Cantrell, G. *Stephen F. Austin: Empresario of Texas*. New Haven, CT: Yale University Press, 2001.

Cunningham, S. P. Cowboy Conservatism: Texas and the Rise of the Modern Right. Lexington, KY: University Press of Kentucky, 2010.

Elazar, D. J. American Federalism: A View from the States 2nd edition. Springfield, OH: Thomas Y. Crowell Publishing, 1972.

Garcia, J. A. *Latino Politics in America: Community, Culture, and Interests*. Lanham, MD: Rowman & Littlefield, 2011.

Grieder, E. "Big, Hot, Cheap, and Right: What America Can Learn from the Strange Genius of Texas." New York, NY; Perseus Books Group, 2014.

Jones, C. A. *Texas Roots: Agriculture and Rural Life Before the Civil War* (No. 8). College Station, TX: Texas A&M University Press, 2005.

Obergefell v. Hodges, 135 S. Ct. 2584, (2015).

McComb, D. G. *Texas: A Modern History*. Rev. ed. Austin, TX: University of Texas Press, 2014.

NALEO Educational Fund. *National Directory of Latino Elected Officials*. New York, NY: 2014.

Olien, R. M. *From Token to Triumph: The Texas Republicans, 1920–1978*. Dallas, TX: SMU Press, 1982.

Orrenius, P. M., M. Zavodny, and M. LoPalo. Gone to Texas: Immigration and Transformation of the Texas Economy. Dallas, TX: Federal Reserve Bank of Dallas, 2013.

Putnam, R. D. *The Comparative Study of Political Elites*. Upper Saddle River, NJ: Prentice Hall, 1976.

Reyes, C. A. *Vocal and Visible: Latino Political Mobilization in the 21st Century*. Santa Barbara, CA; Chicano Studies Institute, 2008.

Roemer, J. "Rationalizing Revolutionary Ideology." *Econometrica* 53, no. 1 (January 1985): 85–108.

Smith v. Allwright, 321 U.S. 649 (1944).

Sweatt v. Painter, 210 S.W. 2d 442 (1950).

Texas State Library. "United States and Texas Populations 1850–2016." Last modified February 8, 2017. https://www.tsl.texas.gov/ref/abouttx/census.html.

US Census Bureau. "U.S. Census Data." Last modified July 1, 2016. http://www.census.gov/quickfacts/table/PST045215/48.

US Census Bureau. "American Fact Finder." http://factfinder.census.gov/faces/tableservices/jsf/pages/productview.xhtml?src=CF.

U.S. Census Bureau, "Urban and Rural Population: 1900–1990." Last modified October, 1995. https://www.census.gov/population/censusdata/urpop0090.txt.

United States Elections Project. "2014 November General Elections Turnout Rates." Last modified December 30, 2015. http://www.electproject.org/2014g.

Wildavsky, A. B. *Leadership in a Small Town*. Piscataway, NJ: Transaction Publishers, 1964.

CHAPTER 2

The Evolution and Impact of the Texas Constitution

A constitution functions as the document that defines the structure, power, and responsibilities of a government. Is such a document designed to stand the test of time at the subfederal or state level?

Historically, the longevity of governing documents or constitutions has varied (Ginsburg 2011). Constitutions and/or governing documents worldwide run the gamut from being extremely short-lived to holding for centuries. But how long is too long? According to Thomas Jefferson, a constitution's ideal longevity hovers around nineteen years. These documents are designed to define specific functions. But, most importantly, they do this as an extension of the public will. Societal change that occurs in the span of nineteen years would logically alter public preferences and thus also the applicability of a constitution.

Unlike Jefferson, the framers of constitutions generally do not see it this way. Neither James Madison (at the federal level) nor the framers of the Texas Constitution meant their constitutions to be temporary. Instead, they saw these constitutions as long-term designs for the structure of government—documents that, through the amendment process, could be adapted to meet the needs posed by societal change. Texas's constitution is an interesting case in point. Instead of having one single document that has been altered, Texas is on its eighth iteration of a governing document. As the state experienced changes (both internally and externally), it was not shy about throwing its constitution out and starting afresh. The first six of those constitutions were adopted in the span of roughly sixty years. During that time, the status of the territory changed: first it was a Mexican territory, then a sovereign nation, and finally a US state. And Texas actually became part of the United States twice, first joining the union and later returning after leaving to be a member of the Confederacy. These events caused seismic changes in how the state operated.

Since 1876, however, Texas's position has stabilized, and its constitution has been amended, rather than rewritten, to fit the changing political and societal landscape. This means that the technology- and energy-driven state we know today is governed by a document that was written during the Reconstruction period, when agriculture was the driving economic force. As of the end of 2016, this document, which is some 150 years old, has 491 amendments.

This chapter attempts to blend an overview of these sequential constitutions with basic theory regarding the role of governing documents and how they function in serving society. In the case of Texas, its constitution has functioned as a blend of concepts and mandates. It offers guidance to the government, protection for individual rights, and a list of provisions that affect both the government and its constituents.

The Role of a State Constitution

State constitutions perform specific roles in the US federal system. In line with the concept of a governing document, state constitutions provide basic guidelines as to how the government is to be structured and where the power will or will not lie. These types of constitutions are among the oldest governing documents in the United States. Still, they are required to meet the "supremacy mandates" outlined in Chapter 3 and must uphold the basic tenets of American democracy while addressing state-based issues.

This chapter examines the role that state constitutions should play and how they best meet their mandates. Although the US Constitution protects individual rights and invests power in certain sectors of the government, state constitutions provide more specific guidance regarding the structure of government and the activity of individuals.

W. F. Dodd (1915) examines these roles and specifies the functions that state constitutions perform. The first function of a constitution is to define legislative power; that is, it limits the power of government agents. There is debate as to the origin of this power. One school of thought maintains that it is inherent, meaning that the legislative body has complete power except where it is restricted by the federal constitution. This concept allows the legislature to use its power in any way as long as it is not specifically restricted from doing so. The converse view is that a state constitution defines the governing body's power by clearly defining the actions that the legislature may take. "Perhaps constitutional limitations may be classed as follows: (1) express; (2) implied, as a limitation upon the legislature is implied from grant of judicial power to the courts; (3) inherent, as limitations implied from the nature of legislative power" (Dodd 1915, 210).

State constitutions must also specify the ways in which government organizations are dealt with. Along with limiting power, constitutions must define the roles and powers of departments and officials. The most basic example of this is defining the power of the various branches. We've touched on legislative power, but there are also the functions and roles of departments within the executive branch. A long-standing aspect of the Texas Constitution is its mandate that the state must provide certain services (such as education) to its citizens. Examples of this power and responsibility include focusing public education in specific areas and the ability to shape the curriculum. Although the federal government can pass laws and mandates, state constitutions have the authority to empower and define the roles of governing boards such as the Texas Board of Education, which establishes policies by which the public schools must abide. The provision limiting debt and governing finance within the state also originates from the Texas Constitution. Government organization was a large part of the reason for and direction of early constitutions, which were traditionally shorter than the increasingly long contemporary versions. Defining this structure is a clear traditional function of state constitutions.

The most important thing is that state constitutions perform the function that the states require of them. Although the national constitution, which is set up to provide fundamental law, provides for a wide variety of functions, the provisions of state constitutions are more specific to the particular needs of that state and its citizens.

> A state constitution is an instrument, a means to an end, and is of no importance for its own sake alone. It may be true that the national constitution should be primarily an instrument embodying fundamental provisions and defining the respective powers of the state and national governments. Yet this is not because the instrument is called a constitution; it is because the successful operation of a federal system requires permanent demarcation of national and state powers. There is no inherent reason an instrument of state or national government should contain only provisions of fundamental law. A constitution must be judged not by its name, but by the function which it has to perform … .The state constitution now serves two purposes, that of organizing and determining the powers of government (whether by limitation, grant or command), and that of serving as an organ of popular will through the embodiment of legislation into the constitution itself. In its accomplishment of both these purposes the newer state constitution far exceeds the limits of what may properly be called fundamental law.[1]

---

1   W.F. Dodd, Selection from "The Function of a State Constitution," *Political Science Quarterly*, vol. 30, no. 2, pp. 215-216. Copyright in the Public Domain.

Texas Constitution's list of provisions and actions connect its fundamental role as a state as defined by the federal constitution to the basic concepts and debates prefaced above. "Each state is free to adopt its own republican constitution. Thus, the geographic, ethnic, religious, socioeconomic, cultural, and historic diversity of the states has meant that each has assembled a constitutional package based on its own conceptions and interpretations of Americans' common republican assumptions" (Elazar 1982, 14). Elazar goes on to note that although the federal constitution is designed to impose limits, it does not answer the question of what the people want their government to be and do. This is where state constitutions step in, acquiring another—and their most important—function. In addition to limiting power and protecting citizens, these governing documents also outline the provisions of day-to-day life and practices in which the government is involved in providing what is wanted by its constituents. Under this mandate, the provisions describing the relationships and functions of local governments come into play. In other words, the Texas Constitution outlines and defines the powers of local governments within the state.

Positive vs. Negative Rights

Governing documents define and limit executive power through their provisions (Usman 2010); they give governments and their actors a road map indicating what they can and cannot do. Here we break these provisions down into two categories of rights: positive and negative. These classifications allow the individuals involved to both take action and understand how it will be limited in specific cases.

Negative rights are provisions that limit the actions that can be taken by governments. They are designed to define a limited role for government in regard to its citizens. The US Constitution can be interpreted as a list of negative rights, as it is geared toward defining and limiting the government's powers and actions. Both it and the US Bill of Rights—which is discussed in depth later in this chapter—are prime examples of documents defining negative rights. The Fifth Amendment prohibits the government from forcing individuals to testify against themselves in a court of law and restricts undue legal persecution. The Fourth Amendment restricts the government's right to force citizens to house or support soldiers. These are negative rights because they place limits on the government's power, especially when potential tyranny or misuse of power is possible. The Texas Constitution also defines negative rights. It includes stipulations similar to those in the US Bill of Rights, in some cases at a more specific level.

Positive rights are provisions that prompt government activity. They give governments the power to take actions that are felt, by vote or mandate of the public, to be in the best interests of the citizenry. Unlike negative rights, which seek to limit government activity and protect people from unfair or undue persecution, these rights give government the responsibility to take action and to provide for its citizens.

An examination of positive rights illuminates a major political argument: the promotion of government activity drives much of the debate between the conservative and liberal ideologies. Social service policy is a manifestation of positive rights. President Franklin D. Roosevelt, for example, cited positive rights as the rationale behind the New Deal. He believed that the government was responsible for ensuring a basic quality of life for its citizens; therefore, he pushed his socially engineered agenda through Congress by citing the needs posed by the Great Depression. A similar example of a positive right would be Texas's responsibility to educate its citizens. Another example would be a clause in the Texas Bill of Rights defining marriage as a union between a man and a woman. This clause defines action that the state and its voters, through the amendment process, believe meets the public will.

Political ideologies differ at a theoretical level, but Texas offers a unique case study. The state is ideologically conservative in its political view, yet its constitution is surprisingly positive in its provisions (Usman 2010). Of its 1,841 provisions, the second most of any state constitution, many are perceived to be a list of dos and don'ts. The Texas Constitution comprises a list of activities and responsibilities that the state must carry out and, in some cases, avoid. Its positive nature makes it appear to be a list of rules; in fact, much debate regarding currently proposed and past changes to the document is centered on decreasing its extremely positive nature.

The Texas Constitution Over the Years

States frequently make changes to their constitutions. In fact, since they first came into the Union, only nineteen states have maintained their constitutions intact. By contrast, Louisiana's constitution has had the most iterations (eleven[2]). Changing the way states are run and re-writing their guiding documents has become a national pastime. Texas falls into this category too, but in a unique way. The first seven constitutions spanned the state's initial sixty-four years, covering its initial designation as belonging to Mexico, then as a sovereign nation, and finally as a US state during the period of Reconstruction. Although the changes made to the constitution were consistent, the fact that they accompanied landmark changes in the state's status or position is unusual. The final iteration was written in 1876 and has remained intact, although it now has 4,891 amendments. These have been adopted in preference to writing an entirely new document.

A historic review examines a case in which the politics of the day influenced the state's governing document. Still, several tenets are consistent throughout the document, including the government's role in education and fiscal affairs and the concentration of power within the state wherever possible.

---

2   Ballotpedia.org, "Louisiana Constitution." Last modified August 28, 2016. https://ballotpedia.org/Louisiana_Constitution.

Constitution of 1827: Mexican Rule and the State of Coahulia y Tejas

During its formative years, Texas was a part of Mexico. After Mexico won its independence from Spain, it wrote its own constitution, which in many ways is similar to the constitution of the United States. The Mexican legislature was bicameral, with upper and lower chambers that were tasked with establishing the law. Delegates to the legislature, elected by the states, chose a president and vice president to head the government. The judicial branch was created with a high court comprising eleven justices as well as an attorney general. The liberties and rights of the people were defined in the document, which also emphasized the importance of education and confirmed Roman Catholicism as the state-sponsored religion.

Under its constitution, Mexico was broken up into three states, with Texas falling within the district of Bexar. Since Texas was a sparsely populated northern land, much of its constitution was designed to strengthen its ties to Mexico and to restrict immigration from the United States. Liberty, security, property rights, and equality were ensured. Property rights were significantly important to the Mexican government, and many of its laws and constitutional mandates were dedicated to protecting the rights of owners and defining their possessions.

Another mandate was the outlawing of slavery. Mexico was not a strong advocate of the practice and therefore often sought to restrict immigration from the American South, where slavery was practiced, into Texas. In addition to defining rights and liberties, the eventual Coahulia y Tejas Constitution allocated two representatives to the state; they would be part of a unicameral state legislature that would control policy, education, and the military. The state had a governor as well as a vice governor; they were elected by the people, although when a majority was not reached, the legislature would make the final decision. All local matters were left to the discretion of the local government, without stringent guidance from the state.

Constitution of 1836: The Republic of Texas

Over time, the people of Texas grew disenchanted with Mexico; they felt that they were losing their identity as a state. Much of the original agreement between Texas and Mexico was aimed at protecting citizens' rights and the structure of a government that upheld the social contract—the obligation to ensure a basic quality of life—in exchange for participation in society. In the Texans' opinion, Mexico had fractured that agreement. Asserting that the government had been dominated by the military and the Catholic Church, Texas pushed for reforms based on the agreements in the Coahulia y Tejas Constitution of 1827. The main points of emphasis were enacting English-speaking schools to go along with Spanish-speaking schools as well making it easier for people from the United States to settle in Mexico. Bringing in immigrants from the United States would promote farming and the economy. However, Mexico tried to restrict such movement to shield Texas from US influence. There were also issues regarding slavery, which existed in Texas but was not promoted by the Mexican government.

By 1835, Texas had begun to move toward separation. Political leaders met and drafted grievances against the Mexican government, producing a declaration of independence that specified how the Mexican government had failed the state. Many of these delegates (thirty-nine of the fifty-nine, to be exact), now living in Texas, were immigrants from the U.S. originally from slave-owning states. There was also significant influence from English-speaking states. An equitable public education system, freedom of religion, and an equitable trial system that enacted peer review and judgment were at the forefront of the demands. Texas professed that, at the basic level, Mexico had stripped them of their liberties. The declaration stated that Texas would separate from Mexico, and when Sam Houston delivered the message to the government in Mexico City, the move away from being a Mexican state began.

After Texas declared its intention to break away, a convention met to draft a constitution for what was to be an independent state. The original intention was to seek statehood in the United States. However, that was not assured, as tensions between northern and southern states regarding slavery and civil rights were rife, and the United States was reluctant to become involved in a dispute with Mexico.

With statehood unlikely at the time, the delegates drafted a constitution that resembled its US counterpart in form and nature. One key deviation from the Mexican regime was the acceptance of slavery. Under the proposed constitution, existing slavery would be protected, while the importation of new African slaves would be prohibited. This allowed the roughly five thousand slaves living in the state to remain. Also, there was constitutional protection for immigrants who owned slaves, allowing them to bring them into the state.

The document offered guidelines for a central government that invested powers in a three-branch system. It provided for the separation of powers (clearly outlining the roles and responsibilities of each branch) as well as checks and balances, giving each branch, as well as the public, the ability to curtail tyranny from another branch. Texas would elect a central executive who would hold considerable power. The legislature would shift to a bicameral system and, instead of one court, the court system would include local courts (justice and district), county courts, and a supreme court.

The constitution included a bill of rights that met the idea of protecting citizens from the tyranny of government. Provisions that protected community property and homestead exemptions from the constitution of 1827 were retained to support the fiscal health of the proposed republic as well as to provide debtor relief. As expected, there was a move to restrict avenues to political positions and power for those in the ministry. Texas did not endorse one religion under its proposed constitution. As this movement progressed and Texas finally won its independence from Mexico, the state passed the Texas Constitution of 1836.

Constitution of 1845: Joining the United States

After Texas became an independent republic, decision makers within the state wanted to petition for statehood within the United States. But Congress was not keen on admitting this new neighbor. Texas was considered a lock to align with states in the South, pushing for proslavery and antifederalist laws. After declaring its independence from Mexico, Texas politics favored states' rights. Therefore, if Texas became a part of the Union, it would mean adding a state that would threaten to work against the Union's priorities. There was also a worry that annexing Texas would lead to war with Mexico, which the United States did not want at that time.

By 1845, these concerns had subsided, and the push to add Texas to the Union grew stronger. Texas was therefore granted statehood with three specific provisions:

1   Texas was required to turn over its military facilities and power to the US government. In return, Texas would participate in the US military and defer to the central government in matters of public safety and foreign defense.

2   Texas would keep claims to unincorporated lands and public debts. At the time, Texas claimed lands that extended into what is now Oklahoma and Colorado. Texas held rights to those lands; it was not until the Compromise of 1850 was signed that the federal government settled the current border, offering payment to Texas. Texas used these funds to pay off foreign debt.

3   Texas was given the right to break into four separate states if its population dictated this.

These provisions allowed Texas to enter the Union, setting into motion the creation of Texas's first constitution as a US state.

Much of this constitution was similar to the one passed in 1836. Separation of church and state was still a tenet; however, it was not necessary because of the supremacy of the US Constitution. Individual rights, separation of powers, checks and balances, and the basic three branches of government were kept intact but altered in small ways. The judicial branch was changed at the highest level by incorporating a three-justice Supreme Court system as well as subjecting justices to the approval of the state senate. Texas's legislature would be divided into two chambers; the house would be responsible for revenue and tax bills and would have the ability to overturn vetoes with a two-thirds vote. These were both also tenets of the US Constitution.

Texas's executive branch was altered the most. The elected offices of governor and lieutenant governor were established, and specific formal powers were outlined. Veto power was invested in the state's executive official, along with the ability to grant pardons and reprieves from criminal sentences. Also, the governor's relationship with the legislature was defined. He was granted the ability to call the body into session and speak to the chambers as well as power over the state's militia. The state was also mandated to create and manage public school funds for the benefit of the community, an idea that had carried through from Texas's time as a Mexican state.

Constitution of 1861: Joining the Confederacy

After joining the Union, Texas did not become a state divided so much as a state fractured, with slavery as the main topic of contention. By 1860, slaves made up 30 percent of the Texas population; the cotton industry was growing and constituted a significant draw for those looking to move into the state. Slavery did not, however, prevail everywhere, nor was it a fully supported practice. Although cotton was booming, the ranching industry was growing considerably in western and northern Texas, and the state was also producing other agricultural products such as corn. Those industries were not reliant on slave labor, which was relegated to the Gulf Coast. This is where the division existed, especially as talk of secession from the Union arose.

The Constitution of 1861 stemmed directly from the decision to secede from the Union. In fact, Texas was happy with its state constitution at the time. The provisions built into the sections regarding education, fiscal rights, and institutional design were popular and successful in directing the structure of the government. The most contentious issues involved slavery and its effects on the state's industry.

While Texas was engaged in a regional debate, its legislature was not. In fact, of the sitting legislators, 70 percent were slaveholders who favored breaking away from the Union. At a special convention on February 2, 1861, the final vote was cast, and Texas declared that it would leave the Union for the Confederacy. The reasoning was that the United States (more specifically, northern states) had overstepped the powers granted by the US Constitution; that is, the government was accused of treating this document as representing supreme law and thus usurping the powers of the states, including Texas.

Furthermore, proponents of secession claimed that the government was "established by the white race" and that the African race was inferior and had no right to the claims of life, liberty, and the pursuit of happiness under either federal or state law. This seems like an archaic idea today. However, in 1861, for most of the lawmakers in Texas, it was an idea that would force them to leave the Union, despite their past vigorous attempts to become part of it.

As Texas moved into the Confederacy, the state's constitution was altered in ways specific to the new situation. Elected officials were required to declare loyalty to the Confederacy and slavery, and states' rights were reinforced. Furthermore, it became illegal to free slaves. The rest of the document was kept intact.

Constitutions of 1866 and 1869: Back to the Union and Reconstruction

After fighting in the Civil War for almost five years, Texas was open to rejoining the Union and to rewriting its constitution once again. Texas had seceded largely because of issues involving slavery—mainly, opposition to the practice on the part of the federalists and the northern states. At this point, Texas had to rewrite its constitution to comply with many of the federal mandates it had once fought against. As the period of Reconstruction began, the former Confederate states were required to accept and enforce the Fourteenth Amendment to the US Constitution, which granted fundamental rights of person and property to all individuals. This would strip Texas of its ability to classify anyone as a slave. However, suffrage and equal civil rights were not included in either the Texas Constitution or the Constitution of the United States. Further mandates included the repudiation of all war debt incurred by the state and the removal of the right to secede.

Outside of those issues, the Texas Constitution remained intact, with small changes to the operation of the government. The governor's term was extended to four years, and a governor could serve only two terms in a twelve-year period. The office of comptroller of public accounts was created to ensure the fiscal direction of the state; this officer would be elected within the executive branch. The position was also granted a salary increase. The Supreme Court was increased to five justices with term limits of ten years, while the legislature was kept as it was, with salary increases and reapportionment (based on the population of white males) happening every ten years. On the surface, the constitution of 1866 did not seem mark a significant shift. Much of the government was the same, and although central government was reinforced, the new document did not wholly undermine the states' rights idea or disrupt power in any significant way.

During this period of Reconstruction, the South was under US and military rule. The Reconstruction Acts of 1867 mandated that states were to be governed by the military. In this case, Texas and Louisiana were paired together under General Winfield Hancock, who would oversee the states' efforts to meet the demands of Reconstruction. Texas was required to ratify the Thirteenth and Fourteenth Amendments, and its state constitution would have to be approved by the federal government.

Hancock called a convention to rewrite the Texas Constitution so that it would fall in line with these provisions. The debate was carried by radical Republicans, staunch federalists who advocated for strong central government and the expansion of fundamental rights, including suffrage, to African Americans based on the Fourteenth Amendment. Although these measures were opposed by the Texas Democrats, who were antifederalists, the Republicans' numbers and the backing of the federal government won out. Thus, Texas ratified the Thirteenth and Fourteenth Amendments, putting the state in compliance with the US Constitution.

The convention also added a clause to the Texas Constitution stating that the US Constitution was the supreme law of the land. African Americans were given the right to vote, and slavery was outlawed. The governor's position became one closely resembling that of the president of the United States, with the power to appoint officials and justices as well as greater power over the executive branch. This move was intended to strengthen the executive branch and place it on at least an equal footing with the state's congress, which was set at ninety members in the House of Representatives and thirty in the Senate. The governor was given the power to appoint justices, and the Supreme Court was again altered, with the number of its justices being brought back to three from five, with each serving a nine-year term.

Under these two constitutions, Texas was repositioned as a steward state under the US government. Much of the states' rights idea ingrained in Texas's political culture was stripped, but with this also came a reinforcement of those ideas. Texas was unhappy with the federal government's oversight: corruption calls against Governor E. J. Davis were loud and common, and oversight from the military further entrenched the state's views opposing true federalism. When Reconstruction ended in 1873, there were calls from within the state to not only revert to its earlier form of government (prior to the Civil War) but also to try to adopt measures that would protect this historic way of life. In truth, the traditionalist political culture discussed in Chapter 1 was established in large part as a result of reaction to Reconstruction as well as to federal rule in the decade following the Civil War. These sentiments would be reflected in the final constitution composed by the state.

Constitution of 1876: Response to Reconstruction

Davis's regime as governor is widely considered to have been corrupt and power hungry, and during his tenure, negative feelings toward the central government increased. An economic depression during the early 1870s did not help matters; as a result, farmers pushed for popular control of the government in hopes that it would pass legislation helpful to agriculture.

In 1875, as the Reconstruction era came to an end, the government called a convention in order to reshape the constitution. This time, unlike six years earlier, most of the delegates were Democrats, with Republicans occupying only fifteen of the ninety seats. Without opposition, the real debate came mainly from a popular controlling faction within the Democratic Party called the Grange, a group that represented farmers who wanted widespread change. The Grange occupied forty of the ninety seats and used that majority to influence the direction of change, in particular wanting to limit the impact of the central government. The convention focused on four areas:

1   Popular control was seen as a way of curtailing corruption within the government. With popular control, decisions and decision makers would be subject to public

referendums. Elections (in which only white males could run or vote) would offer a way of controlling the government. This approach spawned the idea of electing judges and played a role in revising the amendment structure, whereby a popular majority vote would be required to amend the constitution. As many saw it, the move to popular control would restrict the ability of a central entity to extend its power beyond what the will of the people would allow. It also placed the burden of government on the people.

2   Limiting the power of government was another option. The convention debated the issue of whether the power of government should be limited and governmental responsibility spread out among several entities. From this came the idea of the plural executive, whereby the power to govern would be divided among six individuals, including the governor, all of whom would be popularly elected. Also, the legislature would be limited to a part-time role with a strict salary limit. Legislative sessions were limited to one every two years, special sessions notwithstanding, to limit the influence and actions of the government.

3   The economy was a driver of political and governmental debate; that is, it was felt that a fiscally responsible state would not be obliged to raise vast funds. The amount of debt that the state could accrue and its ability to tax the public would be limited. Instead, taxation would be regressive, relying on sales and business taxes to produce revenue. Other ideas for cutting costs were introduced, including placing limits on the sorts of social programs that the state could enact. Most notable was the decentralization of the education system. To save money, education would be left to local governments and special districts, putting the onus on them to carry out state mandates. This had the result of promoting inequality and segregation in the state's schools.

4   Last, agricultural interests had a strong influence on shaping the constitution. The constitution protected property rights and ensured land ownership and low taxes by fortifying the homestead exemptions; that is, the constitution exempted properties (including all homes valued at $3,000 or less at the time) from government taxation and comprised a tiered system of exemptions as the value of such properties increased. There were also limits on the activities of competitive businesses (such as railroads and the enterprises that came with them) and restrictions on the proliferation of banks.

The Texas Constitution Today

After the constitutional convention of 1875, the Texas Constitution of 1876 was ratified, and it formed the basis of the constitution as it exists today. Of the four major areas of focus, three proved to be influential. The emphasis on agricultural needs changed over time, and this calls into question the logic of basing a modern state on a constitution that focuses on policy areas and concepts that may become outdated. However, the multiple iterations and constantly changing nature of the constitution has given way; since 1876, Texas has chosen simply to amend rather than rewrite this document. What we have currently is 139 years of amendments guided by the state's evolving politics and culture.

The Texas Constitution we know today arose from the history reviewed in the previous section. The major long-standing aspect of today's constitution is the will to limit government expansion. Limited government has been the goal of the Texas Constitution since the end of Reconstruction. That is, Texas approved and added provisions to this 289-section document that made it a guide for how to keep government from overstepping its authority. The complexity and strength of the Texas Constitution stems from this premise.

As Texas sought to limit government power, it turned its constitution into a document of policy through constitutional power. This document has grown, and policy (especially specialized policy) has subjected the document to both praise and criticism. Low voter turnout and the ability of special interest groups to influence the public have opened Texas' constitution to special provisions and mandates that may not have the greater good of the state in mind. As we review the constitution, look for these basic emphases and consider how the major concepts that were built into this document—views of education, taxes, business interests, property rights, and power—have or have not been served by recent amendments.

Role of the Bill of Rights

Thomas Jefferson, a noted antifederalist during the creation of the nation, was an advocate for a bill of rights. Arguing against his friend and colleague James Madison, Jefferson maintained that, regardless of the intentions of the government, all publics have the right to acceptable and mandatory protection from government tyranny. From this thought sprang the current US Bill of Rights. Traditionally, its list of amendments constitutes citizens' primary first layer of protection from oppression by the government. Prior to the writing of the US Constitution, most states employed bills of rights to guarantee these types of civil protections. The state of Texas has always incorporated such a bill into its constitution—since 1812, when its first constitution was written, to the current iteration, which was written in 1876 and under which the state operates today.

The Texas Bill of Rights includes many of the same provisions and protections as its national counterpart. There is protection from illegal or unlawful prosecution by the government. There are provisions addressing equal protection, equality of law, and freedom of worship as well as protections for political speech. On the other hand, some guarantees of rights are provided for the government. The legislature has the right to suspend law, to regulate the compensation to victims of crimes, and to oversee the regulation, definition, and use of public beaches.

These last few provisions in the bill of rights instigated a debate over what it should provide regarding the social compact/contract. Traditionally, a bill of rights is a product of negative rights, protecting citizens from government tyranny. Texas moved away from that tradition with provisions that cross into the realm of positive rights, such as promoting the use of public beaches and guaranteeing rights to victims of crimes (e.g., restitution to victims, guaranteed involvement, and notices regarding the corresponding case). In truth, there is no right or wrong answer or a single way to provide the protection Jefferson suggested. A bill of rights, at any level, is a product of the people and their will. In Texas, that will is provided in the current iteration of the bill of rights.

The Power and Structure of Government

Article II lays the groundwork for the structure of government by establishing its three major branches, all of which are given significant power. The key points here are the division (i.e., separation) of power and the basic idea of a system of checks and balances that restricts any branch or branches from usurping the power of another. Akin to a similar article in the US Constitution, Article II sets the definition of power and lines of responsibility for the executive, legislative, and judicial branches of government.

Extending from these provisions are three successive articles that outline the powers and roles of each branch. Article III provides for the basic organization of the legislature. This body is very similar to its federal counterpart. There are two chambers, the House of Representatives and Senate, which are capped at 150 and thirty-one members, respectively, by constitutional order. This article sets the standards for the minimal age for office (twenty-one for the House, twenty-six for the Senate), defines residency requirements, and provides salary guidelines. It limits meetings of the legislature to once every two years. While the details and rules of the branch are there, the article extends further to provide legislative checks in a variety of ways. One of the sixty-seven sections of the article stipulates that the legislature must come under the guidance of the comptroller of public accounts regarding budget estimates and activity. Several sections, however, go beyond legislative power. There are sections outlining the provisions of the lottery as well as portions that define the power that county and municipal officials exercise at the local levels of government. While the article is mainly about the functions and structure of the legislature, many sections also address economic development.

There is no greater example of limited government in the Texas Constitution than Article IV, which fractures the executive branch into a six-sided office. The aim of dispersing power in this way is to avoid empowering one person. The article is much more focused than its legislative predecessor: its sections outline the roles of the plural executive, including those of the lieutenant governor, secretary of state (the only appointed official), comptroller of public accounts, commissioner of the general land office (the powers and limitations of which are outlined in Article XIV), and the attorney general. Each office is given a clear set of directions and responsibilities. As those offices are granted power (to be addressed later in this book), the governor's power is restricted in specific ways. The governor serves four-year terms and has specific formal powers such as addressing and calling the legislature into special session and assigning the power to enact legislation, which can also be used to draft and sign executive orders. The rest of the administrative powers given by the constitution are allocated to the other offices in the plural executive.

Article V defines the judicial branch and establishes a structure for the court system, from the dual high courts all the way down to justices of the peace. The constitution outlines the specific jurisdictions and powers attributed to every level of the court system as well as the duties of all judges (these duties are outlined in Chapter 7). The creation of the dual high courts is an important aspect of the constitution, since it provides for the establishment of the Texas Criminal Court of Appeals and the Texas Supreme Court, the latter dealing with civil cases. In addition to the dual-high-court setup, the election of judges is outlined in the constitution. By constitutional provision, the public is charged with the election of judges. Supreme Court justices (nine in each court) are elected through at-large votes, while local judges are elected by their constituents. The constitution calls for independence and allows for justices to conduct their business without fear of reprisal; however, it also exposes judges to the will and oversight of the people. It is a subject of significant debate and has led to attempts to revise the constitution.

These four articles (II through V) outline the foundations of a limited government. As their sections and provisions mount, they provide evidence for a clear case of mistrust of centralized government power resulting in specific direction and limits of power being placed on the three branches of the government. With that have come several sections that seem out of place. Sections in Article III dealing with economic development stand out by offering opportunities for one branch of government to exert legislative control over another. Judges are charged with making impartial decisions; the inclusion of elections meets the idea of mistrusting the power of the central government, but it can also lead to corruption and pandering to the public in the name of self-preservation rather than being objective in carrying out the law.

Education

As already mentioned, education is a cornerstone of Texas's constitutional history. The concept that a refined education system is an integral part of a successful republic has been a running theme throughout the state's history, from its time as a Mexican state, to its declaration of independence, to today. Each successive constitution has included a dedication to education that makes the state responsible for maintaining and promoting that system. Article VII details that responsibility and gives it direction. Much of Article XII is dedicated to the structure of education at the primary, secondary, and tertiary levels and details the policies and expectations to be met by the state.

The structure of the education system, which is run through special districts and funded by taxation, is outlined in the provisions of Article XII. Article VII gives power to the state government to make decisions regarding curriculum and uniform learning objectives. That article provides for the creation of the state board of education and the Texas Education Agency. Higher education is outlined as a function that is overseen by the state's board of education as well as a board of regents. These executive boards determine funding at the higher education levels and manage the staffing of executive positions at universities. The education system is discussed in multiple chapters in this book, but it has been the subject of much debate regarding the sources of funding as well as the amount of funding allocated to each district. The state budget is routinely held up as school districts and local entities battle for funding and challenge legislative decisions on issues dealing with funds allocation and equity in resources and instruction. Challenges routinely end up in the Texas Supreme Court, which can slow the budget process down.

Local Governments

Articles IX and XI deal with government at the municipal and county levels. These functions are discussed at length in Chapter 4. However, we can note here that there is a clear trend in the provisions governing the legislature's ability to make policy regarding local affairs. The legislature has the power to make decisions and policy that can create and tax a special district in an area that meets specific criteria. The legislature also has the power to define a municipal or county function in regard to how these entities carry out their services and roles. Along with these provisions are basic structural components regarding how municipalities and counties are defined. Again, these are discussed at length in Chapter 4.

Article XVI: The Catch-All

What do pensions, the residences of civil officials, homestead exemptions, mixed beverages, and the oath of office have in common? Apparently not much, but they are grouped together in the Texas Constitution. Under Article XVI, these wildly different policy areas are combined in a section called "general provisions." The article serves the purpose that its title suggests: it is, by default, the catch-all of the Texas Constitution. Amendments and provisions that are general in nature and do not have a stated home in the constitution are petitioned to be entered as general provisions. Although this seems innocuous enough, the existence of this article underlies much of the debate surrounding this document.

The main critiques of the Texas Constitution revolve around its length, dearth of topics, and seeming tendency to overstep the policy or procedural powers defined in some of its parts. The existence and definition of an oath of office is integral to modern democracy. It is necessary to grant power to the legislature, and it is important to define the power of a county assessor, but many of the provisions in Article XVI read like policies passed by the legislature and, in some cases, like procedures for a bureaucratic agency. Within these provisions often lies the granting of power to a government entity to act on or in support of a specific activity. This is where the constitutionality of these provisions comes into contention. For example, Section 20 (regarding alcoholic and mixed beverages) seems out of place in the constitution, as it grants the state legislature the ability to pass provisions regarding the sale of such beverages as well as giving power to municipal and county governments to use and sell them within their jurisdictions. Such a specific and positive-rights-oriented provision calls into question its placement in the constitution. There are similar provisions in this article that might be better suited as policy (especially, at times, local policy) that is debated and passed in the halls of the legislature. Understanding how these provisions find their way into the constitution is the next step in our analysis.

The Amendment Process: Changing the Constitution and the Reasons for Change

Constitutions that can be amended are called living documents, as they can be altered to follow the trends of the population and the time. In that respect, Texas's constitution has lived more than most. The state's traditionalistic political culture shines through in the way it has treated its constitution. "The inclusion of particular governmental institutions or policy type provisions in the constitution indicates that these policy areas are important to the citizens of the state. In this sense, the constitution of the state can be tailored to reflect the political culture or values of the people who live under it" (Hammons 2010, 1342). Over the years, Texas has struggled to let things go. The state has been transformed, especially demographically and economically, as much as any state of the Union. Its governing document has been the subject of continual amendment instead of critical revision. The state has held firm with many of the traditional provisions that were written in 1876 but has also considered 662 amendments. Despite the continual attempts at change, Texas has chosen to keep its connection to the past rather than scrap its constitution fully.

Article XVII guides the amendment process in Texas. The article explains in detail how the constitution can be shaped and reshaped within the context of constitutional law. No amendment can fracture the basic tenets of the constitution, nor can it contradict clauses and amendments within the US Constitution without calling its alignment into question.

The process begins in the legislature, where the proposed amendment to the state constitution is written and presented by a member or members. Each proposal must be written and voted on by both chambers (the Texas House of Representatives and Senate) and receive a two-thirds vote of approval in each chamber. Today, that is one hundred votes in the House and twenty-one in the Senate. If the amendment is approved, the legislators decide on a date for it to be submitted for popular approval through a special election.

All proposed amendments must be written by the secretary of state and provided to all local newspapers in the state to be published. They are also sent to county clerks, who must post the notifications between fifty and ninety days prior to the election and again a week later for public consumption and debate. After public notice is provided, if a simple public majority approves the measure, it is drafted into the current constitution.

The approval process places a burden on the state's constituents to be knowledgeable about proposed amendments. In comparison with the federal constitution, whose amendments are approved by a two-thirds vote of state legislatures, Texas offers its amendments up for the approval of its citizens as a measure of popular control. As with any election, this places the burden on the public to make quality decisions regarding the state constitution; it also gives the amendment process a political tone. As legislators propose amendments and the public approves them, political will and opinion can come to play a part in the process.

It is not surprising that many recent provisions in the Texas Constitution are classified as providing the legislature with more power, while suggested reforms to empower the executive branch have been shot down. In the past twenty years, a common theme for revisions made to the constitution has allowed for the legislature to take power or make policy in areas they would not have been able to otherwise. For example, the legislature is granted power through provision to create and levy taxes on county hospital districts while restricting local policy that contradicts its constitutional power. That provision, passed in 1999, could be an example of the legislature exploiting the amendment process to expand the power of its branch.

Hammons (2010) contends that the amendment process (the ability to tailor a constitution to the state's needs) is mandatory. Texas continues to encounter serious change in its population and social makeup. States can use their constitutions to ensure a way of life or meet the needs of the population. The ability and willingness to use the amendment process to meet those needs is an important tool that a state can use to make sure that government maintains relevance and proper connection to the population it governs. There is concern that political majorities or culture may change over time. But in states such as Texas, which has a tradition of consistent and sturdy politics, the amendment process can provide an opportunity to maintain balance and political connection.

Are Voters Overwhelmed?

Recently, the number of constitutional amendments passed in Texas has declined. While amendments in the 1990s and 2000s were passed as general cleanup movements to reorganize the constitution with a view to making it easier to understand, the process of making amendments to the document has been tough. Part of the reason for this is opposition in the state's legislature. In a traditionalistic state, changing the "way we've done things" can be both tough and politically jolting. For instance, the proposal by Rob Junell and Bill Ratliff in 1999 to revamp the state's constitution would have set the state on a path to a stronger executive official, empowered local voters, and turned the state's appellate courts over to an appointment process. It would also have revamped Texas's government. The amendment was shot down in the legislature, as it was seen as bringing too much change.

Getting an amendment out of the legislature is only half the battle. With final approval coming from the public, a disengaged voter base has become increasingly problematic. Voter participation in off election years is abysmal. Dating back to 1995, the highest level of participation in a special election to amend the constitution has been 17 percent.[3] Getting voters to the polls and involved in discussions about proposed constitutional amendments is becoming tougher by the year.

A part of the problem is when votes are scheduled. One factor affecting voter participation is voter burnout, or the idea that if voters are faced with a long ballot of choices, especially ones that seem unfamiliar, their willingness to participate in an engaged manner will decline. The response to this is to place amendments on special ballots. This addresses the voter burnout issue but requires voters to become engaged off schedule. In election years since 1995, when constitutional amendments were on the ballot, participation has ranged from 51 to 59 percent, a sharp increase from the 4 to 17 percent seen in off years.

The amendments themselves also contribute to this issue. Innocuous changes are met with apathy and lower voter turnouts. When issues are intriguing or connect to the public, the participation levels rise. In 2005, when 17 percent participated, the marquee amendment centered on same-sex marriage; the amendment defined marriage as a union between one man and one woman. This was a hot-button issue around the nation, and large amounts of money were poured into the debate as both sides and their activists rallied support. All that has had a positive effect on voter engagement and participation.

Duplicating that engagement on other amendment votes or votes that do not carry the same cachet is much tougher. Without watershed decisions, voter participation falls dramatically, begging the question of whether the amendment process works. If the mandate for public approval of an amendment is needed, does the low voter turnout nullify a sense of popular control, considering that only a small segment of the population participates? In considering revisions to this process, the state must evaluate this effect, since low voter turnout can be manipulated by the legislature and interest groups. It also degrades the popular control on which the constitution is predicated.

---

3   Texas Secretary of State, www.sos.state.tx.us.

The US or Texas Model: Which Constitution Fits Best?

A popular movement among academics and constitutional historians is to reform state constitutions to more closely resemble the type seen at the federal level. These calls for reform center on two basic ideas: flexibility and applying a framework on which to build (Lutz 1994; Przeworski 1994). Conceptually, the format of the US Constitution allows for actors in the government to use its clauses and amendments as guides for political and government activity. In many cases, the US Constitution does not give explicit instruction; instead, it offers implicit concepts for those in government to interpret and build upon. Because of this, cases that are explicit carry the full weight of supreme law. The idea of adding a list of provisions that resemble public law and policy is a foreign and unaccepted practice under this model. The idea, then, is that states would be better off applying these same concepts and structures to their own operations, allowing their constitutions to act as frameworks while letting the branches of government decide and administer law. In fact, reformers see the sheer number of provisions in most state constitutions as an impediment to the effectiveness of a state or governing document.

At the state level, the constitution is treated differently. Instead of letting the document be a framework, it is a source of action and power, often mixing the concepts of positive rights and negative rights seen in its federal counterpart. Part of this stems from the different roles the two layers of government play. As we'll discuss in Chapter 3 about federalism, each layer of government plays a specific role and performs different functions. At the federal level, a framework-oriented constitution is useful because of the limited nature of federal government. States, on the other hand, are more "hands on." Part of their primary function is to carry out services rather than enact policy. Much of this responsibility is defined by the Tenth Amendment of the federal constitution, which states that all actions and clauses that do not fall to the national government fall to the states. This amendment ensures that the two layers of government will carry out different functions. The different responsibilities make pushes for reform difficult, as one style does not fit the other.

Although politics drives many of Texas's decisions away from an active government, the 491 amendments to its constitution have gone through a significant legislative process, with much of the activity geared toward defining the role and proper action of government and further explaining specific issues. Including these provisions within the constitution allows for greater clarity and empowerment of the government when needed at the action-oriented state level.

This is not to say that Texas has not attempted constitutional reform in the past. In 1921, Governor Pat Neff proposed revising the constitution to catch up with the modern economy and social changes in the state. At the top of Neff's list of changes was an expanded role and term (from two to four years) for the governor and a shift to annual legislative sessions. His reform did not pass.

After political and financial scandals, the voters approved a constitutional convention in 1972 that would revise the constitution in such a way as to help weed out corruption and financial irregularities on the part of the government. After two years, the convention came back with a trimmed-down version of the document that proposed (1) annual meetings for the legislature, (2) judicial appointments at the state level, (3) the prohibition of mandatory union membership through a right-to-work clause, and (4) widespread school funding reform. These last two, among other provisions, killed the reform's popularity with conservatives and liberals alike, and the revision fell three votes short of approval.

Moving forward, there are areas of discussion for change. Texas has long since examined its selection process for state judges, debating the virtues of the election-based accountability system vs. the appointment-based independence system. There is also the streamlining of bureaucracy that constantly comes under scrutiny and debate in a state prone to less action. Still, streamlining the system and even sources of funding are areas that reformers could tackle in the future. Such changes, however, will probably come through amendments rather than a rewrite of the state's governing document.

Summary

After a period of immense and rampant change, Texas settled on the ways in which its government should function. After quickly evolving through several constitutions (which included influences from Mexico, Spain, and the United States as well as a fear of the central government), Texas had a constitution that changed and grew through amendments while retaining its basic structure and tenets over time. Today, limited government remains a focus. Texas has continued to promote and strengthen its limitations on government while also putting greater emphasis on economics. This is discussed in more detail in later chapters.

While the bones remain the same, what we've seen is that the Texas Constitution has changed over time for better and worse, depending on one's viewpoint. The document in its final iteration has become rigid and cumbersome, but that does not represent failure. Diverging from the federal level, the Texas Constitution is still a living document that is based on a traditionalistic viewpoint. It has guided the state to where it is today.

References

Ballotpedia.org, "Louisiana Constitution." Last modified August 28, 2016. https://ballotpedia.org/Louisiana_Constitution.

Banning, L. *Jefferson and Madison: Three Conversations from the Founding*. Lanham, MD; Rowman & Littlefield, 1995.

Bruff, H. H. "Separation of Powers Under the Texas Constitution." *Texas Law Review* 68 (1989): 1337.

Calvert, R. A., A. De Leon, and G. Cantrell. The History of Texas. Hoboken, NJ: John Wiley & Sons, 2013.

Crouch, B. A. "'Unmanacling' Texas Reconstruction: A Twenty-Year Perspective." *The Southwestern Historical Quarterly* 93, no. 3 (1990): 275–302.

Dodd, W. F. "The Function of a State Constitution." *Political Science Quarterly* 30, no. 2 (1915): 201–221.

Elazar, D. J. *American Federalism: A View from the States 2nd edition.* Springfield, OH: Thomas Y. Crowell Publishing, 1972.

Elazar, D. J. "The Principles and Traditions Underlying State Constitutions." *Publius* 12, no. 1 (1982): 11–25.

Hammons, C. W. "State Constitutional Reform: Is It Necessary?" *Albany Law Review* 64 (2000): 1327.

Ginsburg, T. *Constitutional Endurance.* Cheltenham, UK; Edward Elgar, 2011.

Lutz, D. S. "Toward a Theory of Constitutional Amendment." *American Political Science Review* 88, no. 2 (1994): 355–370.

May, J. C. "Constitutional Amendment and Revision Revisited." *Publius: The Journal of Federalism* 17, no.1 (1987): 153–179.

May, J. C. "State Constitutions and Constitutional Revision, 2000–2001." *The Book of the States* 34, (2002): 3–11.

Przeworski, A. (1994, December). Comment on "The Impact of Constitutions on Economic Performance" by Elster. In *Proceedings of the Annual World Bank Conference on Development Economics 1992.* Washington D.C.; International Bank for Reconstruction and Development, 1993.

Texas constitutions, all iterations, Tarlton Law Library; Austin, TX. http://tarlton.law.utexas.edu/Constitutions/.

Usman, J. O. "Good Enough for Government Work: The Interpretation of Positive Constitutional Rights in State Constitutions." *Albany Law Review* 73 (2010): 1459.

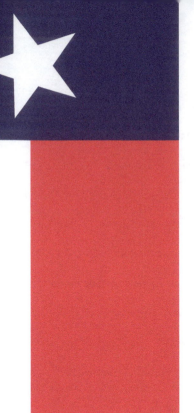

CHAPTER 3

Federalism and Texas

I n 1787, the United States was in shambles. The states were wasting time trying to decide how to best to manage their populations, and the federal government was struggling to work under a structure that was confining at best and limited in the power and actions it could take. Instead of a nation working in harmony, the states were struggling just to figure how to work together, much less how to make the nation prosper.

How to piece the nation together came down to one question: James Madison vs. Montesquieu? The French philosopher was enthralled with the US style of government; however, his disapproval of a strong federal government was clear. Given the issues of time and space and the lack of connectivity to decision makers over a vast land, an effective federal government would be nearly impossible. That is, the government requires a structure able to address all the many issues that may arise in the course of meeting the needs of the public. The alternative was a sovereign nation-state with a loose confederacy. Madison directly opposed that view. Before the Articles of Confederation were deemed ineffective, the Founding Fathers championed a strong but monitored central government, extolling the virtue of oversight.

Deciding which would be better for the United States was the key, and this would have a major impact on every state that then existed or would exist in the future. How the relationship and responsibilities of two distinct layers of government were defined would determine how the nation functioned. Providing states with sovereign powers would invest power in entities that were believed to be more manageable, closely connected to their constituents, more likely to be economically secure, and free from overarching political squabbles. The downside to this type of union would be the pitfalls that the Articles of Confederation brought to the forefront. The Union would be based on voluntary cooperation, which could not be ensured. A federalist or compound republic, as advocated by Madison, suggested oversight, economic stability, security, and defined authority, which would make for a stable nation. The fear was overextending power to a disconnected political/governmental body that would always have the option to overstep its bounds.

Defining this relationship is one of the major questions in political science and the study of government. Some 230 years later, Madison's system has won out. Texas functions in this system and has shown the positives and negatives of both approaches over time. How has this system played out, and what is its impact on the Lone Star State?

US Federalism and Basic Governing Systems

In discussing the topic of federalism, we are looking at how the system of government works. Within this system, state governments such as Texas's are given specific responsibilities and powers derived from the federal government. We'll talk later in this chapter about where those powers come from and what they are, but first it is important to understand the system or systems comprised by the national government.

The basic idea is that the United States operates by way of a three-layer system. The top layer is the federal government, and its power is granted by the Constitution. Its Supremacy Clause (Article VI, Clause 2), which we'll discuss in depth later, has precedence over any law made at the state level. Therefore if a law exists at the federal level, the states, unless they have proven they are sovereign on the issue, must follow that law.

This delineation is best illustrated by the topic of same-sex marriage rights. Until the recent decision by the US Supreme Court, Texas was left to define what marriage was and how the state would act in that regard. Prior to the decision, Texas's constitution had stated that marriage was a union between a man and a woman. The Supreme Court took that issue out of the states' hands, as it is now deemed that any such distinction is a violation of the Fourteenth Amendment of the US Constitution.

The second layer of the system is where Texas comes in. This is the state layer. States are granted power over policy areas and government activity that is not specifically outlined in the federal constitution or covered by a standing federal law. As we discussed in the last chapter, with the US Constitution being oriented toward negative rights, Texas is granted a large amount of power in a significant number of areas. The major role of this layer of government is to carry out government policy issued at the federal level, oversee day-to-day policy, and provide oversight on state laws and areas of policy that the federal government has not addressed.

For example, the decision about whether to grant citizens the right to obtain a license to carry a concealed handgun is left to the states. Currently, Texas is one of forty-one states that have "shall-issue"[1]-allowed CCL licenses. Because this law is not strictly connected to the Constitution, Texas is free to rule and pass a law as its legislature sees fit (under the rules of federalism), and Texas has pushed the idea of open carry.[2] As of January 1, 2016, Texas became the fifteenth state to pass a law allowing citizens with concealed handgun licenses to carry their weapons in open view. The law complies with licensing and federal laws but was made at the state level.

The final layer of federalism is local government. Because there is an entire chapter dedicated to local governments, I will not belabor the issue here. However, an important distinction to be made here is that the local layer is the lowest layer in terms of federalism and must abide by both US and Texas laws. This restricts municipal and county governments' ability to pass laws, limits their activity in carrying out laws passed at the first two levels, and affects their ability to manage local fiscal affairs and social services.

Understanding the division of these layers helps us to understand the basic structure of the system. Regardless of how the layers work together or how the system is defined, these layers exist to provide specific services to the public.

Systems of Federalism

Although the three layers do not change, the system in which the relationship is carried out can be defined and redefined. The United States has seen three distinct systems of federalism that have greatly affected the states, including Texas.

The first system is cooperative federalism. This system is commonly called marble-cake federalism. Although the three layers of government are still present, the lines of power are not clearly defined. In fact, in the absence of clear supremacy, each layer can define and acquire power as it sees fit. The federal constitution still defines lines of power and responsibility; however, states can share power and responsibility on specific policies. Under marble-cake federalism, Texas would share the power over education with the federal government and, where there is an absence of clear federal superiority, would be the decision maker or final authority on the subject. An alternative to this system, historically, is a dual-federalism, or layer-cake, system. Under layer-cake (dual) federalism, the lines of activity and responsibility are clearly defined and the layers of government have specific powers and areas of policy in which they can take charge. Under cooperative federalism, the lines of power and supremacy

---

1   A "shall issue" state is one that requires a concealed handgun license that is granted by the state.

2   Per Texas law, open carry is the practice of carrying a handgun in plain view. To be able to do this, the person must have a concealed handgun license. Public sentiment about this law has ebbed and flowed as businesses have taken up their constitutional right to post signage that bans the practice in their establishments.

are ironclad, and crossing or blurring them is prohibited. In this case, Texas would have only the power that is absent at the federal level and that its constitution provides.

These two systems have ruled our government since the Civil War. As the country has shifted between the two, marble-cake federalism has taken hold. States are granted greater power as the federal government deals with a conflict of identity as to where its power lies. These debates have led to an increasing number of Supreme Court cases, and—as states have fought and won the right to enact or maintain laws and policies that go against federal policy—these have further blurred the lines of power.

Although federalism today is mainly a question of dual versus cooperative, a debate over states' rights has pushed the nation into a battle that strongly involves Texas. When Texas entered the Union in 1845, it entered as a southern state that was in favor of confederacy. A confederacy is a loose union that invests little power in the central government, which is defined by its member states, and instead invests most power and classification regarding laws and policy areas in the states. This was the system under which the US existed after the passage of its original constitution. Antifederalism was the theme of the first ten years of the nation's history, but it became difficult when revolts and intranational squabbling among the states threatened to fracture the Union. When the South, which Texas joined, seceded from the Union, it returned Texas to the status of a confederal state. With Texas—a former nation that was not on board with a strong national government—as a new part of it, the Confederacy was born. Eventually, however, this relationship, which never became productive, was lost with the South's defeat in the Civil War.

The Role of the States

Dual and cooperative federalism faded in and out of control of the government for the better part of two centuries. This relationship has traditionally been protected by the Tenth and Eleventh Amendments of the Constitution. These two amendments have protected many of the lines of power between the nation and its states regarding the policies and actions relegated to each layer of government. Strictly speaking, states are sovereign and can pass all laws that conform with these two amendments.

Texas, traditionally a state that has resisted big government and federal power, has relished this. The state is given the power to make decisions and policy in all areas not covered by the constitutional clauses or amendments that directly enumerate the powers of the federal government. That is the basic concept of the Tenth Amendment. Originally, the federal government was seen to have power over matters of national security, economics, and other standing federal areas of policy. These pared-down policy areas left Texas to administer policy and, most commonly, services to the state's individuals and parties. Texas is left to administer and oversee services such as education, healthcare, transportation, and other day-to-day policy areas that involve government.

Article VI of the US Constitution (the Supremacy Clause) mandates that there is an order to law. With the Constitution setting the main law of the land, this governing document is the ultimate law. Its precedence and the lines of power it provides govern the acts of the federal government and, by extension, grant power to the states where no constitutional power exists. Following that are federal policy and treaties agreed to by the nation. This sets the standard that where federal law exists the national government has jurisidction under the express powers granted to it by the nation's governing document.

Article I, Section 8, Clause 3 includes the Commerce Clause, which mandates that the federal government shall handle matters of both inter- and intrastate commerce. All agreements, laws, and policies regarding commerce fall under the federal government and its ability to make supreme law in these areas. The Commerce Clause is commonly used to enforce federal regulations on market and economic activity.

Last, Article I, Section 8, Clause 18 (the Necessary and Proper Clause) prevents the federal government from making policy that does not pass a rational test, stating that federal policy is necessary to address the policy issue. These three clauses are designed to define and, in their original intent, restrict the federal government's ability to overstep its power in policy areas not specifically outlined in the US Constitution. Where significant gaps exist, states like Texas are mandated to step in and provide guidance and policy in those areas. There is no direction on how or what political direction those actions should take. Such decisions are truly left to the state.

Use of the Necessary and Proper Clause and the Commerce Clause to Develop Informal Power

Article I, Section 8 of the US Constitution has been a source of much debate in federalism. In attempting to act as both a restrictor and definer of power, the Constitution provides clear guidance as to the lines of power in regard to policy and law but leaves much open to interpretation. The coming of the Necessary and Proper Clause and the Commerce Clause has given ground to fights that challenge them. Throughout the years, the federal government has attempted to use these clauses to expand its informal powers.

While the federal government is imbued with a significant amount of delegated powers, the role of government is to expand, and, as we have seen, the US government has done so through Section 8. With the mandate that the government make policy where it is necessary and proper to uphold the basic tenets of the Constitution and natural rights, the government has pushed the boundaries of policy and in effect expanded its power.

The New Deal of the 1930s was the trendsetter for such modern policy. With the Great Depression and the nation's economy in shambles, public perception of the

The Role of the States | **53**

government started to change. Hunger and economic hardship affected millions of people, including policy influencers, and the federal government was prompted to act. Under President Franklin D. Roosevelt, the government passed a laundry list of policies that would provide protection to individuals. Social Security, Medicare, Medicaid, unemployment insurance, and other policies were all passed at this time. However, this legislation originally drew the ire of the Supreme Court, which declared the policies unconstitutional because they violated the federal government's delegated powers. Revisions to make the policies economic in nature and connect them to delegated powers addressed the issues and thus enabled the government to make policy for individuals because it was needed and the states were unable to manage the crisis. Those powers were otherwise remanded to the states.

Commerce has posed challenges to the federalist system. With the Commerce Clause backing it, the federal government has often stepped in to regulate markets that existed within the states' boundaries. The regulation of interest rates, price caps, and monopolies has been carried out by the federal government under the Commerce Clause.

We have seen these attempts backfire. On March 10, 1992, Alfonso Lopez Jr. was arrested in San Antonio for violating the state law prohibiting firearms on school premises. He was later charged with the federal crime of violating the Gun Free School Zones Act of 1990. The act was passed under the Commerce Clause with the rationale that, since the federal government has the mandate to regulate commerce and education was a form of business, the federal government could supervise the education system to ensure safe economic practices. However, the Supreme Court overturned Lopez's conviction, stating: "The Act neither regulates a commercial activity nor contains a requirement that the possession be connected in any way to interstate commerce. We hold that the Act exceeds the authority of Congress "[t]o regulate Commerce … among the several States." U. S. Const., Art. I, §8, cl. 3.

Power in these areas is derived from the Tenth Amendment, which specifically states that where there is no delegated constitutional power to the federal government, the state has power to create policy. This provides Texas with the ability to make policy where there is a gap in federal power, and it protects the state from federal coercion.

The Eleventh Amendment reinforces the state's power by insulating it from federal prosecution. This amendment protects the state from being sued in federal court by individuals or other states in areas where the states are given sovereign immunity. This means that an individual cannot sue or make a claim against a state in a federal court if the claim is based on an area of authority over which the state has authority. If an individual wanted to challenge Texas's allocation of the education budget, they would have to make a case in a state court, without the ability to take the issue to a federal court. This restricts the ability to subject Texas to the control of the federal government. However, there are four exceptions to this:

1   Political subdivisions in a state (i.e., municipalities, counties, special districts) can be brought to suit in a federal court.

2   Sovereign immunity can be retracted if a state violates the Fourteenth Amendment. Subjecting or fracturing the Equal Protection and Due Process Clauses without reason can subject a state to federal judgment.

3   If a state is in conflict with a federal law, it can be taken to federal court. An example would be if Texas refused to issue a marriage license in a case of same-sex marriage. Here, the individuals involved could take the state to federal court for violating the ruling issued by the Supreme Court.

4   The state can waive its right to sovereign immunity and allow the case to be heard in a federal court.

These four exceptions exist to ensure that states do not overstep their boundaries. However, they also reinforce the significant amount of power the states have under these two clauses.

Delegated Powers: Federal vs. State

Delegated powers are expressly granted in the US Constitution. Powers and limitations are provided to both the state and federal governments.

Federal Delegated Powers

The US government is granted specific powers. These powers were originally intended to strictly define what the federal government can do regarding policy. The original delegated powers can be traced to issues raised by the Articles of Confederation, under which the federal government become powerless to alter and govern the group of states. These powers include the following:

- Regulation of foreign and interstate commerce
- Borrowing and coining money

- Managing the postal system
- Declaring war
- Raising and supporting a national defense through a navy and army
- Levying and collecting taxes
- Governing naturalization

State Powers: Constitutional Guarantees

Texas, as well as all the other states, is granted guarantees for policymaking and powers of administration which accompany statehood. These guarantees ensure that Texas operates under equitable circumstances and help to protect the state's sovereignty. The guarantees are as follows:

- A state cannot be divided or combined with another state without consent of the legislature. This nullified the clause stating that Texas would be able to divide into as many as five states when it was annexed.
- States are guaranteed to function in a republican form of government, thus ensuring the election of representatives by popular vote.
- States are allocated two senators and at least one representative in the House of Representative to ensure their roles in the central government; their number can be altered by changes in proportional representation.
- States are ensured a role in the presidential selection process through the Electoral College, which is selected by state senates and takes the final votes in the election. The number of electors is determined by a state's legislative representation. Texas currently has thirty-eight votes.
- States are assured control over the Constitution and its amendment process. All amendments must be ratified by a three-fourths vote in either the state legislatures or at state conventions. This process has been used for all but one US Constitutional amendment, the Twenty-Fourth.
- States are entitled to protection from attack or domestic violence from the federal government and can operate and maintain a standing state militia. Texas currently operates the Army National Guard, Air National Guard, and State Guard.
- States are assured that trials by federal courts for crimes committed in Texas will take place within the state's borders.

Although the states have guarantees, they also have reserved powers. As we will discuss later in this book, the US Constitution is defined as much by what is not written as by what is written. Government entities have expanded power with informal or, in this case, reserved powers that are implied by clauses and sections of the document. Because the Tenth Amendment leaves room for interpretation regarding state and federal powers and responsibilities, several areas of informal powers are applied to the states.

Public education is an area where the state has reserved power. Although the federal government has pushed policy in this area, within state borders, states govern the actions and policies on education. *Lopez v. Texas* (1964) challenged this when federal policy attempted to restrict the use of firearms on public school property, and the Supreme Court upheld the state's power to govern activity on school property. Conversely, the state's power over education was seemingly diminished with the administration of the No Child Left Behind Act, which set national standards and funding decisions based on federal guidelines, essentially lessening the state's control over performance and evaluation.

Law enforcement is another area where the state has control. Enforcement of federal and state law is delegated to state law enforcement agencies. Within that, the state is responsible for preserving the health, safety, morals, and general welfare of its citizens. The federal government levies taxes, but the state also has the right to levy taxes. An individualistic state, Texas resists personal taxes such as an income tax, but it has employed its ability to tax property, sales, and corporations, among others, to raise the revenues needed to pay for state policy and public officials' salaries, establish a rainy-day fund, and pay state debts.

Property ownership is a unique power reserved to the state, as it allows the state to guarantee public ownership of property for use of services. This power gives the state the ability to purchase and own land for roads, highways, airports, schools, and any other service the state is delegated and mandated to provide. Property ownership can provide the state with revenue. Texas has seen an expansion of toll roads, on which drivers must pay fees to access highways.

This also leads to the controversial topic of eminent domain. States can acquire private property at a fair and equitable price for public projects. This has most commonly come into play with the construction or reconstruction of roads and highways. The ability to buy the land needed to build a highway, which must be justifiable, is provided to the state. In 2005, the Fifth Amendment was expanded to allow local governments to acquire lands (under the eminent domain mandate) for public projects. One common effect of this involves building publicly owned or partially owned professional sports stadiums. In 2011, the city of Houston and Harris County purchased land (again, such purchases must be made at fair prices) to build the BBVA Compass Stadium for the Houston Dynamos, a major league soccer franchise. The area around the land became a "tax reinvestment zone" designed to provide revenue to the city.

State Limitations

States do not have carte blanche or free rein. Texas is granted several rights and powers by the Constitution, but there are still lines that the state cannot cross. Many of these lines deal with jurisdiction and actions that cross state borders. The Constitution gives Texas the right to pass and uphold laws as it sees fit under its guarantees and reserved powers. It must also honor those same distinctions and privileges for persons crossing state lines.

Article IV protects the rights of visiting citizens. It states that any person visiting a state is entitled to the same privileges and immunities, including protection from the government; protection of life, liberty, and the pursuit of happiness; and all rights granted by that state and the federal constitution as defined by the Supreme Court. This restricts a state from treating visitors improperly or attempting to restrict certain rights and privileges because of the visitors' status. It does not mean that a state must obey and apply laws from visitors' home states to those individuals.

All persons in Texas must abide by the laws of the state, regardless of any conflicts with the laws of other states. This is reinforced by the Full Faith and Credit Clause, which mandates that any government action by another state must be recognized by officials in all the states. All of Texas's laws, state constitutional clauses and amendments, deeds, marriages, divorce rulings, and civil decisions must be honored in relation to people who have crossed the border into another state. Issues with this clause arise when another state has a contradictory clause or law which would take effect if a person were in the state.

One notable exception involves criminal cases. If a person is found guilty of a criminal charge in Texas, he or she cannot be tried for that transgression by another state. If the charge fractures federal law, the federal court system can move the case from the state court to its own jurisdiction to pursue the case. Persons charged with a crime in another state who are apprehended in Texas fall subject to extradition agreements between states.

The relationship between states is important because states can form understandings and partnerships to enhance certain aspects of government. An example is memorandums of understanding regarding state military assistance in times of crisis or natural disaster. States are not, however, compelled to dedicate military resources unless they are called to do so by the federal government.

States are also no longer free to leave the Union. Although Texas pushed for this right as it was petitioning for statehood, the Supreme Court found, in *Texas v. White* (1869), that the Constitution sees the Union as binding, an agreement between the states that cannot be fractured for any reason.

The Rise of Coercive Federalism

Defining federal and state power is one of the major tasks of the government. A by-product of this is that both layers (federal and state) have fought, at different times and by different means, to broaden those definitions. Depending on which system of federalism was involved, each layer has wielded more power at some times than at others. Over the past thirty-five years, the federal government has pulled ahead, as coercive federalism has taken control (Cranston 1979; Kincaid 1996, 2008; Posner 2007).

"US federalism today can be described as 'coercive' because major political, fiscal, statutory, regulatory, and judicial practices entail impositions of many federal (i.e., national government) dictates on state and local governments" (Kincaid 2008, 1). Most recently, the federal government has taken actions to expand its power. Where has that expansion taken place?

Taking a page from Roosevelt and the New Deal, the national government has moved into the realms of social and fiscal policies. Most notably, federal policy has begun to incorporate mandates that are directed at individuals and the entities that represent them rather than the traditional path, which involved state mandates or directives that then extended to the individual. This trend of policy directed to the individual (or individual entities) has sparked more federal government involvement in the country's day-to-day affairs, and some states have argued that it goes beyond constitutional powers and increases limitations on the states.

Furthermore, with the advent of technology, access to federal policy makers has become easier. Social and special interest groups have direct lines of access to policy makers. Benefits from federal programs for the public now flow directly from the federal government to the individual rather than being filtered through state or local governments; reducing the subnational government functionality. The federal government has made policies—whether they are financial, ideological, access-granting, or restricting—through congressional acts and executive orders that are centered on addressing constituents directly and, by extension, bypassing states.

In this sense, several factors regarding federal power come into play. One way the government can obtain power is through increasing the states' reliance on pass-through funds and federal grants-in-aid. The nation's economy and operating budget have increasingly become dependent on federal funding. With budget allocations to gain, states must often adhere to federal regulations and policy to obtain the funds they need to operate programs.

Under the No Child Left Behind laws, education policy falls into this category. States are left to govern education within their borders, but federal funds are used to provide those services. When the bill was enacted, those funds were tied to student achievement and compliance with the program. The "power of the purse strings," as it is colloquially called, can be a driver into a coercive state.

There is also the practice of federal earmarks, or "pork-barreling," which allocates money from the federal government to specific areas, and this can be used to expand power. Taxation has also played a role, as the federal government has preempted the states' ability to tax citizens for services such as the Internet or to impose undue sales taxes.

Federal preemptions have also paved the way. As Kincaid (1996, 2008) points out, preemptions have become a useful tool for legislators, allowing them to usurp states' powers and rights. Preemption suspends a state's power, thus enabling the federal government to institute a statute or policy that would otherwise encroach upon its constitutional power. States can and have challenged preemptions in the US Supreme Court, but these challenges routinely fail; the justifying rationale is that the preemptions enact policies that involve no state-to-federal or state-to-state conflict.

One such case that affected Texas was the National Defense Authorization Act of 2006, which gave the federal government and the president the power to command any state's National Guard during a state of disaster or emergency. That control has historically been focused within each state's executive (per the Constitution), allowing any state to allocate its forces to other states or the federal government with its governor's approval. The National Defense Authorization Act preempts this power when the case of emergency comes into play.

These activities have driven a wedge in political relationships between state and federal governments. Texas, a state in favor of increasing the powers it has been granted, has routinely butted heads with the federal government on political matters. Texas pushed back in the early stages of allowing same-sex marriage licenses when the decision was passed down by the Supreme Court. The state also rejected federal aid after Hurricane Ike caused damage to the state's Gulf Coast and eastern cities. Recently, Texas has opposed allocating resources to other states and fought the government over federal preemptions. Governor Greg Abbott deployed National Guard troops to the Rio Grande Valley (on the US border) after President Barack Obama's executive order absolving immigration claims. The state filed an injunction in a federal district court in Texas to halt the order, which is currently being discussed.

Federal disputes play out in the federal court system. States have the opportunity to challenge federal policy, and they have come up on both sides of the decision. Most recently, Texas won a battle against coercive federalism regarding the state's power to conduct redistricting (i.e., drawing the boundaries of its electoral districts). As of 2010, the state's increased population mandated a redrawing of the lines. To comply with the Voting Rights Act of 1965,[3] the state's plan was submitted to the federal government for preclearance (i.e., acceptance that the revised plan was not discriminatory). While the plan was being discussed, the 2012 election was approaching, and the federal court in San Antonio redrew the lines as it saw fit. Texas argued that the district court was politically motivated and that redistricting power should lie with the state. The Supreme Court agreed.

Coercive (or creative, as some have called it) federalism has not stymied bureaucratic activity. While political relationships have faltered at times, bureaucracy and the work between

---

3   Voting Rights Act of 1965, 42 U.S.C. (1973).

government agencies at the federal and state levels have not been affected. State and local governments continue to work together to provide services from the federal government while performing their own administrative duties. Policy implementation is rarely coercive in nature; there is no benefit to be gained by obstructing policy administration at the state or local level. These layers of government have a long history of working together; this has continued while political players have struggled to find balance.

In truth, federal coercion, while impactful, has not usurped a great deal of the states' power. While areas such as healthcare and the military have been affected by policy and political decision making, the Constitution has not been altered to expand the direct power granted to the federal government, nor have the guarantees of power and limitations been altered for the states. There are areas of policy that are left to the state government to administer. While federal criminal laws are on the rise, the states remains responsible for carrying out law enforcement. Texas still manages systems such as transportation, immigration, and social services. Those actions can still fall under challenge, but the states' power to make policy and carry it out has not been impaired.

The Effects of Federalism

Devolution

In the 1980s, the US fell into an economic recession. Funds were low, and under President Ronald Reagan, the national government looked to trim down. Devolution was the answer. An administrative concept, devolution involves reducing the role of the federal government by reappropriating responsibility to lower governments. A popular theory in Western democracy, devolution is the idea of empowering local governments to carry more of the administrative workload while the federal government functions more as an oversight mechanism.

True devolution has yet to be reached. Even though Presidents Reagan, George H.W. Bush, and Bill Clinton committed to the concept, the federal government is still very active in public administration. Where we have seen devolution play out is in the allocation of funds—namely, through formula grants. These grants are based on a specified formula that determines the funding needs of states or governments carrying out policy and allocates money after taking certain variables into consideration.

Devolution has created a competition for funds amongst states. Texas now must push to the front of the line for many pots of money whose allocation depends on formula-based decision making. A traditionalistic-individualistic state like Texas has been forced to unwillingly engage in activities to obtain federal funding. Texas has resisted this trend and has traditionally paid the federal government more in taxes than it's received in federal funds. One area in which this has come into play is Medicare. Medicare is a program under which the federal government provides matching funds to states. Texas contributes up to 51 percent[4] to its Medicaid fund—the second largest allocation in the nation.

As federal programs operating in Texas have risen in activity, so have the allocations to operate those programs. A significant number of military installations operate in the state. Transportation and education are other areas that have seen cost hikes over the past three years.

Deciding where state and federal government jurisdictions begin and end has been a contentious point, and US Supreme Court cases show the process through which jurisdiction is decided. Texas has been in the thick of working through where the federal government's jurisdiction truly lies, and its political culture makes it a constant challenger to the federal government's attempts to expand its authority. Texas has challenged laws on many fronts and was particularly active under the current governor, Greg Abbott, who had formerly served as the state's attorney general. Most notably, Abbott challenged the Voting Rights Act's preclearance clause,[5] which prevented the state from implementing its voter ID law.

The state's ID law (passed in 2011 but suspended as it worked through the legal system) required voters to show one of seven forms of identification to cast a ballot. Under Section 5 of the Voting Rights Act, Texas was one of nine states[6] that were required to have preapproved legislation that addressed voting access or rights to ensure a lack of discrimination. The federal government argued the state's voter ID law would disenfranchise minority voters; Abbott argued it would reduce cases of fraud. As will be discussed in Chapter 10, the Supreme Court declared Section 5 unconstitutional in 2013, and the voter ID law was put into effect.

As of 2016, Texas was litigating fourteen cases in the Supreme Court, eight[7] of which revolve around environmental protection. Many of the acts attempt to restrict business activity while increasing the state's responsibility for managing regulation.

Challenging decisions and federal policy in the high court is one way to restrict the government's reach. Nullification—the refusal to enact or carry out federal policy—is another. By suspending a federal law within a state, nullification is the process a state employs to limit the federal government's reach for power within its borders.

The most recent challenges to federal power have come within the past decade against the enacting of tax and natural rights policies passed at the federal level. The idea put forth by the South was that the government is set up by and serves the states; therefore, if a law was considered unacceptable, the states could refuse to enact it. Texas was the leader of a twenty-six-state[8] coalition that filed an injunction against President Barack Obama's executive

---

4   Legislative Budget Board. "Texas Medicaid Program and Mental Health Overview and Funding." http://www.lbb. state.tx.us/Documents/HAC_Summary_Recs/84R/2225_Texas_Medicaid_Mental_Health.pdf.

5   Preclearance is no longer part of the legislation as of 2016. This is discussed in Chapter 10.

6   Other states that fell under preclearance law included Alabama, Alaska, Arizona, Georgia, Louisiana, Mississippi, South Carolina, and Virginia.

7   Office of the Texas Attorney General, https://texasattorneygeneral.gov/.

8   Office of the Texas Attorney General, https://texasattorneygeneral.gov/.

order to aid immigrants. The federal circuit court judge granted the stay, and the legislation is pending a decision before being carried out in Texas.

Laboratory Effect

As states operate and pass policy legislation, the laboratory effect comes into play. States are workshops for policy. As issues arise, states define power and limitations by developing and advancing policy. When a policy is fleshed out by one state, other states take notice. States with similar structures, ideologies, and models can use policy made by other states as a template for their own. What often emerges is "copycat legislation."

Texas has engaged in copycat legislation, as both standard-bearer and reenactor, in several areas. Texas's 2007 Religious Viewpoints Anti-Discrimination Act (RVAA) allows prayer and the exercise of religious beliefs on school property in Texas. The legislation was a reaction to the decision in *Santa Fe ISD v. Doe* (2000), which restricted the right to have an invocation performed before school events. The RVAA allows Texas to endorse and allow religious activities. Opponents of the legislation believe the bill could be used to establish a base religion or to force religion on students, which would then cross the line between church and state. Tennessee and Virginia soon followed Texas, passing similar laws in similar incidences that prompted action.

Immigration legislation has also been a topic of discussion in Texas. One example is the 2010 decision by Arizona to pass SB 1070,[9] which introduced immigration status checks as a duty of local law enforcement. The bill was challenged in the Supreme Court in 2012,[10] and while components of the bill were blocked by an injunction, the ability of law enforcement to check immigration status was upheld. In 2011, Texas deliberated Texas House Bill 12,[11] a similar law that would have allowed law enforcement officers to question detainees about immigrant status and to keep records of those interactions. It was significantly less severe than its Arizona counterpart (which was by design, considering the public backlash). That bill ultimately failed; however, Texas has continued to explore immigration reform in the years

---

9   The debate surrounding Arizona SB 1070 centered on the state's ability to pass law that could usurp federal power over immigration. The state law made it a misdemeanor for an illegal immigrant to be in Arizona without carrying registration documentation and cracked down on assistance for or hiring of illegal immigrants. The law worked its way through the court system after protest as the US justice department filed the case on July 6, 2010 claiming the law infringed on federal laws. The injunction was upheld in the district court as federal resources would be taxed. Arizona appealed the decision with the support of nine states including Texas. The district court's decision was upheld and the case reached the Supreme Court December 12, 2011. On June 25, 2012, the court struck down the documentation requirements, arrest power for suspicion of being an illegal immigrant, and the provision to make it illegal for an illegal immigrant to search for a job as they preempted federal statute. However, power for investigation of individuals detained for being an illegal immigrant was upheld.

10   Arizona v. United States, 567 U.S. (2012).

11   Texas HB 12 was a point of much contention. The law was a copycat of the segments of Arizona's SB 1070 that were upheld in the Supreme Court.

since. As of 2013, Texas had the most (ninety-six)[12] of the nation's 311 immigration laws[13] on the books to govern policy towards illegal and undocumented aliens.

Summary

The sovereign nature of the state of Texas has always been a point of contention. Traditionalists believe that the nation was not made to be a coalition of governments subservient to the federal government. Instead, Texas has fought to maintain its ability to make policy decisions and maintain the powers and guarantees granted to it by the US Constitution.

Federalism has been the battleground for those discussions. The US and states, including Texas, have attempted to find the balance of which federal system works best. While states and the federal government are connected as actors serving the interests of similar people, the evolution from cooperative and dual federalism to a state of coercive federalism has seen the federal government and Texas battle for power and jurisdiction. Texas is currently leading the charge on this fight, challenging fourteen[14] separate cases regarding federal power. Defining these lines and establishing jurisdiction is a vital function of government, and an understanding of where power is invested and which layer of government has responsibility over services and responsibilities is necessary for any individual attempting to understand the process of government. The fact that these lines are not static—they are, in fact, constantly moving—makes the study of federalism an important component of civic knowledge.

References

Arizona v. United States, 567 U.S. (2012).

Corwin, E. S. "Passing of Dual Federalism." Virginia Law Review. 36 (1950): 1.

Cranston, R. "From Cooperative to Coercive Federalism and Back." Federal Law Review. 10 (1979): 121.

Elazar, D. J. *American Federalism: A View from the States*. Thomas Y. Crowell: Springfield, OH, 1972.

Elazar, D. J. *Cooperative Federalism: Competition among the States and Local Governments: Efficiency and Equity in American Federalism*. University Press of America: Lanham, MD, 1991.

Epstein, L., and K. O'Connor. "States and the US Supreme Court: An Examination of Litigation Outcomes." *Social Science Quarterly* 69, no. 3 (1988): 660.

Inman, R. P., and D. L. Rubinfeld. *The Political Economy of Federalism*. Robert D. Burch Center for Tax Policy and Public Finance, Berkeley, CA, 1994.

---

12   Texas Legislature, http://www.lrl.state.tx.us/.

13   These laws are directed to oversee and maintain the right of a person to become a naturalized citizen without being impeded because of race, sex, or marriage. These laws are defined by the federal government and enacted by the states.

14   Office of the Texas Attorney General. Austin, TX. https://texasattorneygeneral.gov/.

Inman, R. P., and D. L. Rubinfeld. "Rethinking Federalism." *Journal of Economic Perspectives* 11, no. 4 (1997): 43–64.

Kincaid, J. *The Competitive Challenge to Cooperative Federalism: A Theory of Federal Democracy. Competition Among States and Local Governments: Efficiency and Equity in American Federalism.* Washington, DC: Urban Institute, 1991.

Kincaid, J. (2008). "Contemporary US Federalism: Coercive Change with Cooperative Continuity." *Revista d'estudis autonòmics i federals* 6 (2008): 10–36.

Nathan, R. P. "Federalism and Health Policy." *Health Affairs* 24, no. 6 (2005): 1458–1466.

Posner, P. "The Politics of Coercive Federalism in the Bush Era." *Publius: The Journal of Federalism* 37, no. 3 (2007): 390–412.

Santa Fe ISD v. Doe, 530 U.S. 290 (2000).

Texas v. White, 74 U.S. 700 (1869).

U.S. Const. amend. X.

U.S. Const. amend. XI.

U. S. Const. art. I, §6.

U. S. Const. art. I, §7, cl. 3.

U. S. Const. art. I, §8, cl. 3.

Zimmerman, J. F. *Contemporary American Federalism: The Growth of National Power.* SUNY Press: Albany, NY, 2009.

CHAPTER 4

The Role of Local Governments in Texas

As the structure of the government evolves from federal to state, many of the same discussions crop up regarding the role of local governments. As the most intimate form of government, local governments in Texas perform specific functions directly for their citizens. Local governments provide services and govern day-to-day relationships between citizens and corporations regarding taxes, services, and special districts.

As the local governments in Texas serve those functions, it is important to understand that all local governments function as part of the state's government. Due to Dillon's Rule (a common legal concept applied in many states that defines power between local and state governments), the state constitution confirms that local governments in the state are extensions of the state. The three-pronged rule defines the role of governments and guides decisions regarding those areas. The three types of power accorded to local governments under Dillon's Rule are as follows:

1   Power is granted in the express words of the statute, private act, or charter creating the municipal corporation.

2   Power is necessarily or fairly implied in, or incident to, the powers expressly granted.

3 Power is one that is neither expressly granted nor fairly implied from the express grants of power but is otherwise implied as essential to the declared objects and purposes of the corporation.

This rule governs how power is distributed and establishes the state as the key rule maker in the relationship of federalism. In short, local governments only have power that is granted to them by the state government.

It also attempts to protect local governments in a usually unsuccessful way. An interpretation of Dillon's Rule is that local governments are not given unreasonable and or unfunded mandates. As the state passes statutes and legislation demanding action by the local government—an extension of the state government—there are times when the state places unfair expectations on local governments. However, unfunded mandates have been an issue for local governments and local taxpayers. The "pass the buck" idea of passing legislation and mandating action without sufficient funds is a common practice of both the federal and state governments.

Unfunded mandates are not intentional. Recent debate in the past three legislative sessions has started to question unfunded mandates regarding individual policy, especially because local officials and representatives push hard to keep the idea in the legislative arena. These mandates are commonly seen when the state sees a budget shortfall. To cut costs, indigent care was left to the local governments in 2003, when Texas faced a $10 billion[1] shortfall. Education has seen the same treatment over the years. In 2005, House Ways and Means Committee Chair Fred Hill detailed the effects of unfunded mandates. Still, proposed constitutional amendments restricting them have not made their way out of session in the past five legislative sessions.

Types of Government

There are three main types of local governments currently operating in Texas. Local governments are either counties, municipalities (cities), or special districts. Most powerful of these three are municipalities, as they are granted the most power and governance, but all three serve specific purposes when it comes to local activity. These three types of government substantiate the process and function of the local layer of the federal system. As of the 2010 census, there were 1,216 cities, 254 counties, and 2,300 special districts (including 1,265 school districts) in Texas.

---

1 Aguilar, Julian. "State Faces Worst Budget Deficit in Eight Years." *Texas Tribune*, February 10, 2010.

Municipalities (Cities)

Municipalities, or cities, are the most common type of local government. Of the three types of government, municipalities are granted, by far, the most responsibility for functions and services. Cities in Texas are granted thirty-nine general areas of powers and functions. Thirty-six of those powers are classified as governmental. These powers range from the ability to pass and enact ordinances to the ability to oversee street construction and emergency services. These thirty-six functions provide the municipalities with their power of governance. There are three major proprietary functions: the operation and maintenance of a public utility, amusements owned and operated by a city, and any activity that is abnormally dangerous or ultrahazardous.

City councils oversee these functions as the legislative body of municipal government. Councilors are elected from within city districts. Depending on the municipal charter, the officials are elected in one of two ways. First, district or ward elections can elect councilors. These elections aim to ensure that representation comes from within the area the councilor will represent. Like legislative elections, municipalities set standards regarding residency and participation in the district or ward to ensure accurate representation from those seeking election. At-large elections do away with district lines. In at-large elections, every registered voter in the city can vote in each election. A common formula is to have a mix of district- or ward-elected councilors to go with at-large councilors. City councils are tasked with reviewing and passing legislation as well as overseeing the administration of agencies and departments.

To go with the city councils, municipalities elect mayors to serve as their de facto executive officials. In Texas, mayors are elected in at-large elections, and their power and roles vary in their respective cities. Candidates for mayor, especially in larger cities, go through rigorous elections that mirror those of state and federal officials. Background, experience, personal lives, and political beliefs all come into play as cities seek to elect their executive officials. Candidates participate in primaries to seek nomination, but mayoral elections routinely see more than two candidates in the general election. Municipalities are nonpartisan, meaning party affiliation is not a factor on the ballot. If that happens and no one receives 50 percent of the vote, a runoff election is conducted to decide the race between the two highest vote getters.

As municipalities control much of the goings-on and services, they receive the most attention. How those powers are divided comes down to the general acceptance and conditions set in each municipality. These governments function in one of two major forms: council–mayor or council–manager.

In a council–mayor system, the powers and responsibilities to administer and oversee government services are split between the two main legislative entities. In most cities, the relationship is traditional: legislative matters are passed by the council, and the mayor has informal policy/political powers to oversee the administrative form of government. The balance of power is determined by whether the city operates in a weak-mayor system or a strong-mayor system.

The former is more common in Texas amongst smaller cities, as the executive official is the weaker of the two entities. In a weak-mayor city, the council controls most policy decisions and has power over administration. Mayoral powers in these cities are usually relegated to administrative practices such as appointing department heads, but any political or decision-making power is minimal. This system allows for a diverse legislative body to carry the load while the executive official remains weak—a tradition in Texas.

Strong-mayor systems are just the opposite, and the state's ten most populous cities practice it in some form, with Houston having the strongest mayor. The balance of power is traditional: the mayor has power to oversee administration, recommend a budget, and participate in council politics. Annise Parker is an example of a strong mayor, as she was intimately involved in the politics and decision making in Houston and made herself a strong political figure. Her ability to push politics defined her terms as mayor, despite being a liberal in a conservative state.

The council–manager system places political power with the council. These cities have mayors, but the position is mostly ceremonial and has minimal powers. In fact, in these cases the mayor is often appointed rather than elected by the people. Much of the administrative and political decision-making powers rest with the council. It is tasked with budgetary decisions, policymaking, and overseeing the political aspects of administration. One of those powers is the ability to hire and oversee the city manager. While the council fulfills the legislative and political powers, the manager works for the council to administer government. While the council controls and has decision-making power, the manager operates day-to-day functions and has the power to appoint and hire employees without council approval. This is the most popular form of government in Texas, particularly in midsized cities.

A third form of government, the commission form, has existed in the state since 1900. This was seen in Galveston after a hurricane decimated the city. The state installed the commission form to help the city recover. Under this form, the city operates with five to seven commissioners who operate the administration, with each taking control of a department or area of city government. In fact, commissioners are typically selected based on their expertise in these areas. This style of government has not caught on in the state. While it is extremely efficient in theory to have both the legislative and executive function under one body, it has been much less popular than the council–mayor and council–manager systems.

General Law vs. Home Rule

City governments derive their power from the state of Texas. The type of charter and how the local government is set up is determined in many cases by the state. From its inception in 1836, as Texas looked to incorporate local governments, the state took a strict hand in setting the legal standards and actions its local governments could take. General Law charters were developed for local governments. The charters provided basic sets of laws and definitions of government action by which cities must abide. The state legislature developed initial General Law charters. These charters served specific functions and provided direction in six key areas:

1 Description of the city's governmental and proprietary powers

2 Provisions establishing the city's form of government (council–mayor, council-manager, and so on) and its legislative and judicial machinery

3 Organizational provisions establishing the administrative structure of the city government and the means for financing its operations

4 Provisions governing the procedures of the city council, advisory boards, and commissions and procedures for granting franchises, assessing and collecting taxes, and conducting annexations

5 Popular controls over the city government, such as elections, referenda, initiatives, and recalls

6 Provisions relating to procedures for amending the charter

Without specific permission, local governments were required to fall under the state-adopted charter despite some inconsistencies on the part of the legislative body. In 1913, those inconsistencies led to home rule.

Cities or municipalities with five thousand citizens or more were granted the ability to pass their own charters based on their locales and the needs of their citizens. Per 2010 census data, there are 354 home rule cities in Texas. With the provision that cities not pass anything outside of (or that contradicted) the formal powers granted and approved by the state, municipalities that eclipsed the five-thousand-citizen mark were given the ability to write their own charters. Home rule gives the local government the inherent authority or power (i.e., the ability to perform an act without the specific consent of the state) to serve any public purposes unique or germane to the population.

Municipalities are therefore free to make decisions regarding their charters based on local consent by election or local government. This empowers the population in these locales to pass referendums and initiatives and to even take part in recall elections that provide policy guidance and rules. Major areas in which these powers can be exercised are the following:

1 Decide the form of government (council–mayor, council–manager, commission) as well as how these officials will be selected

2   Decide administrative structure regarding representation, size of city council, administrative procedure, and processes

3   Define districts and structure of elections

4   Provide power to create administrative boards and commissions

While these are basic areas, some have come under much debate. First, home rule charters lead to the approved use of Article XI, Section 5 of the Texas Constitution, which allows municipalities to annex neighboring territories that are unincorporated without the consent of those citizens. This is a source of contention, as annexation can have a significant effect on local taxes. In one example, the city of Kingwood went through a popular annexation by the city of Houston; the annexation imposed city taxes on the affluent suburb and stripped it of its classification as falling under the government of Harris County. Per the latest census data, Texas has some of the fastest-growing cities in the nation, including Houston and Austin. Both have benefitted from home rule charters establishing and entrenching the unilateral annexation policy.

Charters also established the role of initiatives. This is legislation brought forth by the public. Charters outline the process used in the absence of state direction. Initiatives begin with a local petition that must have a defined number of signatures. Once the petition is certified by the city secretary, the city council either adopts the measure or puts it to a popular vote. Referendums—when the public seeks to repeal an unpopular city ordinance—follow a similar process. The public must collect a predetermined number of signatures and, once these are certified, the ordinance is brought for public vote and repeal.

This occurred in Houston with the Houston Equal Rights Ordinance (HERO).[2] The ordinance passed by a significant margin in a city council vote. However, activist groups took umbrage at the law and collected signatures to have the ordinance brought up as a referendum. As discussed in the public policy chapter, the campaign and route to a referendum was aggressive and hard-fought. The city did not certify the signatures, but Texas upheld them, forcing the city to bring the ordinance up for a vote. After a heated campaign, the public voted down the HERO law by a 68 percent vote.

Another popular election tool in home rule charters is the ability to force a recall election. This allows the public to petition for a call of no confidence in an elected official due to lack of performance or an inability to uphold the tenets of their office. If the required petition numbers are met, a recall vote is convened, and citizens vote "yes" or "no" to keep the official in office. If "no" wins out, an election takes place to replace the recalled official. Cities determine the number of signatures needed to initiate a recall election, but ten percent of registered voters is a common standard.

---

2   Full text of the law available at https://archive.org/stream/equal_rights_ordinance/equal_rights_ordinance_djvu.txt.

Charters are determined and written by the governing city council. The local government code allows for citizens to push for amendments to the city charter by obtaining twenty thousand signatures. Along with popular amendments, there are limitations to home rule charters. Charters cannot usurp the state constitution, nor can they go against election code. Charters also can set the tax rate, regardless of state statute. In Texas, cities can tax property up to $2.50 per $100. If the city charter sets a lower rate than that, the city law would take precedence.

Counties

While cities represent the typical government structure, counties are more service oriented. Without the ability to make policy, counties in Texas are tasked with providing basic services, as the Texas Constitution classifies them as an arm of the state government. With that, counties are tasked with very specific functions and service commands. These services range from tax collection to law enforcement but encompass the action arm of the state government. These powers are derived from Article IX of the state constitution and from Vernon's Civil Statutes, which is a collection of provisions that cover topics ranging from retirement proceedings to law enforcement to the way the county will handle economic development.

Constitutional provisions for counties:

1   Administration of elections at the national, state, and local level, not including special districts or city elections

2   Law enforcement in the areas of protection, a security force, and administration of incarceration

3   Overseeing transportation on county roads

4   Record keeping, including documents for the following: courts, marriage certificates, birth certificates, public safety and driving, and deeds and titles

5   Collection of taxes and state fees

Counties can also elect to oversee the following:

1   Outdoor business regulation

2   Maintenance of parks and public cemeteries

3 Obtaining and participating in intercounty agreements regarding emergency services dealing with law enforcement, medical services, and fire safety

4 Funding and overseeing the administration of libraries

5 Administering and establishing county hospitals and clinics

A county judge oversees these powers at the executive level. Elected by an at-large process, the judge serves as the administrative leader of each county and heads the commissioner's court. Each of Texas's 254 counties has the same structure, regardless of size, by mandate of the Texas Constitution. Elected to four-year terms, the county judge has little to nothing to do with legal proceedings. In fact, in counties with a population greater than fifty thousand, the judge does not need to be a lawyer. The judge instead has a set of powers and administrative duties that include overseeing the budget process (unless it is a large county that employs an auditor), using the veto, and proposing their own budget. The judge also oversees the county commissioners and the issuing of alcohol permits, can perform marriages, sits on county boards such as the hospital board, sits on the election board, and fulfills certification duties regarding election results.

Commissioners are elected to four-year terms by district and are often called road commissioners. As road maintenance and construction is a prime duty of the court, commissioners' power is concentrated in their ability to oversee a specific form of the budget for road maintenance. Many counties divide this budget equally and allow commissioners to manage their portions of the budget as they see fit. Commissioners represent one of the main differences between cities and counties. While councilors for the city can pass ordinances, commissioners are more administrative oriented. Two powers the court does maintain are the powers to pass the county budget and impose countywide taxes. Without the power to alter its structure or opt into home rule charters, commissioners are limited to these express powers per state mandate. The state has considered allowing counties to participate in home rule structures and to have county administrators, like managers, who would be appointed to oversee government activity.

In addition to these, there are other elected positions that participate in county government. Per the *Guide to Texas Law for County Officials*, elected officials have specific roles. The following lists define the powers and roles of the county judge, commissioner, tax assessor, sheriff, clerk, and district/county attorney.

Judge[3]

- Presiding officer of the commissioners court
- Represents the county in many administrative functions

3 "County Judge." Copyright © 2017 by Texas Association of Counties.

- Serves as budget officer in counties with fewer than 225,000 residents
- Most have broad judicial duties such as presiding over misdemeanor criminal and small civil cases, probate matters, and appeals from the justice of the peace court
- Serves as head of emergency management

Commissioner[4]

- Adopts the county's budget and administers the tax rate
- Approves all budgeted purchases of the county
- Fills vacancies in elective and appointive offices
- Sets all salaries and benefits
- Has exclusive authority to authorize contracts
- Provides and maintains all county buildings and facilities

District Attorney

- Represents the state in prosecuting felony criminal cases
- Works with law enforcement officers in the investigation of criminal cases
- Presents cases to the grand jury
- Represents victims of violence in protective orders and represents the state in removing children from abusive households

County Attorney

- Represents the state in prosecuting misdemeanor criminal cases
- Works with law enforcement officers in the investigation of criminal cases
- Provides legal advice to the commissioners court and to other elected officials
- Brings civil enforcement actions on behalf of the state or county

Sheriff

- Serves as a licensed peace officer and is responsible for enforcing the criminal laws of the state
- Manages and operates the county jail

---

4   Selections From "Who Are County Officials?." Copyright © 2016 by Texas Association of Counties. Reprinted with permission.

- Provides security for the courts
- Serves warrants and civil papers
- Regulates bail bondsmen in counties with no bail bond board

County Tax Assessor

- Calculates property tax rates for the county
- Collects property taxes for the county
- May collect taxes for cities, schools, and other local taxing entities
- Processes motor vehicle title transfers
- Issues motor vehicle registration and licenses
- May process boat titles and registrations
- Registers voters and may conduct elections
- Collects various other fees for the state and county

County Auditor

- Appointed by the district judge(s)
- Prepares and administers accounting records for all county funds
- Audits the records and accounts of the various county departments
- Verifies the validity and legality of all county disbursements
- Forecasts financial data for budgetary formulation purposes
- Serves as budget officer in counties with more than 225,000 residents (counties with more than 125,000 residents may opt for an appointed budget officer)

This structure of officials controls and manages administration of county governments. As the county is responsible for major services, local officials work to oversee aspects of services for their residents. Issues, however, can erupt due to jurisdiction. As counties and cities overlap, disputes sometimes arise between executive officials about the activities that take place in the jurisdictions.

Political issues can also crop up between people at different levels of leadership. Former Houston Mayor Annise Parker, a Democrat, and Republican former Harris County Judge Ed Emmett routinely butted heads in political arenas. A major area of contention was the administration of sports teams in Houston. As Harris County has power over amusement, the Harris County Sports Authority controls the lease and agreements for all major sports stadiums in Houston. While the HCSA controls the agreements and oversees activity, many of the city's arenas and stadiums are built on city land. The overlap in jurisdiction requires the two governing bodies to overlap; this came to a head during Major League Soccer's Houston Dynamo's attempts to build a stadium in downtown Houston. The franchise was forced to receive approval from both the city and county, making political deals and impasses a part of the six-year process to obtain rights to the land and permission to build BBVA Compass Stadium.

Special Districts

While municipalities and counties serve the general area and general purposes, there are services that neither entity provides. Services such as local education, water and gas supply, and, in some cases, medical services are not provided out by the municipality or county. In the absence of those services, Texas relies on special districts. Each of these districts serves one function and provides a singular service. With that power, they can levy taxes on the population that receives the services. As these services are specific, special districts only serve a limited population and have jurisdiction only over that group of citizens in their service area.

Urban sprawl has dominated population patterns, and Texas has seen a significant surge in suburbs and population areas located further and further from city centers. To avoid inundating counties with service responsibility, special districts have stepped in to fill the void. With close oversight from the state and legislature, each of the more than forty types of special districts must be created in a separate fashion. For example, to create a hospital district, one hundred residents in the proposed area must first submit a petition to the county judge; the district is then confirmed by a majority vote in a general election. Other districts, such as those administering utilities, must have the signatures of 50 percent of the landowners in the area before the Texas Commission on Environmental Quality (TCEQ) will render a decision. County commissioner's courts oversee these districts, but they have their own administration and leadership hierarchy.

Of the more than 2,300 special districts in Texas, more than half are water or utility districts. These districts oversee and provide services, mainly the use of water, in their areas. With the expanse of suburbs and exurbs (small population centers surrounding housing developments adjacent to cities), water districts have become necessary in Texas. Referred to as Municipal Utility Districts (MUDs), their basic function is to provide water, power, and gas as well as emergency services like local fire protection, medical care, and law enforcement to residents in specific areas.

As MUDs have become necessary to service large suburban areas, these districts have become convenient funding mechanisms for developers. With the ability to tax and accrue revenue, MUDs are commonly created before developments are constructed. While these districts require the approval of TCEQ, the projected development is enough of an incentive to create the district to provide economically advantageous circumstances for housing and economic developers. These districts can issue bonds, which are essentially loans, to developers that can be paid off over time through repayment with interest or through taxes and service fees.

Independent School Districts (ISDs) are another type of special district. These are the most visible and commonly identified special districts. In Texas, ISDs are the decision makers and administrators of local education. While the Texas Board of Education and Texas Education Agency guide education policy implementation, the management and administration of schools is carried out by school boards elected by constituents. Like MUDs, ISDs can tax local property owners to supplement funds that come from the state budget. School boards are mandatory per state law and must be staffed by three to seven publicly elected trustees who serve 3–4-year terms. If the population in a district exceeds 764,000, the board can be increased to nine members. The board is headed by a publicly elected superintendent who serves as the executive official. This board operates as the legislative and executive body governing policy and education in the district. Decisions regarding administration at individual schools, school size, and appropriate activity to meet state standards are governed by ISDs.

The main source of funding for school districts comes from the state. As detailed in the financial policy chapter in this book, a significant amount of state funds contribute to ISDs. No funds are provided from municipalities or county governments. The formula used to determine the funds is often called into question as the state and its ISDs debate how to keep education equitable across social and economic demographics.

In addition to state funds, property taxes are a major source of funding for ISDs. Through power granted from the Texas Constitution, ISDs, like MUDs, can levy taxes on all property owned in their districts. The ability to levy these taxes is different from the service fees seen with MUDs, as property owners must pay the tax, regardless of whether they have a child in the school system. The fact that these property owners must pay taxes for a service they do not use is a common point of contention. Debate has taken place on the equity of a tax for a service from which the payer does not benefit.

Once collected, these funds are at the discretion of the school board and its population. Funds can be used on brick-and-mortar projects, supplies, technology, or school resources. This can lead to interesting debates, as school projects (not just for those expenditures involving academics) are routinely brought up for general election in the form of bond elections. The city of Allen, Texas passed a proposition calling for more than $60 million to be used to build a state-of-the-art football stadium. On the outside, the project was met with ridicule from those who believe taxpayer funds should be used on academics. The town and local school responded with the fact that the decision had been made through a referendum that passed with 68 percent of the vote; the approval of the use of the funds came from those who paid them.

In addition to ISDs, community college districts are special districts created to oversee and provide education services. Designed to meet the needs of students who cannot attend traditional four-year universities, community college districts were created to bridge the education and, in some cases, technical gaps between public education and the needs of the workforce. Overseen by the Texas Higher Education Coordinating Board (THECB), these districts are controlled by a body of elected trustees that sets rates for tuition and other fees and services in addition to dipping into the property tax tool to provide funding.

Per the Texas Association of Community Colleges, 1,427,690 students enrolled in community college programs in 2011, and 710,337 community college students made up 53 percent of the student population attending all Texas public higher education institutions in 2013. A popular mechanism for those at a financial or academic disadvantage, community college districts have been successful at offering alternatives in education. As of 2013, tuition rates per credit hour for in-district residents hovered around $827, compared to $1,300 for nonresidents. As of 2016, there were fifty community college districts operating in Texas.

In 2015, President Barack Obama advocated that the first two years of community college education be free for students. His message, given in the annual State of the Union address to Congress, was that young Americans need programs to develop skills and work with businesses to help the United States catch up in the need for skilled workers. In the summer of 2015, Obama introduced the American Graduation Initiative, which would work to make funding available to pay the first two years of tuition for students seeking an education at a community college. That would include students in Texas, but it yet to be considered by the US Congress.

Another type of special district is a hospital district. Both counties and special districts can operate hospitals. In the case of special hospital districts, voters have approved the creation of a district hospital that would be funded by local taxes and user fees. These facilities are normally geared to provide medical care for the indigent or for those who cannot afford private medical services. Taxes are the largest source of income for these districts, but they can take payment from federal programs such as Medicaid and Medicare. Currently, there are twenty-seven special hospital districts operating in Texas.

While special districts serve specific needs otherwise not addressed, they are not without criticism. Critics worry that oversight from the state is not conducted closely enough. Also, the relatively small nature of special districts calls into the question the district's ability to function properly and without issue due to a lack of infrastructure, resources, and scope of influence. One debate surrounding special districts is the apathy toward and lack of information about special districts amongst the general population. While many district leadership positions are elected, public or civic knowledge of how these districts operate and what their powers and jurisdictions are is uneven in many service areas. This lack of knowledge can lead to an absence of quality oversight and accountability from the public. Still, special districts are growing as fast as the Texas population. The process of obtaining approval for these districts has been called into question, in part because the public vote is conducted only among those living in the district at the time. Especially with new developments, that could be fewer than ten voters. There is also the issue of voters approving the bond (which will be paid over time) and then leaving the area, requiring others to pay off the bond with higher taxes.

As cities continue to grow and outstretch their current land areas, special districts will continue to be called upon to provide services that other local entities refuse to deliver or lack the ability to carry out. Issues raised within the privatization debate surrounding public services such as education and sanitation, however, will continue. For voters and those approving funds, the question will be: Where does the decision to create these districts cross the line from using public money to improve areas to being an avenue for private gain?

Council of Governments

While local governments would like to be autonomous, the truth is that they may not be equipped to offer the services needed by their communities. Medical and emergency services can be overwhelmed in times of disaster or high need. This is evidence of one of the major issues facing local governments today: having the resources to meet the needs of a population.

With this as a main issue, the state passed the Regional Planning Act of 1965 to provide the ability to create a council of governments (COGs). These organizations operate on contracts and/or agreements that traverse county local jurisdiction to provide a service to a broader area and, in many cases, pool resources. COGs are considered regional planning boards composed of local officials and members of the community, as designated by the agreement. In these regional commissions, two-thirds of the members must be local elected officials, and they operate under policies and guidelines that govern their interaction and influence. Originally, structure was created to oversee them and ensure that basic federal standards—usually concerning utility functions such as water, sewage, etc.—were met. Over the years, agreements have expanded to include emergency services, transportation, services provided to specific populations, the environment, and, most notably, economic development.

Summary

Local governments are the service providers in the federalism system. This layer of government functions as a necessary avenue to govern activities and provide services to the population. Under Texas rule, local governments have found a niche for themselves. While not given much in the way of legislative power, these entities have increased their scope of influence in the services they provide and the responsibilities they have taken on.

While local governments have expanded their scope of influence, questions remain regarding their role in a coercive federalism system. While they act autonomously in certain areas, the state of Texas, as a major provider of funds, still holds a considerable amount of influence over this layer of government. When dissecting the relationship between Texas and the local governments, the issue of unfunded mandates and the carrying out of Dillon's Rule create questions. As seen in the situation surrounding the HERO law in Houston and the discussion of the ability of cities to challenge funding decisions in education in San Antonio and in the Rio Grande Valley (discussed in Chapter 3), the relationship between the state and local governments is one to examine.

References

Aguilar, Julian. "State Faces Worst Budget Deficit in Eight Years." *Texas Tribune*, February 10, 2010.

Blair, T. *Leading the Way: A New Vision for Local Government*. Institute for Public Policy Research: London, 1998.

Bridges, A. *Morning Glories: Municipal Reform in the Southwest*. Princeton, NJ: Princeton University Press, 1997.

Brook, D., and G. J. G. Upton. "Biases in Local Government Elections Due to Position on the Ballot Paper." *Applied Statistics*, 23. (1974): 414–419.

Calvert, R. A., A. De Leon, and G. Cantrell. *The History of Texas*. John Wiley & Sons: Hoboken, NJ, 2013.

Davidson, C. *Race and Class in Texas Politics*. Princeton, NJ: Princeton University Press, 1992.

Dillon, J. F. *Commentaries on the Law of Municipal Corporations*. 3. Boston, MA: Little, Brown, 1911.

Driessen, Katherine. "Houston Equal Rights Ordinance Fails by Wide Margin." *Houston Chronicle*, November 4, 2015.

Duncombe, H. S. *Modern County Government*. Washington, D.C.: National Association of Counties, 1977.

Imazeki, J., and A. Reschovsky. "Is No Child Left Behind an Un (or Under) funded Federal Mandate? Evidence from Texas." *National Tax Journal*, 57, no. 3, (2004): 571–588.

Kelly, J. "Unfunded Mandates: The View from the States." *Public Administration Review* 54, no. 4 (July/August 1994).

Miller, C., and H. T. Sanders. *Urban Texas: Politics and Development*. College Station, TX: Texas A&M University Press, 2000.

CHAPTER 5
The Role of the Executive Branch in Texas: Weak Lead Officials and the Administration They Function Within

Historically, the evolution of the office of the governor has gone from historically subdued by the legislature or foreign appointed official from Mexico in the state's early years, to overseeing the military and administration, to a position without clear or immense power. Originally, a governor's chief responsibility was overseeing and executing laws, taking on specific formal powers in the administration. Time and the expansion of state authority and administration has propelled that eighteenth-century idea into what is seen today.

Modern governorships are a hodgepodge of power in the United States, and definitions of power for executive officials are outlined by the state constitutions. In states where there is a large and influential government, the governor could be given supreme executive authority. In this case, all aspects of administration and government activity would be routed through the governor's office. The role and constitutional framework resembles that of the federal government. The executive official has power of administration, significant legislative influence and power, and control of the state's military resources.

While supreme executive authority became popular in the mid-nineteenth and early twentieth centuries, there were still places for officials beyond the governor in the executive branch. Breaking down responsibilities and empowering departments became the norm as states grew in authority. In states where the governor was strong, the officials reported to him. The less supreme the governor's power, the more autonomous the other officials in the executive branch would be.

This brings us to Texas. With a mistrust of government as a rallying cry, the state has created a system that is the opposite of supreme executive power. Instead of empowering a governor to carry out the state's business, the official is limited by constitutional mandate and left to obtain power and influence more from informal powers than formal ones.

A complex plural executive is one of Texas's calling cards. Seven officials, not one, oversee and execute the administrative aspects of the government. While theory on administration provides that rigid and defined power is important, Texas views that power as being too influential to leave in the hands of one person. In this chapter, we'll examine how the governor's position is shaped in Texas, look at the role of the remaining six officials in the plural executive, and debate whether it is the best arrangement for an effective government in the state.

Reading 5.1

Selection from "Governors Turn Pro: Separation of Powers and the Institutionalization of the American Governorship"[1]
from *Political Research Quarterly*
Ann O'M. Bowman, Neal D. Woods, and Milton R. Stark

Reading Introduction

When attempting to pin down the role of a governor, gaining context on current and historical use of power and power attribution provides a mixed bag of results. The examination of how states across the nation address power at the executive official level can provide a myriad of results, from the strongest governors who have significant power to the weakest. Tracking the development of that role and those powers is critical to understanding how the lead official in states is addressed. Ann Bowman, Neal Woods, and Milton Stark address the evolution of the office of the governor. Their study provides some insight into the role governors play and how that has evolved nationally, which provides great context for an examination of the weak lead official role in Texas.

GOVERNORS AND STATE GOVERNMENT

The reforms that state governments undertook in the twentieth century shared a common aim: to provide the three branches of government with sufficient resources to function effectively (Hedge 1998; Teaford 2002). In effect, the goal was to make them truly institutions, possessing the Huntingtonian (Huntington 1968) characteristics of autonomy, adaptability, complexity, and coherence. The empowerment of the governor was intended "to place governors in a strong position to direct, control, plan, organize, evaluate, and coordinate the activities of the executive branch—to fulfill the role of manager in the classical sense" (Beyle 1983, 82).

Institutional Change

Along with the other branches of state government, the office of the governor is now more institutionalized and less personalized.[1] As Thad Beyle wrote in 1983, "Governor's offices are becoming larger, gubernatorial staffs are increasing in size and in actual and potential influence, and in some states, a more institutionalized organization is developing around the governorship itself" (p. 158). Studies of the governorship in the mid-1950s reported that average staff size, including both clerical and professional staff, was 11 employees, with a range of 3 to 43 employees. Two decades later, average gubernatorial staff size had nearly tripled (29 employees), ranging from 7 to 245 employees. By 2004, the number of staff members averaged nearly 59, with a range of 8 (Wyoming) to 310 (Florida) (Beyle 2006). An increased staff size affords the governor more flexibility and support in the various roles he or she plays (Fisher and Nice 2005; Beyle 2006). Figure 1 shows the trends in both gubernatorial staff and real expenditures of the governor's office from 1983 to 2004.[2] Although both staff and expenditures have increased over time, the rates at which they increased vary somewhat. Clearly, by both these indicators, the American governorship has become substantially more institutionalized during this period.

The institutionalization of the governor's office has been accompanied by an increase in formal gubernatorial powers. Reformers had long advocated strengthening the governor's office by lengthening the governor's term of office, allowing consecutive succession in office, broadening the veto power, increasing appointment and removal power, and increasing budgetary authority (Teaford 2002; Beyle 2004). States have generally responded by adopting many of the reformers' propositions, and by late in the twentieth century, most governors enjoyed significantly enhanced formal powers. Nonetheless, the formal powers of the governor appear to be unrelated to the number of staff in the governor's office. In a cross-sectional study of gubernatorial staffing in 2004, Fisher and Nice (2005) found that neither formal powers nor other plausible explanations such as a state's ideology or its affluence were consequential; what mattered were explanations related to the workload of state government. Moreover, staffing patterns in 2004 appeared to be connected to the amount of legislative activity in 2003, reflecting perhaps not only workload but also institutional rivalry.

Governors Differ from Presidents

Governors, although similar to presidents in many important ways, also differ from them in at least one important respect: the extent of executive branch fragmentation. Governors typically share responsibility for administering the executive branch of state government with an average of six separately elected officials (Beyle 2004). Key administration officials such as the attorney general, treasurer, and secretary of state are elected in at least 75 percent of the states, not appointed as they are at the national level. In many states, the heads of the state's education agency, agriculture department, and insurance department are elected as well (Council of State Governments 2006).[3] The extent of this plural structure varies by state. At one extreme is North Carolina, where the governor leads an executive branch in which nine other cabinet-level officials are elected statewide; at the other extreme is New Jersey, where the governor is the sole nonfederal, statewide elected official.[4]

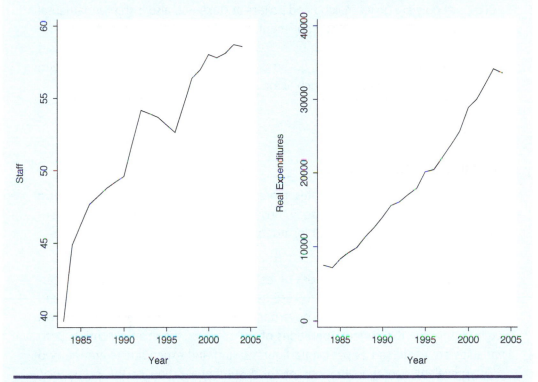

FIGURE 5.1 Average Gubernatorial Staff and Real Expenditures of the Governor's Office, 1983 through 2004

Furthermore, many state agencies are headed by boards and commissions or by executives who are not appointed by the governor and thus are only nominally under his or her control. Even in instances in which the governor has the power to appoint department heads, confirmation by a legislative body is often required.

A governor's ability to act unilaterally, essential to the accomplishment of policy goals, is severely impeded under these circumstances (Lewis 2005). The executive branch, far from an integrated structure with a governor at the apex, is instead an amalgam of separate fiefdoms with which a governor must negotiate. To be a successful manager of this fragmented executive branch, a governor must establish a series of circumjacent relationships (Simmons 1965). Not surprisingly, a fragmented executive structure is frequently criticized for diluting a governor's effectiveness and reducing accountability (Beyle 2004).

Governors who share responsibility with separately elected officials and with agency heads not subject to gubernatorial control may face significantly greater coordination problems in administering the executive branch. Adding staff and increasing expenditures may be the governor's way of grappling with the fragmentation of authority that he or she confronts. This process of internal bargaining may supersede the process of external bargaining discussed by Dickinson (2000, 2003); not only are policy making and politics at stake—so also is the fundamental executive branch role in policy implementation. Thus, we expect that a greater number of independent executive branch officials will lead to significant increases in the institutionalization of the governorship, to bargain and coordinate with these independent executive branch actors.

DATA AND METHOD

Dependent Variables

As the foregoing discussion indicates, there are various manifestations of executive branch institutionalization. This study thus employs two separate dependent variables to assess two dimensions of institutionalization:

(1) number of staff in the governor's office and (2) real expenditures of the governor's office. The former variable represents the total number of professional and clerical full-time employees in the governor's office. The latter reflects a state's real expenditures for the current operations of the office of the chief executive. Both variables are expressed as per capita figures.[5] Staff and expenditures are the two most prevalent operationalizations of the institutionalization of the presidency, capturing the Huntingtonian concepts of complexity (an internal feature) and autonomy (an external dimension), respectively (Ragsdale and Theis 1997). Some prior research has suggested that these different facets of executive institutionalization may be subject to different dynamics (Dickinson and Lebo 2007).[6]

NOTES

1 See Berry, Berkman, and Schneiderman (2000) for a discussion of legislative institutional-ization and Lightcap (2003) for a review of reforms in state judiciaries.

2 All dollar values are expressed in constant (2000) dollars.

3 Even the lieutenant governor is elected separately from the governor in eighteen states.

4 In 2005, New Jersey voters amended the state's constitution by approving the election of a lieutenant governor, effective with the 2009 state elections.

5 Governor's office staff is obtained from the *Book of the States* (Council of State Governments various years). Governor's office expenditures are found in the *Annual Survey of State and Local Government Finances* (U.S. Bureau of the Census various years-a). Both measures are closely related to the size of the state; therefore, expressing them in per capita terms allows for meaningful comparisons across states.

6 These are the most commonly used measures in the national literature as well. Some presidential studies have used additional indicators; unfortunately, comparable measures are not available at the state level.

REFERENCES

Beck, Nathaniel, and Jonathan Katz. 1995. What to do (and not to do) with time series cross-section data. *American Political Science Review* 89:634–47.

Berry, Frances Stokes, and William D. Berry. 1990. State lottery adoptions as policy innova-tions. *American Political Science Review* 84:395–416.

Berry, William D., Michael B. Berkman, and Stuart Schneiderman. 2000. Legislative pro-fessionalism and incumbent reelection: The development of institutional boundaries. *American Political Science Review* 94:859–74.

Beyle, Thad L. 1983. Governors' offices: Variations on common themes. In *Being governor,* ed. Thad L. Beyle and Lynn R. Muchmore. Durham, NC: Duke University Press.

———. 2004. The governors. In *Politics in the American states: A comparative analysis,* ed. Virginia Gray and Russell L. Hanson. Washington, DC: CQ Press.

———. 2006. Being governor. In *The state of the states,* 4th ed., ed. Carl E. Van Horn. Washington, DC: CQ Press.

Council of State Governments. Various years. *The book of the states.* Lexington, KY: Council of State Governments.

Dickinson, Matthew J. 2000. Staffing the White House, 1937–96: The institutional implica-tions of Neustadt's bargaining paradigm. In *Presidential power: Forging the presidency for the twenty-first century,* ed. Robert Y. Shapiro, Martha Joynt Kumar, and Lawrence R. Jacobs. New York: Columbia University Press.

————. 2003. Bargaining, uncertainty, and the growth of the White House staff, 1940–2000. In *Uncertainty in American politics,* ed. Barry C. Burden. New York: Cambridge University Press.

Dickinson, Matthew J., and Matthew J. Lebo. 2007. Reexamining the growth of the institutional presidency, 1940–2000. *Journal of Politics* 69:206–19.

Dilger, Robert Jay. 1995. A comparative analysis of gubernatorial enabling resources. *State and Local Government Review* 27:118–26.

Dilger, Robert Jay, George A. Krause, and Randolph R. Moffett. 1995. State legislative professionalism and gubernatorial effectiveness, 1978–1991. *Legislative Studies Quarterly* 20:553–71.

Ferguson, Margaret Robertson. 2003. Chief executive success in the legislative arena. *State Politics and Policy Quarterly* 3:158–82.

Fisher, Patrick, and David Nice. 2005. Staffing the governor's office: A comparative analysis. In *The book of the states, 2005.* Lexington, KY: Council of State Governments.

Granato, Jim, and Mitoshi Suzuki. 1996. The use of the encompassing principle to resolve empirical controversies in voting behavior: An application to voter rationality in congressional elections. *Electoral Studies* 15:383–98.

Hamilton, Alexander. 1788/1961. Federalist no. 70. In *The federalist papers,* ed. Clinton Rossiter. New York: New American Library.

Hedge, David M. 1998. *Governance and the changing American states.* Boulder, CO: Westview.

Hibbing, John. 1999. Legislative careers. *Legislative Studies Quarterly* 24:149–71.

Hill, Larry B. 1974. Institutionalization, the ombudsman, and the bureaucracy. *American Political Science Review* 68:1075–85.

Hsiao, Cheng. 1986. *Analysis of panel data.* Cambridge, UK: Cambridge University Press.

Huntington, Samuel. 1968. *Political order in changing societies.* New Haven, CT: Yale University Press.

Klarner, Carl. 2003. Measurement of partisan balance of state government. *State Politics and Policy Quarterly* 3:309–19.

Krause, George A. 2002. Separated powers and institutional growth in the presidential and congressional branches: Distinguishing between short-run and long-run dynamics. *Political Research Quarterly* 55:27–57.

Krause, George A., and Jeffrey E. Cohen. 2000. Opportunity, constraints, and the development of the institutional presidency: The issuance of executive orders, 1939–96. *Journal of Politics* 62:88–114.

Lewis, David E. 2005. Staffing alone: Unilateral action and the politicization of the executive office of the president, 1988–2004. *Presidential Studies Quarterly* 35:496–514.

Lightcap, Tracy. 2003. Issue environments and institutionalization: Structural change in U.S. state judicial institutions, 1975–1995. *Justice System Journal* 24:183–203.

March, James G., and Johan P. Olsen. 1989. *Rediscovering institutions: The organizational basis of politics.* New York: Free Press.

Moe, Terry M. 1985. The politicized presidency. In *The new direction in American politics,* ed. John E. Chubb and Paul E. Peterson. Washington, DC: Brookings Institution.

————. 2006. Power and political institutions. In *Rethinking political institutions: The art of the state,* ed. Ian Shapiro, Stephen Skowronek, and Daniel Galvin. New York: New York University Press.

Neustadt, Richard E. 1960. *Presidential power: The politics of leadership.* New York: John Wiley.

Orren, Karen, and Stephen Skowronek. 1996. Institutions and intercurrence. In *Political order, NOMOS XXXVIII,* ed. Ian Shapiro and Russell Hardin. New York: New York University Press.

————. 2004. *The search for American political development.* New York: Cambridge University Press.

Plumper, Thomas, and Vera E. Troeger. 2007. Efficient estimation of time-invariant and rarely changing variables in finite sample panel analysis with unit fixed effects. *Political Analysis* 15:124–39.

Polsby, Nelson W. 1968. The institutionalization of the U.S. House of Representatives. *American Political Science Review* 62:144–68.

Ragsdale, Lyn, and John J. Theis III. 1997. The institutionalization of the American presidency, 1924–92. *American Journal of Political Science* 41:1280–1318.

Rudalevige, Andrew, and David E. Lewis. 2005. Parsing the politicized presidency: Centralization and politicization as presidential strategies for bureaucratic control. Paper presented at the annual meeting of the American Political Science Association, Washington, DC, September.

Sanford, Terry. 1967. *The storm over the states.* New York: McGraw-Hill.

Selznick, Philip. 1957. *Leadership in Administration: A Sociological Interpretation.* Evanston, IL: Row, Peterson.

Shafer, Byron E., and Anthony J. Badger, eds. 2001. *Contesting democracy: Substance and structure in American political history, 1775–2000.* Lawrence: University Press of Kansas.

Simmons, Robert H. 1965. The Washington State plural executive: An initial effort in interaction analysis. *Western Political Quarterly* 18:363–81.

Teaford, Jon C. 2002. *The rise of the states: Evolution of American state government.* Baltimore: Johns Hopkins University Press.

U.S. Bureau of the Census. Various years-a. *Annual survey of state and local government finances.* Washington, DC: Government Printing Office.

———. Various years-b. *Public employment in [year].* Washington, DC: Government Printing Office.

———. Various years-c. *The statistical abstract of the United States.* www.census.gov/compendia/statab/past_years.html.

Wilson, Woodrow. 1885. *Congressional government: A study in American politics.* Boston: Houghton Mifflin.

———. 1908. *Constitutional government in the United States.* New York: Columbia University Press.

Qualifications for the Office of Governor

Qualifications to take the office of the governor are stipulated in the constitution. A person must be thirty years of age, a citizen of the United States, and a resident of Texas for at least five years preceding the election in which they could become governor—not a strict list of qualifications and not the whole picture. The minimal qualifications are designed to open the office to a wide range of individuals and make the position one that is accessible. The governor's salary (a plump $150,000 per year) makes the position attractive, and access to planes, cars, and travel aids and reimbursements make the financial side of the position even more appealing. Coupled with a mansion to live in and a sizable staff (currently at 266), the attractiveness of the position is evident despite the lack of formal powers, which we'll get to. While these formal qualifications set a very low baseline, there is a profile of qualifications.

Becoming governor is not simply completing a checklist of formal qualifications. A person must be a significant campaigner and fundraiser to obtain the position. In 2014, Greg Abbott spent $103 million to defeat challenger Wendy Davis for the position. The ability to make connections and raise funds is a requirement for the position. The ability to thrive in a cutthroat political environment is necessary as well. The battles for the position of governor can be nasty as experienced politicians vie for the position. A record of accomplishment in Texas government or high social profile is necessary to "qualify" for the job. Professionally, the breeding grounds for governors have been ranching, business, and the legal profession. Dating back to the nineteenth century, these fields have produced many of the state's governors. Abbott moved into the position from the attorney general spot. George W. Bush, before becoming president, worked both the rancher and businessman profiles to reach success.

Examining Formal and Informal Powers

In Texas, establishing power for the governor and defining the executive role are important. Examining the current role of the governor, the seeds of mistrust that were laid at the state's inception are evident today. As Texas avoids large government and an overly active executive, the goal is to minimize the impact of the position. Establishing those lines of power is a necessary step to developing an accurate conception of what the executive official is in Texas. While the rewards and salary for the job are good and the path to higher office is established, what is the part that the position plays in the administration of Texas government?

Reading 5.2

Selection from "Do Governors Matter? Budgeting Rules and the Politics of State Policymaking"[2]
from *Political Research Quarterly*
Charles Barrilleaux and Michael Berkman

Reading Introduction

A baseline for gubernatorial power is hard to pin down. When it comes to roles in policymaking and the administration of government, defining the parameters of power and actions is tricky. As this examination of the Texas governorship will show, the power meter rises and falls dramatically, both in issue areas and times on the calendar. Charles Barrilleaux and Michael Berkman studied the power

---

of governors, estimating how their power is used and to what extent. In this excerpt, they address how power is defined and provide a brief but needed base for discussing the formal and informal powers and roles of a governor.

GOVERNORS AND POLICYMAKING IN THE STATES

Systematic tests of executive effects on state policymaking take two approaches. The first casts the governor as the leader of a party team whose success is a function of the governor's leadership and political skills. The second focuses on the institutional powers of the governor, suggesting that the ability to lead depends upon the resources and design of the governorship.[1]

Governors as Team Leaders

As a member of a *party team*, a governor's success or failure is viewed as a function of his ability to lead that team (Morehouse 1998). The strength and cohesion of the party organization is a crucial tool at a governor's disposal, but individual ability to use those resources largely establishes whether a governor will succeed or fail. Related to this view, governors are cast as the "legislator in chief" and their effectiveness a reflection of their individual ability to work with the legislature (Bernick and Wiggins 1981). This view is supported by evidence from studies of redistributive policies that find that Democratic governors, like Democratic legislators, promote more redistribution (Dye 1984; Winters 1976). The team-leader approach, in general terms, leads to a focus on the party of the governor, and tends to see the governor's constituency in terms very similar to that as a legislator from the same party.

Clearly the governor's leadership of her legislative party is important. But it also the case that within any party each individual office has its own constituency and organization; Schlesinger (1985, 1994) refers to these as party *nuclei*. Because governors draw upon distinct constituencies we expect that the governor's nucleus differs systematically from that of the average legislator. These constituencies, along with other characteristics of the nuclei, may push different officeholders from the common preferences suggested by a party focus. Party organizations devote considerable effort to trying to "link the nuclei together" (Schlesinger 1985: 1153) to get them to cooperate with one another. The extent to which this linking occurs "is not a fixed or stable quantity" (ibid.) but depends upon political conditions. This means that not only may different officeholders within the same party have different policy interests, but also that the notion of a team is variable and conditional. We suggest below it is possible to identify when governors have the incentives to act independently or otherwise.

Governors' Powers

A second approach emphasizes the governor's formal and informal powers (Mueller 1985; Beyle 1996; Schlesinger 1971) conditioned by political circumstances. For example, powerful governors are more successful when they enjoy strong electoral margins and legislative majorities (Sigelman and Dometrius 1988) and the same party controls both branches (Clarke 1998). But commonly used measures of gubernatorial power are not designed to discriminate *when* particular powers matter because they mix budgetary powers with others (such as appointment powers; see for example Schlesinger 1971 and Beyle 1996). Therefore, they can obscure the issue of influence and fail to measure power over the legislature in the stage at which the legislature is most involved—the formulation of budget totals and priorities.

To estimate gubernatorial influence properly we need to isolate governors' power over the specific stages of the budgetary process relative to the power of the legislature.[2] This is emphasized in some congressional work on the budgetary process (Thurber 1997) as well as in the comparative cases studies of some states done by Clynch and Lauth (1991). But only a handful of studies look at how a small number of these rules affect governors' abilities to achieve their preferences (Crain and Miller 1990; Poterba 1997). Not only are these studies limited in the kinds of rules they consider, they also conceptualize gubernatorial interest as simply reducing legislative spending, rather than the pursuit of particular types of spending objectives rooted in their distinctive constituencies.

ELECTORAL INCENTIVES AND POLICY PREFERENCES

Our model borrows from both of these approaches. But we put in the forefront gubernatorial preferences embedded within the institution. To derive these we draw upon legislative studies, which offer a theoretically rigorous analysis of institutionally derived preferences that are advanced and mediated by institutional capacity. Influential studies of Congress recognize that legislators' electoral incentives cannot be explained solely in terms of the demography partisanship, and the ideological profile of their constituencies. Legislators, irrespective of party, are parochial in their preferences (Mayhew 1974) eager to deliver particularized benefits to their constituencies (Tullock 1962; Weingast, Shepsle, and Johnsen 1981). While our understanding of how distributive politics operates would not be possible without an appreciation of how legislators' preferences are rooted in geographically defined constituencies, this approach has had more limited influence on state-level studies.[3]

Governor's preferences, too, should be rooted in their geographic constituencies. Governors cannot spread the costs of particularized programs for their constituents among others' constituents, the way legislators can; their constituency is statewide, or "at-large" so their "benefit-cost calculus for appraising government programs" is not the same (Crain and Miller 1990: 1030). Therefore, they may seek to lower legislative spending, which may reduce overall spending totals (Crain and Miller 1990). Yet governors may have constituency driven preferences of their own that go beyond their desire to suppress spending by the legislature and their own budget-maximizing agencies. Thus, in contrast to legislators' interest in policies "with district-specific benefits" (Crain 1999: 678), governors should prefer to fund policies with statewide benefits.

Peterson, who characterizes policies as "redistributive or developmental" based upon their geographic impact, has advanced this argument. Developmental programs, (frequently called distributive) provide "physical and social infrastructure" (1995: 17) and "are generally perceived to be a concentrated benefit" (Peterson 1995: 41). Redistributive programs "reallocate societal resources from the 'haves' to the 'have-nots'" (Peterson 1995: 17), are structured by class rather than geography (Wong 1989), and have costs and benefits that are "geographically diffuse" (Peterson 1995: 43). Providing statewide benefits best rewards governors, who must appeal to statewide constituencies (Schlesinger 1994). If governors are politically ambitious (as many seem to be), their focus should be on the U.S. Senate—a statewide office—or other national office, so they are again best served by providing benefits to a broad constituency. But evidence for this is scarce. Mark Peterson (1990) finds that presidents introduce more redistributive proposals than any other kind, and Winters (1976) finds that governors push for redistributive measures. But we find no direct tests of hypotheses based upon the assumption that governors and legislators are motivated to support different types of policies.

NOTES

1 Another important approach less applicable to our study of aggregate spending differences across states concerns the budgetary requests of executive agencies (e.g., Sharkansky 1968; Clarke 1998).

2 Gross (1989) argues that most measures of legislative and gubernatorial strength covary positively and that gubernatorial power should be measured relative to that of the legislature. See also Dometrius (1987) and Mueller (1985).

3 Examples include Wong (1989), Crain and Miller (1990), Crain (1999), and Peterson (1995).

Formal Powers of the Texas Governor

Military Power

Military power is often seen as a power that is relegated to the president. While the traditional view of the military places control with the president, the Texas governor has troops at his or her disposal.

Most common amongst this group is the National Guard. The governor has command of the National Guard if they are under Title 32 of the US Code. This designation places the forces under the control of the Texas governor. As the commander in chief of the military and military activity in the state, the governor controls the National Guard, which is made up of reservists operating in Texas. If needed for a federal action, however, the guard would be classified under Article II of the Constitution, and its availability and the power to command it would be transferred to the president. When not mobilized for national service, the guard functions as an entity of the state of Texas.

In addition to the National Guard, Texas has a Texas Guard. This is a group that functions as the state's militia. This groups falls under the sole purview of the governor and cannot be taken from his or her control. This guard has the same characteristics of the traditional perception of militias: it is made up of retirees, part-time troops, and volunteers. The main advantage is that the president has no control over these troops. The eight-regiment outfit can be called into action only by the governor. They function in three areas: as an army guard, an air guard, and a maritime guard. Both divisions fall under the control of the Texas adjutant general, who is appointed by the governor. The adjutant general (currently, Major General John F. Nichols) oversees training and has a responsibility to comply with both federal and state command.

The guard is used in most cases to keep the peace. While they do not have express or consistent powers in law enforcement or peacekeeping, they have powers granted by the governor. The most recent deployment in the state has been in response to immigration, as both Rick Perry and Greg Abbott have deployed troops to the border in response to what was termed "a growing number of child immigrants." The initial deployment in 2014 came after an executive order issued by President Barack Obama regarding immigration practices. The move to deploy troops to support border patrol has drawn the ire of federal officials and shows the division that can take place between the state and federal layers of government.

Executive Power: Executive Orders, Administration, and Appointments

Much of the governor's formal powers lie in the executive arena, but even those are measured and called into question. What power the governor has over the administration differs depending on the governor and the interpretation of the constitution. One interpretation is that, as the chief executive officer, the governor serves as the overseer and manager of the administration in Texas. That reading would provide the office with a significant amount of power—power would extend into day-to-day activity and open the administration up to the direction of the governor.

Rick Perry followed this reading and attempted to push the boundaries. Perry tried to extend his power over the government's administration through the use of executive orders. Executive orders are a source of debate at any layer of government. The ability of an executive official to direct administration through mandate is something that is delineated at the federal level in the US Constitution. However, there is no mention of it there or in the Texas Constitution. Instead the executive official is given the ability to make decrees or take administrative action to carry out the executive function of the government. This allows executive officials to make these decrees and signed them into mandatory order which must be followed by administrators and requires no legislative approval.

The use of the executive order is designed to follow the interpretation that gives the governor more power. Perry pushed that and signed several orders, including where education funds must be spent by mandating that 65 percent be spent in the classroom. He also tested his informal and formal powers by signing an executive order mandating HPV shots for all females in the sixth grade. The order was met with opposition from both parties, as religious Republicans felt it would lead to promiscuity, and Democrats and Republicans alike worried about the health of the girls and the safety of the vaccination. Perry reversed course in 2011, four years after signing the order, as he tried to appeal to the masses in a failed presidential campaign. This level of control, however, would lend itself to the formal bureaucratic structure that Weber lines out.

Other interpretations of the role of the governor in administration suggest that, instead of directly influencing administration, the official's job is to advise and direct. Take the appointive powers of the governor as an example. The governor has the task of appointing officials to several key positions in the government. Examples include the adjutant general, secretary of state, and commissioners of education and health and human services. These appointments stay in office during staggered six-year terms. It is estimated that a governor can make over two thousand appointments in a four-year term. The longer a governor stays in office, the more influence he or she has. The opposing side of that argument is that, once appointed, the officials act of their own accord. The governor has no removal power; that would require a two-thirds vote by the Senate, and no sitting governor can remove an appointment of a previous official midterm.

Legislative Powers: Messages and Special Sessions

Formal powers are very rare when reality sets in for the governor, and nowhere is this more evident than when dealing with the legislature. The structure of Texas government is designed to keep the governor out of the legislative business of the state until the very end of the process. In short, until the final say is necessary, the governor really does not have much power; where they do have formal power is in the following four areas.

Message power is something governors can use to their advantage. Formally, the governor gives a "state of the state" address at the beginning of every session. In this speech, the governor outlines the state of politics and well-being in society. Governors use this message to give directives to the legislature on political agendas they believe will benefit the state. Also, they will try and impress upon the legislature a focus on certain issues. The effectiveness of this message can rest on the informal power of the governor. If the person is well liked or has relationships within the chambers, the message will be favorably received and followed. If not, the message could be ignored.

In line with message powers, the governor can mandate focus on a policy area by calling a special session. These thirty-day sessions can be convened when the executive official believes there are topics that need immediate attention. The focus of these sessions is usually very narrow and can be called because the legislature is out of session and the need for policy debate has arrived. While there is a thirty-day time limit, there is no rule against calling multiple special sessions to extend the time.

While the sessions are usually conducted to address a pressing need, there have been times where they have been called for political reasons. After Wendy Davis and the Democrats ran time out on the abortion bill in 2013, Rick Perry called a special session to discuss the issue, and the bill was tweaked and passed despite the filibuster efforts during the regular session. Along these lines, the governor can classify a policy or issue area as an emergency item. These items do not fall prey to the session's schedule and can be voted on during the first sixty days of session, which are normally relegated to introduction and committee activity. Emergency issues can deal with natural disasters, civil unrest, or any matter that is shown to be a pressing need.

Veto Power: Control over Budget and Policy

One executive power that has carried over to the state level is the power to approve (or not approve) policies. The veto gives the governor of Texas the ability to nullify the actions and decisions of the state legislature. One of the governor's most significant powers, it gives the executive official a leg up in the legislative process on all policies. While it is a way for the governor to show strength, it is also one of the most negative powers the governor has. The governor is given ten days to decide on a bill once it is passed out of the legislature—twenty if the session is adjourned during the initial ten days. During that time, the governor wields an immense amount of power. A strong veto would signify he or she is using that power and show force in the legislative process. That show of force can be interpreted as a very negative and reductive step, however, making future negotiations tough and straining the relationship between the executive and his or her counterparts in the legislature.

In truth, vetoes work better as a threat. Signaling that a policy measure will not be signed is more effective in some cases than employing the veto at the end of the process. If used during the legislative process, it could lead to changes or amendments that create a better or more acceptable policy, which is the reason for the process in the first place. Governor Abbott used the veto forty-two times in 2015; this accounted for less than five percent of all bills passed, according to legislative records. A two-thirds vote in the legislature can formally override any veto, but that is difficult to achieve due to party lines and the fact that many bills are passed at the end of the session, when there is no time to vote to overturn.

The veto is not an option for some bills. The budget is a necessary bill that must be passed for the state to follow the constitution. Instead of employing a straight veto, the governor can choose to employ a line-item veto. A power that was stripped from the president in 1992, it allows the governor to strike specific budget appropriations from the bill. Because the governor has this power, it increases the slim influence they have over the budget process.

Reading 5.3

Selection from "Why do Governors Issue Vetoes? The Impact of Individual and Institutional Influences"[3]
from *Political Research Quarterly*
Carl E. Klarner and Andrew Karch

Reading Introduction

Vetoes are a tricky business. The act of undoing the work of the state legislature is no easy task and can put the governor in a tough situation. While that is the case, the veto is seen as a significant power for any executive official because it grants de facto final say on whether a bill is made a law. That role in the legislative process is not understated, but does fluctuate in influence and can be used in different ways, depending on the structure and governmental environment. Andrew Karch and Carl Klarner examine the factors, both individual and institutional, that lead to a veto and provide a framework for examining the activity. In Texas, the veto

3   Carl E. Klarner and Andrew Karch, Selection from "Why Do Governors Issue Vetoes? The Impact of Individual and Institutional Influences," *Political Research Quarterly*, vol. 61, no. 4, pp. 575-578, 583-584. Copyright © 2008 by SAGE Publications. Reprinted with permission. Provided by ProQuest LLC. All rights reserved.

is not a popular tool of the governor, and this excerpt provides insight into the factors that lead to its infrequent use.

INDIVIDUAL AND INSTITUTIONAL INFLUENCES ON USE OF THE VETO

A major objective of existing research on veto activity is to "untangle individual and institutional influences ... in order to understand their relative contributions to the observed behavior" of the executive (Gilmour 2002, 199). The relative contributions of these two sets of factors illuminate the broader relationship between the legislature and the executive branch. If individual influences dominate, such a pattern suggests that veto use is best explained by factors specific to the time, bill, constituents, or personalities involved. But if institutional influences dominate, such a pattern suggests that presidents or governors in similar situations will behave in similar ways. Scholars disagree about the relative significance of individual and institutional forces, with some privileging the former (Herzik and Wiggins 1989) and others privileging the latter (Shields and Huang 1997). This section introduces specific individual and institutional variables that may affect veto activity. [...]

INDIVIDUAL INFLUENCES

The president-centered perspective posits that individual influences affect the president's propensity to veto. It emphasizes the unique points of view that executives bring to their posts. The general flexibility or inflexibility of the executive potentially affects veto activity as does the executive's view of his or her role as active or passive. For example, some executives might view veto use as a way to assert control over the legislature while others might view veto use as a sign of executive weakness. The logic of this approach also applies to the relationship between governors and state legislatures. For example, Herzik and Wiggins (1989, 855) attribute veto use to specific circumstances in a state, the bill at issue, and the personalities involved in the conflict. Their conclusion that veto activity is "state specific rather than cross-sectionally based" resonates with the president-centered approach. In this article, we examine five hypotheses that attribute veto use to the personal traits and resources that the governor brings to office independent of the institutional perquisites of his or her post.

First, we examine whether Democratic governors have a greater propensity to veto legislation. The partisanship hypothesis has sparked a heated debate amongst presidency scholars. Lee (1975) finds that, all else equal, Democratic presidents are likely to issue significantly more vetoes than their Republican counterparts and speculates that Democrats may be more inclined to believe that executives should provide forceful legislative leadership. Other scholars have criticized the partisanship hypothesis on theoretical and empirical grounds (Hoff 1991; Ringelstein 1985). For example, Copeland (1983) attributes the large number of vetoes under Democrats to the outlier presidencies of Grover Cleveland and Franklin D. Roosevelt. His finding reveals an advantage of examining the partisan hypothesis at the state level. Our analysis incorporates a larger number of actors and is therefore less likely to be affected by extreme outliers, enabling us to have greater confidence in any inferences we draw. It includes a dichotomous independent variable indicating whether the governor is a Democrat.[1]

Second, we examine the impact of the governor's electoral mandate. Specifically, we hypothesize that veto activity will be negatively related to the percentage of the popular vote that the governor received in the previous election because legislators may be more willing to challenge an executive who won a close election. The electoral mandate hypothesis builds on a common line of inquiry in the presidential veto literature. Many analyses posit that presidents who can draw on a reservoir of public support will be more effective in persuading Congress and that Congress will be more accommodating of such a president (Rohde and Simon 1985; Hoff 1991; Woolley 1991; Shields and Huang 1995, 1997). Similarly, governors might be better able to convince state legislators to modify a bill if they are perceived as popular, and they might therefore resort to the veto less frequently.[2] Our analysis includes the percentage of the vote received by the sitting governor in the previous election.[3]

Third, we examine the impact of legislative experience. Former legislators may be more sympathetic to legislative prerogatives and may consequently issue fewer vetoes once they become governor. Governors who were exposed to vetoes as a state legislator or a member of Congress may recall the frustration that such vetoes caused and use their veto pen reluctantly. In addition, governors who previously served in the state legislature may issue fewer vetoes because they are better able to steer their priorities through the policymaking process. They may have cultivated friends and allies who will support them (Beyle 2004, 206). Our analysis therefore includes two dichotomous independent variables, one indicating whether the governor previously served in the state legislature and one indicating whether he or she was previously a member of Congress.[4] We posit that veto activity will be negatively related to both forms of legislative experience.

Fourth, we examine the impact of the governor's gender. Women make up an increasing percentage of state legislators, and many scholars have examined the impact of this shift. The influx of female state legislators has been linked to changes in legislative agendas, operations, and policy outputs (e.g., Thomas and Welch 1991; Saint-Germain 1989). In a similar vein, the presence of a female governor may affect the frequency of conflict between the state legislature and the executive branch. Such conflicts may be due either to differences in policy priorities or to systematic differences across genders in terms of gubernatorial personality. Although we do not have a clear expectation about the direction of its impact, our analysis includes a dichotomous independent variable indicating whether the governor is a woman.

Finally, we examine the impact of gubernatorial experience. As they spend more time in their posts, governors may gain a better understanding of what to expect and what is expected of them. Furthermore, they may cultivate allies who will support their policy priorities. Governors with more experience may therefore be better able to enact their legislative agendas and, as a result, issue fewer vetoes. To assess this hypothesis, our analysis includes the number of years that the governor has been in office prior to the current legislative session.[5]

INSTITUTIONAL INFLUENCES

The institutional perspective attributes veto use to factors that lie beyond the control of the chief executive. Institutional structures constrain executive behavior in ways that are not affected by election results or the partisanship or gender of the person holding the office. They affect the relationship between the governor and the state legislature by shaping both the tendency of the legislature to provoke a veto and the executive's propensity to veto. In this article, we examine three broad hypotheses about institutional influences on veto activity.

Formal Powers

We posit that governors with greater formal powers will issue more vetoes. The state level is an especially appropriate environment in which to examine this hypothesis empirically. While presidential veto powers are largely constant across administrations, there has been a general trend toward stronger veto power at the state level (Prescott 1950; Bowman and Kearney 1986). Gubernatorial veto powers continue to vary across states, however, allowing us to assess the formal powers hypothesis in a compelling way.

We examine the impact of four constitutional provisions that affect the strength of the governor's veto power.[6] The first two provisions affect the likelihood of a veto override. When executives and legislatures disagree, executives may be more willing to issue vetoes if they think that an override is unlikely. The first provision is the percentage of legislators who must vote to override a veto. The more stringent this requirement is, the more difficult it is for the legislature to override a veto. As a result, we expect a positive relationship between the override percentage and veto activity. The second provision is the "absolute veto," an especially powerful form of the pocket veto that makes a legislative override impossible. When the legislature passes a bill at the end of a session and the governor issues an absolute veto after the session has ended, the state legislature cannot meet to override it. There is no possibility of a legislative response. We posit that the absolute veto increases the governor's propensity to veto since it gives the executive the "final word" on a bill. Our empirical analysis includes a dichotomous variable indicating whether the governor possesses this authority.[7]

The third and fourth institutional provisions relate to the length of time governors have to consider legislation. State legislatures pass a large number of bills, many of them at the conclusion of a legislative session. Facing severe time constraints, the executive branch may find it difficult to process the information contained in the legislation. Extending the time frame that the governor has to consider legislation helps to address this problem of incomplete information. Governors who possess more time to consider bills may be better able to identify objectionable legislation and may therefore issue more vetoes than their colleagues who possess less time. We therefore consider the number of days within a session and after a session ends that the governor has to consider legislation. We expect the relationship between these variables and veto activity to be positive.

Partisan Composition of the State Legislature

Building on existing research, we posit that the partisan composition of the state legislature affects veto activity. We examine three specific relationships. First, we assess the relationship between veto activity and "simple divided government" (Bowling and Ferguson 2001), the condition that exists when both chambers of the state legislature are controlled by the same political party but the governor does not belong to that party. This alignment may increase the legislature's willingness to challenge the executive, therefore increasing veto activity. Several presidential studies provide empirical support for the simple divided government hypothesis (Clarke 1998; Lee 1975; Copeland 1983).[8]

Second, we examine the impact of a "divided legislature," a form of divided government that exists when two different political parties control the two chambers of the legislature. This partisan alignment does not seem likely to affect veto use because one chamber will be controlled by the party of the governor and may share the governor's policy preferences or at least be more willing to accommodate those preferences. A split legislature may therefore moderate the legislature's willingness to challenge the governor.

Third, we examine the relationship between veto activity and a specific form of "simple divided government." Sometimes a governor faces a state legislature in which the opposing party possesses a veto-proof majority in both chambers. While this partisan alignment may increase the tendency of the legislature to provoke a veto, governors in this situation may be less willing to issue a veto given the increased likelihood of an override. As a result, the relationship between this partisan alignment and veto activity is uncertain. This is an important empirical question, however, because governors were opposed by veto-proof majorities of the other party almost ten percent of the time between 1971 and 2002. To examine these three relationships, our empirical analysis incorporates dichotomous independent variables that indicate whether "simple divided government," a "divided legislature," or a veto-proof majority existed in a state in a particular biennium.[9]

Electoral Cycle

Our third institutional hypothesis is that the electoral cycle affects veto activity. Several studies conclude presidential veto activity increases in an election year (Shields and Huang 1995, 1997; Rohde and Simon 1985; Woolley 1991; Lee 1975; Hoff 1991). Legislatures and executives must respond to different constituencies to win reelection, giving legislators an incentive to address parochial concerns that might conflict with executive preferences. We expect a gubernatorial election year to produce heightened executive attention to legislative matters, thereby enhancing the likelihood of executive-legislative conflict (Rohde and Simon 1985, 403). Our empirical analysis incorporates a dichotomous variable indicating whether the governor is up for reelection, and we expect this variable to be positively related to veto activity.

The electoral cycle might also affect veto activity through the operation of gubernatorial and legislative term limits. Building on Axelrod's (1984) observations about the evolution of cooperation, both legislators and governors may be less inclined to cooperate with elected officials with whom they will not serve in future sessions. The presence of "lame-duck" governors in the last biennium before their terms expire may increase inter-branch conflict and cause the governor to issue more vetoes. Similarly, we expect legislative term limits to produce greater conflict between the two branches. Our empirical analysis includes a dichotomous variable that indicates whether a governor is a lame duck (Congressional Quarterly 1998; Council of State Governments, Various Years) and a variable that measures the percentage of legislators facing term limits at the end of the biennium (National Conference of State Legislatures 2004).[10] We expect both variables to have a positive effect on veto activity.

NOTES

1 Our dataset will be available at www.klarnerpolitics.com on January 1, 2009. We assign fractions for midyear changes in the governor's party, following Klarner (2003).

2 Gilmour (2002, 207) characterizes presidential popularity as an institutional variable "because it is largely ... beyond the control of the president." We treat the electoral mandate as an individual influence because it depends on the occupant of the office. Our decision resonates with the literature on gubernatorial authority that describes the electoral mandate as a "personal power" (Beyle 2004, 205–8).

3 These data are from Congressional Quarterly (1998), the *Book of the States* (Council of State Governments, various years), and numerous state-specific sources. We account for changes in the party of the governor when no election has taken place by using the percent of the vote the opposing party received in the previous election.

4 "Former State Legislator" indicates whether a governor served in the state legislature within eleven years of their initial election to the governorship (Council of State Governments, *Supplement I*, various years). "Former Member of Congress" indicates whether a governor served in the U.S. Congress at any time prior to their initial election. The congressional data are available at the U.S. House Web site, http://bioguide. congress.gov/biosearch/ biosearch.asp (accessed May 23, 2007).

5 These data are from Moore, Preimesberger, and Tarr (2001), with updates from the *Book of the States* (Council of State Governments, various years).

6 Governors' formal powers were determined by examining the *Book of the States* (Council of State Governments, various years). If these formal powers changed over time, we also consulted numerous state-specific sources, such as state constitutions, to verify that the *Book of the States* was not in error; sometimes it was.

7 In some states, the governor can issue pocket vetoes but the legislature can override them in special sessions. Thus, the "pocket veto" is distinct from the "absolute veto."

8 Woolley (1991, 298) concludes that divided government reduces the number of major vetoes issued. Since we do not distinguish between major and minor vetoes, we cannot evaluate this particular claim.

9 All partisan balance data are from Klarner (2003).

10 Our term limits measure is an average of both legislative chambers.

REFERENCES

Axelrod, Robert. 1984. *The evolution of cooperation*. New York: Basic Books.

Berry, William D., Richard C. Fording, and Russell L. Hanson. 2000. An annual cost of living index for the American states, 1960–1995. *Journal of Politics* 62:550–67.

Beyle, Thad. 2004. The governors. In *Politics in the American states: A comparative analysis*, ed. Virginia Gray and Russell L. Hanson. 8th ed. Washington, DC: CQ Press.

Bowling, Cynthia J., and Margaret R. Ferguson. 2001. Divided government, interest representation, and policy differences: Competing explanations of gridlock in the fifty states. *Journal of Politics* 63:182–206.

Bowman, Ann O'M., and Richard C. Kearney. 1986. *The resurgence of the states*. Englewood Cliffs, NJ: Prentice Hall.

Clarke, Wes. 1998. Divided government and budget conflict in the U.S. states. *Legislative Studies Quarterly* 22:5–22.

Congressional Quarterly. 1998. *Gubernatorial elections, 1787–1997*. Washington, DC: Congressional Quarterly.

Copeland, Gary W. 1983. When Congress and the President collide: Why presidents veto legislation. *Journal of Politics* 45:696–710.

Council of State Governments. Various years. *The book of the states*. Lexington, KY: Council of State Governments.

———. Various years. *The book of the states, supplement I: State elected officials and the legislatures*. Lexington, KY: Council of State Governments.

Davenport, Christian. 2005. The case of the U.S. Government against the Republic of New Africa. *Journal of Conflict Resolution* 49:120–40.

Fairlie, John A. 1917. The veto power of the state governor. *American Political Science Review* 11:473–93.

Ferguson, Margaret R., and Jay Barth. 2002. Governors in the legislative arena: The importance of personality in shaping success. *Political Psychology* 25:787–808.

Gilmour, John B. 2002. Institutional and individual influences on the President's veto. *Journal of Politics* 64:198–218.

Greene, William H. 2000. *Econometric analysis*. 4th ed. Upper Saddle River, NJ: Prentice Hall.

Hager, Gregory L., and Terry Sullivan. 1994. President-centered and Presidency-centered explanations of presidential public activity. *American Journal of Political Science* 38:1079–1103.

Herzik, Eric B., and Charles W. Wiggins. 1989. Governors vs. legislatures: Vetoes, overrides, and policy making in the American states. *Policy Studies Journal* 17:841–62.

Hoff, Samuel B. 1991. Saying no: Presidential support and veto use, 1889–1989. *American Politics Quarterly* 19:310–23.

Honaker, James, Anne Joseph, Gary King, Kenneth Scheve, and Naunihal Singh. 2001. *Amelia: A program for missing data* (Gauss Version). Cambridge, MA: Harvard University. http://Gking.Harvard.edu/.

King, Gary, James Honaker, Anne Joseph, and Kenneth Scheve. 2001. Analyzing incomplete political science data: An alternative algorithm for multiple imputation. *American Political Science Review* 95:49–69.

Klarner, Carl. 2003. Measurement of partisan balance in state government. *State Politics and Policy Quarterly* 3:309–19.

Lee, Jong R. 1975. Presidential vetoes from Washington to Nixon. *Journal of Politics* 37:522–46.

Moore, John L., Jon P. Preimesberger, and David R. Tarr. 2001. *Congressional Quarterly's guide to U.S. elections*. 4th ed. Washington, DC: Congressional Quarterly.

National Conference of State Legislatures. 2004. Members Termed Out: 1996–2004. http://www.ncsl.org/programs/legman/about/ termedout.htm.

Prescott, Frank W. 1950. The executive veto in American states. *Western Political Quarterly* 3:98–112.

Ringelstein, Albert C. 1985. Presidential vetoes and classification. *Congress and the Presidency* 12:43–55.

Rohde, David W., and Dennis M. Simon. 1985. Presidential vetoes and Congressional response: A study of institutional conflict. *American Journal of Political Science* 29:397–427.

Saint-Germain, Michelle A. 1989. Does their difference make a difference? The impact of women on public policy in the Arizona legislature. *Social Science Quarterly* 70:956–68.

Shields, Todd G., and Chi Huang. 1995. Presidential vetoes: An event count model. *Political Research Quarterly* 48:559–72.

———. 1997. Executive vetoes: Testing presidency- versus president-centered perspectives of presidential behavior. *American Politics Quarterly* 25:431–57.

STATA Corporation. 2003. *STATA: Cross-sectional time-series.* College Station, TX: STATA Press.

Thomas, Sue, and Susan Welch. 1991. The impact of gender on activities and priorities of state legislators. *Western Political Quarterly* 44:445–56.

Wang, T. Y., William J. Dixon, Edward N. Muller, and Mitchell A. Seligson. 1993. Inequality and political violence revisited. *American Political Science Review* 87:979–994.

Watson, Richard A. 1988. The President's veto power. *Annals of the American Academy of Political and Social Science* 499:36–46.

Wiggins, Charles W. 1980. Executive vetoes and legislative overrides in the American states. *Journal of Politics* 42:1110–7.

Woolley, John T. 1991. Institutions, the election cycle, and the presidential veto. *American Journal of Political Science* 35:279–304.

Informal Powers of the Governor

By design (as discussed before), the governor does not have much in the way of formal powers. That does not handcuff the governor. A governor's position and stature can really be defined by his or her ability to increase influence outside the formal realm. This can be done through informal powers.

These powers are tough to quantify and even more difficult to define when it comes to the ways they are assumed and exercised. Many of these powers are developed through relationships and the ability of a governor to conduct business. The longer governors serve and the more successful they become, the more informal power they wield. This power can come mostly from the people around them. In this case, it is namely support they collect over the years from both officials and the public. If legislators and the public are on the side of the governor, then his or her informal powers will increase, making the ability to maneuver in the job easier. If he or she cannot curry favor, the political road will be much tougher to navigate.

Many of these informal powers come through leadership. Texans perceive the governor to be the top-ranking and dominant official in the state. In truth, no official has that role, but that also means that there really is no official above the governor. If the governor can capitalize on his or her political power and work with those in their political party, this can show quality leadership. That leadership is what many in the public see. While the expectation that the governor is the strongest (or even merely a strong) official is not realistic, if the officeholder can make it seem that way, he or she can capitalize on that perception.

The easiest path to this is leading in times of dissent or crisis. Rick Perry's multiple terms in office showed his popularity and success within the state. Perry led the Republican Party and the state through periods of crisis. His quick and strong reactions during the disasters following hurricanes Katrina and Rita showed a strong leadership style as he took accountability and quality action to help the state recover and aid neighboring states in turmoil.

Governors can also curry this support by leading politics. Being the face of the party is as important as being seen and acting as the face of the state. A governor can increase his or her power by taking the lead on major issues and publicizing the party's platform. Increasing this influence could allow the governor access to decision making that formal powers would not normally grant.

Applying Theory to Texas Administration: Max Weber and Georg Hegel

At the state level, the function of bureaucracy was determined quite often through the federalism system. The state falls prey to the federal government, and the roles it plays and authority it has is often shaped by what the federal government does. Many of the powers attributed to the state, in fact, are found in the US Constitution, not in the Texas Constitution. Still, how bureaucracy, which is the administration of law, is structured and carried out is not lost on state government. Applying these theories, especially where the governor and executive branch are concerned, is essential for examining the structure in Texas.

German sociologist Max Weber provides the dominant theory of modern administration. Weber's theory relies on the fact that bureaucracy is a rational entity that serves two basic mandates: efficiency and effectiveness. The goals of administration should be to achieve those two mandates. In short, Weber believes that bureaucracy serves the purpose of organization. Through this organization, the administration of government becomes rationalized. That organization is best served by rules that are derived from policy and statutes. Through these rules, under a Weberian civil society, administration would be able to provide a stable and structured set of activities and governance to best serve the people.

To achieve this, Weber believed that a hierarchy model best served government. Clear lines of communication and power would create a defined chain of command. That chain would oversee the system and ensure that all its cogs worked together to serve the system. Rigid division of labor and defined lines of authority would guide the system. In addition to this, there was no room for individuality. A worry of Weber's was that the best way to serve the rationalized version of bureaucracy and administration was to remove the individual nature from it and rely on qualifications; which meant using credentialism to choose and advance employees based on merit and experience. The worry was that employees would lose their connection with the population and find themselves in an "iron cage" with little to no regard for the public or desire for advancement.

> Only within the bureaucratization of the state and of law in general can one see a definite possibility of a sharp conceptual separation of an "objective" legal order from the "subjective" rights of the individual which it guarantees. ... These distinctions presuppose the conceptual separation

of the "state," as an abstract bearer of rights of domination and the creator of legal norms, from all personal authority of individuals. These conceptual distinctions are necessarily remote from pre-bureaucratic, especially from patrimonial and feudal, structures of authority (Weber 1978, 998).

Weber's worries have been substantiated and led to many of the stereotypes we see attached to bureaucracy today. While the system pushes against American idealism and individuality, it does provide a baseline model for an effective administration—one in which the system is the focus (not the individual) and rationality leads to the organization and structure that best serve the society.

Weber believed that administration is a necessary process to ensure organization and rationality. Therefore, it is devoid of much individuality. Hegel's theory of bureaucracy offers a different point of view. In truth, the two theories share many of the same characteristics. Both suggest that administration should be focused on organization that is derived from a structured system. In the United States, the Constitution develops that system. According to Hegel and Weber, that system should be adhered to and cultivated. Officials, or civil servants, should work in a hierarchy, and there should be a separation of personal rights and systematic benefit.

Instead of relying on the rigid system, this theory puts a modern spin on bureaucracy. "For [Hegel], the executive mediates between the state and civil society. Its distinctive function is to execute and maintain existing legal norms. In its relation with civil society, the executive upholds universal interest among pursuits. Its specific mode of activity is designated as subsumption" (Shaw 1992, 382). With that, officials are pillars of the state, and the issues dealing with individuality and advancement that Weber identifies are put aside. The strict stratification of employees is replaced by a system that has more flexibility as a means for universal service and activity. For Hegel, that should be the goal of the administrative employee and not the preservation of the organization or system. They should be selected and given tasks based on knowledge and not technical application of expertise. A major deviation is that Hegel believed power is derived from political sentiment, meaning that power is derived from those who can obtain it and interpret it, as opposed to the rules-based Weberian system.

Administrative theory (and here, Weber and Hegel) provides a clear view of what the function of government can and should be: the preservation of order, rationality, and logic through systematic rule. While there is an impact on political regime and interaction with the public, in Hegel's theory more than Weber's, the will of the administration should come from structure (in this case, the Constitution) and not from those in office or with political influence. The end goal is to protect and serve the people.

Reading 5.4

Selection from "The Governor and the Executive Branch"[4]
from *Texas Politics: Governing the Lone Star State*
Cal Jilson

Reading Introduction

The plural executive is meant to establish an executive branch that is free from the constraints of one single powerful entity. Cal Jilson outlines the structure of the executive branch and examines the roles each independent administrator plays. Along the way, the definition and confirmation of their power is defined.

INFORMAL POWERS

The formal powers of the Texas governor are fewer than those of most other governors, but one must be careful not to dwell exclusively on these limits. Even if the governor has limited powers, so does everyone else in Texas politics and no one has *more* power than the governor. It is common to suggest that the lieutenant governor may be the most powerful figure in Texas politics. But politics is about winning and using power. So ask yourself this: has any governor ever capped off his or her political career by running for lieutenant governor? (Hint: the answer is no.)[1]

Former Governor Dolph Briscoe (1973–79) explained quite well the expectations that Texas governors face and the limits on their ability to meet them. Briscoe wrote,

> Texans perceive the governor to be the head of state government. They look to the governor for leadership, and they hold that person to be responsible for the condition of the state. These are understandable expectations. The reality is, however, that the Texas Constitution does not establish a form of government in which the governor controls the executive branch.[2]

Governors must act as if the public expectations of executive leadership are legitimate and realistic, even while knowing that the bluff can be called at any time. Nonetheless, Texas governors are generally able to establish themselves as the leading figure in the state's politics. There are several important reasons for this. First, the governor is the face of his party; he is expected to develop an agenda

4   Cal Jilson, Selection from "The Governor and the Executive Branch," *Texas Politics: Governing the Lone Star State*, pp. 118-125, 186-187. Copyright © 2011 by Taylor & Francis Group. Reprinted with permission.

for the legislature and to speak to major public issues. Second, the governor is the only figure who has a finger in every pie. While his powers do not allow him to control most events, he is in a position to influence them. Third, when the legislature is not in session, which is most of the time, the governor dominates the stage in Austin. Finally, most Texans are only vaguely aware of the real limitations on the power of the governor. They assume that, as governor, he is the leader of Texas state government. Governors use this visibility, centrality, and presumption of authority to direct events more authoritatively than their formal powers alone might allow.

THE BUREAUCRACY

To exercise the influence and leadership that most citizens and voters expect, the governor must distinguish himself on a crowded stage. The lieutenant governor, AG, comptroller of public accounts, commissioner of public lands, and agriculture commissioner are also elected statewide, and with the exception of the lieutenant governor, who is principally a legislative official, they are executive department heads. Hence, Texas is often said to have a **plural executive**. The lieutenant governor is paid a legislative salary of $7,200 a year, plus *per diem*, while the others draw a salary between $137,500 and $150,000.

The executive branch of Texas state government is made up of about 275 separate departments, agencies, boards, and commissions. Each executive branch office is headed in one of four ways: by elected or appointed single administrators, or by elected or appointed multi-member boards or commissions. These executives direct the work of about 340,000 state employees. 750,000 Texans work in county and municipal governments.

SINGLE-ELECTED ADMINISTRATORS

Like the governor, the lieutenant governor, AG, comptroller of public accounts, land commissioner, and agriculture commissioner are elected to renewable four-year terms.

Lieutenant Governor. While the lieutenant governor is one of the top officials in Texas government, the office is almost exclusively legislative rather than executive. [...] [T]he lieutenant governor serves as acting governor when the governor is out of state or incapacitated. If the

Plural executive
An executive branch featuring several officials with independent constitutional and legal authority.

Q3

What other statewide elected officials share power with the governor?

governor should resign or die, the lieutenant governor ascends to the governorship for the remainder of the open term. If the lieutenant governor becomes governor, and then dies, or is forced to resign, the Senate selects one of its own to serve as lieutenant governor until the next general election.

Lieutenant Governor David Dewhurst, formerly a U.S. Air Force officer, C.I.A. and State Department official, and Houston businessman and rancher, first won statewide office as Texas Land Commissioner in 1998. In 2002, Dewhurst was elected lieutenant governor by defeating former Democratic Comptroller John Sharp, 52 percent to 46 percent. Dewhurst was easily re-elected in 2006 and 2010.

Attorney General. The Office of Attorney General (OAG) is mandated by the Texas Constitution. The AG is one of the state's most visible public officials. Texas Supreme Court Justice Greg Abbott was elected AG in 2002 and easily re-elected in 2006 and 2010. The OAG has 4,200 employees, more than 400 of them lawyers, in seventy offices located throughout the state. Most of the department's responsibilities involve legal representation of state agencies and civil administration.

The AG is the principal legal advisor and advocate for Texas state government. The AG represents the officers and agencies of Texas state government in court when they are party to a suit. Moreover, the AG's Opinion Committee issues opinions to the legislature and other state agencies concerning whether existing or proposed laws and regulations comply with the requirements of the U.S. and Texas Constitutions. While these opinions are not legally binding, they are seldom challenged or disobeyed.

Most of the thirty-eight divisions in the OAG engage in civil administration; they punish delinquency and enforce compliance with Texas laws and regulations. The OAG investigates and punishes violations of family and tax law, consumer and environmental law, antitrust legislation, and worker's compensation and Medicare fraud. Key divisions of the OAG include the Child Support Enforcement Division, the (Tax) Collections Division, the Consumer Protection Division, and the Cyber Crimes Unit.

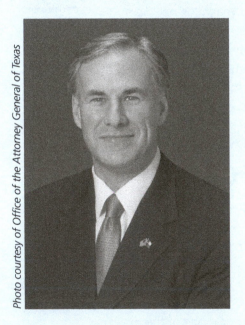

Photo courtesy of Office of the Attorney General of Texas

Greg Abbott, Attorney General of Texas.

Comptroller of Public Accounts. The Texas Constitution has mandated a Comptroller of Public Accounts since 1835. Only a dozen other states have an elected comptroller; the rest have appointed comptrollers or state treasurers. The comptroller is the state's chief accountant, auditor, tax collector, and investment officer. Many credit the legendary Bob Bullock, Texas comptroller from 1975 to 1990 and lieutenant governor from 1990 to 1998, with modernizing the comptroller's office and making it one of the most powerful offices in Texas politics.[3] Carole Strayhorn was elected comptroller in 1998 and 2002. She ran unsuccessfully for governor in 2006. Susan Combs, Texas Agriculture Commissioner since 1998, was elected comptroller in 2006 and re-elected in 2010.

The key to the comptroller's political influence lies in her constitutional responsibility to produce a **revenue estimate** at the beginning of each legislative session. The revenue estimate may be updated during the session, but the legislature cannot pass and the governor cannot sign a budget that expends more money than the comptroller predicts will be available. Tensions can build between the governor, legislative leaders, and the comptroller because the comptroller tends to make conservative revenue estimates that other leaders feel make budgetary discussions more difficult than they need to be. In the 2003 and 2005 legislative sessions, these tensions led to open conflict between the governor, legislative leaders, and the comptroller. Tensions have eased since Susan Combs became comptroller.

Revenue estimate
The Texas Comptroller is empowered to make revenue estimates that the Texas state budget must stay within.

Land Commissioner. Texas has had an elected land commissioner since independence. The land commissioner oversees the General Land Office. David Dewhurst was land commissioner before he was elected lieutenant governor in 2002. Jerry Patterson, a former state legislator, was elected land commissioner in 2002 and re-elected in 2006 and 2010.[4] He oversees 20.3 million acres of land and 2.2 million acres of Texas submerged lands (often called tidelands) extending three leagues (10.3 miles) into the Gulf. The land commissioner is responsible for leasing state land for oil and gas exploration, mining, and grazing. The commissioner is also responsible for maintaining the environmental quality of Texas lands, waters, wetlands, and coastal areas. Finally, the land commissioner administers the Veteran's Land Board, which provides veterans with loans and other assistance to purchase Texas public lands.

Agriculture Commissioner. The office of agriculture commissioner was established by statute in 1907. Governor Rick Perry first won statewide election as agriculture commissioner in 1990. Susan Combs succeeded Rick Perry in 1998 and was easily re-elected in 2002. Republican Todd Staples, a former member of the Texas House (1995–2001) and Senate (2001–06), was elected agriculture commissioner in 2006 when Combs moved up to comptroller. He was reelected in 2010.

The agriculture commissioner oversees the Texas Department of Agriculture (TDA). The TDA has the dual responsibility of regulating and promoting Texas agricultural interests and products. As a regulator, the TDA enforces laws and regulations regarding land use, pesticide use, product certification, and inspection. The TDA also inspects and certifies measuring devices like gas pumps, electronic scanners, and scales. Finally, the TDA promotes Texas agricultural products through research and public education.

SINGLE-APPOINTED ADMINISTRATORS

The governor, with the approval of two-thirds of the Texas Senate, is empowered to appoint several key officials of the executive branch to renewable two-year terms of office. While these are not officials of the first rank, they do oversee and administer important elements of Texas state government.

Secretary of State. The Secretary of State (SOS) is the chief election officer for Texas. The SOS interprets the election code, enforces election laws throughout the state, and maintains the voter rolls. Prior to election day, the SOS trains election officials and distributes election supplies. On election day, the SOS receives, reviews, and officially reports election results. Between elections, the SOS receives reports of campaign contributions and maintains a list of lobbyists registered with the state. Finally, the SOS issues corporate charters and licenses notary publics.

The incumbent SOS, Esperanza "Hope" Andrade, was appointed by Governor Perry in 2008. In addition to the traditional responsibilities of the office, Secretary Andrade will serve as the governor's liaison on border and Mexican affairs.

Commissioner of Insurance. The Commissioner of Insurance (COI) monitors and regulates the insurance industry in Texas. Governor Perry named Mike Geeslin to be insurance commissioner in 2005. The commissioner's office educates the public on insurance matters, licenses agents and investigates complaints against them and their companies, and monitors the financial health of insurance companies operating in the state. In recent years, the COI has attempted to roll-back home and auto insurance rates.[5]

Commissioner of Health and Human Services. Governor Perry named Tom Suehs to be Executive Commissioner of Health and Human Services (HHSC) in 2009. The executive commissioner has oversight, coordination, and review responsibility over five health and welfare agencies, running 200 programs from 1,300 locations around the state. HHSC employs 55,000 workers. Each agency is administered by its own appointed board or commission. The commissioner's responsibility is to review their activities, identify overlaps and redundancies, and recommend efficiencies.[6]

Adjutant General. The Adjutant General, the top military official in Texas state government, is appointed by and reports to the governor. He oversees and manages the Army and Air National Guard and the Texas State Guard.

ELECTED BOARDS AND COMMISSIONS

Much of Texas state government is administered by multimember boards and commissions. The members of most boards and commissions are appointed by the governor with the consent of the Senate, but a few of the most important win their seats in partisan elections.

The most important elected board is the Texas Railroad Commission (TRC). The TRC was founded in 1891 to regulate the railroads. Over the course of the 20th century, the TRC's regulatory mandate was extended to cover the oil and natural gas industries. The modern TRC's principal responsibilities involve regulating oil and natural gas exploration, drilling, recovery, storage, and transportation while protecting the state's environment. Critics always contend that the commission leans toward exploiting natural resources rather than environmental protection.

The three members of the TRC are elected statewide to staggered six-year terms. One member is up for election every two years and the member next up for election serves as the commission chair. Elizabeth Jones, first appointed by Governor Perry in 2005, was elected to a full term in 2006. Michael Williams was appointed to the TRC by Governor George W. Bush in 1998. He won a full term in 2002 and another in 2008. Victor Carrillo, appointed by Governor Perry in 2003, won a full term in 2004, but was beaten by David Porter in the 2010 Republican primary. Porter went on to defeat Democrat Jeff Weems in the general election. The commission oversees a professional staff of 750.

Q4

What roles do elected and appointed boards and commissions play in Texas?

The SBE is composed of fifteen persons, elected to four-year terms from single-member districts. The governor appoints a member of the SBE, currently Gail Lowe of Lampasas, to serve a two-year term as chair. The SBE is responsible for reviewing and adopting textbooks for use in the state's public schools, setting curriculum standards and graduation requirements, as well as promotion criteria and passing standards for achievement tests.

The SBE nominates three persons to be Commissioner of Education, from whom the governor, with the consent of the Senate, picks one to serve a four-year term. Governor Perry appointed Robert Scott in 2007 to be Texas Commissioner of Education. The Commissioner of Education is the chief executive officer of the SBE and head of the 1,200-employee Texas Education Agency (TEA). The Commissioner, SBE, and TEA set and administer policies and standards for the state's 1,227 school districts and 7,900 individual campuses. Texas public schools employ 590,000 teachers and staff to teach more than 4.5 million students.[7]

APPOINTED BOARDS AND COMMISSIONS

With the consent of two-thirds of the Senate, the governor appoints members to more than 275 agencies, boards, and commissions. Most gubernatorial appointees serve for a six-year renewable term without pay. The boards and commissions of Texas state government set general policy for their agencies, approve agency budget requests and major personnel decisions, hire the agency's executive director, and oversee agency implementation of state and federal law.

Governors try to appoint people who are accomplished and knowledgeable and who share their partisan and ideological commitments and principles. Surprisingly (or not), governors often find their appointees among their political contributors. One-third of Governor Perry's appointees between December 5, 2002 and February 22, 2006 were contributors. They contributed an average of $3,769 to his campaigns. The more important the board, the more likely the appointee was a contributor, and the more likely that the contribution was large. Appointees to the higher education governing boards gave an average of $10,616 to Governor Perry's campaigns.[8]

To serve on some boards and commissions, generous contributors will also need to have appropriate professional credentials. For example, there are thirty-eight examining boards that license individuals to practice particular professions, from dentistry to home building. Service on these boards allows members of these professions to ensure that state law aids the profession and does it no harm. Finally, all gubernatorial appointments are scrutinized for appropriate regional, racial, ethnic, and gender balance.

Gail Lowe is chairman of the State Board of Education.

While the appointment power gives the governor the opportunity to set the general direction of state policy, as well as to elevate his friends and deny his opponents, dangers lurk. Each appointment makes one person happy, but disappoints several others. And as former Governor John Connally observed, "If you want to talk about real 'in fighting,' try making an appointment to the Board of Cosmetology."[9]

Table 5.1 shows that while white men still fill most seats on state boards and commissions, qualified female and minority candidates are present. Governor Ann Richards, a female Democrat, directed 41 percent of her appointments to women, 13 percent to blacks, and 18 percent to Hispanics. Governors Bush and Perry, both male Republicans, gave almost two-thirds of their appointments to men. Perry did somewhat better than Bush in regard to black and Hispanic appointments, giving 10 percent of appointments to blacks and 15 percent to Hispanics.

TABLE 5.1 Gubernatorial Appointments: Gender, Race, and Ethnicity

	Texas Population	Ann Richards Administration	George Bush Administration	Rick Perry Administration
Male	50%	59%	63%	65%
Female	50%	41%	37%	35%
Anglo	46%	67%	77%	73%
Black	12%	13%	9%	10%
Hispanic	38%	18%	13%	15%

Source: Peggy Fikac, *San Antonio Express-News*, October 21, 2009.

EXECUTIVE BRANCH REFORM

Q5

What reforms do analysts propose for the executive branch?

Texas's plural executive and extensive use of independent boards and commissions has created a weak and diffuse executive branch. Historically, Texans have been wary of executive power. But today's Texas is the second most populous state in the Union, with three of the nation's ten largest cities. Some Texans wonder whether the powers of the governor and the structure of the executive branch are adequate. The most frequently mentioned reforms involve making the executive branch in Texas work more like the executive branch at the national level. The goal of these reforms would be to make Texas state government stronger and more hierarchical.

Advocates of reform contend that the governor's ability to energize and direct the executive branch would be dramatically enhanced by the adoption of several key reforms. First, candidates for governor, like candidates for the presidency, should pick their running mates. A lieutenant governor, selected by and working with the governor, would pull together the executive branch. The Senate would likely reduce the power of the lieutenant governor as a presiding officer, making him more of an executive than a legislative figure, but that would allow him or her to take on major tasks assigned by the governor.

Cabinet government An executive branch in which the governor has broad appointment and budgetary powers.

Second, reformers argue that the governor, like the president, should have the power to appoint and remove executive branch department heads. These department heads would then form the governor's cabinet. **Cabinet government** would empower the governor to initiate, coordinate, and implement executive policy. Advocates of reform also propose that many of the state's boards and commissions be rolled into the major departments of the state government.

Third, reformers argue that the governor, again like the president, should have the power to initiate and submit an executive budget. Today, the governor just goes through the motions of drafting a budget proposal because the legislature favors the budget drafted by the Legislative Budget Board. Reformers suggest that the Texas legislature must be able to consider and revise the governor's budget proposal, but that proposal should be the basis for the legislature's budget considerations.

Finally, many believe that if the powers of the governor are seriously enhanced, a two-term limit should be set.

NOTES

1 For a full list of Texas governors, lieutenant governors, statewide elected officials, and a description of key agencies, see the *Texas Almanac, 2008–2009*, pp. 466–471, 481–495.

2 Elizabeth C. Alvarez, *Texas Almanac: 2008–2009* (Dallas, TX: *Dallas Morning News*, 2008), pp. 466–467.

3 John J. Harrigan and David C. Nice, *Politics and Policy in States and Communities*, 9th ed. (New York: Pearson Longman, 2006), p. 222.

4 The governor's office provides a list of all the agencies, boards, and commissions to which the governor makes appointments and the number of appointments made to each. See http://www.governor.state.tx.us/divisions/appointments/positions.

5 Christy Hoppe, "Does Perry Really Have the Power?," *Dallas Morning News*, February 23, 2007, A1, A6. See also Corrie MacLaggan, "Abbott: Perry's HPV Mandate Does Not Carry the Weight of Law," *Austin American-Statesman*, March 13, 2007, A1.

6 Dennis L. Dresang and James L. Gosling, *Politics and Policy in American States and Communities*, 6th ed. (New York: Pearson Longman, 2008), p. 257.

7 House Research Organization, "Writing the State Budget," 81st Legislature, State Finance Report, no. 81–1, p. 7.

8 Jason Embry, "Perry Seeks to Hold the Line This Session: Speech Offers Few Bold Initiatives," *Austin American-Statesman*, January 28, 2009, A1.

9 Legislative Budget Board, *Fiscal Size-up, 2010–11 Biennium*, "Adjutant General's Department," pp. 308–309.

10 T.R. Fehrenback, *Lone Star: A History of Texas and the Texans* (New York: Macmillan Publishing Company, 1968), p. 437. See also George Norris Green, *The Establishment in Texas Politics: The Primitive Years, 1938–1957* (Norman, OK: University of Oklahoma Press, 1979), pp. 16–17.

11 Dolph Briscoe, *Dolph Briscoe: My Life in Texas Ranching and Politics* (Austin, TX: University of Texas Press, 2008), pp. 203–204.

12 Dave McNeely and Jim Henderson, *Bob Bullock: God Bless Texas* (Austin, TX: University of Texas Press, 2008), p. 89.

13 S.C. Gwynne, "This Land Is His Land," *Texas Monthly*, pp. 146–151, 254–259.

14 W. Gardner Selby, "Four Years After Emergency: Texas Still #1 in Homeowner Insurance," *Austin-American Statesman*, April 23, 2007, A1.

15 Carrie MacLaggan, "State Has Little to Show for Social Service Innovation Plan," *Austin-American Statesman*, April 25, 2007, A1.

16 http://www.tea.state.tx.us/sboe_history_duties.html.

17 Jane Elliott, "1 in 3 Perry Donors Get Post," (This story title was later corrected to say one-third of appointees were donors, not one-third of donors got posts) *Houston Chronicle*, April 11, 2006, B2; see also Christy Hoppe, "In Perry Appointees: Dallas Lagging Across the Board," *Dallas Morning News*, August 7, 2006, A1, A2.

18 James Reston, Jr., *The Lone Star: The Life of John Connally* (New York: Harper & Row, 1989), p. 309.

Summary: How Powerful Should the Governor Be?

While the state's traditionalistic culture wants limited government, through the years, its governors—as all executive officials do—have worked to expand the power of the office, whether through formal powers (very rare) or the more common informal power. Governors have come and gone, and the ability to expand the power of the office is a common measure of a governor's success in office. While several individuals have done this, the most recent and successful has been Rick Perry. He was able to capitalize on his lengthy time in office and a seemingly never-ending line of appointments to increase the power of the office. His appointive powers and ability to be relatable and work with the Texas legislature set him apart in terms of power.

How much of that power should be passed on? While the governorship of Texas is a significant position, the state has stuck to its guns to keep it weak. Texas imbues its governor with some of the strictest limitations, from a formal standpoint, of any US state. When examining that against theories set forth by Hegel and Weber, is the Texas governor powerful enough? Would a stronger executive official lead to better organization and more hierarchical management?

The answer to that question is double-edged and tough. For Texas, there is importance in viewing the executive branch with all its heads rather than just one. While the governor has the leadership role for the state, the remaining six members of the plural executive certainly help meet the administrative mandates set forth by theory and practice.

Still, questions remain about whether the governor's role should be reformed. Would patterning the state's structure after the federal government, giving the governor more power over administrative leaders—namely, through increasing the appointive powers of the office— make for a more efficient administration? Should the governor have more say in who takes the roles in the plural executive rather than leaving the choice to the public accountability system, which may or may not have a firm grasp on what functions those positions perform? Should the office's powers be limited so it doesn't take too much informal power? Perry's informal powers were harnessed as much from his longevity as his ability to function as a politician. Would term limits help assuage concerns about a strong executive and make the state more willing to increase the office's powers in favor of a strong administration? These are debates the state will continue to have as over 250 agencies attempt to perform the executive function.

References

Barrilleaux, C., and M. Berkman. "Do Governors Matter? Budgeting Rules and the Politics of State Policymaking." *Political Research Quarterly* 56, no. 4 (2003): 409–417.

Beyle, T. L. "The Governor as Innovator in the Federal System." *Publius: The Journal of Federalism* 18, no. 3 (1988): 131–152.

Dometrius, N. C., and D. S. Wright. "Governors, Legislatures, and State Budgets across Time." *Political Research Quarterly, 63.* (2009): 783–795.

Dresang, D. L., and J. J. Gosling. *Politics and Policy in American States & Communities*. Saddle River, NJ: Pearson Higher Ed, 2012.

Fairlie, J. A. "The Executive Power in the State Constitution." *Annals of the American Academy of Political and Social Science* 181, no. 1(1935): 59–73.

Key, V. O., and A. Heard. *Southern Politics in State and Nation*. Knoxville, TN: University of Tennessee Press, 1950.

Sager, F., & Rosser, C. "Weber, Wilson, and Hegel: Theories of Modern Bureaucracy." *Public Administration Review* 69, no. 6 (2009): 1136–1147.

Salter, M. *Hegel and Law*. United Kingdom: Taylor and Francis Ltd, 2002.

Shaw, C. K. "Hegel's Theory of Modern Bureaucracy." *American Political Science Review* 86, no. 2 (1992): 381–389.

Fehrenbach, T.R. *A History of Texas and the Texans*. Cambridge, MA: Da Capo Press, 1968.

Weber, M. *From Max Weber: Essays in Sociology*. London: Routledge, 2009.

Weber, M. *The Theory of Social and Economic Organization*. New York, NY: Simon and Schuster, 2009.

Williams, C. H. "The 'Gatekeeper' Function on the Governor's Staff." *Western Political Quarterly*, 33, (1980): 87–93.

CHAPTER 6

Texas's Republican Legislature and the Impact it has on the State

What drives decision making for the betterment of a society? What, in a plainer sense, is the goal of a legislature? As they have developed over time (and most recently in the US and its states), legislative bodies consist of representatives who are tasked with making decisions that have the best interests of the people—the greater good—in mind. Policy decisions should be made to serve the population that has tasked the government—and by extension, the legislature—with making decisions for their well-being, thus fulfilling government's part of the social contract. After all, the instincts and freedoms that individuals give up to the society are in exchange for quality decision making by leaders who have their best interests at heart.

Is this possible?

The collective action principle provides a simple view of decision making: those tasked with deciding what is best for the group are left to come up with the best possible way to move forward on a specific issue. Under this principle, the decision makers in a society would reach a conclusion based on what is best for the collective and not what is best for individual constituents. The collective action principle, a theory grounded in sociology, suggests that, when tasked, individuals will work to make decisions and direct actions in a way that serves the collective.

There's been much discussion through the years about the legitimacy and efficacy of this theory. While collectivity is a goal of many decision-making bodies, is it possible? While the decision made by a group is an attempt to serve the collective, how does an individual remove self-interest from the decision-making process? Furthermore, how likely is the collective to be served if there is nothing to be gained by the individual?

These are key points as we start to discuss the legislature. The legislature is designed to serve the collective action principle. As we examine the Texas legislature, this is a central question as to how it functions. James Coleman examined legislators' application of the collective action principle to rebuff the theory.

> First, suppose we put back this single decision into the context from which it was abstracted—taking for simplicity a legislature as the context, with a whole sequence of collective decisions on which to act. In such a situation, is it possible to express intensity of preference? The answer is that legislators do so by using the resources at their disposal. These resources consist of a number things, depending on their positions within the legislature. But the simplest case, and a relatively frequent one, is an exchange of resources: legislator X agrees to vote as Y wishes on one action in return for Y's agreement to vote as X wishes on another action. They do so because each sees a gain. Each loses his vote on an action where the outcome makes little difference to him but gains a vote on an action where the outcome matters more. Each has in that exchange expressed something about his intensity of preference. Each has given up a vote on an issue in which the utility difference between alternatives is less than the utility difference between alternatives on the vote he has gained.[1]

In an equation that has a series of outcomes that inherently creates winners and losers, how can legislators in Texas serve the best interests of the public if it means personal or political loss? Why are concessions made, and how do the structure and rules of the legislature make that process easier?

Understanding Legislator Behavior

What Is a Legislator's "Home Style"?

Legislator behavior is something that can cause constituents much consternation. What a legislator will respond to and focus on is a prime question. How should we communicate with them? What interest does the legislator serve? What influences a legislator the most? These are all questions regarding how legislators conduct themselves while in session and at the important moments of seeking reelection.

---

1   J. S. Coleman, Selection from "Foundations for a Theory of Collective Decisions," *American Journal of Sociology*, p. 620. Copyright © 1966 by University of Chicago Press.

To begin to form a quick profile of legislator behavior, the first thing to focus on is how a legislator defines or chooses his or her "home style" (Fenno 1978). Fenno classified two home styles that are dominant in legislators. The first is the service-oriented style. This style prompts a legislator to curry favor with voters by offering and providing them with services. Legislators in this case are much more likely to respond to correspondence regarding service requirements than policy inquiries; this style favors interaction about a service the government provides and how to adjust it rather than engagement in a policy discussion.

Fenno's second style is an issue-oriented style termed "articulating the issue." Under this style, a legislator would rather engage voters about the tenets of policies and decision making rather than actual government activity. There is a strict level of education involved here; traditionally, part of a legislator's profile has been as an educator. From the beginning of the Union, legislators have been conduits for information about government activity. It is one of the basic tenets of representative democracy. Fenno's second style feeds into this when a legislature is engaged in concept and theory of policy rather than calls for services.

The prominence of either style is dependent on the state and the political climate within it. Early research shows that service home styles are easier to maintain and have the most tangible payoff come election time.

> First, service allows legislators the opportunity to cultivate an image or reputation for helpfulness, sympathy, courtesy, and hard work. Second, legislators may sincerely feel that an important part of their duty or responsibility is to assist constituents when they have questions or difficulties, especially as government becomes larger and more complex. Finally, service may also be a method for defending local interests or pleasing local activists by solving a problem of special interest to those back home (Butler, Karpowitz, and Pope 2012, 476).

However, research shows that polarization, the product of staunch issue-oriented politics, has refuted that. The current political climate is moving away from service; as voters become more politically educated and entrenched, their ambition is to seek out representatives who share their views and who will engage them and push for them.

In Texas, the examination of service versus policy styles is intriguing. Unlike those of other states, Texas's legislators are predominantly grouped together on the political ideology spectrum. With Texas being a conservative-leaning state,[2] the theory of policy orientation comes into play less often. As there is little to no real debate regarding the overall ideology of the legislature, the debate over policy in Texas is how the issue or dominant view will be

---

2   Debate exists on just how Republican Texas is. The state ranks eighteenth among states reporting to be Republican, according to a 2014 poll, but young adults in Texas report as 41 percent conservative, and 32 percent of moderates report as Republicans. Texas has also not elected a Democrat to a statewide position since 1996.

served. That entrenchment pushes past the policy home style towards a service-oriented one in the state.

Trustee vs. Delegate

Just as what drives a legislator to act is a major subject of debate when it comes to congressional activity, how the legislator makes decisions is also a primary factor to consider. The historic debate surrounding legislative decision-making procedures has centered on two predominant points of view: trustee versus delegate. They focus on where the legislator receives his or her major influence.

On the surface, this seems like a simple debate. A delegate is a legislator who follows the direction of his or her constituency; a trustee seeks information to form an opinion and acts on that. Theoretically, both types are seeking to make the decision that is best for their constituency and that meets the greater good principle of democracy—selecting the option that provides what is the best for the population. However, the debate goes much deeper.

There are three factors to consider in the debate about the two hegemonic types. First is the aim of the decision maker in regard to focusing on the greater good versus the individual or small-group benefit. Second is the source of judgment for the legislator: is it internal or influenced by outside voices? The final factor is the decision maker's degree of responsiveness to outside influences such as interest groups, sanctions, or reelection. Andrew Rehfield categorizes the characteristics in his argument that the two designations are not enough.

> Collapsing these three aspects of political activity, "trustees" are generally described as (1) looking out for the good of the whole (the nation's interests), (2) based on their own judgment about that good (rather than the judgment of their constituents), and (3) less responsive to sanctioning (acting instead according to civic virtue), whereas "delegates" are generally described as (1) looking out for the good of a part (the interests of their electoral constituents), (2) defined by a third party (their constituents' rather than their own judgment), and (3) more responsive to sanctions (in particular, the hope of reelection) (Rehfield 2009).

While Rehfield argues against the dual designation, the archetypes are predominant when discussing the behavior of legislators.

In Texas, legislative influence is a significant topic of discussion. How legislators behave and how they respond to public pressure in decision making is a great debate in a state that, as is covered later in this chapter and subsequent chapters, is significantly influenced by outside parties. When viewing Texas legislators and the legislative process, identifying these types of styles is important. As is the case at most levels of government, public and legislative agendas are congruent when there is a high level of understanding on both sides. When the balance of that understanding shifts or becomes one-sided, legislators tend to act in a way that is not consistent with their constituents' wishes or interests. That is true for Texas as well.

As with many aspects of US democracy, Texas strives to define the roles of its government's branches. This concept falls in line with the federal conventional wisdom, but Texas doubles down where checks and balances and separation of powers are concerned. Much of the power in Texas government is diffused among various entities. Popular sovereignty is defined by the maxim that all the power of the government derives from the consent of the people. Texas invests a significant amount of authority in the state legislature. In fact, we see the aspects of legislative authority in many of the subjects touched on previously in this chapter—in particular, the power to make law. That role, however, can be pushed. Many legislators over the course of the state's history have pushed for reforms that strengthen the authority of government bodies despite the limitations laid out in the state's constitution.

Structure of the Texas Legislature

Texas is one of the states in the Union whose view of legislative activity diverges from that of the federal Congress. In fact, as do most states, Texas avoids the term "congress" when describing its legislative body, opting simply for the "state legislature" instead. The norm for legislative activity and structure is a two-chamber system with different powers invested in each chamber. From the structure of sessions to the activities within the chambers, Texas's legislative body strays and creates quirks that impact its legislative ability.

Bicameral Structure and Makeup of Elected Officials

Texas's structure starts with the setup of the two-house system. Upon its introduction into the United States, the state shifted to a bicameral system. The two-chamber system is designed to provide a dual layer of examination to law. Laws can be introduced in either chamber or concurrently. As will be outlined later in this chapter, law is best produced when it is based on a rigorous form of deliberation. Adding a layer to the passage of law introduces an additional element to this deliberation.

The debate about this structure centers on the effect of the dual-chamber setup on the passage of policy. Conventional wisdom suggests that adding the extra layer of deliberation will reduce the passage of frivolous laws and policies. Functioning as a self-check, this extra layer is designed to, in a basic sense, keep the legislature honest and working towards policies and directives from the constitution and the legislator's constituencies. However, the additional layer could cause the process to stall out or become stymied where producing quality legislation is concerned. While each chamber has veto power over the other, the fact that both can produce legislation could bog down the system. That will be an important factor when discussing the effects of the biennial sessions, which relegate the state legislature to meeting just once every two years. The concept that bicameralism can restrict legislative power, however, is appealing and aligns with Texas's view on restrictive government power.

As Texas's legislative body falls into the bicameral mode, each chamber has its own make-up. Per the state constitution, the number of members in the Texas House of Representatives is fixed at 150;[3] officials are elected by districts of 175,000 people. The Senate houses thirty-one members from districts of 850,000 people. These seats are filled on a two-year basis for the House and a four-year basis for the Senate, prompting mass elections in November of even-numbered years, when all 150 seats in the House and half the seats in the Senate are voted upon.

Member requirements restrict the persons who can run and serve in these positions. To serve in the House of Representatives, a person must be at least twenty-one years of age, a US citizen, a registered voter, and a resident of Texas for at least two years (one of which must be in the district he or she seeks to represent). In the Senate, a person must be twenty-six years old, a US citizen, a registered voter, and a resident of Texas for five years (two of those in his or her district). Formal requirements govern who can enter an office, but there are certainly informal qualifications that apply to Texas legislators.

Traditionally, the characteristics of legislators have followed the historic archetype: white males who are professionals, well educated, and middle-aged. Even though the state is culturally diverse, this described most Texas legislators until the mid-twentieth century. Over the past thirty years, however, that has changed. As Texas's population grows to be one of the most diverse in the nation, the demographic makeup of the legislature in the state has followed suit. According to data provided by the legislature, the percentage of seats occupied by Anglos has taken a sharp downturn over the past thirty years, dropping from 78.5 percent to 64 percent.[4]

Minorities and women have taken advantage, moving their numbers in a positive direction over that span of time. Women currently occupy 20.6 percent[5] of the seats in the legislature and had an all-time high of nearly 24 percent in 2009. While not a high number, it is growth that is welcome, as until 1970 there was only one female member in either chamber. The issue, however, is that these numbers have stagnated in the past twenty years. Women in Texas are more Republican than Democrat, and breaking through the gender barrier has been difficult in the past two decades. African Americans have also struggled to increase representation

---

3   All legislative numbers originate from the Texas legislature website, http://www.capitol.state.tx.us/.

4   Legislative Reference Library of Texas. "Membership Statistics for the 85th Legislature." http://www.lrl.state. tx.us/legeLeaders/members/memberStatistics.cfm.

5   All listed percentages come from the legislature website and the *Tribune* source cited in this chapter.

for the past thirty years. Making up 12 percent of the population, African Americans have occupied between 8 and 11 percent of the seats in the legislature.

While women and African Americans are searching for their next significant gains, Hispanics have made considerable strides. Currently, the Hispanic population makes up 38 percent of the state. They have seen their numbers grow, but there is criticism as to why they have struggled to turn the numbers more in their favor. While they are approaching Anglos (who make up 47 percent of the population, as the majority, they still only hold 23.2 percent of the seats in the legislature. Lack of citizenship is a considerable reason for the lag, but a lack of political knowledge and willing participation is at fault as well. Hispanics have traditionally shied away from the voting booth, and that has shown in their level of representation. Still, the 23.2 percent number shows a rise of nearly a full 10 percent in the last thirty years.

While minority status and diversity in the makeup of the legislature is growing, financial and personal support is moving at a slower pace. Legislators in Texas are a hybrid, not because of a lack of expertise or staff support but because of their salary and time commitments. By contrast, professional legislatures are bodies that provide a significant salary that allows their members to participate full-time. Legislators are provided with funds for staffing purposes and can be required to make the position their full-time position. The converse would be amateur legislatures. States with these types of legislatures often seek citizen legislators, since the pay and staff support are low, as is their requirement to be in session. Traditionally, states that employ amateur legislatures are small in population.

Texas is a hybrid, as mentioned before; legislators receive a low salary and meet only once every two years. However, the staff support and number of resources (such as the legislative resource committees and boards) are in good supply, as is the length of sessions (140 days). Salary is the major issue for legislators. In Texas, the yearly pay is $7,200 per year plus a $150 per diem[6]—set by the Texas Ethics Committee—for any legislative activity. This is a paltry sum when compared to legislators in California, who participate in nearly year-round sessions and earn between $97,197 and $100,113.[7] Staff support, however, is in high demand. While their salaries are low, representatives receive $13,250 per month while in session and $11,925 while out of session to staff offices in both Austin and their districts. Senators receive $38,000 per month to do the same. This is coupled with any donated time or contributions from fundraising.

While the financial reward is not enormous, turnover in the state's legislature is low. Turnover rates hover around 25 percent,[8] per legislative data. In 2015, turnover in the House was 16 percent (twenty-four new representatives) and 26 percent in the Senate (eight freshman senators). Turnover can be a result of several causes, including political reasons (when the incumbent

---

6   Texas Legislature Online, http://www.capitol.state.tx.us/.

7   California State Assembly, http://assembly.ca.gov/sites/assembly.ca.gov/files/Salaries/assembly_members_salaries_-_11jan2016.pdf.

8   Ballotpedia.org, "State Legislative Incumber Turnover in 2014." https://ballotpedia.org/State_legislative_incumbent_turnover_in_2014.

is voted out or steps down), death, or redistricting that causes a political shift. Representatives serve an average of twelve years, while senators serve an average of fourteen years.

Data shows that Texas is an incumbent-driven state. Once entrenched, incumbents have a high record of success at winning reelection and retaining their seats. If a member of the legislature dies, steps down, is impeached, or becomes incapacitated, then the governor must call for a special election. This mandatory meeting to replace that member for the remainder of the term must take place at least thirty-six days after the call and must be held on a natural election day. The exception can be a looming session.

Chamber Leadership

Power in the state legislature is as sought after within the chambers as it is during election time. With the majority party having the most significant influence, the elected leaders of the party enjoy much of the spoils. The one-party state that has evolved under Texas Republican leadership has steered the ship in the legislature since 1997 in the Senate and 2003 in the House of Representatives. That power is solidified within the parties, as the legislature is 63.5 percent Republican. That margin has turned the power in the legislature firmly red.

With their power unchecked, the leadership in each chamber can dominate the discussion, with control over agendas, committee makeup, councils and boards, and floor debate all at their disposal. These two positions are the speaker of the house and the lieutenant governor, who leads the Senate. The power invested in these positions comes from the rules of each chamber and creates positions and an environment based on legislative authority. That authority, however, does not take place in a vacuum.

While both positions hold significant power, they benefit from working together to accomplish outcomes. The pair joint chair several key committees. Chief amongst them is the Legislative Budget Board, which manages the drafting and monitoring of the state budget. The LBB is composed of ten members in addition to the chamber leaders: the chairs of the House Ways and Means Committee, the Appropriation Committee, and the Senate Finance Committee, two representatives appointed by the speaker, and three senators appointed by the lieutenant governor. The chamber leaders also co-chair the Legislative Audit Committee, which monitors and investigates spending and is composed of the leaders, the chairs of the House Ways and Means Committee and the Appropriations Committee, the Senate Finance Committee chair, and a senator appointed by the lieutenant governor. Finally, there is the Sunset Advisory Committee. An essential committee, the SAC oversees the review of agencies in the state. Reviewing efficiency and effectiveness as well as financial positioning, the committee evaluates, on a twelve-year cycle, whether the agency is needed. The membership, including the two leaders, includes five appointed members from the Senate and House as well as two members of the public appointed by the presiding officers.

Each chamber leader is exceedingly cognizant of the political landscape. As the presiding officers in a dual-authority legislature, they know well that legislation will not pass without the approval of the neighboring chamber as well as the governor. Policy approval is then contingent on dual acceptance. This has prompted people in these positions to seek out and advocate for policy they are sure will be signed off on by their opposite number and the governor; this prompts a significant amount of cross-chamber debate and discussion as well as interaction with the governor's office.

Moreover, leadership must have the support of their chambers. Neither position can overrun the debate or their fellow legislators. While the leaders have been selected for their positions, Texas's legislature is full of experienced and crafty politicians. Consistent aggressive activity or policy disputes would put either of them in a weak position amongst their members. Just as communication is essential across chambers and with the governor, speaking and connecting with chamber veterans is essential.

Lieutenant Governor

The lieutenant governor leads the Senate. Popularly elected, the lieutenant governor serves the will of the people, as the position comes up for public vote every four years. This ties the position's fate to political and policy success more than any business in the actual chamber. Beholden to the citizens of Texas, the Senate leader's actions are much more political than those of his federal counterpart in the US Senate, the Vice President. If the position is vacated during a term, the Senate will select the replacement to finish the term until the next general election is held.

Without a vote to cast, the position's tangible impact on policy debate comes through being active in guiding debate. Often the role requires an official to play the roles of deal maker and peace broker, advocating more for compromise and the greater good than pushing a policy agenda. The lieutenant governor can cast a vote when there is a substantive political point to be made or a tie to be broken.

The Texas Constitution defines the powers of the position as follows:

1 Appoint chairs, vice chairs, and members to all Senate standing, conference, and interim committees

2 Assign bills and resolutions to committees based on political and policy areas

3 Preside over and administer the rules of the chamber

4 Chair (or co-chair, with the speaker of the house) the Legislative Budget Board, Legislative Council, and Legislative Audit Committee

The lieutenant governor wields a great deal of influence. While the position does not have a consistent vote, the ability to administer rules and oversee floor and chamber activities gives the position a considerable amount of power. Also, the ability to route policy to specific committees to be discussed by specific legislators gives the lieutenant governor a substantial measure of control over the policy process.

While the position carries a significant amount of power, it is still subject to the whim of the people. Unlike the speaker, who is selected from within the chamber, the choice of leadership in the Senate is left to who wins the election every four years. Long-serving Lieutenant Governor Bill Hobby was noted for his ability to guide policy debate in the Senate during his eighteen-year run in the position. Recently, David Dewhurst put in a long shift, serving for twelve years before being defeated by Dan Patrick, a former radio talk show host who ran as a Tea Party candidate. Patrick's intention to revitalize the conservative faction of the Senate will be interesting as he attempts to fulfill the role the position has come to perform.

Speaker of the House

While the lieutenant governor is a popularly elected official, the speaker of the house is a different animal with a unique set of requirements. Evolving from a largely ceremonial position, the speaker has become a highly influential political figure who has immense influence on policy debate and activity. Increased policy influence has made the position a target of outside interests such as lobbying groups, and this has caused internal strife.

The constitutional power of the position has remained consistent over the years:

1   Define the jurisdiction of standing committees

2   Appoint committee leadership with chairs and co-chairs

3   Refer all bills and resolutions to committee based on policy area

4   Staff committees

5   Preside over session

6   Appoint members of conference, special, and interim committees

The role of speaker has become synonymous with power and ambition. To win a public election requires campaigning and connecting with constituents; to win a race for speaker, the representative has to convince fellow political figures and interested parties that he or she is are the right person to lead the chamber. Since every speaker so far has been a man, the position has followed the traditional lines of power in the legislature. To obtain the office, representatives seeking the position must be adept at currying favor, aligning allies, connecting with and gaining third-party support (namely from the business community), and winning over a majority, since the race is nonpartisan. While evolving legislation has attempted to make these races more transparent, much of what transpires (including the money that changes hands) is still conducted behind closed doors.

While his or her opposite number in the Senate is chosen by the voters, the speaker is selected internally, meaning a contest between representatives produces the officeholder. Elections for the speaker are held at the start of each session and are overseen by the secretary of state. The power these men have sought since 1940 has been used in a wide variety of matters.

Texas has traditionally been a one-party state, so elections for this position have usually been cases of political battle between partisan colleagues. An example of this came in 2007, when popular incumbent Speaker Tom Craddick (R-Midland) was opposed by Jim Pitts (R-Waxahachie) for the position. Pitts was the chair of the Appropriations Committee; Craddick was a popular speaker because of his role in pushing through a favorable redistricting plan, but he was hit with a negative reputation due to a push for bipartisanship. Pitts campaigned on a platform of intimidation instead of the across-the-aisle approach.

When Craddick won, he summarily punished the opposition, removing Pitts from his powerful committee. The 2007 session became contentious as motions to defy and remove Craddick came to a head three days before the session ended. After the members of the House pushed to vacate the seat, Craddick declared there was no such ability, drawing the ire of his parliamentarian, the person who oversees the rules of procedure. Craddick survived the session despite being branded a dictator. Craddick was later defeated due to those actions when moderate Republicans moved to replace him with Joe Strauss (R-San Antonio) and push for an amendment that would allow the removal of a Speaker midsession.

The battle in 2007 was an example of both how the position can be executed and the political vitriol that can occur. Speakers can use their power to treat (or mistreat) their fellow representatives. Much of their success comes from the power they place around themselves. With roots in traditionalistic and patronage (or cronyism) culture, the speaker is loyal to those who helped him get elected. Members of the group that pushes for election, campaigns for support, and votes for the speaker are rewarded with resources and positive committee appointments. If veteran enough, they are provided with chair positions.

Logjam: The Effects of a Biennial Session?

Legislation in the Texas legislature can be like something out of an avalanche scene. As discussed in the next section, Texas's legislative behavior when it comes to passing policy can be a bit of a procrastinator's dream. Evidence shows that over 70 percent of bills passed are voted upon in the final two weeks of the legislative session.

> No practice of state legislatures' workload management has been more thoroughly condemned than the end-of-session logjam of business. In the closing weeks of the sessions, state legislators are buried in an avalanche of work. In many states, it becomes impossible to find bills, let along secure action on them (Wahlke 1966: 147). Legislative chambers become scenes of madness and mayhem (Berkley and Fox 1978, 84). In the midst of such confusion, legislators vote wildly and blindly on count-less measures they don't know a thing about (Chamberlain 1969, 206; Lorch 1983, 164). The leadership is able to push bills or amendments through hastily without giving the members a chance to deliberate on them (Harrigan 1980, 110). The most important legislation receives the least careful consideration (Burns 1971, 56). The result is legislation of inferior quality (Luce 1974, 155). There seems to be widespread agree-ment among legislators, legislative scholars, and legislative reformers that the end-of-session logjam is endemic and pernicious. For some, the end-of-session logjam seems inevitable. For others, the logjam is a function of legislative workloads or procedures. For yet others, the logjam is a strategy of legislative leaders to enhance their own power. Many observers have identified presumed causes of logjam; some have suggested ways to reduce the size of logjams.[9]

Why does this happen? Theory explains that workload management, when it comes to policy discussion and debate, can be the culprit. As is detailed in the next section, Texas has a firm schedule for the passage of bills. As the state's legislature and informal activity delineate, policy that is introduced goes through a prescribed process. That process and its efficiency are left to the legislators. Also, there is the case of importance placed on bills and where they fall on the agenda. As is discussed later, agenda setting is a key component of the process of passing laws in the legislature.

The most commonly cited culprit, however, is the biennial session. Texas's legislature meets on a biannual basis, meaning that policy is proposed, discussed, and passed once every two years. With no rollover policy, a policy must go from introduction to conclusion within the 140-day period or be subject to a two-year wait unless a special session is convened.

The creation of the biennial session was designed to limit the state legislature's authority. To encourage a reduction in the number of bills discussed and passed, the framers of the Texas

9   Harvey J. Tucker, Selections from "Legislative Logjams: A Comparative State Analysis," *The Western Political Quarterly*, vol. 38, no. 3, pp. 432, 440. Copyright © 1985 by SAGE Publications. Reprinted with permission.

Constitution sought to limit the activity by limiting the amount of time the legislature is in session. With just 140 days to pass legislation, the prevailing thought is that logjams happen due to the lack of time in session.

> It has been suggested that biennial legislative sessions cause greater logjams than do annual legislative sessions (Walker 1948, 297; Harrigan 1980, 110; Harris and Hain 1983). The logic is that legislatures without the option of returning for a second meeting will squeeze as much business as possible into the end of the single meeting (Tucker 1987, 440).

Tucker goes on to remove the assumption, providing evidence that annual sessions are just as likely to have a logjam at the end of session as those that meet every two years. The ability of the governor to call a special session to finish work on important areas, and only those areas, can also relieve the burden. Special sessions are called to address a specific topic mandated by the governor and last for thirty days. During a special session, the legislature can reintroduce and discuss policy as well as introduce and pass new legislation.

The legislative burden has grown over time. In 1985, the legislature introduced 4,021 bills and passed 1024, a 25 percent[10] passage rate. In 2015, 6,276 bills were introduced and 1,322 were passed, a rate of passage of 21 percent.[11] While the numbers have grown and seem insurmountable, the majority of bills never make it out of the committee process or are submitted as non-action bills that do not require decisions and never make it to the floor in either house. Including the use of companion bills, the amount of legislation that is introduced in both the House and Senate, as well as the number of bills that are left for frantic approval, is lower than expected.

Policy-Making Process

Power is something Texas has been leery of when it comes to government institutions, and the legislature is no exception. From the state constitution to tradition to law, it has attempted to keep the legislature from growing beyond its design regarding power—see the structure of sessions to understand more. When it comes to the legislature's power, however, none is greater than its policy-making power. In 2011–2012, Texas had the most bills passed of any state (per Bill Tracker), coming in with 1,582[12] bills passed. The fact that the legislature only meets once every two years affects that, but Texas does produce legislation at a high rate,

10 Legislative Reference Library of Texas, http://www.lrl.state.tx.us/.
11 Legislative Reference Library of Texas, http://www.lrl.state.tx.us/.
12 Legislative Reference Library of Texas, http://www.lrl.state.tx.us/.

making the 140-day session action-packed. The state legislature has averaged 6,340 bills introduced, with a pass rate between 21 and 25 percent.

The passage rates are indicative of a process that is designed to limit power but has a politically active group seeking to maximize its time in office. As legislators are part-time, we see several activities that come up. Bills are introduced to seek passage as important issues face the state, but there is a segment of bills that are introduced with no intent of passage. As Tucker (1985, 1987) points out, bills are not always designed to reach the final stages. Political motives can push a legislator to introduce a bill they know will not make it through process. If a bill is blatantly unpopular in the chamber or the legislature but is a matter of district interest, a legislator will submit it, understanding that no action will be taken or that it will quickly die in the early stages of the process. Consider the fraction of policy that makes it out of the committee process; it is dominated by deliberation and double-checking the need for the law or mandate.

Each chamber has specific rules for the policy-making process, as does the legislature as a whole. One of the rules states that each piece of legislation will receive three readings. The first comes when it is introduced, the second on the floor of the originating chamber, and the third before the final vote. The process is conducted to ensure a deliberate and sometimes intentionally slow process. Every piece of legislation, from the hyperimportant budget to the final bill, must pass both chambers. Bills can be introduced concurrently—traveling through both chambers simultaneously, with sponsors in each—or go through the process in one chamber and, once passed, go through floor debate in the other, with the Senate carrying final approval.

Introduction of Bills

Bills must be introduced by sitting legislators. A bill must have a sponsor and a legislator who will carry the bill; the legislator takes ownership of the bill's progress and works to ensure its progression. Bills can also have cosponsors. While sponsors write and monitor the bill closely, cosponsors are attached to the bill for political or policy reasons. If a bill is assimilated or incorporated into another bill, the bill will gain a cosponsor. A cosponsor with seniority or political standing could be brought in to help ensure passage of a bill.

Once the bill is written, it is introduced into the legislature. Bills can be prefiled during a period before the session begins but must be filed no later than sixty days after the session begins. Only bills dealing with emergency funds, gubernatorial declarations, or a local government can be filed after the deadline. Once filed, each bill is assigned a designation for tracking purposes. Bills introduced in the House of Representatives receive a designation of H.B. followed by a number; for example, the first bill filed will be H.B. 1. Those filed in the Senate follow the same pattern; they are designated with an S.B. and a number.

The head of the chamber oversees the process and often reserves the first numbers for important bills, as those numbers determine their place on the agenda. The budget is reserved to be H.B. 1, for example. All bills dealing with revenue must originate in the House and must comply with the constitutional statute mandating that revenue-oriented bills originate in the chamber of proportional representation. The role of the chamber leadership is significant at this point, not only in the assigning and agenda processes but also in assigning the bill to committee. If the bill is seen as favorable, then it will be routed to a committee that offers the path of least political resistance. If not, it can be routed to a harsher committee that will look to tear the bill apart. After the introduction stage, the bill is given its first reading read by the chamber clerk.

A major point of contention surrounding the introduction stage is the source of the bill. Legislators are tasked with introducing the bill, but the assumption that all bills are penned by legislators is false. Interest groups and outside staffers are often responsible for penning legislation for legislators to introduce. Lobbies have created template forms that legislators can fill out; these speak to the special interest of the bill and advocate for specific aspects of legislation. The practice of lobby-written bills is a concern of modern democracy but is not outlawed by Texas.

Committee Discourse

A bill's landing spot after introduction can be a crucial step. Bills can be doomed to failure if sent to an unfavorable committee, as the purpose of this second stage is to examine and reshape bills to determine whether they are suitable and ready for floor debate. If a bill is looked upon favorably, it will receive positive treatment. The most influential person in this process is the committee chair, who oversees the proceedings and sets many of the rules within the group. Committee chairs are senior members or those who have a favorable relationship with the chamber leadership, as the speaker of the house and lieutenant governor are responsible for assigning all positions. A committee chair can bury a bill if he places it low on the committee agenda, which can cause a time crunch when it comes to finalizing committee business.

There are three major types of committees that operate in the chambers: standing, conference (which will be outlined later in this section), and special/interim. These committees encompass much of the work that is done in the legislature, as they perform their own type of legislative examination. These committees get a close-up look at the details of bills that come through the legislature and are tasked with shaping them ahead of potential floor debate.

Standing committees are integral to the process, as they are the standard groups that examine legislation. These committees are grouped by content area and tasked with examining bills. While they serve a significant function in the process, they are not stable. The chamber leadership can alter the focus, jurisdiction, leadership, and membership of these committees, so they can look very different from session to session.

The House has thirty-eight standing committees, and the Senate has fourteen. The most important of these deal with education, energy, economics, the budget, and state affairs. The political makeup is at the discretion of the leadership in each chamber. Due to the Republican stronghold in both chambers, the makeup of the committees usually follows the makeup of the chambers. Currently, twenty-five Republicans chair committees in the House, versus thirteen Democrats, many of whom chair unimportant committees or don't have good relationships with the speaker.

The types of bills received can also play into the committees' standing and importance. Policy-oriented standing committees examine legislation for policy validity. Power committees oversee the process of legislation and economics. The House Appropriations Committee is an example of a power committee, as it controls the budget and how money will be allocated.

Special and interim committees are temporary, meaning they must be created every session by need. Conference committees fall under this designation and provide a special service in the policy process. These committees are provided with a clear designation of their roles and the services or functions they are to perform. They can be based on policy or on time out of session, and they do not have membership restrictions. The chamber leadership convenes them.

See Table 6.1 below, which is a listing (provided by the legislature) of active committees in the 2015 session:

TABLE 6.1 Active Committees in the 2015 Session of the Texas Legislature

House of Representatives Committees			
Agriculture & Livestock	Energy Resources	Judiciary & Civil Jurisprudence	Special Purpose Districts
Appropriations	Environmental Regulation	Juvenile Justice & Family Issues	State & Federal Power & Responsibility, Select
Business & Industry	Federal Environmental Regulation, Select	Land & Resource Management	State Affairs
Calendars	General Investigating & Ethics	Licensing & Administrative Procedures	Transportation
Corrections	Government Transparency & Operation	Local & Consent Calendars	Transportation Planning, Select
County Affairs	Higher Education	Mental Health, Select	Urban Affairs
Criminal Jurisprudence	Homeland Security & Public Safety	Natural Resources	Ways & Means
Culture, Recreation & Tourism	House Administration	Pensions	
Defense & Veterans' Affairs	Human Services	Public Education	
Economic & Small Business Development	Insurance	Public Health	
Elections	International Trade & Intergovernmental Affairs	Redistricting	
Emerging Issues in Texas Law Enforcement, Select	Investments & Financial Services	Rules & Resolutions	

Continued

Senate committees	
Administration	Intergovernmental Relations
Agriculture, Water & Rural Affairs	Natural Resources & Economic Development
Business & Commerce	Nominations
Committee of the Whole Senate	Property Tax Reform & Relief, Select
Criminal Justice	State Affairs
Education	State Real Property Data Collect, Report & Assess, Select
Finance	Transportation
Government Facilities, Select	Transportation Planning, Select
Health & Human Services	Veteran Affairs & Military Installations
Higher Education	

Source: http://www.capitol.state.tx.us/Committees/CommitteesMbrs.aspx?Chamber=H.

These committees control the process at this stage. Bills that receive significant committee attention go through three stages: hearing, markup, and approval/disapproval. Hearings allow the public to engage in the process of committee activity. Texas's open meetings law mandates that all hearings be publicized five calendar days before a House hearing and one day before Senate hearing. This is to allow sufficient time for the public to obtain information and plan to attend the meeting. Those who would like to be heard can fill out a witness ID card and join the queue to be heard.

Hearings carry the same weight as judicial hearings. If subpoenaed to a hearing by the Texas legislature, a person cannot refuse to show. Hearings can be used simply as a public tool (e.g., to utilize a question-and-answer period regarding the issues connected to the bill in question) or as a tool of political activity. While hearings are mandated in the Senate, they are not mandatory in the House, although they are common for high-profile bills.

Due to the difference in size, the levels of effectiveness and roles of committees are different between the two chambers. Much of the debate over a bill in the Senate happens during floor debate, when members of the smaller chamber can participate in the discourse. In the House, much of the debate occurs in the committee markup sessions. While both chambers employ committees, the House uses the sessions as a more rigorous evaluation of the policy. The committee will go line by line, revising and amending where they see fit. The bill itself determines the length and depth of a markup session. The committee may frown upon a bill, and that could kill its chance to move out of this stage; the bill is a work in progress, and they will offer brief markups, but the bill is unlikely to pass after the final vote.

After the committee revises the bill, the final step in the process occurs with the vote on whether to pass the bill out of committee and send it for floor approval. If the committee votes to deny the bill passage, it falls out of the process. If the bill passes, the chair and staff write up the report describing the intent of the bill, revisions, costs, and certification of funds for it to become law. They then move on to the calendar stage.

Calendars

Once out of committee, bills are destined for what can at times (especially during the final days of session) be considered controlled chaos. As bills flood the floor, their organization and how they'll be addressed is vital to the process on the floor. Determining when the bills will be discussed as well as the rules used to discuss them is vital. Enter the Calendars Committees. Both chambers employ these committees to attempt to ensure orderly function in the floor debate in both chambers. As much of the work is done in the final two weeks (when 80 percent of bills are decided), these committees focus on making sure bills are routed to the right place on the agenda and that high-priority bills such as the budget do not fall prey to the time clock.

The House employs a rigid calendar system. Broken into two major areas (general calendars and local calendars), the House operates six separate calendars to attempt to ensure comprehensive attention. Major bills such as school finance and public works projects are placed on the emergency, major state, or general calendars, which receive priority.

In the House, what constitutes whether bills fall under these categories can be very political. Bills that would usually be considered general can be forced onto the emergency calendar if the right legislator applies pressure. Bills that are considered local or that have a narrow focus are routed to one of the three local calendars that operate. Priority is given to the general calendars, as they contain bills that impact the state at a wider level.

The Senate operates under a single calendar. The regular order (the primary route for bills to be brought to the Senate floor) mandates how a bill is brought for discussion. For a century, the lieutenant governor suspended the rule to allow for bills to flow in a steady fashion. Since, the Senate leaders have used a blocker bill—a bill with little consequence placed at the top of the agenda and not intended to be voted on. Instead, the bill will sit, and all bills must be brought to the floor by a two-thirds vote to suspend the rules. The issue increased the lieutenant governor's power by informally mandating his approval and two-thirds of members' support to initiate floor debate. The rule is disingenuous and a disruption to state policy discussion. Current Senate leader Dan Patrick worked to reform the rule (changing the two-thirds requirement to three-fifths), which will allow for more activity in the current legislature but will certainly lead to an advantage for conservatives due to their numbers in the Senate.

Floor Debate

Once the bill makes it to the floor, in many cases, the real political work begins. Floor debate can seem to be a riot scene out of a movie. Depending on the bill being discussed, the action and fervor on the floor can rise to very high levels.

Operationally, floor debate serves as an avenue to ensure equitable approval. At this stage, the discussion focuses much more on the ideas of compromise and consensus building. The former is the idea that each bill, when presented to a group of politicians, will incur some level of debate and pushback; therefore, a willingness to amend and change the bill is necessary.

Building a consensus is the political aspect of this. While, in theory, reaching a compromise is about component ideas being massaged together, consensus building is geared to gain political acceptance. This can certainly incorporate compromise but introduces the ideas and practices of politics as they are commonly perceived. Logrolling becomes a useful and common tactic. The practice of offering a political favor in return for support is a key bit of currency in the Texas legislature. Political pressure through this or seniority can be effective and influential.

Floor debate is governed by different sets of rules in the two chambers. The House operates in a more chaotic manner. With 150 legislators working to advance their political and individual causes, debate is done in an informal fashion. It is routine for many members to not be present during the actual discussion of a bill, but voters must show up to meet the quorum necessary to have the vote count. A legislator who is absent from votes for more than seventy-two consecutive hours can be held in contempt of the chamber.

The bill is read (its second reading) to begin the debate, and the sponsor or manager of the bill has twenty minutes to present the bill and again receives twenty minutes to close the discussion. Representatives can also request ten-minute slots to present an argument for or against the bill. The chamber operates under open rules, and anyone can amend the bill with majority approval from the sitting members. This is an attempt to restrict unlawful and disingenuous riders—amendments that have nothing to do with the bill but can be used to curry political favor or harm the original bill.

As the debate concludes, the speaker will call for the vote, prompting the straw poll. As representatives cast their votes, many will walk the aisle, holding up one or two fingers. One finger indicates a "yes" vote; two indicates the opposite. The practice is a way for party leadership to influence fellow members. A representative who has not been present for the proceedings could look to other members during this time as guides for casting their vote. If passed, the bill is tabled for a day and met with a final vote before being sent to the Senate.

While the House's activity can seem like a *Romper Room* episode, the Senate is the more composed of the two. Senators work from a stationary position at their desks to minimize the activity, creating a different environment from their House counterparts. For a bill to pass, it must receive the approval of the lieutenant governor and three-fifths of the votes in the chamber. There is no time limit on debate, and senators vote from their desks. This allows for the practice of the filibuster. Filibustering and chubbing (artificially extending debate to stall proceedings in either chamber) occur late in session. If passed by both chambers, the bill moves on to the governor. If there is debate regarding amendments made in the opposing chamber, the bill is moved to conference committee.

The Home of the Filibuster

A Texas tradition, the filibuster is a tried-and-true method for stalling and influencing policy debate. According to the Texas Legislative Reference Library, there are over one hundred filibusters on record, six of which have broken records for length. Debate exists about the ethics of a filibuster, as it is the practice of a senator hijacking the Senate floor and refusing to yield until a resolution is reached that satisfies them. When a filibuster is ongoing, the Senate's business must cease. Largely seen as a political tactic, the stall can only stop if voted on after violation of the rules or when it is voluntarily ended. In Texas, the rules[13] for a filibuster are as follows:

- Rule 3.02 prohibits eating or drinking in the Senate chamber.

- Rule 4.01 requires a member of the Senate to stand at his or her desk to address the Senate. The member speaking may not sit, lean, or use a desk or chair in any way. Bathroom breaks are not allowed.

- Rule 4.03, which governs the interruption of a member who is speaking, allows other senators to raise objections if a speaker does not confine his or her remarks to the issue under consideration or if his or her voice is inaudible.

Staying on topic is the most commonly contested rule, but there are instances when the physical nature of an extended filibuster can take its toll. After three fractures of these rules, the chamber can vote to end the filibuster.

While the practice is uncommon today, Texas sets the pace nationally for long filibusters. Texas Senators Bill Meier (R-Hurst) and Mike McKool (R-Dallas) hold the top two slots for filibusters nationwide. Meier stalled the Senate to stop a bill that would prevent public institutions from accessing records of the Industrial Accident Board. He held the floor for forty-three hours and employed a number of tactics, including sneaking Hershey bars and using an alternative method to address the bathroom issue: a catheter. He ultimately failed in his attempt, relinquishing the floor, and the bill passed. He is on record saying that he went home, ate, and slept for twenty hours. McKool held the previous record—a forty-two-hour, thirty-three-minute filibuster of S.B. 1, which provided support for the

---

13   Legislative Reference Library of Texas, "Seante Rules." http://www.lrl.state.tx.us/whatsNew/client/index.cfm/2011/5/23/Filibusters-and-Chubbing.

construction of state buildings and for state aid to public junior colleges. McKool relied on lemon slices to make it through the near-two-day affair.

The most recent practitioner of the filibuster, Wendy Davis (D-Fort Worth), took a very public stand in 2013. In her second filibuster (the first came in 2011 but lasted only one hour and eighteen minutes), Davis acted against an anti-abortion bill that was the source of public controversy. The bill gained national attention for the restrictions it attempted to place on legal abortion. Knowing she did not have the political advantage to lead a vote against the bill, Davis prepared to filibuster and commandeered the floor for nearly eleven hours. It was not without controversy, and a number of procedural objections were brought up to move her away from the issue. An hour and a half before session ended, the third objection was sustained, and her filibuster ended. The Democrats then worked a system of motions to kill the remaining time. Republicans took a vote, but a mass of protestors that had filled the state capitol with noise stalled a roll call (thus preventing a vote) until just after midnight, killing the bill. Governor Rick Perry called a special session weeks later, and the bill passed.

While her attempt failed and Davis did not run out the clock, her star was on the rise. She was a national sensation and received social media attention from all areas, including from President Barack Obama. She turned that filibuster into political capital, using it to lead her fundraising efforts when she ran for governor in 2015; she was ultimately unsuccessful. The move showed the impact of a filibuster as well as its political aspects. It also questions the role of the tactic and the true merits of its allowance in the Senate.

Conference Committee Effect

One of the most powerful committees, when needed, is the conference committee. This committee is introduced when amendments made in opposing chambers are not recognized by the originating chamber, necessitating further deliberation. In truth, most bills undergo changes that receive a courtesy approval when returned. Only 5 to 10 percent of bills reach this stage; most of these are contentious due to their high level of importance. Considering this, they receive a firmer stance and a willingness to compromise and finalize debate through the conference committee. Addressing these differences allows the conference committee to resolve the issues and rewrite an acceptable bill. Once done, the bill usually receives a rubber stamp in both chambers, as it has already gone through debate and a series of revisions.

Each chamber leader names five representatives to the conference committee. Chief among them are the bill sponsor's and the chair of the committee that approved the bill. Placing these two on the board is a cursory move by each chamber to allow for rigorous defense of the work. Three additional members from each chamber are selected—usually senior members with expertise in the area. Once the chamber has evaluated and conferred on the bill, the committee decides to pass and write up the bill to return to each chamber or to deny passage due to difference. Since 2009, over 80 percent of bills that enter conference committee make it out of the session. To accomplish that, three-fifths of each delegation must accept the rewritten bill. It is then sent to final passage or given the rubber stamp.

Influence of the Governor

Once a bill passes its final stage in the legislature, it is sent on to the governor for final approval. As will be discussed in the chapter on the executive branch, the governor's role in legislative matters is very informal. In fact, it may be the most informal of all the office's powers. The level of influence the governor has on policy is determined by his or her political relationship with the legislature. A popular long-standing governor will have a more influential role, while a newer or disliked governor may be kept at arm's length. Either way, the governor's role in the process is mainly as advisor and discussant until the final stage. Then the available options are the veto, line veto, and passage of the bill. Once signed, the bill is enacted into law. If it is vetoed, the legislature can overturn that veto with a two-thirds vote.

Potential Reform

Reform has hit state legislatures around the nation, but Texas remains steadfast in the process it has curated over time. Reforms in other states have changed membership in state legislative bodies from a part-time activity to a nearly full-time job. All but seven states, including Texas, have moved away from the biennial session, and several states have extended their sessions to mirror the six-month process that takes place at the federal level. The legislatures in New York and California meet year-round. States have seen sharp increases in the time legislators spend on the job (both while in and out of session), and the budget and scope of influence on policy has correlated with this rise in focus.

Texas, however, has remained on its path. A state that has historically fended off power and authority in its institutions, Texas's customs have remained clear. Change has been attempted, however.

Even though the state's constitution has stayed the same, views of the Texas legislature have changed over the years. Much of the current standards in the constitution relegate activity in the state legislature to little more than a part-time job that many in modern democracy are forced to do full-time. The pay scale, a paltry $7,200 per year, lends credence to this and, as has been discussed, opens the system to outside financial and special interests. It also restricts the type of individual willing to run for office to those who can afford the financial hit.

This has led to an unintentional reform towards what is characterized as legislative professionalism. As the ability of citizens to serve as legislators dwindles due to the cost of living and low salary, many of the elected representatives come from occupations with significant income that allow the legislator to leave his or her job for an extended period. The relationships between legislators and special interest groups that many researchers and onlookers are leery of is supported by this structure. A rise in salary would go against the individualistic and fiscally responsible nature of the state, but the current salary scale is so far behind other large states that a shift to higher pay is a topic that should be debated.

There have been calls for the legislature to fall in line with many of its fellow large states. Of the thirty largest states in the US, only Texas's state legislature meets once every two years. The adamant adherence to the biennial schedule has made the Texas session struggle to balance proper governance with a consistent eye on the clock and the calendar. With the legislature routinely examining and discussing over five thousand bills in modern sessions, the time crunch discussed previously has been taken into serious consideration. However, no change has been made.

The final potential change could happen over time and organically. While Texas's population is one of the most diverse in the nation, two-thirds of the membership of the state legislature is white, despite comprising only 45 percent of the state's population.

Summary

The Texas legislature is a body that the constitution and state have sought to limit over the course of the state's rise from a Mexican state to what it is today. The legislature has grown in power to become a leader in political decision making. Since the state's move to pure red status, the legislature has advanced its cause and the causes of those who provide the most support. Bills have pushed the conservative agenda, and the process has been used to make policy that the overwhelmingly conservative state agrees with. As that has taken place, the home styles and approaches to decision making by the legislators sitting in each chamber have followed suit. With a lawmaking process that emphasizes politics and the legislature's power, the branch is growing and moving steadily from the monitored branch of government it was through the nineteenth and early twentieth centuries to one that is a political signpost for Texans.

References

Bowling, C. J., and M. R. Ferguson. "Divided Government, Interest Representation, and Policy Differences: Competing Explanations of Gridlock in the Fifty States." *Journal of Politics* 63, no. 1 (2001): 182–206.

Butler, D. M., C. F. Karpowitz, and J. C. Pope. "A Field Experiment on Legislators' Home Styles: Service versus Policy." *Journal of Politics* 74, no. 2 (2012): 474–486.

Caldwell, L. K. "Strengthening State Legislatures." *American Political Science Review* 41, no. 2 (1947): 281–289.

Coleman, J. S. "Foundations for a Theory of Collective Decisions." *American Journal of Sociology* 71, no. 6 (1966): 615–627.

Cover, A. D., & Mayhew, D. R. "Congressional Dynamics and the Decline of Competitive Congressional Elections." In *Congress Reconsidered*, edited by Lawrence C. Dodd and Bruce I. Oppenheimer, 54–72. Washington, D.C.: Congressional Quarterly, 1977.

Fenno, R. F. *Home Style: House Members in Their Districts*. New York, NY: Pearson College Division, 1978.

Fernandez, Manny. "You Call That a Filibuster? Texas Still Claims Record." *New York Times*, July 3, 2013.

Fox, J., and K. W. Shotts. "Delegates or Trustees? A Theory of Political Accountability." *Journal of Politics* 71, no. 4 (2009): 1225–1237.

Koh, Elizabeth. "Texplainer: What Are the Rules of a Filibuster?" *Texas Tribune*, June 25, 2013.

Legislative Reference Library of Texas. "Membership Statistics for the 85th Legislature." http://www.lrl.state.tx.us/legeLeaders/members/memberStatistics.cfm.

McCullough, Julie, and Alexa Ura. "Meet Your 84th Texas Legislature: White. Male. Middle-Aged. Christian." *Texas Tribune*, January 14, 2015.

Newell, C. "Inflexibility, Traditionalism, and Partisanship: The Texas Response to New Federalism." *Publius* 12 (1983): 185–195.

Pew Research Center. "Party Affiliation among Adults in Texas by Political Ideology." Pew Research Center website. 2014. http://www.pewforum.org/religious-landscape-study/compare/party-affiliation/by/political-ideology/among/state/texas/.

Rehfeld, A. "Representation Rethought: On Trustees, Delegates, and Gyroscopes in the Study of Political Representation and Democracy." *American Political Science Review* 103 (2009): 214–230.

Rogers, J. R. "The Impact of Bicameralism on Legislative Production." *Legislative Studies Quarterly* 28, no. 4 (2003): 509–528.

Rosenthal, A. "State Legislative Development: Observations from Three Perspectives." *Legislative Studies Quarterly* 21, no. 2 (1996): 169–198.

Tucker, H. J. "Legislative Logjams: A Comparative State Analysis." *Western Political Quarterly* 38, no. 3 (1985): 432–446.

Tucker, H. J. "Legislative Workload Congestion in Texas." *Journal of Politics* 49, no. 2 (1987): 565–578.

Tucker, H. J. (1989). "Legislative Calendars and Workload Management in Texas." *Journal of Politics* 51, no. 3 (1989): 631–45.

CHAPTER 7

The Texas Judiciary
By Methias Plank

The Cultural Underpinnings of the Texas Judiciary

Perhaps nothing underscores the attitude of Texas like the slogan "Don't mess with Texas," from the famous 1985 Texas Department of Transportation (TXDOT) public service campaign aimed at stopping the littering epidemic. That one phrase has become a part of the Texas lexicon and typifies the approach the state takes towards crime and punishment. In a sense, that marketing campaign was an extension of the strong historical culture Texas has in being "tough on crime."

Texas has a culture of justice that dates to before the Civil War. It is a vast and complex labyrinth covering everything from routine traffic violations to the ultimate denial of liberty: capital punishment. The state has evolved into a system of overlapping institutions (including local, county, and state courts), which has in turn developed into a bureaucracy with budgets of over $3 billion for crime and corrections and over $175 million for court administration. Furthermore adding to the strain on the judicial system are an ever-growing state population, the conservative nature of the state's political culture, and the continuing debate over how Texas judges are selected. All of this has created a cauldron of controversy and become a rallying cry for widespread reform. Because of the enormity of both the scope and function of the Texas judiciary, it has long been thought that the state has a disconnect in terms of the coordination of philosophy, function, and execution of policy.

Perhaps nothing has highlighted the need for judicial reform like the events in the Tulia drug case of 1999. This case dealt with the multijurisdictional effort of a federally funded task force to target drug trafficking in the state. This multifaceted law enforcement operation yielded thirty-nine convictions, even though no physical evidence was ever produced in the case. Moreover, the case revealed other notable blunders in evidence collection, including failure to secure wiretaps and chain-of-custody issues. The Tulia drug case resulted in a three-year review of the whole operation and uncovered gross misconduct. The investigation led to the formal accusation of the chief detective on the case, Tom Coleman.

The aftermath of the Tulia case set into motion a call for a detailed investigation by Governor Rick Perry and for the Texas State Board of Pardons and Paroles to review all aspects of this multijurisdictional effort. In the end, thirty-five of the thirty-nine convicted were pardoned by Governor Perry (Blakeslee 2005).

In this chapter, we will examine the structure of the Texas court system, the legal framework by which cases are decided, the judicial selection process, and finally, issues related to judicial politics in the Lone Star State.

Structure of the Texas Courts

The Texas court system closely mirrors the federal system in that it follows the same tripartite format. Simply put, a tripartite system is a three-tiered system consisting of trial courts, appellate courts, and a supreme court. Texas has a much more detailed system (including two high courts), and that is the focus of this section. Perhaps one of the major differences between the Texas and federal systems of courts is the way judges are selected. The federal system uses a process in which the president nominates potential judges based on merit selection. Judicial nominees are confirmed by the Senate through a hearing process before they take the bench. Furthermore, federal judges have lifetime tenure, thus insulating them from the vagaries of political whim.

In Texas, judges are elected. Even if the judge was put on the bench by appointment (because death provided a vacancy), the judge would ultimately have to face an election to stay on the bench. This, therefore, creates a system in which not only the voters have a say in the ultimate longevity of a judge, but also a myriad of other political considerations—including conducting campaigns (raising, in some cases, gross amounts of money to keep a seat on the bench), special interest groups, and political parties—can affect the tenure of a judge. A judge will, therefore, face scrutiny from a variety of forces and will need to adapt to the winds of political change. This tension between the political process and the rule of law poses some interesting questions related to judicial ethics and judicial decision making that ultimately affect policy. One of these tensions is related to the area of objectivity—the extent to which the judge can make objective decisions based on the rule of law rather than on political considerations.

Types of Courts

Texas has a large and complex mosaic of courts that has developed over the course of the state's history. The initial level in the Texas court system is municipal courts. These courts have jurisdiction over a number of city ordinances, which are laws passed by city governments. Usually, these are minor violations of the law such as "class C" misdemeanors, for which up to a $500 fine may be imposed with no jail time. The vast majority of municipal court decisions relate to traffic and parking violations. Municipal court judges may also serve search warrants and have limited civil jurisdiction. Texas has 926 cities and towns with municipal courts and 1,559 municipal judges across the state.

The justice of the peace courts make up another category of court that has existed in Texas since 1837. Returning to the theme of state history and culture, justice of the peace courts date back to the beginning of statehood, when a need arose for a legal authority where none may have been readily available. Usually, these were men of good character and community standing who were selected because of their integrity and judgment. They filled a very important role and, in a sense, "wore many hats."

Most justices of the peace are not lawyers and, as such, do not have formal legal credentials. This issue has led to calls for reform. Today, a justice of the peace decides mostly traffic misdemeanors and small claims cases (less than $10,000) and may issue arrest warrants and death certificates in counties that do not have medical examiners. Both municipal courts and justice of the peace courts are referred to as *trial de novo* courts, which are courts that keep no record (written or recorded) of the proceedings and whose decisions can be appealed directly to appellate courts. These appeals would essentially be brand-new cases heard in the appellate court.

A court that was primarily created for large urban areas is the statutory probate court. The main function of this court is to deal with the disposition of property left by a deceased person who may not have had a will. Statutory probate courts also rule on guardianship-related matters for people unable to handle their own affairs. They also have authority over mental health commitments. The vast majority of these matters can be disposed of in a county court, and currently Texas has only eighteen statutory probate court judges.

Statutory county courts at law tend to decide quite a broad range of issues because they were created by statute, over time, as the need arose. The main purpose of these courts is to hear appeals from both the municipal and justice of the peace courts. They are kind of an intermediary between what would be heard at the municipal court level and what would be considered at the district court level. The size, history, and needs of a state with an ever-growing population necessitated the formation of many of these specialty courts, which were designed to take the pressure off an already-taxed court system.

Texas has 254 counties. In each of those counties, the county judge acts as the chief administrative officer and has some limited judicial responsibilities. The county judge presides over the county court. Generally speaking, county judges are more administrators than judges, but they do preside over some uncontested probate matters and more serious misdemeanors that may incur fines above $500 with the possibility of jail time. They also preside over civil matters—usually on a small scale, in the $200–$10,000 range. While the state constitution requires a county judge to be "well informed in the law of the state," it does not require that the judge hold a law degree. Salaries for these positions vary from county to county.

Finally, a county judge can make a name for himself or herself in the way administrative duties are handled in a crisis. For example, Ed Emmet increased his political stature with the way he managed Harris County during Hurricane Ike, which rolled through Houston and southeast Texas in 2008. His targeted and coordinated leadership with then-mayor Bill White was lauded as important in that significant event in Houston's history.

The largest trial courts in Texas are called district courts. In most states, they are referred to as superior courts, and these courts hear serious matters of both civil and criminal law. In essence, they are the workhorses of the Texas legal system. Texas has 456 district courts. The large urban centers usually have several district courts, whereas rural areas may have several counties served by a single district court.

The other unique feature of these district courts is that, in urban areas, they may be much more specialized, with a district court that hears only civil, criminal, or juvenile matters. In rural areas, the district court may need to handle several different kinds of cases. Finally, district courts are trial courts, meaning they are "courts of fact." They are the "triers of fact" and determine (usually by jury) guilty vs. not guilty, negligence, etc.

The courts of appeals are the next step up the ladder in the Texas judicial system. Unlike the trial courts, courts of appeals are appellate courts, which means they are "courts of law" rather than fact. In other words, the job of a court of appeals is to ensure that "the law" was correctly applied at the lower court level. Currently, Texas has fourteen courts of appeal, which are overseen by eighty judges. These courts hear both civil and criminal appeals.

The highest court in Texas—or, for that matter, in any state—is called the Supreme Court, also known as the "court of last resort." Every state has a supreme court, but what makes Texas unique is that it has two high courts: the Texas Supreme Court, which is the highest court in the state for civil appeals, and the Texas Court of Criminal Appeals, which automatically hears all capital murder case convictions. Both courts have ultimate and final appellate jurisdiction within the state. The requirements for serving on the Texas Supreme Court are minimal: the judge must be a citizen of the United States, a resident of Texas, at least thirty-five years old, and have been either a practicing lawyer or a judge for the past ten years. The term of a Texas Supreme Court justice is six years, and the amount of money it takes to run for this elected office has led to calls for reform. The cost to run for a spot on the Texas Supreme Court has shot up monumentally in the last twenty years and has spurred some discussion about the disparate effect special interest groups are playing in filling these spots.

The Legal Framework

All cases in the United States begin as one of two types: civil or criminal. Civil cases deal with disputes between two or more parties and deal with obligations, relationships, and responsibilities. In a civil cause of action, somebody is seeking "damages" for suffering, usually in the form of monetary compensation. For example, two parties were involved in an accident, and one brings a civil cause of action alleging he or she was harmed. Thus, in the case of *Plank v. Smith*, the plaintiff (Plank) is seeking damages (usually in the form of money) against the defendant (Smith). Since nobody is in danger of losing liberty in a civil case, the burden of proof is substantially lower than if it were a criminal case. In this kind of case, the burden of proof is called a "preponderance of evidence" standard. That is, the plaintiff must show that the defendant is more likely than not to be the cause of the harm suffered by the plaintiff. To put it another way, the plaintiff must simply tip the scale in his or her favor; that is, when both sides are evaluated, there is a higher likelihood that the plaintiff has suffered damages than not. This is sometimes referred to as the 51 percent standard.

Civil cases involve countless tens of millions of dollars every year and have bogged down the legal system with many cases that may appear "frivolous." As a result, efforts have been made to reform the system to reduce the amount of damages for "pain and suffering" that a plaintiff may be awarded in a civil case.

Another issue that is hotly debated is making sure those who were truly harmed actually receive the money they deserve in the form of damages. For example, an attorney may take a case on a contingency fee basis, which means that the attorney automatically receives (usually) 33–40% of any jury awards or settlement. This has led to much speculation that cases are often settled out of court to avoid lengthy jury trials while perhaps not allowing the plaintiff to receive maximum damages for injuries.

The matter becomes further complicated in class action lawsuits. A class action lawsuit is one in which many people who were similarly harmed (by a defective product, for example) combine into one "class" instead of having potentially hundreds or thousands of lawsuits. That is a more efficient way of handling these disputes. However, remember that the lawyers get their 33–40% right off the top of any award or settlement. That leaves the remainder for the rest of the class. That may seem great, but say the settlement leaves $2 million to be split among thousands in the class. Potentially, that could mean that the lawyers get hundreds of thousands of dollars but each member of the class (those who suffered damages) ends up receiving only a few hundred dollars.

Criminal cases are the other type of case in the United States. In a criminal case, the defendant has allegedly violated a criminal statute and has committed an act against society. For example, if someone named Jones robs a liquor store in Harris County, TX, that person has allegedly committed a crime in violation of a section of the Texas Penal Code. The case, therefore, would be *The State of Texas v. Jones*. Notice that in this example, Jones is the defendant because he has allegedly violated a criminal statute of Texas. The liquor store is not the plaintiff, because Jones's violation was against the people of Texas.

Furthermore, because Jones allegedly committed this violation of the penal code (constituting a crime), the burden of proof is now elevated. Jones can potentially lose his freedom if he has violated a criminal statute, which provides for the loss of his liberty in the form of a jail term. Therefore, now the burden of proof is now "beyond a reasonable doubt." This means not only that the jury must come back with a unanimous verdict (12–0, 6–0, etc.); it also means that the members of that jury must basically be convinced that there is no other conclusion that a reasonable person could reach other than that Jones did, in fact, rob the liquor store. In other words, it does not mean that there must be zero doubt; it means that 95 percent of the population, having a reasonable take on the evidence, could not come up with any other conclusion than that Jones did it. Remember, this standard is much stricter than the "preponderance of evidence" because someone will potentially lose his liberty if a jail sentence is imposed (or he could even lose his life, if the greatest penalty—the death penalty, which is reserved for capital cases—is imposed.

Crimes can be classified as felonies or misdemeanors. A felony is a very serious criminal offense that usually carries with it jail time (often in the state penitentiary) and heavy fines, and the most serious crimes (e.g., premeditated murder) can carry the death penalty. A misdemeanor is a less serious criminal charge that carries with it a short jail sentence (usually in county jail and no longer than one year) and/or a small fine.

A major consideration is whether to bring charges against an alleged defendant in the first place. For example, in Texas, grand juries consist of twelve persons who sit from two to twelve months with the sole purpose of determining whether the evidence available in each case is sufficient to hold someone over for trial. Grand juries do not determine guilt or innocence; they only decide whether there is enough evidence to warrant a trial. If the grand jury determines there is enough evidence, it will issue an indictment (a written statement that charges a person with a specific crime) indicating that a trial is warranted. Grand jury members can be selected from a general pool; however, they are usually picked by a commissioner system. Usually, a district judge will appoint several grand jury commissioners, and they will then select twelve-member panels to do the work of the grand jury.

One of the issues facing Texas and many states across the country is prison overcrowding. Some efforts have been made to ease this problem. One technique used to try to solve overcrowding (both on the court's docket and in prisons) is the plea bargain. This is a negotiated settlement, approved by the judge, between the prosecution and the defense. Plea bargain arrangements often drastically reduce the number of years a defendant must serve in jail in exchange for admitting guilt; they also save taxpayer resources. For example, someone who was charged with robbing a liquor store (nonviolent) may have been looking at ten years in the state prison. Instead, the defendant agrees to admit to the wrongdoing in exchange for a reduced sentence. The judge must agree to and sign off on the agreement, but this is designed to save society a lot of time and money trying people who would otherwise be convicted.

Judicial Selection

Perhaps one of the most controversial issues in Texas politics surrounds the way judges are selected across the state. Unlike federal courts, where the president appoints the judge and the Senate confirms or rejects that pick, Texas has a system largely centered on partisan elections. Some states use a system called the merit system, or Missouri system, in which judges are initially selected by the governor. The state executive official chooses the judges from a list provided by a screening committee. The judge then serves an initial set term and is then subject to a retention election in which the voters of the state vote on whether to retain that judge.

Several issues surround judicial selection in the Lone Star State, including partisanship, voter apathy, actual qualifications versus name recognition, campaign contributions, interest group activity, and minority representation. While several bills related to this issue were introduced in the Texas legislature between 1999 and 2009, none of them passed, and Texas is left with a partisan election selection process. Part of this has to do with the reluctance of Texas voters to give up the right to directly select judges. In this section, we will examine the framework behind the judicial selection process and why it has been criticized.

While most of the judges in Texas are selected through partisan elections, a number of judges initially get on the bench through the appointment process. For example, the governor fills vacancies on district and appellate courts when they occur before the next election. The governor also appoints judges to newly formed courts in the state. Therefore, a significant number of judges get their initial seats on courts through the appointment process. In 2011, for example, 52 percent of all appellate judges and 37 percent of all trial court judges started via the appointment process.

The partisan nature of Texas judicial elections went into full swing during the late 1970s. Prior to that, partisan elections were not a significant factor. However, with the election of William Clements as governor in 1978, the Republican Party began a period of domination in Texas that transferred to judicial races. Since the governor has the power to fill judicial vacancies, Governor Clements began to appoint Republicans to all these spots, which, for a hundred years after Reconstruction, had largely been held by Democrats. In fact, beginning in the 1980s, many judges who had previously run as Democrats switched their party affiliations to Republican.

As a result of Texas's being a "red" state, there is a marked advantage to having an "R" next to a name at election time. Because of this partisan advantage, Republicans consistently win the majority of judicial elections across the state. Democrats have had some success, particularly in the large urban centers, where Democratic voters have the numbers to sway the outcome (Tolson 2008).

The notable advantage that incumbent Republican judges enjoy does raise the question of how knowledgeable voters actually are when voting in judicial races. For example, many voters are known to vote "straight party ticket," and, because of the potentially dozens and dozens of judicial races being decided during an election cycle, the question arises about how aware voters are of the actual experience and qualifications of those on the ballot. In fact, because many voters are unaware of the responsibilities of many of the courts in Texas, they are very likely to either vote along partisan lines or use name familiarity to select their candidate (Mora and Ruger 2013). Therefore, because of the number of judicial contests and the relative obscurity of the issues facing most Texas courts, voters will tend to rely on party identification as their cue for selecting judicial candidates.

The process of becoming a Texas judge is a costly one. A judge must win not only a primary election but also the general election in a process that takes up most of the year. Moreover, because most voters consider name familiarity and party identification to be the most significant factors affecting their vote, it makes sense that a great deal of money and resources go into creating campaign ads that put an emphasis on name recognition.

It is the norm for Republicans to outspend their Democratic opponents by several times. Not surprisingly, therefore, Republicans are often successful and dominate Texas judicial politics. However, the amount of money raised, as well as where the money comes from, plays a big part in Texas judicial politics. For example, running for the Texas Supreme Court can cost many millions of dollars. Much of this money comes from special interest groups who have cases before the Supreme Court.

To what extent does money pose a conflict of interest for those who need to raise it in order to secure a seat on the Texas bench? For example, in 2008, incumbents running for reelection to the Texas Supreme Court received more than half of their contributions from big corporations and law firms who had direct business before the court. A study conducted by Texans for Public Justice revealed that between 60 and 75 percent of the money received by incumbents on the Texas Supreme Court came from groups that had direct business before the court (Texans for Public Justice 2008). The issue of judicial impartiality comes up because the selection of the cases that are heard before the Texas Supreme Court often appears to be directly traceable to interests who gave the largest amounts in campaign contributions.

Still another concern related to the partisan election system in Texas is minority representation and diversity. For example, one major worry is that countywide partisan elections make it difficult for minorities to get elected. Furthermore, while women make up slightly more than 50 percent of the population, they fall well below that number in Texas judgeships. Males make up 72 percent of the judges in Texas (Champagne 2012).

Another problem area lies with the lack of minority judges. This lack of racial diversity is a problem across the nation, but in Texas, nearly 92 percent of the judges are white. This has caused many civil rights groups to argue that large urban county districts, by definition, prevent minority candidates from getting elected because white voters effectively dilute the minority vote. Some have suggested creating smaller judicial voting districts that have a higher population of minority voters in order for any significant progress to be made. Yet another issue is that most minority candidates for judicial office run as members of the Democratic Party, which further hurts their chances because of the partisan advantage Republicans hold in the state. Finally, there is an overall shortage of minorities who hold the requisite credentials to run for these positions.

The controversy surrounding minority representation continued to brew in Texas for much of the 1980s, and minority and civil rights leaders were determined to find ways to remedy these disparities. In 1989, the case of *League of United Latin American Citizens v. Mattox* (1991) was filed, challenging the process by which judges were selected in ten of the largest countywide districts in the state.[1] Minority voters contended that these large countywide districts violated the Voting Rights Act of 1965.

The lower court judge ruled in favor of the plaintiffs and ordered that the elections be held on a nonpartisan basis and the actual districts be made smaller. The case ultimately made its way to the US Supreme Court, where the justices ruled that provisions of the Voting Rights Act did apply. The court remanded the case back to the Fifth Circuit Court of Appeals (composed of Texas, Louisiana, and Mississippi); the issues were whether the countywide system did, in fact, dilute the minority vote and whether there was a state interest in keeping the status quo. The case was finally decided in 1993 by an *en banc* Fifth Circuit ruling that said it was the party affiliation of the minority candidates and not the candidates' actual race that was the cause of their failure to win these contests. Furthermore, the ruling left intact the countywide system by rejecting the need to reduce the size of these districts.

Since that ruling, minority leaders, candidates, and groups have continued to fight for reforms in the system. Because the federal court issued a definitive ruling, the apparent option would be to change the system through reforms in the legislature. These efforts have included attempts to reduce the size of countywide elections but have failed to gain support. One notable exception was offered by Lieutenant Governor Bob Bullock, who created a task force to develop an acceptable selection alternative.

In 1995, the task force offered a constitutional amendment that passed in the Texas Senate but failed in the House. Under the plan, the governor would have the power to appoint all appellate judges. District judges, on the other hand, would be selected from county commissioner precincts in nonpartisan elections. After serving on the bench for a period of time, the judges would then be subject to a retention election, which would be a countywide election

---

1   The trial court's opinion was unpublished.

in which a simple "yes" or "no" vote would determine whether or not that judge kept his or her judicial seat.

These reform proposals seemed to have little apparent downside. The governor would have the opportunity to appoint appellate judges, and those judges would have job security and would not have to worry about raising the often-large sums of money necessary to protect their seats. This, in turn, pleased business interests across the state, because they understood that as long as Republican governors kept winning office, they would have conservative judges looking out for their interests. On the other hand, the idea of nonpartisan elections would help to mitigate the "straight party ticket" voting and would reduce voters' reliance on simply voting based on party.

Ironically, a split among the minority groups actually contributed to making the plan fall through. While African American groups were largely in favor of the plan, Latino groups opposed it. Their belief was that the size of the districts needed to be smaller in order to get Latino judges elected. In addition, the political parties themselves were not in favor of the compromise. While the plan would preserve the judges' interests, the political parties actually would be weakened by nonpartisan elections. The "Bullock proposal" ended up passing in the Texas Senate but never gained the support in the House and ultimately died. Unfortunately, the Bullock plan was probably the best chance at reforming this area of the judicial selection process, and nothing has come along since to gain significant support (Champagne and Harpham 1998).

Judges across the United States are selected by a variety of means according to the laws of each state. Another way in which judges are selected in Texas is by the governor making the initial appointment, with approval by the Senate. This takes place whenever a new court is authorized by the Texas Legislature or when a death or resignation occurs during the current term before the next election. This process is similar to the way federal judges are selected, with the president making an appointment and the Senate voting to confirm or reject. Interestingly, this system does not garner widespread favor in Texas because of its historical culture that mistrusts powerful governors.

Still another alternative for judicial selection would come in the form of nonpartisan elections. In this system, political parties and their powerful labels would be diminished. Candidates for judicial office would no longer be able to rely on party identification, and it would become that much more difficult to get their messages across to the voters of the state. Moreover, it would actually make judicial campaigns more dependent on the contributions of donors, causing the amount of money involved to skyrocket.

Perhaps the most popular proposal offered by reformers of the judicial selection process is called the merit selection method. In merit selection, a blue-ribbon committee made up of lawyers and citizens is responsible for coming up with a small list of qualified names to give to the governor to fill a judicial vacancy. The governor would select a candidate from the list and, after that judge serves for a period of time, he or she would face a "retention election." In this process, the judge's name would be on the ballot as the incumbent, but there would be no opponent. The voters would simply vote "yes" or "no" regarding the job the judge has done. One outcome of this system is that incumbents enjoy overwhelming retention rates and seldom lose one of these elections. In fact, one study shows that only 1.6 percent of incumbent judges lose in these retention elections (Carbon and Berkson 1980).

Another reform advanced in recent years is called "appoint-elect-retain." In this hybrid style, the governor would appoint a judge, and then the Senate would have to confirm the judge by a two-thirds vote. When the judge is up for reelection the first time, he or she would run in a contested, nonpartisan election. Then, in subsequent elections, the judge would be subject to retention elections as described above. This reform plan has features of many of the systems covered above.

Finally, the Judicial Campaign Fairness Act is a reform that has had a significant impact on the role of money in judicial races in Texas. In fact, Texas is the only state to have such a bold initiative. The most significant feature of the law is to limit campaign contributions in judicial elections. For example, a candidate in a statewide judicial election can receive a maximum of $5,000 from a person in any election. Furthermore, law firms are limited to maximum donations in statewide elections of not more than $30,000 per candidate. Although these amounts still seem rather high, the law has managed to significantly curtail the overall amount of contributions. Finally, a recent revision of the law now requires that any judge who is receiving donations from litigants in a lawsuit or from lawyers to a party in a lawsuit must recuse himself or herself from participating in that matter. Money continues to be a hot-button topic for those who want to reform the system, and many see it as having a corrupting influence on Texas judicial selection. On the other hand, money will continue to be a necessary evil to effectively run in statewide judicial elections (Becker and Reddick 2003).

Issues Related to Texas Judicial Politics

One of the key issues surrounding judicial politics in Texas is tort reform. Essentially, tort reform is a movement to limit the amount of damages a plaintiff may receive in a civil case. Tort cases are civil cases in which the actions of one party bring harm to another party. Usually, damages are sought by the plaintiff for things like pain and suffering. The Texas Supreme Court sets the tone for civil cases, including tort cases, across the state.

In the early to mid-1980s, plaintiffs often did quite well in matters dealing with tort law. Plaintiffs were quite successful in suing big companies, medical professionals, and insurance companies, for example. A shift, however, took place in 1988 as more and more Republican judges took the bench. These Republican judges tended to have sympathy for big-money interests across the state and were far less willing to hand out large awards to plaintiffs in these matters. For example, there has been somewhat of a shift in the Lone Star State with regard to medical malpractice, one variety of tort claims.

Essentially, then, decisions shifted from the early to mid-1980s when more "plaintiff" judges, carryovers from a strongly Democratic bench, tended to favor those seeking damages in civil cases. Since the late 1980s, and especially since the 1990s, judges now tend to favor the defendants in these matters—defendants who usually represent big business, the medical community, and insurance companies. Simply put, the bench has most recently favored big business. The Texas Supreme Court, for example, is made up completely of Republican justices who have ruled in favor of big-business interests (Anderson 2007).

Crime and Punishment in Texas

Looking historically at crime in Texas, we see a cultural bias toward being "tough on crime." Prisons and the system of corrections were used largely as a place to "house" undesirable elements of society, dating back to when Texas opened the state penitentiary in Huntsville in 1849. Years later, after the Civil War, prisons in Texas were largely used to control the newly freed African Americans. As a result, African Americans have always been overly represented in the state prison system as compared to their overall population within society. A few issues have been impacted by this cultural bias toward being "tough on crime," including the death penalty, juvenile justice, and the overall subject of rehabilitation of criminals in the state (Jillson 2012).

The Death Penalty

The death penalty has long been thought to be a deterrent to crime in the United States, and it has been used in states like Texas to support the campaign for being tough on crime. In 1972, the United States Supreme Court, in *Furman v. Georgia* and *Branch v. Texas*, ruled that the death penalty has been applied disproportionately to minority groups, and a moratorium was adopted that was to remain in place until the fifty states could come up with plans to put safeguards in place. In 1976, the Court ruled in *Gregg v. Georgia* that as long as certain guidelines were in place, states could resume the use of the death penalty.

While Texas did not resume using the death penalty again until 1982, it used the penalty at a much higher rate than did the rest of the states. In fact, while Texas had always used the death penalty more frequently than other states, by the 1990s Texas was using it at a much greater rate than it ever had historically and a great deal more than any other state. Moreover, African Americans represented 36 percent of those put to death in Texas between 1982 and 2010, or about three times their percentage of the population.

The vast majority (82 percent) of death penalty sentences are carried out in southern states. This is consistent with the South's dominant traditionalistic culture. Moreover, there seems to be a willingness on the part of southern juries (at even a greater rate than judges) to use the death penalty as an option for serious crime. As of October 1, 2011, Texas had 317 death row inmates. Texas has the third-largest population on death row, behind only California and Florida. Moreover, the large percentage of those placed on death row come from the state's large urban centers such as Houston and Dallas.

Two major factors contribute to the disproportionate number of death row inmates in Texas. First, the statutes pertaining to the death penalty the Texas Penal Code give juries the latitude to issue death sentences when the accused has been found guilty of a capital crime. Essentially, the jury must answer "yes" to two questions: 1) Did the defendant commit the act intentionally, and 2) Does the defendant pose a threat to society in the future? With these diminished standards and the overall traditionalistic culture of the state, juries are more than willing to impose a death sentence.

The second reason for Texas's higher rate of capital punishment is that the Texas Court of Criminal Appeals rarely reverses a death penalty sentence. Moreover, the governor rarely uses his or her pardon and clemency powers to reverse these sentences. Finally, again tied into Texas political culture, voters in the state offer broad popular support for the death penalty. In fact, in a 2012 Gallup Poll study, nearly 73 percent of Texans supported the death penalty, compared with about 61 percent surveyed nationally. Thus, the two things that remain constant are that Texas continues to have a very high rate of death penalty sentences and that minorities, particularly African Americans, are sentenced to death at a disproportionate number in Texas as compared to the national average.

Juvenile Crime

With regard to juvenile crime in Texas, some interesting dynamics are at play. For example, Texas is a fairly young state (compared to much of the rest of the United States), with just over 27 percent of its population under the age of eighteen. In Texas, the "age of majority" is seventeen, and the concept of juvenile justice includes not only criminal and civil acts committed by those under this age—juveniles are also wards of the state.

Because criminal law is largely dictated and shaped by the states themselves and not the federal government, the juvenile justice systems of the fifty states vary based on the level of responsibility the state assigns itself with regard to its legal duties. In Texas, the state takes on three general roles related to the administration of justice and minors. The first is *in loco parentis*, which basically describes the responsibility of the state to act in the best interests of the minor even if there is no formal, legal relationship. Second is *parens patriae*, which gives the state the power to protect those who are not able to protect themselves. Finally, under the police powers doctrine outlined in the federal constitution, the state takes on the power of protecting the health, safety, and welfare of its citizens, including minors, for whom the state acts as the caretaker of their legal interests.

These very broad general areas have created a complex system of juvenile justice in Texas. This detailed system of juvenile justice creates a labyrinth of state and local authorities who unite to consider what is in the juvenile's best interest. Judges must determine this as well as at what point the juvenile must be considered an adult under the law. In addition, the state has a complex system of caseworkers, mental health professionals, and other experts working together to help the court determine what is in the best interest of the juvenile.

In Texas, juvenile justice falls under the jurisdiction of family law, which is covered under Title III of the Texas Family Code, Chapters 51 through 61. A myriad of issues is considered under this section, which gives great discretion as to how the juvenile offender is to be treated under the law. Much of how any case will be decided by the court will hinge on the prior record of the juvenile, the mental state of the offender, the intent of the juvenile as determined by the court, and the severity and number of crimes committed by the juvenile.

One of the reforms called for is changing the way minors are designated as adults. This whole process tends to be quite random, and part of the problem lies in its arbitrary and inconsistent nature. For example, if a minor is tried as an adult, he or she cannot be given life in prison or the death penalty if under the age of eighteen. One of the biggest problems is the fact that while many of these offenders are not the worst criminals, the stigma of being tried as an adult can follow them the rest of their lives.

Because of the complexity of the Texas court system in general, the way juvenile justice is meted out varies from county to county. Moreover, while the court system is responsible for administering juvenile justice, a large, complex bureaucracy of state agencies processes and maintains the juvenile population. As a result, at least 168 local probation departments must work with attorneys, case workers, and other juvenile justice professionals to perform the full list of tasks, including investigation, intake, prosecution, probation, and other services.

Until 2011, juvenile justice was largely carried out by two state agencies: the Texas Youth Commission and the Texas Juvenile Probation Commission. Because of widespread controversy regarding these agencies, the Texas legislature abolished them in 2011 and combined them into one agency, the Texas Juvenile Justice Department, which now fulfills the duties of those former agencies.

The future of juvenile justice policy in Texas is uncertain. Since 2008, rates of crimes committed by juveniles have declined. This overall decline suggests some hope for the Texas Juvenile Justice Department as it takes on its most daunting task: overhauling the entire system.

Rehabilitation

In Texas, as is the case in other states, the criminal justice system's purposes are to deter future criminal activity, punish convicted criminals, and rehabilitate those who commit crimes. Unfortunately, there appears to be little solid evidence that much rehabilitation takes place in Texas's system of corrections. While we do see some evidence that crime in the Lone Star State is either in decline or stagnant, incarceration rates in Texas are still among the highest in the nation. Although the trend toward decreased crime is positive, Texas built ninety-four prisons between 1980 and 2004; it has increased spending for those facilities by 1,600 percent over the same period and has had a 566 percent increase in its prison population (Perkinson 2011).

Thus, while the level of crime and incarceration is leveling out or declining, the rate of spending on corrections resources continues to grow. One of the state's paramount challenges is to decrease the rate of recidivism—the rate at which offenders return to prison after serving their sentences. Recidivism rates have stabilized in recent years. According to the Texas Department of Criminal Justice, recidivism rates remained the same or dropped slightly between 2009 and 2011 in all areas for adults, except for those convicted of substance abuse and the therapeutic community.[2]

Two areas of alarm stand out. First, many repeat offenders find their way back into the system for crimes that are different from those they first committed. Also, over half of repeat offenders are imprisoned for violating a technical, minor condition of their parole. In other words, Texas has to do a better job of focusing on areas of rehabilitation, whether through increased funding for rehabilitation programs or through the use of faith-based organizations.

Summary

To think about the Texas judicial system, one must take into account the traditionalistic political culture of the state and its people. Furthermore, to understand the system of justice in the Lone Star State, one must examine the historic conditions of the state. Indeed, the size of the state and the various demands that have historically been placed on the justice system have paved the way for its complex judicial landscape.

While Texas has the same kinds of cases and controversies found in every other state, cultural, political, and regional differences make for a very interesting structure for the administration of justice. The process by which Texas chooses its judges allows a system of interest groups and big-money interests to permeate the politics of the state. Moreover, the "red" nature of the Lone Star State tends to support big business interests. Finally, the state's widespread growth and the migration, both from within and from outside the US, of people looking for job opportunities, lower taxes, and an overall high quality of living have further solidified conservative, "red state" values.

The future of Texas's judicial politics will largely be a function of the continued cultural shifts in a landscape which heretofore has been very traditionalistic in its approach. Because of the urban-centered nature of Texas state politics, only time will tell what, if any shifts, will take place towards a more progressive agenda.

---

2   Legislative Budget Board of Texas, http://www.lbb.state.tx.us/Documents/Publications/Policy_Report/1450_CJ_Statewide_Recidivism.pdf.

References

Anderson, D. A. "Judicial Tort Reform in Texas. Review of Litigation." *Review of Litigation* 26, no. 1 (Winter 2007).

Becker, D. and M. Reddick. *Judicial Selection Reform: Examples from Six States*. Chicago, IL: American Judicature Society, 2003.

Blakeslee, N. *Tulia: Race, Cocaine, and Corruption in a Small Texas Town*. New York: Public Affairs, 2005.

Carbon, S. and L. Berkson. *Judicial Retention Elections in the United States*. Chicago, IL: American Judicature Society, 1980.

Champagne, A. *Texas Politics: A Reader*. 2nd ed. Edited by A. Champagne and E. Harpham. New York, NY: W.W. Norton, 1998.

Champagne, A. *Texas Politics: A Reader*. 3rd ed. Edited by A. Champagne and E. Harpham. New York, NY: W.W. Norton, 2012.

Gallup Inc. (2012). "Death Penalty." Accessed December 1, 2015. http://www.gallup.com/poll/1606/death-penalty.aspx.

Houston Lawyers' Association v. Attorney General of Texas, 501 U.S. 419 (1991).

Jillson, C. C. *Lone Star Tarnished: A Critical Look at Texas Politics and Public Policy*. New York, NY: Routledge, 2012.

League of United Latin American Citizens Council v. Clements, 999 F.2d 831 (1993).

Miller v. Alabama, 567 U.S. (2012).

Mora, S., and W. Ruger. *The State of Texas: Government, Politics, & Policy*. Columbus, OH: McGraw Hill Education, 2013.

Perkinson, R. *Texas Tough: The Rise of America's Prison Empire*. New York, NY: Metropolitan Books, 2011.

Texas Family Code, Section 51.041(a).

State of Texas. (2014). "New Commitment profile." http://www.tjjd.texas.gov/about.aspx.

State of Texas. (2015). "Statewide criminal and juvenile justice recidivism and revocation rates." http://www.lbb.state.tx.us/Documents/Publications/Policy_Report/1450_CJ_Statewide_Recidivism.pdf.

State of Texas Government Code § 411.081.

State of Texas Government Code § 58.003.

State of Texas Government Code § 58.203.

State of Texas Judicial Branch. (2010). Profile of appellate and trial court judges. http://www.txcourts.gov/about-texas-courts.aspx.

State of Texas Judicial Branch. (2014). Profile of appellate and trial court judges. http://www.txcourts.gov/media/683430/3-Judge-Profile-9_1_14.pdf.

State of Texas Penal Code, Section 8.07.

Texas Office of Court Administration. (2012). Annual Statistical Report for the Texas Judiciary Fiscal Year 2012. http://www.txcourts.gov/oca/.

Texans for Public Justice. (2008). "Courtroom Contributions Stain Supreme Court Campaigns." http://info.tpj.org/reports/courtroomcontributions/intro.html.

Tolson, M. "Democratic Sweep Revives Debate on Election of Judges." *Houston Chronicle*, November 9, 2008. http://www.chron.com/news/houston-texas/article/Democratic-sweep-revives-debate-on-election-of-1780514.php.

US Census Bureau. (2015). "United States Quick Facts." http://www.census.gov/quickfacts/table/PST045215/00.

CHAPTER 8

Views on Public and Social Policy in a Conservative Texas

Where does the willingness to make decisions that benefit the public interest come from? In the first chapter, we briefly discussed a democracy model that is based on rational choice. The idea is that rationality is a potential indicator of political activity and policy decision making. Is this a given? As we have seen in politics, a policy is not always meant to serve the greater good. Policy can be considered singular in focus when it crosses the line into pork-barreling or has a focus other than the whole.

The idea is that rational thought guides decision making and can be traced back to the rationality principle. Karl Popper (1949) presents the basic theory that "agents always act in an appropriate manner to the situation in which they find themselves." Popper's theory is that, when faced with a problem or situation, the inherent human decision is to make the choice that is logically based on the factors within the circumstance. The assumptions, then, are that humans always act appropriately or rationally and that is in an individual's best interest to do so. Interestingly, Popper himself debated (and even refuted) his theory alongside several political and social scientists. The question then becomes: Can the irrational activity be considered rational?

When examining this idea, I applied the question to policymaking in Texas. Ideally, policymaking is a process whereby deliberation and debate are used to find the best possible solution to a problem facing a community. Texas is steeped in the individualistic and traditionalistic political cultures of government, which often translate into specific legislative proposals and agendas. As we have noted in previous chapters, Texas constituents guide policy makers in specific directions. While the rationality principle suggests that decisions are made in the context of what is appropriate, the case can be made that, under Texas policy, rationality takes a back seat to what is politically and electorally acceptable.

Within that context, I discuss Texas policymaking regarding social and public policy. The state has traditionally been a slow mover when legislating policy for programs that fall into the social service category. Spending is frowned upon within the state. However, even though policy in its basic form is an answer to a problem, can we assume that the rationality principle applies simply with a few caveats from outside influences that drive decision making or that rationality is based on either one form of reasoning or another? Does social policy in Texas take on a new or altered rationality?

Understanding Policy: A Look at the Policy Process Framework

One way to understand policymaking is to conceptualize the course of a policy's ascension to its potential termination. Understanding this systematic framework can help individuals grasp the role it plays and how policy makes an impact beyond the basic structure and processes learned in the legislative chapter. Policy is designed to address issues, but the process of creating, implementing, and evaluating solutions describes how policymaking takes place. In their book *Foundations of Policy Analysis*, Gary Brewer and Peter DeLeon address this by providing a six-step framework for understanding the stages a policy goes through. It can be used, then, to understand the Texas process of policymaking.

1. Policy initiation: The initiation stage encompasses a policy's inception. The idea for a solution usually comes from the local and expert discourse on the potential issue. The first step in this stage is to identify the issues. If the issue refers to low test scores in schools, for example, work will be done to identify the factors affecting those test scores. Considering any environmental or institutional parameters, one goal of this stage is to engage in discussion to better understand an issue.

Lack of resources in a classroom would be considered an institutional parameter. A lack of attention to homework or provocation from family or parents would be environmental. Identifying these parameters is important, as it allows groups of involved individuals to assess and understand the issues by working to put the information together. Once these groups discuss the issue/problem, they will come to some agreement on the goals and objectives of a policy and start to form what an ideal solution will include.

2. Policy estimation: While the initiation stage is designed to produce an ideal outcome, the estimation stage of the framework involves making the policy realistic—feasibility is the goal instead of creating an ideal solution. The work done at the initiation stage is captured and evaluated to estimate what can practicably be done about the issue. To achieve this,

the resources that can be put towards the problem are estimated, and there is an evaluation of what can reasonably be done. Using these metrics, policy is in a sense formed through estimation as the problem is rationalized and potentially feasible policy starts to take shape.

3. Policy selection: After issues are identified and rationalized, policy reaches its critical stage: selection. This includes the legislative process, during which policy is formed, written, critiqued, and debated upon to determine whether a solution will be approved. This stage is a carbon copy of the legislative process discussed in the chapter on the legislature. As the legislature in Texas debates policy, it fulfills the framework's selection mandate. The goal of this stage is to produce quality policy based on consensus building—gaining a general understanding of the policy and the effects of the issue—and conflict resolution.

4. Policy implementation: Once a policy is selected and passed, it is rolled out to the public. As policies are solutions by nature, this involves implementing the approved plan of action in a public setting. As policy implementation unfolds, bureaucrats and legislators will work to estimate its impact. The overall idea is to gather data on how the rules of the policy are working, whether the policy meets the goals set forth, and if the policy does address the major components of the problem. The goal of this stage is to achieve a data set that can be used to evaluate a policy.

5. Policy evaluation: As policy changes and matures, one main question will arise: Is it working? Answering that question involves taking the data from the implementation stage and analyzing it against stated goals and objectives. Policy can be evaluated for:

   a. Efficiency—the path to achieving an outcome versus reasonable resources

   b. Effectiveness—does it achieve the desired outcomes?

   c. Adequacy—does the policy address the issue in a sufficient manner and within an acceptable period?

   d. Equity—is it fair and accessible, and does it have equal affects across populations?

This evaluation can determine if a policy lives or enters a discussion of termination.

6. Policy termination: The final stage of the framework addresses whether a policy will continue its current course. If a policy is deemed to not meet the basic mandates in the evaluation stage, it can be put up for discussion to be eliminated or changed. Full termination would be eliminating the policy and its funds in favor of creating a new solution. Another option could be partial termination: the policy is altered or redirected to better address the initial issues or those that have arisen throughout the process.

This framework provides a systematic view that helps us evaluate and understand the public policy system. As Texas works through a number of policy debates (which I will chronicle in this chapter), having a framework for understanding policy decisions and the effect they can have—as well as comprehending their function and the process by which they are made—is integral to understanding the state of policy in Texas.

Social and Public Policy in Texas: Major Debates

Education

Texas has a jaded history with education. It was one of the prime issues involved with the break away from Mexico, and Texas has consistently worked to establish a quality education system. Funding for education has been the subject of a constant battle within the state. Traditionally, funding is done by district; each special district is in charge of using property taxes and user fees, along with a subsidy from the state government, to fund education.

There has been a consistent push and pull regarding the equality of education funding in the state. School districts in richer or more affluent areas have benefitted from higher funds. Poorer school districts have struggled to keep pace: they fall behind in both academic performance and resources used to maintain a productive environment, and teacher compensation has been low. The battle for education funds has routinely ended up in court. Two landmark cases drove the debate on equitable funding in Texas.

San Antonio v. Rodriguez shed light on the ability to assess property taxes, which in turn called education equity into question. The issue centered on Edgewood ISD, a poor district in an area with high property taxes. Due to restrictions on property taxes (based on a cap on taxable property values), the district could only raise $37 in taxes per student, while the surrounding districts in the same area could raise $413 per student. The argument to equalize the ratio (framed as a breach of the Fourteenth Amendment and Equal Protection Clause) was upheld in district court after Texas was unable or unwilling to address the inequality. However, it was overturned by the US Supreme Court, which stated that those clauses did not pertain to state public education.

Edgewood ISD v. Kirby, however, managed to force a change. William Kirby, the commissioner of education at the time, was sued; the claim argued that the inequality in Texas's education funding (which came from property taxes) fractured the Texas Constitution's provision on providing quality education. With the assistance of the Mexican American Legal Defense and Education Fund (MALDEF), the eight original districts claimed the state was derelict in providing needed funding while basing the system solely on property taxes.

After a lengthy legal battle, the Texas Supreme Court found in favor of Edgewood and the sixty-seven districts that had joined the suit, charging that Texas had violated the efficient system and equal protection clauses of the Texas Constitution with regard to education. Another lengthy battle ensued as the Texas Legislature dragged its feet on abiding by the court's ruling on how to equalize funding to school districts. Plans ranged from forcing richer districts to subsidize poorer districts through the Robin Hood plans to the current plan: capping the taxable value of homes at $284,000 and choosing an outlet for any balance that property tax accrues. This has created several challenges, and it has become custom for the education budget to be challenged in the state court system.

Texas's current education budget is currently working its way through an appeals process as poorer school districts fight for a larger piece of the budget, which they believe should be based on need. The Texas Board of Education and the legislature believe an equitable allocation regardless of need is the most productive standard. Spending per student has slipped over time as well, according to the US Census Bureau. In 1950, Texas was on par with average US spending per student; however, it has lagged since. In 2000, Texas ranked twenty-eighth in spending per student but dropped to forty-ninth as of 2012, with just $8,400 spent per student.[1]

Funding is not the only battleground for education. Historically, the state has struggled with minority education. Dating back to the middle of the twentieth century, Texas has fought against change in its schools and resisted integrating minorities within the system. Desegregation to make education equitable was the subject of a major fight in Texas. After *Plessy v. Ferguson* (1896) was overturned due to inequalities in education spending and procedures between minority and predominantly white districts, the state was forced to equalize education.

Salvatierra v. Del Rio ISD (1930) and *Delgado v. Bastrop ISD* (1950) were both cases that challenged the way Hispanics were educated in Texas. Those cases claimed that separate but equal education was not successful, as Hispanics were given minimal resources and education was largely restricted to vocational training. Treatment of minorities in Texas schools continued to be a point of contention within the state. In 1957, *Brown v. the Board of Education* overturned *Plessy* and mandated that school districts integrate immediately to help curb the inequality of education. Some Texas school districts resisted as the state leadership and legislature passed bills to attempt to resist the proposed change in *Brown*. Other districts, such as those in San Antonio, were quick to abide by the mandate. Cal Jillson (2015) examines the rate of minority success in Texas schools and points to the differences in performance associated with the ratio of minorities in Texas public schools. While schools have a growing population of Hispanics, students in predominantly Anglo school districts are performing better.

Evaluation and assessment models have also been a source of debate. Texas has traditionally used accountability through testing to measure student success and progress. Versions of standardized testing have ranged from the TAKS test to the STAAR test, which gauges student advancement and attainment. This model has come under scrutiny. While pass rates have been consistent for Anglos (according to the US census), minorities' ability to gain the necessary exam-rate passage has fluctuated. Furthermore, the move to the STAAR test system, which consists of multiple end-of-course exams, had adverse effects: test fatigue set in for both teachers and students, and corresponding fail rates followed—especially among freshman and sophomores, who had a higher than 50 percent fail rate.

---

1   U.S. Census Bureau. "American Fact Finder." https://www.census.gov/newsroom/press-releases/2015/cb15-98.html.

This assessment model became widely known in 2009 when President Barack Obama introduced his "Race to the Top" policy, which aimed to allocate over $4 billion in federal funds to states that performed well in education and met progressive standards. Texas, which uses the accountability through testing system, believed it was at the top of the curve. However, before the application could be submitted, Governor Rick Perry instructed that Texas withdraw from the system.

Curriculum debates have evolved over time as well. In the early twentieth century, there was a push to remove any mention of anti-Southern rhetoric from the education system as veterans of the Reconstruction and Civil War eras and their descendants fought to remove unforgiving treatment from the system. Contemporary debates have centered on abstinence as the primary form of sex education, and it is the only sex education advocated for in the majority of the state's school districts.

This broaches the subject of the religious influence in education that has become prevalent in Texas. In 2009, there was a move to discredit the concept of evolution: teachers were prompted to "thoroughly examine" all scientific theories in order to give a "complete review" of existing theories. Of most importance was the theory of evolution. The feeling amongst the members of the board of education was that Darwin's teachings flew in the face of religion and that they should be treated as uncertain or flawed.

Reading 8.1

Selection from "Vestigial Parts"[2]
from *Big, Hot, Cheap, and Right: What America Can Learn from the Strange Genius of Texas*
Erica Grieder

Reading Introduction: Armed on Campus—Discussing Security and Civil Rights on College Campuses

Erica Grieder examines policy debates in Texas. As the state becomes increasingly conservative, policy and policy decisions have followed suit. Grieder examines the concealed-carry-on-college-campuses policy debates. Texas has made several contested policy decisions in the last decade regarding colleges; these policies deal with activities on campuses in the state as well as cost. What is found is that current policy maintains a conservative view of the issues of safety and rights on college campuses.

Consider Oak Hills, a San Antonio megachurch. The head pastor, Max Lucado, has written about twenty best-selling books, and he ministers to half a million followers on Twitter. "Guess who is thinking about u today? God is," and so on. Lucado trained in the Church of Christ, but Oaks Hills (like most megachurches) is nondenominational, and the approach is resolutely user friendly. In one typical message, Lucado explains grace by telling a story about how his puppy got in the trash and made a big mess. So he cleaned it up, and when he came back, the puppy was looking at him with a hangdog expression. But the puppy didn't need to be so worried because Lucado had already and implicitly forgiven the puppy for its misbehavior. For a heady, cerebral kind of Christian—an Episcopalian?—this kind of message might seem facile. Yet compared to Joel Osteen, who heads America's biggest megachurch and runs a spin-off self-help empire (*Your Best Life Now!*) in Houston, Lucado is practically St. Augustine.

In other words, while Texas occasionally produces a pastor like John Hagee, of the Cornerstone megachurch where I learned how to get rid of my demons, most of its religious leaders are temperate enough. Nor do the people seem overly zealous. On polling, Texans are generally in line with national opinion. The same is true in practice. The typical Texan doesn't, for example, seem unusually homophobic, even when you leave the liberal enclaves such as Austin. In 2011, cities guru Richard Florida ranked the greater San Antonio area as America's friendliest metro area for gay couples raising children. According to census data, fully one-third of same-sex couples there have children under eighteen; around the nation, the figure is slightly less than one in five. In August 2012, Mary Gonzalez, a Democratic state representative from El Paso who was the first lesbian to serve in the state legislature, announced that she was actually the first pansexual to have that job.

Even in the eastern part of the state, which is conservative and heavily religious, Texans have pushed back against the worst displays of bigotry. In 2012, the Westboro Baptist Church, a virulently homophobic group from Kansas, came to College Station to protest a funeral that was being held at Texas A&M University for a 1993 graduate, an Army officer, who had been killed in North Carolina. (The church has frequently protested at the funerals of soldiers; its reasoning, such as it is, is that soldiers support the United States, and the United States supports gays.) Some 650 Aggies gathered around the church, forming a human wall to keep the Westboro people away.[1] "In response to their signs of hate, we will wear maroon," wrote Ryan Slezia, the Aggie who coordinated the vigil. "In response to their mob anger, we will form a line, arm in arm." On that day, at least, the most deranged people in Texas were Kansans. Maybe Thomas Frank has a point?

At times, in fact, Texas's churches are more liberal than its politicians. In 2010, Andrew Doyle, the bishop of the state's Episcopal diocese, and James Baker, a former secretary of state, produced a "plan for unity" in response to growing internal debate over the church's teachings on homosexuality. After discussions in

Houston, they agreed that the Texas diocese would allow its individual priests to decide whether to officiate gay unions.[2] The priests can't officiate gay marriages, though; the state doesn't allow those.

The strangest detail of all, however, is that if you want to get technical, Texas is *less* Protestant than the country as a whole. Nationally, according to the most recent American Religious Identification Survey, 50.9 percent of Americans were Christians other than Catholics. In Texas, non-Catholic Christians (including Mormons) were slightly less than half of the population.[3] Only one major religion was significantly overrepresented in Texas. About a third of Texans, 32 percent, were Catholics. Around the country, the figure was 25.1 percent. Texas's Catholic population is growing too; in 1990, the figure was just 23 percent. The reason, of course, is the growth in the state's Hispanic population.

And yet despite all of that, Texas has, as noted, proven to be an unusually happy hunting ground for the religious right. In 1995, for example, the state revised its education code to specify that schools should make it clear, in their sexuality education courses, that abstinence is best for teenagers. It's not a mandate, and the state has no way to force schools to comply; the local school boards still get to decide how this kind of guideline is carried out. But abstinence-only sex ed quickly became de facto policy across the state.

Several years ago, David Wiley and Kelly Wilson, both professors of health education at Texas State University in San Marcos, decided to figure out what exactly the schools were teaching teenagers about sex. Working in conjunction with the Texas Freedom Network (TFN), a nonprofit that works for church-state separation, they requested the relevant documents from all of Texas's school districts—the state has more than 1,000—and 990 replied.

Of these, only 4 percent provided anything like comprehensive sex education; 2 percent said they ignored the topic altogether, largely to avoid controversy, although one interim superintendent told the researchers that he figured most of the kids learned everything they needed to know from helping out with the farm animals. The vast majority of the school districts that provided the researchers with materials, 94 percent, were teaching kids only about abstinence.[4] And those districts weren't necessarily confining themselves to the narrow point that abstinence works when diligently pursued; a lot of them were adding scare tactics and lies: condoms don't work, no one wants to marry a slut, and so on. "We knew it was bad. We didn't know it was this bad," said Wiley, who was at home recovering from knee surgery when I called.

The problem, he said, was one of collective distraction and apathy. Texas school districts are atomized; they're not under the control of the counties. The superintendents knew what was going on, but they wanted to steer well clear of politics. The teachers knew too, but some of them were part of the problem, asking their pastor to come in for a guest talk and so on. The parents, in too many cases, weren't paying attention to what their children were supposed to be learning.

But when confronted with what the schools were teaching, Wiley said, the parents took notice: "If they found out that the youth minister came up and said Jesus wants you to be abstinent or whatever—I think parents are put out by that." Since Wiley and Wilson's report was released, the issue has attracted more attention. In November 2011, TFN released a new survey: 25.4 percent of Texas school districts had started giving their students basic information about contraception;[5] "ignorance, it seems, remains a central pedagogical strategy in Texas classrooms." Still, it was a lot better than the 4 percent from three years before.

The religious right has caused other national controversies. One of the recurring myths about Texas is that the State Board of Education has been taken over by creationists and ideologues who have devoted themselves to rewriting the state's history and science textbooks according to their preferred worldview. This is a national issue, the critics say, because Texas textbooks effectively go national. About 10 percent of America's school-age children live in the state, so as a business matter textbook publishers are bound to make sure their books conform to Texas standards. If the smaller states want to buy textbooks, they're stuck with the options approved for Texas.

In 2011, Texas republicans introduced a bill that would have allowed college students to carry concealed weapons on campus at the state's public colleges and universities as long as they were otherwise authorized to carry concealed weapons. For Texans, this wasn't an abstract issue. In 1966, a sniper had ascended the tower marking the center of the University of Texas's campus in Austin and opened fire, killing seventeen people and injuring thirty-one more. It was America's first mass school shooting and the worst until the 2007 attack at Virginia Tech.

At a Senate committee hearing on the campus carry law on March 22, Austin's police chief, Art Acevedo, pointed to a grim coincidence: earlier that school year, in September, a student had entered the University of Texas's main library with an assault rifle. It turned out that he was only planning to kill himself, which he did. This, Acevedo explained, was precisely why it was a bad idea to allow concealed weapons on campus: an armed student might well have tried to stop the guy with the rifle, triggering a crossfire situation.

A series of students, some of them distressed, also testified against the bill. They didn't like the idea of guns in their dorms and lecture halls. "I am sorry that it makes you feel uncomfortable, but comfort is not a right," said a witness on the other side, a student who identified himself as a veteran, a vegetarian, and not a hunter. Some of the witnesses in favor of the bill had an air of persecution, as if they were facing a war on guns, just as evangelicals sometimes complain about a supposed war on Christianity. On that point, the senators weren't hugely sympathetic. "I would argue that Texas is a pretty gun-friendly state," said John Whitmire, a Democratic state senator from Houston.

Even the Democrats, however, seemed to be resigned to the bill's passage. The state allows people to carry concealed weapons in most public spaces, and opponents were struggling to come up with an airtight case that a college campus is an intrinsically different sort of space. In primary schools, that is, concealed weapons are disallowed because those places are crawling with kids. One witness, a professor of biology, offered a similar argument, observing that major mental illnesses such as schizophrenia may not emerge until a person reaches the midtwenties. But the state already allows youngsters to have guns: at eighteen a kid can take up arms, and at twenty-one a young person can carry a concealed weapon. Eventually, however, the bill was undone by a different line of argument: allowing concealed weapons would be too expensive. The universities might have to pay more for their insurance.[6]

It wasn't the only time that Texas's hang 'em high tradition has been checked by fiscal conservatism. Texans are reluctant to bankrupt themselves even in the name of punishment. In 1876, delegates to the state constitutional convention argued for minor criminals to be punished at the whipping post rather than the penitentiary, because the cash-strapped state could barely afford its prisons.

Another check is Texas's pragmatic streak. That's why all Texas's major cities have sanctuary policies, meaning that police don't ask about someone's legal status unless it's directly related to the matter at hand. That way they don't spend all their time detaining and deporting people, and unauthorized immigrants, most of whom are lawabiding, can have at least some small measure of safety.

There's even evidence that Texas is getting more fair, although it has a long way to go. Since 1992, the Innocence Project, a nationwide legal organization, has helped forty-seven people (as of November 2012) get exonerated via postconviction DNA testing—including several men who had spent decades in jail for crimes they hadn't committed and several who were on death row.[7] Given how hard it is to get an exoneration after the fact, the real number of the wrongfully convicted has to be higher than that. In 2002, the Houston Police Department Crime Lab closed down its DNA lab altogether after investigators found that hundreds of cases had been bungled.[8]

In 2007, the legislature passed a new law, the Tim Cole Act, in response to one of these exonerations. Timothy Cole was a college student at Texas Tech University in Lubbock when he was charged with raping another student and sentenced to twenty-five years in prison. He maintained his innocence for years, turning down parole hearings because to have a chance at early release, he would have had to admit to a crime he had never committed. In 1999, he died in prison after a bout of asthma triggered a heart attack. Eight years later, when another man confessed to the crime, Cole was exonerated posthumously. The new law was intended to help the wrongfully convicted rebuild their lives once released. It provided for $80,000 in compensation for every year served, college tuition, and other forms support.[9] For once, no one tried to bluster through the issue and no one begrudged the expense.

Implementation has been tricky, however. In 2010, another man, Anthony Graves, was denied compensation after having served eighteen years. The issue was that he technically hadn't been exonerated— when he finally convinced the state to give him a new trial, the district attorney determined that the evidence against him was so flimsy he couldn't even be charged. He was presumed innocent, but not proven so. It took an additional year of wrangling before the state worked through the issue.

As for the death penalty, as mentioned before, a large majority of Texans still support it in concept, but over the past decade the number of death sentences issued in Texas has plummeted, for two specific reasons that no one would guess offhand. The first is that in 2005 Texas passed a law giving juries the option to sentence a murderer to life without parole; it was one of the last states to make such a provision. Life sentences were already an option, but due to the crowding in the prisons, parole was a distinct possibility. Once life without parole became an option, the number of death sentences handed down in Texas dropped overnight. In 2004, Texas juries issued twenty-three death sentences, according to the Death Penalty Information Center; in 2005, the number was fourteen; in 2006, it was eleven.[10] Jurors were less willing to send a killer to death if permanent incarceration could be genuinely guaranteed.

The second blow to Texas's death penalty pipeline came in February 2008, when Chuck Rosenthal, the Harris County district attorney, abruptly resigned. Rosenthal had been America's most ardent death penalty prosecutor. In an interview in 2007, Rosenthal had explained to me that his approach was simply to seek the death penalty whenever there was a chance the jury might go for it. His attitude about that was unusual, even among prosecutors. The law says that the death penalty is an option only if the murder was exacerbated by an additional factor (such as premeditation or rape) and there are no mitigating circumstances (such as youth or mental illness). In practice, most Texas district attorneys are more reluctant than Rosenthal was about asking for a death sentence. As a result, Rosenthal's office brought in more death sentences than any other county. Since 2001, when he took the job, Harris County alone had accounted for about a third of Texas's death sentences.

The events that prompted Rosenthal's resignation were unrelated to all of this. In 2002, Houston police had arrested a pair of brothers who were taking pictures of a drug raid happening to their neighbors and seized their film. The brothers had sued the city for the civil rights violations, and their lawyer, wanting to see what the district attorney's office was doing about the case, had subpoenaed Rosenthal's e-mails. Rosenthal deleted some 2,500 e-mails, a panicky move that drew public scrutiny to the e-mails he did turn over: chain e-mails that included racist jokes, and evidence of an extramarital affair—love notes to his secretary.[11] That the latter helped seal his downfall was a fine bit of irony; it was Rosenthal who had gone to the Supreme Court in 2003 to defend Texas's sodomy ban, which was declared unconstitutional in *Lawrence v. Texas.*

Since Rosenthal left, the number of capital sentences in Harris County has come down. Texas still has America's biggest death row and will no doubt lead the nation in executions for years to come, because there are so many people already on death row. But on the sentencing side, the change is clear. In recent years, Texas has become less draconian—not just in its use of the death penalty, but also in its approach to criminal justice more generally. It's just like the textbooks say: evolution happens, even if it doesn't happen overnight.

As for evolution, the United States has been getting safer since the 1990s, and Texas has seen the same trend. In 1996, according to data from the Texas Department of Public Safety, there were 1,476 murders in Texas—about 1 for every 13,000 people.[12] By 2010, the number of people in Texas had grown by about 5 million and the number of murders had dropped to 1,248. Only 1 in every 20,000 Texans was a victim of murder; the murder rate had dropped by slightly more than a third. The rate of rape had dropped by a third; of robbery, by a quarter.

Texas has a presumption of goodwill and cooperation between the public and private sectors. Private citizens pour money into political campaigns. "Had I known you could raise $3 million, I'd have been here long ago," Mitt Romney said on a 2012 trip to Midland. Elected officials, in turn, are generally chummy with lobbyists. The exceptions are few enough to be enumerated. Sam Rayburn was one; at one point an oilman sent him a beautiful horse, and he sent it back. Ron Paul is another.

But even Texas liberals are more sanguine about lobbyists than you would think. For Molly Ivins, the criticisms leveled at the state on these grounds had an off-putting piety: "I know a number of pols I count as honest who never did anything in return for such favors. Is it any ranker than getting a large campaign contribution from someone with a special interest in legislation? For virtue, try Minnesota."[13]

That is a Texas tradition that isn't going to change any time soon. You have to dance with the one that brung you, I guess.

In fact, Texas Democrats even, on occasion, scold their national counterparts for letting down the cause. "If there was one thing that Texas Democrats did well in the '60s," wrote Ben Barnes, the former lieutenant governor, in his memoir, "—and one thing today's struggling Democratic party ought to emulate—it was creating this bridge between conservative business interests and progressive constituencies."[14] For Barnes, it isn't just about tactics. He reminisces about the meetings Texas politicians used to have with business leaders who wanted to help raise money and bat ideas around: "They weren't afraid to take a hit now for improvement later, and their efforts are a big part of the reason why we were able to effect such dramatic improvement in the social and civic life of Texans."[15] Maybe Barnes would say that. He is, after all, a lobbyist now. On the other hand, maybe he is a lobbyist because he would say that.

Either way, Barnes was right in line with Texas Democratic tradition. That's worth keeping in mind as Texas turns blue: the Texas version of blue might not be quite the same as the national shade. Wait—is Texas turning blue?

NOTES

1   Sonia Smith, "Aggies Build Human Wall to Keep Westboro Baptist Church from Protesting Funeral," TexasMonthly.com, July 6, 2012, http://www.tmdailypost.com/article/education/aggies-build-human-wall-keep-westboro-baptist-church-protesting-funeral.

2   Jon Meacham, "Of God and Gays and Humility," *Time*, July 30, 2012, http://www.time.com/time/magazine/article/0,9171,2119 924,00.html.

3   http://commons.trincoll.edu/aris/publications/aris-2008-summary-report/.

4   David Wiley and Kelly Wilson, "Just Say Don't Know: Sexuality Education in Texas Public Schools," Texas Freedom Network Education Fund, February 2009, www.tfn.org/site/DocServer/SexEdRort09_web.pdf?docID=981.

5   "Sex Education in Texas Public Schools: Progress in the Lone Star State," Texas Freedom Network Education Fund, November 2011, http://www.tfn.org/site/DocServer/Report_final_web.pdf?docID=2941.

6   Reeve Hamilton, "Campus Carry Debate Likely to Return Next Session," *Texas Tribune*, April 4, 2012, http://www.texastribune.org/texas-issues/campus-carry/campus-carry-debate-likely-return-next-session/.

7   The Innocence Project's list of exonerations in Texas is available online at http://www.innocenceproject.org/news/state.php?state=TX.

8   Steve McVicker and Roma Khanna, "New Tests Urged in HPD Crime Lab Final Report," *Houston Chronicle*, June 13, 2007, http://www.chron.com/news/houston-texas/article/New-tests-urged-in-HPD-crime-lab-final-report-1530898.php.

9 Hilary Hylton, "Texas: The Kinder, Gentler Hang 'Em High State," *Time*, September 19, 2009, http://www.time.com/time/nation /article/0,8599,1924278,00.html.

10 Death Penalty Information Center, http://www.deathpenaltyinfo.org/death-sentences-united-states-1977–2008.

11 Ted Oberg, "Why Rosenthal Had to Turn over Email," KTRK-TV, January 31, 2008, http://abclocal.go.com/ktrk/story?section=news/in_focus&id=5926157.

12 http://www.txdps.state.tx.us/administration/crime_records/pages /crimestatistics.htm.

13 Molly Ivins, "Texas-Style Ethics," in *Molly Ivins Can't Say That, Can She?* (New York: Random House, 1991), 60.

14 Ben Barnes, *Barn Burning, Barn Building* (Albany, TX: Bright Sky Press, 2006), 94.

15 Ibid., 95.

Healthcare

Texas's pro-business culture has an adverse effect on healthcare in Texas. With a political culture that mandates economic frugality, Texas has resisted using public funds for any social program, including those associated with healthcare. While the federal government has made a significant financial commitment to healthcare in recent years ($43 billion in 2014[3]), Texas has refused to use state money or match the federal government's contribution to programs in Texas. In the 2014–2015 budget, Texas allocated $30 billion to healthcare in the state—a significant sum, but far less than the federal contribution. Texas has a history of avoiding using public funds, both state and federal, as a fear of entitlement and unnecessary (and potentially coercive) mandates has weighed on decision makers.

Healthcare has been a point of contention in Texas since the mid-1800s. Healthcare and the provision of basic medical needs have been topics of discussion in governments through the history of the nation. Texas addressed this question in what would be considered the "Texas Way": Wealthy individuals and families sought the best healthcare possible. That entailed paying for house calls and traveling to see doctors or to undergo necessary surgeries. Texans without the means to seek out this type of healthcare were left to make do with what was available. Home remedies were popular, as were traveling physicians who performed medical procedures.

At the turn of the twentieth century, all social programs were treated as money pits of sorts, and lawmakers resisted investing in the social climate of the state in favor of an individualistic

---

3   Expenditures in the Texas state budget 2014–2015 can be found here: http://www.lbb.state.tx.us/Documents/ GAA/General_Appropriations_Act_2014-15.pdf.

view of maintaining a basic quality of life. Within this view was an aversion to spending on healthcare reform. Change came with the Great Depression. After President Herbert Hoover placed economic and social recovery on the heads of local communities, President Franklin Roosevelt took a hard-line stance. Texas and other states were coerced into increasing funds for social programs at the risk of losing federal funding. Texas responded immediately and pumped $20 million into social services despite the state party leadership's distaste for expanding the federal government.

That trend defined the century. Texas continued the "Texas Way," relying on low taxes and few services to drive its economically concerned activity. Thus, Texas has continually approached spending with a tightfisted nature, resisting any call to invest where unnecessary and relying on federal funds when needed.

That outlook has pervaded Texas's history and direction towards healthcare policy over the years. Texas has continually been ranked at the lower end of the spectrum when it comes to healthcare. Routinely shuffling budget expenditures away from the issue, Texas ranked fiftieth in the nation in terms of treatment of needy citizens, according to a 2009 study conducted by the *New York Times*.

Medicaid and Medicare have been at the forefront of the recent debate on healthcare. Medicaid is a jointly funded program, with the federal government providing matching funds—funds that are given in relation to state contribution—to provide healthcare services to the poor and needy. Care is based on need and was designed to be a final stop or last resort for these communities in regard to treatment. While these were the target groups, 1980 brought a focus on expanding eligibility to poor adults by raising the income requirement to include more individuals in the program. Texas responded by working in the opposite direction. Medicaid-eligible communities were limited and there was a cutback in state contributions. According to data from the Texas Medicaid program, Texas spends roughly 84 percent of the national average of state funds on the program. That number was as low as 72 percent in 1990.[4] Today, Texas has earmarked $60 billion for the program, $35 billion of which is from federal funds. The state has remained focused on limiting the eligibility and services available to keep costs from rising.

Medicare is a federal program that is geared to providing care for the elderly and children. The program has a high cost, but at the state level, it seeks to set the rates for medical services—including emergency room visits, procedures, physician visits, and other medical costs—that would then be billed to the federal government.

Texas has had one of the highest user rates of any state in the nation since the inception of Medicare. The costs of services have increased dramatically in the state since the creation of the program in 1965. Until 1981, according to available Medicare data, costs in Texas were roughly 95 percent of the national average. Since then, Texas has exceeded the national average and is now ranked fourth highest among the fifty states for expenditures per Medicare enrollee; Texas expenditures are 112 percent of the national average.

---

4   Texas Health and Human Services. https://www.hhsc.state.tx.us/medicaid/.

The businesslike nature of healthcare in Texas has opened up the system to exploitation. With providers seeking to bill for services, there have been cases of billing fraud: providers will fraudulently claim payment from the federal government for procedures they don't provide. The inclusion of home healthcare as a viable service has increased the incidence of this type of fraud in recent years.

The Affordable Care Act has brought about the last change in Texas's healthcare policy. The federal policy, which was upheld in 2012 by the Supreme Court, seeks to increase the provision of government-sponsored healthcare by providing enhancements to the states. Texas was a vociferous opponent, as representatives, senators, and lobby groups from the state worked to kill the bill. During the debate, the state threatened to leave the Medicaid system—which the Affordable Care Act sought to inflate and not deflate—if the policy passed. However, the potential loss of nearly $20 billion in federal funds was too great to make that move.

With the passage of the Affordable Care Act, states like Texas caught a break and were not forced to expand eligibility or increase the rate of services. Texas has spoken out against the policy, continuing to charge that the healthcare system is broken due to poor-quality services, that it is a system easily taken advantage of, and that it has poor oversight. Instead, Texas has clung to the individualistic political culture the state is known for and sought to keep healthcare in the state within those lines.

Moral Policies

There is a battle taking place within the dominant political party in Texas, and it is having a major effect on policy. Social conservatives and fiscal conservatives are battling to take over the direction of the Texas Republican Party. Fiscal conservatives advocate that economic policy decisions drive the policy debate. Their focus is on policy that will benefit the state and its businesses—a very traditional view of state politics. Social conservatives advocate for social or moral policies to control the direction of the debate; in their view, the focus should be on instilling a morality that creates an acceptable way of life in the state. As that debate wages, there have been several recent instances when the social faction has been able to push policy in the state.

One recent example is the attempt to pass strict abortion laws in Texas. In 2013, the Texas Legislature introduced a bill that would strengthen restrictions on abortion in clinics in Texas. The 2013 debate centered on the ability of abortion clinics to operate at what the legislature felt was a "less than surgical" level. The bill met considerable opposition from abortion rights groups, and their cause was championed by Wendy Davis, who conducted an eleven-hour filibuster to halt the bill. When Lieutenant Governor David Dewhurst asserted that Davis went off-topic in the tenth hour by talking about sonograms, a vote was held to end the filibuster. While Republicans attempted to pass the bill (by a vote of 19–11 in favor of passage), procedural inquiries and considerable distractions from a full gallery of protestors forced the vote to be delayed. After debate regarding the timing of the vote, Republicans conceded that the vote to pass had come after the midnight deadline and the session had closed, providing a brief stay on the vote. That result was eventually negated, as then-governor Rick Perry called a special session a month later, and the bill was passed into law.

The stated intent of the bill was to reform these clinics in order to ensure the safety of patients. Among the reforms was the mandate that all abortion clinics meet the same level of surgical qualification as any regional medical facility; failure to do so would preclude their continued operation, including the ability to admit patients. Those restrictions forced nearly half of the eighteen abortion clinics operating in Texas at the time to shut down.

The law also mandated that no abortion could take place after the twentieth week of pregnancy, going against the decision in Roe v. Wade (1973), which set the mark at twenty-four weeks.[5] The law's provisions were upheld in 2015 by a federal circuit court but are being challenged in the US Supreme Court at the time of this writing. The justification that Texas Republicans and their leadership provide for the bill is that the safety of abortions and the women who seek them should be a high priority. This viewpoint guided the restrictions to ensure safety and medical standards.

Texas Attorney General Ken Paxton has accused abortion clinics of being more concerned with profit than with safety. If upheld, the bill will leave abortion clinics close to urban areas, with a total of six that meet current standards. Opponents of the bill have asserted that it is not an issue of safety but rather a way to infringe on the choice of women to have abortions by limiting their options. Their argument also centers on the assertion that the socially conservative legislature is using the bill to circumvent their civil rights. In addition, they have questioned the safety argument of the bill's proponents, arguing that instead it could prompt women to seek illegal or unsafe abortion procedures that could harm their health.

While abortion laws are new to the state, one long-running policy debate pushed by social conservatives surrounds the emboldened Texas Religious Freedom Restoration Act.[6] Texas's version of the policy has been on the books for fifteen years and has drawn little attention. The law entrenches an individual's right to practice religion and allows for challenges to any state law that "substantially" infringes on one's religious liberties. As written, the law takes an additional step toward ensuring that no one's individual religious liberties can infringe upon another person's religious or civil rights or liberties.

After Indiana passed a similar but stricter law in early 2015, the discussion about Texas's version of the policy sprang to life. Indiana's version allows individuals to act based on their religious beliefs. The intent of the law is to curtail any perceived infringement on actions taken with a religious undertone or direction. After the law had been passed, a national debate began on the informal intent of the law. While the law allows for activities to be undertaken by individuals in the name of religions, opponents of the law saw it as a way for persons to be restricted from services or civil rights, such as a business owner refusing service to those who disagree with their faith.

---

5   Civ. Stat. §§4512.5, H&S 245.001 et seq.

6   Religious Freedom Restoration Act. "Enacted Texas Religious Freedom Law." http://rfraperils.com/texas/.

Most notable amongst the law's opponents was the lesbian, gay, and transgender community, which sees the law as an avenue for religious business owners to refuse service to LGBT customers in the name of their faith, which would transform the law into a tool for discrimination.

Texas legislators followed suit, pushing later in 2015 to strengthen the state's religious freedom laws to resemble the tenets of those in Indiana. State Representative Tony Krauss of Fort Worth has proposed that the state add a religious freedom amendment to the Texas Constitution. Krauss believes this move will increase the work of an already productive law. While some see the advocacy as an attempt to court an increasingly socially conservative right win in Texas, others see it as an avenue to restore the state's willingness to allow individuals to act on their religion.

Reading 8.2

Selection from "The Coming Crack-Up"[7]
from *Big, Hot, Cheap, and Right: What America Can Learn from the Strange Genius of Texas*
Erica Grieder

Reading Introduction: The Republican Stand Against Planned Parenthood

Erica Grieder (2008) examines one of the moral battlegrounds in Texas: the operations of and opposition to Planned Parenthood in the state. As Texas has become an entrenched Republican state, the ideas and clauses surrounding it have shaped some of these moral debates. Grieder examines the actions of the political structure and their impacts.

Texas was, relatedly, an early adopter of public education for the second sex. In New England, the civilization of women had long been considered a private affair; if genteel parents wanted elegant daughters, they could make their own arrangements. Texas, lacking the genteel parents, needed to intervene, for everyone's sake. "The *girls*, we will not say young ladies, will grow up like mere parrots," wrote Dr. Francis Moore Jr. in 1841. "What a contrast will there be between these dull, shiftless, stupid females, and the intelligent, refined, active, and accomplished ladies who adorn the first society of the United States."[1]

On the other hand, Texas politicians never took much interest in women's civil rights. Pa Ferguson, the populist but crooked governor from the 1910s who later put his wife up for governor in his stead, was against women's suffrage. It was Texas's restrictive abortion laws that triggered the lawsuit that led to *Roe v. Wade*. (At the same time, it was a Texas woman, Norma McCorvey, who brought the lawsuit, and a Texas woman, Sarah Weddington, who won the case at the Supreme Court.)

The right to vote, the right to reproductive freedom, the right to be seen as equals—no. The right to work, the right to an education (education always being seen as an economic issue in Texas)—suit yourself, little lady.

So the passage of the sonogram bill wasn't a surprise, per se. Voters also weren't surprised when the state announced that it would stop providing any funds for Planned Parenthood, a nonprofit reproductive health care organization that provides access to abortion—never mind that abortion is a tiny part of Planned Parenthood's activities. But the latter, in particular, will probably come to look like an example of the Texas Republicans taking things too far.

The sonogram bill inspired an angry backlash from liberals, but polling found that a majority of voters approved it, and in any case, the details of the process of getting an abortion probably weren't directly visible to enough voters, male or female, to inspire a widespread movement. The attack on Planned Parenthood, however, was different. The majority of Americans, in Texas and elsewhere, support access to contraception in general and Planned Parenthood in particular. It's been around for more than a century and has, over that time, been the reproductive health care provider of first and last resort for millions of women. It elicits some loyalty around the country.

That had become apparent in 2012 when the Susan G. Komen Foundation, a nonprofit that raises money for the fight against breast cancer, announced that it was going to stop contributing money for Planned Parenthood to provide breast cancer screenings, also because Planned Parenthood's offerings include abortions. The move got way more attention than Komen could have intended and turned into a massive windfall for Planned Parenthood, as people around the country, realizing that America was suddenly having a gilded-era-style war on contraception, opened their checkbooks.

Surveys corroborate the point. In 2012, Public Policy Polling did a national poll for Planned Parenthood and found that 56 percent of likely voters supported the idea that employer-sponsored health plans should cover birth control.[2] A separate survey, also by Public Policy Polling, found that 58 percent of Texans thought Planned Parenthood should continue to receive funding from the state's Women's Health Program.[3] It has a higher approval rating in Texas than Rick Perry.[4] (As an aside, the national head of Planned Parenthood is Cecile Richards, who is the daughter of Ann Richards and the founder of the Texas Freedom Network.)

Defunding Planned Parenthood, in other words, was exactly the kind of move that could backfire on Texas Republicans. On social issues, Texans are generally in line with national norms—which is to say, moderate. In a May 2012 Gallup Poll, 38 percent of Americans described themselves as social conservatives.[5] That sounds like accurate self-reporting. There's some variation depending on the particular issue at hand, but as a rule of thumb social conservatives make up a plurality of voters, but not a majority, in both Texas and the United States.

In 2011, for example, according to a national survey from the First Amendment Center, 67 percent of Americans agreed that the First Amendment requires the separation of church and state.[6] In 2010, a Texas survey found 68 percent of likely voters agreeing that separation of church and state is a key constitutional principle.[7] So in 2012, when Rick Perry blamed Satan for the separation of church and state—"Satan runs across the world with his doubt and with his untruths and what have you"—he was well outside the mainstream of both Texan and American opinion.[8]

Texas's political leadership is socially conservative for the same reason that the United States sometimes gets socially conservative leaders: social conservatives are more likely to organize around social issues than moderates or liberals are. We can refer back to that Gallup survey that put the percentage of social conservatives at 38 percent. They're not the majority; they are on the back foot, and some of them know it. "We are in a crisis and so far most of the church fails to recognize we are in a battle," said the demonization PowerPoint that day at Cornerstone.

Social conservatives are, however, the biggest bloc; 31 percent and 28 percent of Americans described themselves as moderate and liberal, respectively. When moderates and liberals agree, they win. That's why abortion is legal, contraception is widely available, and gay marriage—which as recently as ten years ago was barely considered a serious suggestion—is making progress throughout the states as moderates come around to the idea. The social conservatives win, however, when moderates agree with them, which is why gay marriage isn't legal in all the states yet. They also win when they make an effort and moderates and liberals aren't paying much attention.

That's what's happened in Texas. For so many years, the state's Republican majority has been a party driven by business issues. Its sideline in Bible-thumping has mostly been confined to the rhetorical level and has therefore been easy for moderates to ignore, given that in practice Texas isn't noticeably more repressive than any other state. "The questions were always there between the social conservatives and the business conservatives," says Aaron Wheat of Texans for Public Justice, a watchdog organization.[9] "The all-or-nothing approach of the Tea Partiers is sort of bringing it to a head."

Social conservatives, emboldened as they are, may be at risk of going too far. In 2012, John Carona, a Republican state senator from Dallas, told the *Dallas Voice* that he supported several gay rights measures, including offering partner benefits to employees at state universities. He was even, he allowed, thinking about gay marriage.[10] It was, as the *Voice* put it, "a rare if not unprecedented move for a Republican state legislator," and the response from the religious right was predictably outraged. But while Carona had clearly gone out on a limb, he wasn't out of step with public opinion.

There are other trouble spots looming for Texas's Republican coalition. Immigration is one; while the state party has been more moderate than its national counterparts. As the sanctuary cities bill suggested, some of the newer legislators might want to revive the issue. The budget is going to be another contentious issue between the moderates and the far right. The severe budget cuts of 2011 didn't elicit that much anger among voters at the time. Everyone had heard about the downturn. But in January 2013, the comptroller projected that the state would have $101.4 billion for general purpose spending in the 2014–2015 biennium—including almost $9 billion left over from the previous cycle, because revenues had been higher than projected. If the Tea Party–type Republicans seek further cuts, moderates might balk.

In 2011, the fact that the sanctuary cities bill failed in the legislature showed that the moderate Republicans still had the upper hand. But the fact that the sonogram bill succeeded suggested that the moderate Republicans were choosing their battles. It's not clear which wing of the Republican Party will have the upper hand in 2013. An interesting detail from the 2012 elections, however, was that, although Ted Cruz won his Senate race by a whopping margin, and despite all the attention paid to his candidacy, he got fewer votes in Texas (about 100,000 fewer) than Mitt Romney. The fact that the Republican coalition has gotten so big might, in other words, be a good thing for Democrats over the medium term. If the Republicans keep fighting among themselves, it could create an opportunity for Democrats to make a pitch for moderates. Obama was right, then, to say that Texas is becoming a battleground. In the short term, however, the battle will be within the Republican Party.

NOTES

1 Ibid., 143.

2 "Our Polling on the Birth Control Issue," Public Policy Polling, February 10, 2012, http://www.publicpolicypolling.com/main/2012/02/our-polling-on-the-birth-control-issue.html.

3 Emily Ramshaw: "Poll: Voters Want to Keep Planned Parenthood in WHP," *Texas Tribune*, March 5, 2012, http://www.texastribune.org/texas-health-resources/abortion-texas/poll-voters-want-keep-planned-parenthood-whp/.

4   Thanh Tan, "A Closer Look at UT/TT Poll on Planned Parenthood," *Texas Tribune*, June 6, 2012, http://www.texastribune.org/texas-health-resources/reproductive-health/closer-look-ut-tt-poll-planned-parenthood/.

5   Jeffrey M. Jones, "In U.S., Nearly Half Identify as Economically Conservative," Gallup, May 25, 2012, http://www.gallup.com/poll/154889/nearly-half-identify-economically-conservative.aspx.

6   "Who Knows What About Religion," Pew Research Center, September 28, 2010, http://www.pewforum.org/U-S-Religious-Knowledge-Survey-Who-Knows-What-About-Religion.aspx#Public.

7   "Poll: Texans Back Church-State Separation," Texas Freedom Network, May 20, 2010, http://tfninsider.org/2010/05/20/poll-texans-back-church-state-separation/.

8   Casey Michel, "Rick Perry Blames Satan for Separation of Church and State," *TPMMuckraker* (blog), September 20, 2012, http://tpmmuckraker.talkingpointsmemo.com/2012/09/rick_perry_satan_church_state.php.

9   Author interview.

10 "John Carona Among First Republican Legislators in Texas to Back Gay Rights," *Dallas Voice*, October 23, 2012.

Environmental Policy

Per the Energy Information Administration, Texas produced 10 percent of the nation's electricity in 2010, nearly double the 5.5 percent it accounted for in 1950.[8] As the need for fuel and energy has risen, Texas has worked to keep up with policy and political decision making, looking to encourage the energy industry in Texas.

Part of that encouragement revolves around passing policies that make the state attractive to energy corporations. With the low taxes and services model as well as the dependence on property taxes for education, Texas has been successful at attracting corporations to the state. Policy that has allowed for progressive businesses and a soft landing spot for employees is attractive when a company is looking to headquarter or operate in the state. With that has come a battle to keep industrial policy from inhibiting economic affairs.

Texas is one of the states that have led the charge in battling policy and strict requirements from the Environmental Protection Agency (EPA). The federal branch of the EPA can create

---

8   EIA.gov.

standards regarding energy output and activity, and under Democratic presidents Bill Clinton and Barack Obama, these became targets for EPA regulation battles. Texas is the top-producing polluter (according to the Department of Energy and the EPA), as 50 percent of its energy output is geared toward industrial use.[9] With that number in mind, Texas has been the subject of inquiries and attempted regulation of energy use, production, and pollution, especially in Houston. State policies, however, have worked against the federal restrictions.

In 1999, the state senate passed a bill that was intended to lower the cost of electricity to consumers through deregulation. The bill removed what were deemed unnecessary taxes and regulatory costs at the state level and allowed the energy market to operate more freely. The intent of the bill was to lower the cost of energy to below the national average. Sixteen years later, the costs remain consistent with the national number. Another battle has been waged over pollution and revolves around a difference between two regulatory agencies: the EPA and its Texas counterpart, the Texas Commission on Environmental Quality (TCEQ), which is tasked with preserving the state's resources and health while also promoting economic development.[10]

Texas has demonstrated in the past that the economic development portion of the TCEQ is the driving factor in its activity. The TCEQ has routinely battled the EPA to limit the impact of federal restrictions, especially where energy production and pollution are concerned. The state regulatory board has consistently landed on the side of economics and businesses when it comes to these issues. Critics argue that the board is too economically driven and has shirked its responsibility when it comes to protecting the public. Governor Rick Perry and the board see it as a healthy balance struck through light regulation and economic responsibility.

While the TCEQ is responsible for regulating the energy industry, Texas has remained the nation's top polluter since 1991 (per the EPA) in the areas of hazardous waste and greenhouse gas emissions. With over one hundred refineries, Houston is home to the main culprits.[11] Texas is the leader in air pollution, another area of EPA focus. The TCEQ develops the state compliance plan, which all cities and corporations must follow, but the plan must be overseen by the EPA. As the federal agency, it has pushed for stricter standards that Texas, behind the lead of former Governor Rick Perry, has pushed against, claiming they would hurt economic development in the state.

In 2010, Texas Attorney General Greg Abbott and Governor Perry filed suit against the EPA's emission standards after the agency's "endangerment findings" laid the groundwork for the claim that carbon dioxide leads to an unhealthy living environment. With the Texas Oil and Gas Association by its side, Texas asserted that the findings were based on bad science and would harm economic development. The federal district court upheld the EPA's ability to pass

---

9   EIA.gov and EPA.gov.

10   Information on services and responsibilities can be found at http://www.tceq.state.tx.us/. Information on the challenge can be found here: http://www.tceq.state.tx.us/agency/ozone_proposal.html.

11   EPA.gov.

regulation. In 2012, the Fifth Circuit Court upheld Texas's appeal, finding that the EPA's seizing control of 167 of the state's largest facilities was a breach of responsibility.

One Texas policy that is not completely pro-business is its policy dealing with coal. While coal is the most economically advantageous source of energy, in 2011, Texas supported it energy needs with 38 percent natural gas, while 31 percent came from coal.[12] Natural gas is more abundant and cleaner than coal but has spurred a debate regarding fracking—the process of using water, chemicals, and other additives to break open the earth and extract natural gas. There has been a national push opposing the use of fracking, claiming it to be dangerous to the local water supply and the environment.

The General Land Office has worked to ensure the ability to use hydraulic fracturing to extract natural gas. With the backing of the Texas Oil and Gas Association, the state has passed legislation that allows fracking, with some level of regulation. The Texas Railroad Commission, which oversees the energy industry, regulates the activity, and requires corporations to disclose the materials used in the process. Still, the allowance of the measure has set off a firestorm of debate and prompted one city, Denton, to ban the activity within its authority. The ban was brought to the city council and voted down before organizers obtained two thousand signatures and passed the ban by popular referendum.

While natural gas has caused debates, Texas is a leader in wind energy production. West Texas is a hub for wind energy corporations, and the science, led by Texas Tech University, has sparked many advancements in the industry in Texas. Nuclear energy is another source Texas has encouraged and consumed. However, these two sources of energy pale in comparison to coal and natural gas, making up less than 10 percent of the state's output and usage (according to the US Census Bureau as of 2012).

Summary

Policy in Texas has transitioned over time. Throughout the state's history, the economically conservative nature of the state has dominated the formulation of policy. Guided by a specific model that promotes economic paths to attainment, the state has created and sustained an environment that cultivates economic success and, by extension, individual success. The influence of fiscal conservatives has had a significant impact on that process. While Texas has thrived economically, social policy has taken a curious turn as the state attempted to blend the two areas, and motives for social policy have skewed over time.

Education policy is currently the subject of a continuous economic battle that has seen discussions of low test scores and questionable performance accompanied by seemingly never-ending battles over funding and equity across the state. Energy and healthcare have taken

---

12   American Gas Association, AGA.org.

on a significant economic theme as well. As we look back on social and public policy, the battle between fiscal and social conservatives has taken center stage. Social conservatives have pushed for policy that places a higher importance on a perceived moral consciousness. Fiscal conservatives are pushing an agenda that seeks to keep economics as the driving factor in the state's policy decisions. As these battles develop, Texas's conservative party, which houses a majority of the state's decision makers, is undergoing a redefinition regarding the importance placed on policy and the types that are given the most attention.

As Texas moves forward, the question is: Which path will the state's policies take? Will policy continue to trend towards a more conservative social awareness, or will economics remain the state's catalyst for decision making? One thing seems certain: the state looks well placed on a path that produces policies consistent with the low taxes, low service ideal, which places the burden of responsibility on the individual rather than the government.

References

Associated Press. "Texas Won't Seek 'Race to the Top' Education Funding." *USA Today*, January 14, 2010.

Brewer, G. D., and P. DeLeon. *The Foundations of Policy Analysis*. Belmont, CA: Dorsey Press, 1983.

DeLeon, P. "The Stages Approach to the Policy Process: What Has It Done? Where Is It Going?" *Theories of the Policy Process* 1, no. 19 (1999): 19–32.

DeLeon, P., and L. DeLeon. (2002). "What Ever Happened to Policy Implementation? An Alternative Approach." *Journal of Public Administration Research and Theory* 12, no. 4 (2002): 467–492.

Edgewood ISD v. Kirby, 761 S.W. 2d 859.

Evans, C. E. *The Story of Texas Schools*. Austin, TX: Steck Company, 1955.

Grieder, E. "Big, Hot, Cheap, and Right: What America Can Learn from the Strange Genius of Texas." New York, NY; Perseus Books Group, 2014.

Jillson, C. *Lone Star Tarnished*. New York, NY: Taylor & Francis, 2014.

Ladino, R. D. *Desegregating Texas Schools: Eisenhower, Shivers, and the Crisis at Mansfield High*. Austin, TX: University of Texas Press, 2010.

Lagueux, M. "Popper and the Rationality Principle." *Philosophy of the Social Sciences* 23, no. 4 (1993): 468–480.

Lagueux, M. "The Forgotten Role of the Rationality Principle in Economics." *Journal of Economic Methodology* 11, no. 1 (2004): 31–51.

Nicks, Denver. "Wendy Davis on the Filibuster that Mattered Most to Her." *Time*, September 10, 2014.

Peters, B. G. *American Public Policy: Promise and Performance*. Washington, D.C.: CQ Press, 2015.

Plessy v. Ferguson, 163 U.S. 537 (1896).

Popper, K. R. "Towards a Rational Theory of Tradition." *The Rationalist Annual* 66 (1949): 36–55.

Popper, K. "The Rationality Principle." In *Popper Selections*, edited by D. Miller, 357–365. Princeton, NJ: Princeton University Press, 1985.

Potoski, M. "Clean Air Federalism: Do States Race to the Bottom?" *Public Administration Review* 61, no. 3 (2001): 335–342.

Prindle, D. F. *Petroleum Politics and the Texas Railroad Commission*. Austin, TX: University of Texas Press, 2011.

Rapoport, Abby. "Texas Eligibility Unclear, Federal Education Grant." *Texas Tribune*, November 12, 2009.

Roe v. Wade, 410 U.S. 113 (1973).

Satija, Neena. "Texas vs. the Feds: A Look at Lawsuits." *Texas Tribune*, July 31, 2015.

Walker, B. D., and J. D. Thompson. "Special Report: The Texas Supreme Court and Edgewood ISD v. Kirby." *Journal of Education Finance* 15, no. 3 (1990): 414–428.

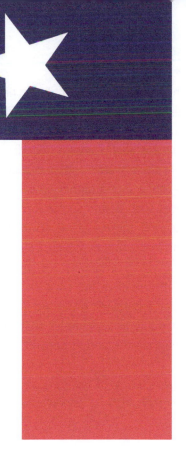

CHAPTER 9

Economics and the State of Texas

O ver time, Texas has become attached to its approach to policy. Dating back to the fiscally conservative early constitutions, Texas has cloaked itself in the idea that it is a powerful economic state. Following its fiscal success, the policy culture promotes individual attainment and is as attractive to corporations and businesses as any other state in the Union. Political officials in the state have developed this model around its individualistic fiscal approach, expanding on it in recent years with policy that emboldens the state's identity. Texas has pushed the boundaries with several interesting economic decisions.

This prevailing thought process has led several political scientists to study the state's activities and provide an in-depth explanation of Texas's economic approach. At the most basic level, the Texas model is centered on the idea that the government should work to be small and allow economics to drive attainment within the state. Putting the responsibility on the individual makes it easier for the legislature to cut services, which bears out in the "Texas Way" approach to healthcare, under which the state contributes a small amount of its own funds to services (such as Medicare) that it uses at a high rate. Contentious debate surrounds the state's application of its model, but it is consistently ranked as one of the nation's best states in terms of revenue, production, and savings, and where economic viability and attractiveness is concerned, the state is amongst the best. Corporations see the state as a friendly environment that will not only provide them an incentive to operate but will engage in policy debates and disputes in the name of preserving the favorable fiscal environment in which they seek to succeed.

While the business side continues to rise, there is another story to be told. Texas has worked to enhance the abilities of the private sector, but the budget and economy in Texas are not immune to crisis. For much of the past decade, the state legislature has been forced to make tough decisions regarding state spending on programs and services; with dwindling coffers, the state has struggled to support its needs and, in some cases, wants. Highly debated funding cuts have been made to education at the primary, secondary, and higher education levels as well as to social programs, including essential services such as transportation and subsidies to local governments. While corporations have done well and are attracted to the state, poverty in Texas remains above the national average, both in the rate by which it affects citizens and in income levels, according to census data.

Texas's economic model has created a culture that feeds into the idea that fiscal success in the private sector increases economic success for the public in general. As discussed in the chapter on the executive branch and alluded to in the social and public policy chapter, that can create interesting bedfellows and economic decisions that leave the state and its constituents debating the economic and budgetary approach.

In this chapter, I will discuss these debates and present the basic tenets of Texas's economic outlook by examining the primary tax approaches, the budgetary process, and where the money is spent as well as the effect on citizens.

Reading 9.1

Selection from "The Texas Model"[1]
from *Big, Hot, Cheap, and Right: What America Can Learn from the Strange Genius of Texas*
Erica Grieder

Reading Introduction: The Texas Way explained

Erica Grieder provides an outlook on Texas's view of economics. As the Texas Way prevails, Grieder examines the model and explains the state's basic points of view toward economic policy and its approach to fiscal responsibility.

Texas's republican leaders can describe their governing philosophy in three words ("the Texas model") or four if they need to explain what the Texas model is ("low taxes, low services"). In Perry's telling, the Texas miracle was proof of how well the Texas model works. During his brief presidential campaign, he offered a four-part "recipe" for economic stewardship as part of his stump speech: low taxes, low regulation, tort reform, and "don't spend all the money." That had worked in Texas, he said, and it could work for the whole country.

The idea is almost as simple as he described. The state's Republicans don't like taxes. Texas is one of the seven states that don't collect an individual income tax (the others are Alaska, Florida, Nevada, South Dakota, Wyoming, and Washington). It's also one of four that don't collect a corporate income tax; it has a gross receipts tax instead, meaning that most businesses pay a small tax on all of their sales, rather than only on their profits. About two-thirds of the state's general revenue funds come from the sales tax.

Texas's taxes are indeed low, albeit regressive. For FY 2009, the Tax Foundation put the Texas tax burden at $3,197 per capita (the thirty-ninth highest in the nation), compared to $4,160 in the United States as a whole and $4,910 in California (the sixth highest).[1] Texas's aversion to taxes is partly principled, partly structural (the state constitution severely limits state taxing authority), and partly pragmatic. The idea is to create a business-friendly climate. That's also why Texas isn't big on regulation or lawsuits.

This model mostly predates Perry. Texas never had high taxes. Technically speaking, he's even raised a few little taxes over the years.[2] His biggest move came in 2006 when he engineered a "swap" that lowered property tax rates—Texas has some of the highest property tax burdens in the country—with the intention of offsetting those declines via an increase on the cigarette tax and a new margins tax on most businesses. Those new revenue streams haven't made up for the decline in property-tax receipts, though; Republicans describe the swap as a net tax decrease, and Democrats call it a structural deficit.

Similarly, the governor inherited the state's minimal regulatory framework. His administration has resisted new federal regulations, in some cases by offering new state regulations as an alternative. Perry also signed a major tort reform bill in 2003 and a follow-up "loser pays" reform in 2011.[3] The connection between tort reform and job creation is empirically dubious, but these reforms may have served as what economists call a "signaling device"—a sign that the state was serious about its commitment to conservative principles. The reforms certainly sent some signals to the Texans for Lawsuit Reform, one of the state's most powerful lobbies.

As far as being business friendly, Texas has succeeded. The Tax Foundation rates it as the nation's ninth best climate for business. Notably, the state gets top-ten billing even as the Tax Foundation also dings Texas for high corporate taxes; though the state's gross receipts tax has plenty of exemptions and loopholes, it still yields the thirty-seventh highest business tax burden in the country. The reason the state's business climate is regarded so highly might have more to do with the lack of a personal income tax, which millionaires like just as much as anyone else does, and the lackadaisical regulatory climate.

As far as taxes and spending go, Texas practice what it preaches, for the most part. Outsiders sometimes assume the state must be hypocritical, that its leaders rail on about taxes and spending while begging for federal money—which is true of many red states, including most of the American South. "Among states that voted Republican in the last three elections, all but one gets more money back from the federal government than it pays in taxes," noted Jonathan Cohn, a progressive journalist, on the eve of the 2012 elections. "For most Democratic states, it's the opposite."[4] So when Perry accepted stimulus funds after railing against the stimulus for months, the schadenfreudists did some smirking.

But as Cohn mentioned, there is one red state that gives more to the federal government than it takes. From 1990 to 2009, according to a 2011 analysis from *The Economist*, Texas was among the twenty states that paid more in federal taxes than they received in federal funds.[5] Many of the state's recent battles with the federal government have been in defense of its right to run a tight-fisted ship. The stimulus package, for example, involved supplemental money for the states' unemployment insurance funds. Texas took some of that money, but only the funds that came without federal strings attached. Taking all of the money on offer would have required the state to change its eligibility standards for unemployment funds. When the federal money dried up, after a few years at most, Texas would be on the hook for more spending—indefinitely. For Texas's Republican leadership, that wasn't an acceptable trade, especially given that Texas still had some money in its unemployment fund. (In South Carolina, by contrast, Governor Mark Sanford had joined Perry in threatening to turn down some of unemployment funds but soon backed down because the state fund was running dry.)

People can agree or disagree with the Texas Republicans on that position, but it wasn't an incoherent argument. Perry later argued—logically enough—that it was fair for Texas to accept some of the other stimulus funds. Texas didn't want the stimulus, he explained, but if it was happening anyway, Texas taxpayers might as well get their share of it.

If we're trying to figure out whether Texas is sincere in its commitment to limited spending, we can look at earmarks as another proxy. Of course, federal pork reflects a lot of things other than state policy—the specific composition of a state's congressional delegation, perhaps, or unusual infrastructure needs. There are blue states that don't get many earmarks (New York and Illinois) and red states that do (Alaska, North Dakota, Utah). With that said, an analysis by the *Congressional Quarterly* found that Texas had the ninth-lowest rate of earmarks per capita in the country in FY 2010: $17.03, compared to, say, $64.37 in New Hampshire, where it seems they live free or die on other people's dime.[6]

Texas has been assiduous in seeking federal contracts, but that's not quite the same thing as seeking federal support. The state has, for example, been the beneficiary of significant increases in military spending. Since 2005, when the military had its most recent round of Base Realignment and Closure, the federal presence at Fort Hood (just outside the town of Killeen), Fort Bliss (El Paso), and Fort Sam Houston (San Antonio) has ballooned. But the army isn't the Works Progress Administration. The Center for the Intrepid—a new rehab facility for veterans returning from combat, at Fort Sam—isn't just there for show. And the Department of Defense isn't expanding its presence in Texas in some kind of misguided effort at redistribution; it's picking the sites that make sense. One of the reasons for the expansion at Fort Bliss, for example, is that the post offers access to miles and miles of training and testing space at the White Sands Missile Range, just across the border in New Mexico.

The state also picks winners and losers through more conventional economic development tools. In 2001, a new law authorized property-tax credits for companies that created facilities for manufacturing, R&D, clean coal, renewables, and so on, as long as they were willing to locate in certain parts of the state and expected to create a certain number of jobs.[7] In 2010, the Comptroller's Office reported that the state had awarded $733 million to sixty-four renewable projects since that time, most of them related to wind power, yielding a grand total of 487 jobs—a cool $1.5 million per job.[8]

At the same time, the goal of the law wasn't strictly to create jobs; it was to goose certain industries. In that respect the credits were more successful. Texas now leads the nation in wind power production. Even the governor's funds have got some things right. In 2009, Texas A&M University received a $50 million award from the TETF to build the National Center for Therapeutics Manufacturing. The award looked like an instance of overt cronyism. "Unfortunately, the infusion of taxpayer money is showing some disturbing symptoms that have been found in other state economic development deals," wrote Loren Steffy, the business columnist for the *Houston Chronicle*, describing a tangle of connections between A&M and the governor's office. The university's new associate chancellor for economic development had just come over from the governor's office, where he had served as the TETF's director; in 2008, A&M had announced a partnership with Introgen Therapeutics, whose founder was on the finance committee for Perry's reelection campaign.[9] Even apart from that—Texans can be oddly sanguine about cronyism—the grant seemed overly optimistic. A&M was well positioned to expand its research in life sciences. The university's expertise is in subjects such as agriculture and engineering. But it had already stumbled several times in its attempts to become a vaccine hub. Three months after A&M announced the partnership with Introgen, for example, the company filed for bankruptcy.

In 2012, though, the federal Department of Health and Human Services announced that A&M was one of three sites around the country to become a new national biodefense center (the other two sites would be led by companies: Emergent Manufacturing Operations in Maryland and Novartis in North Carolina).[10] The federal grants to Texas would add up to $285 million, $176 million over the first five years; the state's expected contribution was estimated at $40 million. The first part of the Texas center opened in July 2012. The university's chancellor, John Sharp, explained that part of the reason A&M won the contract was because it had already built some of the relevant facilities—sterile pods and so on—using the money from the 2009 grant.[11]

Such direct supports can be controversial, even among the beneficiaries. "We're not really big believers in huge subsidies," said one executive at a solar company in Austin; it had received a property-tax abatement from the city of Austin and a grant from the governor's slush fund, but neither sweetener, she argued, was big enough to keep the company going if its products weren't selling.[12] The subsidies and incentives might not be strictly necessary either. Texas's greatest competitive advantage, in the end, might be that it's come closer than most states to mitigating policy uncertainty. You don't have to wonder what's going to happen in Texas next year or ten years from now or, probably, a hundred years from now: what's good for business is what's going to happen. In the end, that's the gift Texas gives business executives once the direct handouts run dry.

Once the Texas miracle started, it proved to be somewhat self-fueling. People looking for jobs moved to Texas in droves. Over the years, the rate of population growth actually exceeded the rate of job growth, causing Texas's unemployment rate to rise and further muddle Rick Perry's figures. Even so, by being here, these newly minted Texans saved the state a lot of trouble. Once there, their presence helped to create even more jobs—in restaurants, in retail, in the schools, and so on.

On balance, some of the critiques of the Texas Miracle were salient, but none were sufficient to explain it away entirely. Some factors in the miracle were put in place when Perry was still a Democrat. Others demonstrably had nothing to do with him. Oil and gas are still major drivers of the state economy, but Texas has diversified from its oil, land, and cattle traditions. These days, its riches also come from technology, renewable energy, and defense and from manufacturing, trade, and transportation, with the latter having been transformed since the North American Free Trade Agreement (NAFTA) was passed in 1994. In 2011, Texas's exports totaled $251 billion—17 percent of America's total and up 21.3 percent from the year before.[13] So when one industry takes a hit—as manufacturing did during the recession or as agriculture is during the current drought—Texas is well hedged.

As for whether the Texas model is safe for export, Krugman was correct when he observed that some of the factors that helped Texas through the recession can't be simply extrapolated to other states or scaled to the nation as a whole. Even if the Texas model could be exported, other states might not want it. Texans have gotten used to having a limited government; the state constitution, which was written in 1876, effectively guarantees that. The people of this state are accustomed to the virtues and the flaws of this approach (which are, of course, two sides of the same coin): the model means that Texas is open to aspirational upstarts, in business and in politics, but sometimes the people who seize the opportunities in either sphere are cranks, crooks, or cronies. People in other states might prefer a more predictable system, even if the result is more static.

The most effective critique of the Texas model is just that jobs aren't everything. It may be that keeping taxes low and regulations scarce and services minimal is a good way to attract business. It nonetheless has consequences, because it means the state inevitably has less money for health care and education and infrastructure than some of its peers. All told, Texas spends less per capita than all but two other states (Nevada and Florida)—$3,703 per fiscal year in 2010. The national average then was $5,251, which was just about where California came in.[14]

And Texas does lag behind the nation as a whole in many respects. It famously ranks poorly on a lot of indicators of social welfare: one of the worst poverty rates, one of the worst high school dropout rates, dead last for the percentage of people with health insurance.

For Democrats, this is no coincidence—it's proof that low taxes can have a high cost. Republicans, however, maintain that the abstemious approach is the best one. A bigger safety net would require more spending, which would require more taxing, which they're against. When it comes to helping people in the most dire straits— feeding the poor or housing the homeless—their suggestion is that other actors, such as churches, charities, or community groups, should pick up the slack. While Texas Republicans do agree with Democrats that the state needs better schools, they're often skeptical about whether money is the answer, especially because Texas's public schools aren't actually that bad. If you control for demographics, they sometimes look quite good.

One thing's for certain, though: the Texas model isn't going to change in the short term. Indeed, there are some serious structural barriers to change. The state constitution calls for an extremely limited government, one of the most limited in the country. Texas Democrats would like to see some changes, but they are so far out of power that sometimes they seem like the state's third party, after the Republicans and the Tea Party.

Perhaps more to the point, even Texas Democrats don't want to change the model altogether. Compared to their national counterparts, they're in favor of business and skeptical of taxes. If transplanted to California, a typical Texas Democrat would be reclassified as a moderate Republican.

NOTES

1 Scott Drenkard, ed., "Facts and Figures Handbook: How Does Your State Compare?," Tax Foundation, February 15, 2012, http://taxfoundation.org/article/facts-figures-handbook-how-does-your-state-compare-0.

2 Meghan Ashford-Grooms, "Gov. Rick Perry Says He Has a Track Record of Not Raising Taxes," PolitiFact Texas, November 1, 2010, http://www.politifact.com/texas/statements/2010/nov/01/rick-perry/gov-rick-perry-says-he-has-track-record-not-raisin/.

3 "Sorry, Losers," *The Economist*, May 19, 2011, http://www.economist.com/node/18712311.

4 Jonathan Cohn, "Blue States Are from Scandinavia, Red States Are from Guatemala," *New Republic*, October 5, 2012, http://www.tnr.com/article/politics/magazine/108185/blue-states-are-scandinavia-red-states-are-guatemala.

5 "Greek Americans," *The Economist*, July 30, 2011, http://www.economist.com/node/21524887.

6 "Federal Appropriations Earmarks by State," CQ.com, http://innovation.cq.com/media/earmarks2010/.

7 "What's It Worth to You?," Economist.com, September 16, 2011, http://www.economist.com/blogs/freeexchange/2011/09/job-creation.

8 "An Analysis of Texas Economic Development Incentives 2010," Texas Comptroller of Public Accounts, December 22, 2010, http://www.texasahead.org/reports/incentives/cost.php.

9 Loren Steffy, "Politics Infect A&M Research," *Houston Chronicle*, August 1, 2009, http://www.chron.com/business/steffy/article/Politics-infect-A-M-research-1735057.php.

10 "Building Up the Arsenal," *The Economist*, June 30, 2012, http://www.economist.com/node/21557773.

11 Author interview.

12 http://www.economist.com/blogs/freeexchange/2011/10/great-green-jobs-hope.

13 http://www.census.gov/foreign-trade/statistics/state/data/tx.html.

14 http://www.statehealthfacts.org/comparemaptable.jsp?ind=32&cat=1.

Monetary Versus Fiscal Policy

There are two types of policies that guide most discussion when it comes to the budget: monetary and fiscal. These policies are macroeconomic in that the decisions and policies are designed to achieve some type of economic stabilization. Fiscal policy deals with the revenue of a state or government. Monetary policy deals with regulation and how spending is monitored.

This latter type of policy is not a huge driver of economic policy in Texas. The goal of monetary policy is to attempt to stabilize the economy through regulation and oversight. This is achieved in four direct ways: 1) protecting the citizen from unnecessary harms caused by activities of the economic system; 2) ensuring fairness in the economic market by not allowing inequitable advantages or policies and practices that favor one entity over another; 3) monitoring the safety of the economic industry by ensuring controlled working environments and best practices; and 4) ensuring the stability of the economic system by not allowing it to place unnecessary pressures on or cause harm to citizens.

Handled with a hybrid approach by the federal and state governments, monitoring the flow of money and regulating business is not something Texas legislators are eager to participate in or support. Economic regulation is frowned upon in the halls of the Texas legislature. It is seen as a threat to economic success and, therefore, the model outlined at the beginning of the chapter, as many federal regulations and state mandates are enforced through taxes and penalties; an overreach here would violate the state's model, the Texas Way approach.

Still, there is a need for agencies to ensure basic quality of life, safety, and fairness. Much of this regulation is enforced by Texas agencies but is passed and overseen at the federal level. The struggle between the EPA and TCEQ, discussed in the previous chapter, is often a component of monetary policy. Enforcing safety standards and policies set forth by OSHA or the Food and Drug Administration is also a form of monetary policy.

Fiscal policy encompasses any policy that is meant to generate revenue or require expenditure. In short, these types of policy govern what revenue Texas will accrue and how those funds will be spent. Taxes are the main source of revenue under fiscal policy. As a highly conservative state, Texas continues to argue (at both the public and legislative levels) about the tax code; this debate focuses on attempts to define how the state should generate revenue. Unsurprisingly, the topic of a state income tax has been taboo for much of Texas's existence. This type of tax is a major source of revenue for both for the nations' richer states and the federal government, but Texas has shied away from employing such a measure. Even though the tax would generate a significant amount of revenue for the state, Texas has taken a hard-line stance on refusing to implement it, as it would fracture its economic approach.

Income Tax in Texas

Resistance to a state income tax is one of the defining characteristics of Texas. Long looked at as a bastion for businesses, the state has actively tried to make itself an appealing candidate for emerging businesses looking for a home. Much of the state's success in attracting new business has been attributed to its ability to posture itself as a viable, attractive option, in large part due to its lack of a state income tax.

Three main types of income tax currently exist. A flat tax is descriptive in nature; it equalizes the rate of taxes paid, regardless of income or earning potential. Advocates of the flat tax cite equity and fairness as their main points of support. Its supporters say the approach would eliminate any sense of economic targeting, either toward the wealthy or the impoverished. Detractors of the approach contend that a flat tax would be ineffective and unfair to those on the lower side of the wage scale, as their share of the burden would outstretch their means, while the wealthy would benefit from increased surplus. No state in the nation employs a flat tax.

The more common approaches fall between a progressive and regressive tax structure. A progressive tax structure seeks to obtain more of its revenue from the wealthy; the tax rate is increased as you move up the wage scale. In this system, the wealthy carry the burden, as they are taxed more than those on the lower end of the wage scale. The idea behind this is to place the largest burden for funding activities on those who make the most money while leaving people with less money a higher percentage of their wages to spend. Detractors of this method argue that it restricts economic growth by limiting the amount of economic stimulus from those who achieve and places an unfair burden on the high-wage class to carry the load for services they may never use.

A regressive tax does the opposite. Instead of placing the tax burden on higher earners, those on the lower end of the wage scale would carry the burden. Taxes are geared toward increasing the contribution of persons who make less to ensure they pay into the system while giving higher earners greater flexibility to stimulate the economy.

Regressive taxes rarely come directly from income taxes. Texas is considered to have one of the most regressive tax structures in the nation despite the absence of an income tax. Much of that revenue is replaced by property taxes and sales taxes on goods. Property tax contributions and sales taxes on products and production are regressive taxes. In a 2013 study by the Institute on Taxation and Economic Policy, Texas was found to be the fifth most regressive state in regard to its revenue source. The study found that those in the state's lowest percentile pay 12.6 percent of the tax burden, while those in the highest five percent carry eight percent of it.

Despite budget shortfalls and past attempts, Texas has rarely come close to implementing an income tax. The most recent serious attempt came after a lengthy debate in 1993, when Texas was looking for new ways to generate revenue to solve a mounting budget crisis. A committee chaired by former governor John Connelly recommended a corporate and personal income tax. After passing a legislative vote, the bill was sent in November as a referendum to the voters, who quickly voted against the policy. In light of that vote and the advancement of Texas's economic culture over the past twenty years, it is unlikely that Texas voters or their representatives would attempt to pass or even seriously consider implementing a state income tax, regardless of the state's budget situation.

Current Texas Taxes

While the idea of an income tax is a pipe dream in Texas (one of only seven states that doesn't employ the measure), the state has come up with a number of ways for the public to fund the government. Texas still generates much of its revenue from taxes, both on individuals and corporations, but Texas still sticks by its low taxes, low services mantra. Texans pay roughly $1,000 less in state taxes than the national average, and the state ranks forty-sixth in per capita tax rate.[2] There are ways to make up for those lost revenues, however. While being income and business friendly, Texans still foot their share of the bill through alternative taxes. Tax collection in the state increased by nearly eight percent from the 2013 budget to the one passed in 2015.[3]

At 6.25 percent, Texas's sales tax, which can be added to by local governments, is the twelfth highest in the nation.[4] Sales taxes can be assessed on any nonessential good purchased. The tax can be assessed on cars, property, nonessential foods, and several other items. It is the major source of revenue in Texas, accounting for 55 percent of the most recent budget passed in early 2015.[5] The larger the sale, the larger the tax. Texas takes advantage of this and applies the same 6.25 percent tax[6] on the sale of motor vehicles. This high-volume industry is a good source of revenue, but between 2010 to 2012, economic slowdowns and rising gas prices caused a decline in the revenue generated from this tax. It has since rebounded and accounted for $8.8 billion in the most recent budget (Grieder, 2013). Along with sales of new motor vehicles, taxes are also assessed on rentals, and the first 65 percent of a manufactured home is taxed at a rate of five percent. The tax on motor fuels has produced a boom for the Department of Transportation and Public Safety. Taxes on gas and fuel (currently $0.15 per gallon sold) were estimated to have raised over $6 billion in 2014–2015.[7]

---

2   Tax Foundation. "State General Sales Tax Collections Per Capita, Fiscal Years 2007–2011." http://taxfoundation.org/article/state-general-sales-tax-collections-capita-fiscal-years-2007–2011.

3   Legislative Budget Board of Texas, http://www.lbb.state.tx.us/.

4   Tax Foundation. "State and Local Sales Tax." http://taxfoundation.org/article/state-and-local-sales-tax-rates-2015.

5   Office of the Texas Comptroller, http://comptroller.texas.gov/comptrol/fnotes/numbers.php.

6   All tax rates can be found at the website for the Texas comptroller: http://comptroller.texas.gov/taxinfo/taxrates.html.

7   Office of the Texas Comptroller. "Transperancy." http://www.texastransparency.org/State_Finance/Budget_Finance/Reports/Revenue_by_Source/.

Property taxes are based on the appraisal value of an individual's home or the property, which includes rentals. Over the past decade, property taxes have become a source of great debate in the state. Texans carry the fifth-highest property tax burden of any state in the nation, paying roughly $3,300 on average, which is $1,200 more than the national average.[8]

Texas property taxes are used in large part to fund education and local government services. As such, the driving force in the education debate is the concept that school districts with the highest property taxes have better schools. The issue has sparked court cases over whether the education funding model is inequitable due to the discrepancies in funds allocated. This has led to a dispute over state policy and funding, which I will cover fully later in this chapter.

The debate over property taxes and the ways they are used guided the election for state comptroller in November of 2015. Challenger Glenn Hegar, a Republican, campaigned on the premise of eliminating the property tax altogether. Hegar felt, as a large segment of Republicans do, that the practical effect of property taxes is that individuals do not truly own their homes. Democratic nominee Mike Collier responded to Hegar, stating that in the absence of a property tax, the state would be left with only the sales tax as its major source of revenue and would have to hike that to nearly 20 percent in order to compensate for the shortfall.

Sin taxes are prevalent in Texas. The concept of a sin tax revolves around the theory of taxing something that is deemed bad for your health and using the revenue for other services. In theory, the taxes can serve as a deterrent, but in reality, higher taxes on products such as cigarettes and alcohol have failed to curb consumption. In 2006, tax reform on tobacco levied an average of $1.59 per pack, depending on size and weight. The reform was designed to provide property tax relief and to contribute to a loan repayment fund for physical education. Alcohol taxes are used in a similar way, and taxes on the two contributed $4.9 billion to the 2014–2015 budget.

Currently, the legislature and people in Texas are contemplating the possibility of legalizing gambling in order to increase state revenue. Texas is a close neighbor to Louisiana (a prime gambling state), and citizens from east and southeast Texas routinely cross the state line to exercise their right to gamble. The same is true in other parts of Texas that border pro-gambling states: the northern section, which borders Oklahoma, and the western region, next to New Mexico.

The argument for gambling in Texas is that a taxed and controlled system would bring a potential revenue windfall and possibly eliminate some illegal activity—mainly, illegal card and casino rooms operated by citizens. A bill was introduced in 2015 to move forward with legalizing gambling, but it was unsuccessful.

While Texas is staunchly conservative, the prospect of greater sin tax revenue could lead the state to consider following in the footsteps of Colorado: since the Rocky Mountain state legalized and subsidized the sale of marijuana two years ago, it has seen an influx of revenue

8   Lincoln Institute of Land Policy, http://www.lincolninst.edu/subcenters/significant-features-property-tax/upload/sources/ContentPages/documents/Pay_2013_PT_Report_National_FINAL.pdf.

(which hit the $91 million mark in 2014) and has allocated the money to fund substance abuse and education in the state.[9]

Businesses do not escape the tax burden in Texas. While Texas is a pro-business state and its legislators have worked to curb individual taxes to make it more attractive, it has not shied away from taxing corporations and production. Texas's economy has seen a rise in revenue in the oil and natural gas industries. As discussed in the previous chapter, Texas has battled to open paths that increase the development of natural gas and the production of oil. The state's benefit in those fights comes in the way of a tax on production. With oil and gas production up over 50 percent in the past four years (in large part due to the use of fracking and horizontal drilling as well as other pro-business measures), Texas has seen a significant increase in tax revenue. The state's latest budget will get a $6.5 billion contribution from the tax.

Texas taxes each barrel of oil produced in the state at 4.6 percent to go along with a 13/16-cent tax. Natural gas production is taxed as well. Texas places a 7.5 percent tax on the production of natural gas in the state. As previously discussed, Texas has seen an increase in this area in the past five years. Revenue from natural gas is estimated to produce nearly $3 billion in the current budget year.

In addition to taxes on oil and natural gas, businesses are required to pay a franchise tax. Along with the tobacco tax, the franchise tax was geared to alleviate the property tax burden in the state. The tax was passed in 2008 and is designed to levy the rate on taxable capital and surplus, making it a margin tax. The tax is determined in one of four ways: 1) total revenue minus $1 million, 2) total revenue minus costs of goods sold, 3) 70 percent of a business's total revenue, or 4) total revenue minus total compensation and benefits. Reform legislation was introduced in 2013 to deter businesses from dodging the tax. Most businesses pay 1 percent on their taxable margin but could pay less, depending on if the business is a wholesale or retail corporation. The 2013 reform was designed to eliminate escaping the tax to aid the Property Tax Relief Fund.

These are the major taxes that exist in the state today. Taxes such as insurance occupation, hotel and motel taxes, and others make up the remainder of the taxes levied at the state level. While Texas is a low-tax state, the $98 billion raised from taxes makes up 47 percent of the total 2014–2015 budget. The remainder of the budget is funded through other sources, including interest revenue, the lottery, land use, fees and fines, and federal subsidies.

One major pot of money is the lottery, which was created as a way to exploit the sin tax model. Texas, a state that has resisted gambling and game playing, introduced the lottery in 1991 to a mixed reception. Texans passed this form of gaming by an overwhelming majority, but the moralistic view of exploiting gambling for positive gains was met with a level of disdain. Texas does not currently allow onshore gambling in the state, but the lottery was passed as an acceptable way to boost the state's revenue. The connection to gambling was met with dissension from the social conservatives in the state as well as those who feel that,

9   State of Colorado, https://www.colorado.gov/pacific/revenue/colorado-marijuana-tax-data.

with its high tax and low odds, the game takes advantage of people. Still, the benefits remain: Texas generated $2 billion from the lottery tax—funds that went into the Foundation School Account—in 2014 and 2015.

Matching funds from the federal government are also a large source of revenue, making up 35 percent of the state's budget.[10] With the expansion of services—from transportation to law enforcement to healthcare—since the late 1970s, Texas has seen a rise in funds from the federal government. The level of funds fluctuates because they are matching funds, meaning the federal government will match whatever the state budgets for a service. This method is intended to encourage states to contribute more of their money to specific areas, but it can lead to the coercive federalism issues discussed in Chapter 3. Even though Texas has a checkered past with regard to matching funds, it received $36 billion from the practice in 2014–2015.[11]

Recently, Texas has shown a willingness to avoid increasing services in order to obtain more funds. Education funds from the Obama administration focused on federally mandated school reform were met with disapproval by Governor Rick Perry in 2010. Medicaid, the program that provides basic healthcare to the elderly and impoverished, is the largest program source of matching funds in the state in the most recent budget.

State Funds and Spending

Taxes make up half of the state's budget. However, a significant portion of the state's account is filled through outside entities. The most common of these are funds. The state treasury is currently operating over four hundred funds that devote money to different areas of state government. Funds are used in a general sense or have specific earmarks and creation structures in specific areas, including education supplements, allocations to retirement funds, transportation, and more.

The state's General Revenue Fund (GRF) serves as its primary operating fund. There are two parts to the GRF: the dedicated and nondedicated. The nondedicated side is where the state's general funds flow. Fees, taxes, and regulation are funneled through the nondedicated avenue and have little restrictions on use. Dedicated funds are earmarked for specific use and have specific sources.

The Economic Stabilization Fund (ESF), or the rainy-day fund, is likely the most talked-about and debated fund that Texas operates. It is the largest of its kind in the nation, and Texas has used this pot of money over the years to bail the state out of tough situations or emergencies, as decided by a two-thirds vote by both chambers in the legislature. The fund was developed

10   Office of the Texas Comptroller, http://comptroller.texas.gov/.

11   Office of the Texas Comptroller, "Transperancy." http://www.texastransparency.org/State_Finance/Budget_Finance/Reports/Revenue_by_Source/.

in 1988 as an avenue for addressing budget shortfalls and to provide the state with a safety net. Any unused revenue is automatically moved into the ESF, along with any allotment the legislature agrees to by two-thirds vote. The major source of funds comes from the ESF's accrual of 75 percent of all tax revenue that exceeds oil and gas taxes that were collected in the 1987 budget year. As the price of oil and gas have skyrocketed, so has the amount of taxes collected, and the ESF has grown exponentially. The original allotment was $18.5 million in 1990. That number grew to $700 million in 2003 before it was used to cure a $10 billion budget shortfall. The most recent ESF estimation has that number at $9.3 billion.[12]

Over the years, the ESF has been accessed to cure budget ills in several areas. In 2005, the Texas Retirement System, Texas Education Agency, and transportation projects were helped along by the ESF. In 2011 and 2013, funds were used to cure a budget shortfall. With transportation and education projects booming as the state grows in population, the state will call on the ESF again in 2015 to aid in keeping the state from going over budget.

While the ESF is the most notable fund in Texas, others operate at a high level as well. The Permanent School Fund (PSF) and Available School Fund (ASF) provide funds for primary and secondary education in the state.[13] The PSF, which started in 1854, was at $20 billion in 2009 and rose to $29 billion by 2013. It is accrued by accounting for the average in the market value of the fund in the previous sixteen fiscal quarters as well as setting distribution rates to ensure that it does not jeopardize future allotments, making the fund forward-thinking and attempting to ensure that it will not be empty for future generations. It is distributed based on attendance and insures local school bonds to make them active in the bond market themselves. The ASF is a fund that is meant to meet the constitutional mandate to provide education. It is funded in part by distributions from the PSF and in part by accruing 25 percent of the state's motor fuel tax.

Together, these funds address the state's education needs as seen by the Texas Board of Education, which administers them. Funds are used to increase equity among school districts and to ensure that instructional materials are provided when necessary. Currently, the funds combined total $3.25 billion, making them the largest of their kind in the nation.

Public higher education is heavily funded in Texas. Through two major pots of money, the Permanent University Fund (PUF) and Higher Education Fund (HEF), the state funds institutions that carry out its education mandate. A majority of funds go to two specific school systems: the University of Texas system and the Texas A&M system. These systems are the major source of public higher education in Texas; because of their size, they receive most of the money available for higher education. Including medical schools, there are fourteen schools in the UT system and eleven in the A&M system.

---

12   Pew Research Center, http://www.pewtrusts.org/en/research-and-analysis/analysis/2016/01/19/why-states-save -a-look-at-texas.

13   Texas Education Agency, "Texas Permanent School Fund." http://tea.texas.gov/psf/.

Those funds come predominantly out of the PUF. The money in this fund comes from earned income on land the state owns in west Texas. Beginning with one million acres, the state now owns 2.1 million acres, and it has used the Land Grant Fund program to lease the lands out for public and private use, devoting those funds to the PUF. Lease funds, combined with mineral income, have pushed the fund's coffers to the north of $14 billion today. UT currently receives two-thirds of those funds, with A&M receiving the remaining one-third per a 1999 amendment to the state constitution.

The two school systems are the state's higher-education flagships, and funding disputes have led to conflicts with smaller public schools and school systems. In 2015, the UT system announced plans to expand to the Houston area, with intentions of building a campus in west Houston. The University of Houston, a school that has built a smaller school system and worked to earn tier-one status as a research institution for its main campus, has since cried foul, arguing that UT, a state institution that already gets the dominant amount of funds from the state, was horning in on their student base.

Schools such as UH pull from the HEF. These funds are available for any public institution of higher education (such as UH and Texas Tech University) in the absence of PUF funds. The Texas Higher Education Coordinating Board makes recommendations to the legislature regarding allocations and how the funds should be used. Funded through the state's general fund, the HEF is a fraction of the PUF (which the UT and A&M systems pull from) and gets $525 million in the current budget.

The Budget Process

Funds and taxes make up the state's revenue, but many of the decisions about the way it is used are left to the Texas legislature. Although much of the budget is mandated through federal programs (whose standards do not fall under discretionary review), every two years, the state's representatives and senators battle over where the money should go. With influence from the public, private corporations and interests, and political agents, the legislature is tasked with creating a budget that works for the state. The budget runs for the entire two-year cycle that the state legislature is not in session. One key issue is that the budget, as a piece of legislation, is subject to the same 140-day cycle as all other legislation. That means that the state's financial plan must be created and adopted within that time period, making budget discussions and decisions a priority for the legislative body.

Three state provisions provide guidance for the budget process. By constitutional amendment, Texas is a "pay as you go" state: Article III mandates that the state must operate a balanced budget. Debts are not allowed and, working with the comptroller, the legislature is mandated to provide and pass a budget that does not put the state in financial peril. If the budget is not balanced, the state must act to do so before it can be implemented. That can be done in one of two ways: cutbacks or moving funds from one pot of money to another. Cutbacks are an unpopular method of balancing the budget. Withdrawing money from one expenditure or program and giving it to another can create a significant political problem. The state can also use the ESF, or rainy-day fund (as it did in 2013 to fix a $2.6 billion deficit), to avoid any violations.

Texas also has constitutional spending limits. Per Article III, Texas is not allowed to spend more than 1 percent of its budget on welfare programs. The constitution provides state funds for services to dependent children and individuals, but the hard spending limit of 1 percent caps how much the state can contribute, which has a significant effect on the matching funds it receives. One caveat is that Medicaid spending is not calculated into this limit. There is also a 5 percent limit on debt payable on the budget. If debt paid or owed by the state is greater than 5 percent on average for three budget cycles, the state cannot incur more than 5 percent in the fourth cycle.

Article VIII provides that any increase in state expenditures that are not mandated by the federal government or state constitution cannot exceed the growth rate of the economy. This is another attempt to keep the state fiscally responsible, as it is designed to ensure that, if the economy recedes, spending on programs will recede as well. The Legislative Budget Board (LBB) provides these fiscal recommendations and is tasked with forecasting the rise and fall of the economy and keeping the budget in line.

The LBB is made up of seven legislators: the speaker of the house and the lieutenant governor (who co-chair the board) plus two representatives and three senators, including the chairs of the House Ways and Means and the Senate Finance committee. This board leads the process by working with the governor, comptroller, and agencies—which they also provide performance reports on and finalizes strategic plans for—to create a budget. By law, it is not allowed to submit a budget to the legislature until it has met the spending limits provision in Article VIII.

The LBB's role in the budget process is significant. It not only develops the budget but also has execution authority when the legislature is not in session. If there is a case where an agency must stop spending, money must be transferred, or the purpose of appropriations change, the LBB can act without the legislature being in session. Working with the LBB, the Governor's Office of Budget, Planning, and Policy attempts to develop a strategic plan for the state. In the absence of a true budget submitted by the governor, the best the official can do is provide a budget outline as well as use message power that spawns potential budget allocations.

The governor can submit a budget; this must be done in the first week. While current governor Greg Abbott has chosen to submit a budget, a more common use of budget power is through the State of the State address, with reminders of policy and agency importance and subtle notices that the office still holds the final say on the end product. The comptroller provides estimates for anticipated revenue and attempts to provide the governor and the LBB with the projected funds they will be able to allocate. The product of this collaboration is a budget that is sent to the legislature for consideration and due within the first week of the session.

The second step is introducing the budget into session, thus entering it into the legislative process. It is then moved to the House Appropriations Committee (HAC) and Senate Finance Committee (SFC) for concurrent review. These committees, which are made up of twenty-seven representatives and fifteen senators (appointed by their respective chamber heads), respectively evaluate the budget and potential appropriations for the budget process. The HAC was most recently chaired by John Otto (R-Dayton), with Houston's new mayor, Sylvester Turner (D-Houston), serving as vice chair. The members of the committee are routinely asked to strengthen ties between the budget committee and other standing committees. The committee breaks into five subcommittees (education, health and human services, criminal justice, economic development, and current fiscal conditions) to focus on and evaluate allocations in these areas. The SFC was led by Jane Nelson (R-Flower Mound) and vice chaired by Juan Hinojosa (D-McAllen). Instead of breaking into subcommittees, most of the work was done with the fifteen members in attendance while breaking into four "working groups" dealing with hearings, markup, floor debate, and conference committee deliberation.

These four areas are very similar to those that deal with the legislative process (as discussed in the chapter on the legislature). The hearing work is designed to elicit expert opinion and deliberation within the committee or subcommittees. While there is no bill writing *per se* to accomplish in the markup stage, the budget is examined and defended as it is polished for a full debate in the committee under the watchful eyes of the chamber leaders who served on the LBB, which wrote the draft.

Once the budget passes out of the committee stage, it is introduced for floor debate. This stage follows the same rules as open policy debate in both chambers. In both chambers, the budget has priority in the calendar process and is placed high on the agenda. While amendments are allowed, there is a limit to their impact; they cannot alter the "bottom line" in a way that causes the budget to violate the mandates in Article III of the state constitution. This means that an amendment to add a program or money to the budget must be accompanied with one to cut corresponding funds from other allocations. The budget must pass by majority vote in the House of Representatives but needs the approval of the lieutenant governor and a two-thirds vote of the Senate to move on from the chamber floor. Considering that half of the Senate sits on the SFC, most of the changes have been ironed out in committee, and there is little change during the floor debate process.

After floor debate, the amendments to the budget that was submitted by the LBB must be addressed. As with all policy that has objections between the chambers, the budget reaches the conference committee stage. Appointed by the chamber leadership, ten members of the legislature (five from each chamber) are selected to contemplate and deliberate on the changes made. The ten-person committee, which is normally staffed by senior members from the SFC and HAC, is assembled in the final days of the session and works under considerable pressure to finalize the budget, move it on to what is normally a rubber-stamp approval from the chamber floors, and pass it to the governor for approval.

Once it receives approval, the comptroller reenters the process to certify the budget. This official works to ensure that the state has the funds to meet the allocations that the budget requires; he or she has ten days to do so, meaning the legislature must give him or her time to act.

In the final step, the governor receives the budget for final consideration and approval. Three possible actions can follow: the governor can sign the budget intact (which sometimes happens), veto the entire budget (which rarely happens), or employ the line-item veto. As mentioned in Chapter 5, the executive official can strike an appropriation from the budget if he or she deems it inappropriate. Governor Abbott struck $300 million from the state budget in 2015 before signing into law.

Budget and Economic Policy Debates & Crisis

The legislature's work produced a $200.4 billion budget. That number includes state funds produced from the regressive tax structure outlined above and follows the Texas model discussed early in this chapter. While the state's funding abides by the cost-saving measures, there are still plenty of battles being waged regarding spending, with various groups and individuals charging that Texas is spending too much in some areas and too little in others.

Education Funding

Education spending is at the top of the list of disputed budget topics. Of the $200 billion of Texas funds spent, $74.2 billion is dedicated to Texas's traditional top expenditure. That number makes up 37 percent of Texas's budget, which is actually down from the 44 percent it consumed in the 2013 budget. Of that number, more than two-thirds ($54 billion) is dedicated to secondary and primary education, while the remaining $18 billion is earmarked for use in higher education.

The battle over this pot of money has continually been waged over time. Clashes based on race and socioeconomic status have put the education budget in the court system eight times in the past forty years. Disputes over the formula Texas uses to distribute its funds, the inequity in how those funds are allocated, and the education system itself have contributed to this debate. This leads to a very clear conclusion: fiscal debates are not just about fiscal policy. While the dollars and cents are ostensibly what the battle is about, the provocation for that battle is usually steeped in public relations and equity within and among communities.

The disparity in funds dedicated to minority districts has long been a point of contention. Texas's education roots are set in the debate over equity and access to fair education and how that was impeded for a number of years in minority districts through both fiscal and social policy decisions made by a primarily white legislature. While the twentieth century brought change in the form of increased funds and services for minority districts, access to fair and equal education is still a topic of hot debate. *Del Rio ISD v. Salvatierra* (1930) and *Delgado v. Bastrop ISD* (1948) claimed that the state provided inadequate funding to districts that were predominantly Mexican American. While Jesus Salvatierra was unsuccessful, the 1948 federal court decision in *Delgado* ruled that differences in those districts and segregation of Mexican American students were illegal; this was reinforced six years later by the decision in *Brown v. Board of Education* (1954), under which all segregation and the idea of separate but equal were declared unconstitutional. The decisions opened the door for more funds to these districts, but the change was incremental.

Texas attempted to loosen the purse strings and provide better pay and more money to districts by eliminating nearly 2,600 districts through the Gilmer-Aiken laws in 1949. Following the legislation, the Board of Education (BOE) and Texas Education Agency (TEA) were tasked with overseeing both the state's education and its education budget. The decision in *Plyler v. Doe* (1982) mandated that states provide free education to illegal immigrants who caused costs in many disadvantaged and minority districts to rise beyond their funds.

Equal funding became the focus of a major dispute. Texas encountered several battles as it tried to make the education funding system blend with the conservative model that drives fiscal decision making by mandating that school districts fund much of their own education. The idea that property taxes would fund education overall raised concerns, which were eventually realized, that poorer areas would not be able to generate enough revenue to properly satisfy the constitution's education mandate. *Edgewood ISD v. Kirby* (1986) used this idea to claim discrimination against poorer school districts and residents of the state, arguing that the disparity in economics and taxes violated the state's constitution, which mandates "efficient" education for all Texans.

The response to this was Senator Bill Ratliff's (D-Wichita Falls) 1993 bill, commonly known as the Robin Hood bill. Affluent school districts were ordered to submit a portion of their property tax revenue to a state fund that would be redistributed. The offering was an attempt to equalize education across the state and prevent poorer students from being subjected to a substandard education due to the incomes in their surrounding areas. The change has not taken effect. Poorer school districts are still operating at a lower level and with insufficient funds, despite reaching the property tax maximum cap of $1.50 per $100. Richer school districts are at the max as well because a large portion of their taxes is sent to the state. The Robin Hood bill was declared unconstitutional in 2006; the state supreme court declared it a violation of state law because it mandated a statewide property tax, which violates the constitution.

Since 2006, the state has attempted to use business and sin taxes to alleviate the property tax burden. According to the Census Labor Statistics, Texas currently ranks thirty-eighth in the nation in per capita funding per student, with $9,559 per student.[14] The $200 billion spent

---

14   U.S. Census Bureau, https://www.census.gov/newsroom/press-releases/2015/cb15-98.html.

by the state provides 46 percent of the funding for education, while local taxes make up 44 percent and federal funds supply the remaining 10 percent.

Summary

From a frugal take on economics to a look at how Texas accrues its funds, policy in the state has revolved around keeping true, as much as possible, to a conservative fiscal model. The state under a number of regimes has looked to keep itself solvent in terms of funds and away from being held to conditions from the federal government. However, Texas is not the strict low tax, low services state that it is portrayed to be by its citizens and representatives.

As we see in this chapter, the state relies quite a bit on a tax structure built on economic participation at every level. From sales taxes to corporate taxes to sin taxes, Texas relies on funds from it citizenry to manage a multibillion-dollar budget that has seen its share of difficulties. This all comes with significant aid from the federal government in areas where the state has historically resisted committing funds. Economic reform has come in recent years in the areas of education and taxes. The discussion and actions taken on property taxes, as well new revenue streams such as gambling, will continue to be front and center when the legislature meets to discuss the budget in 2017 and beyond.

References

Alexander, G., and J. Kato. *Regressive Taxation and the Welfare State*. New York, NY: Cambridge University Press, 2005.

Andrews, Paul S., ed. "Notes: Progressive Income Taxes." *Columbia Law Review* 12, no. 5 (1912): 443–445.

Asimakopulos, A. "Keynesian Economics, Equilibrium, and Time." *Canadian Journal of Economic/Revue Canadienne D'economique* 11 (1978): S3–S10.

Barnett, M. "Property Tax Livens Comptroller's Debate." *Dallas Morning News*, October 30, 2014.

Basinger, S. J., and M. Hallerberg. "Remodeling the Competition for Capital: How Domestic Politics Erases the Race to the Bottom." *American Political Science Review* 98, no. 2 (2004): 261–276.

Batheja, A. "Budget Debate Tackles School Funding, Incentive Programs." *Texas Tribune*, March 31, 2015.

Brueckner, J. K. "Welfare Reform and the Race to the Bottom: Theory and Evidence." *Southern Economic Journal* 66, no. 3 (2000): 505–525.

Cline, R. J., & Shannon, J. "The Property Tax in a Model State-Local Revenue System." *Proceedings of the Academy of Political Science* 35, no. 1(1983): 42–56.

Collier, K. and Alexa Ura. "Texas Public Schools Are Poorer, More Diverse." *Texas Tribune*, December 9, 2015.

Friedman, M. "The Methodology of Positive Economics." In *Essays in Positive Economics*. Chicago: University of Chicago Press, 1953.

Grieder, E. "Big, Hot, Cheap, and Right: What America Can Learn from the Strange Genius of Texas." New York, NY; Perseus Books Group, 2014.

Grieder, E. "Texas has an Unexpected 8.8 Billion Surplus." *Texas Monthly.* January 21, 2013. http://www.texasmonthly.com/politics/texas-has-an-unexpected-8-8-billion-surplus/.

Hibbs, D. A. "Political Parties and Macroeconomic Policy." *American Political Science Review* 71, no. 4 (1977): 1467–1487.

Jillson, C. *Lone Star Tarnished*. New York, NY: Taylor & Francis, 2014.

Johnson, C. M., and K. J. Meier. "The Wages of Sin: Taxing America's Legal Vices." *Western Political Quarterly* 43, no. 3 (1990): 577–595.

Lyon, A. B., and R. M. Schwab. "Consumption Taxes in a Life-Cycle Framework: Are Sin Taxes Regressive?" *Review of Economics and Statistics* 77, no. 3 (1995): 389–406.

Russo, B. "An Efficiency Analysis of Proposed State and Local Sales Tax Reforms." *Southern Economic Journal* 72, no. 2 (2005): 443–462.

Williams, J. T. "The Political Manipulation of Macroeconomic Policy." *American Political Science Review* 84, no. 3 (1990): 767–795.

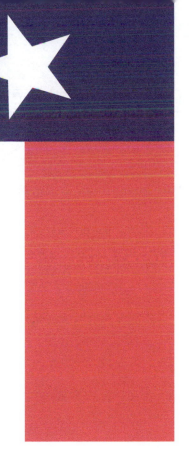

CHAPTER 10

Opinion, Ideology, and Voting in Texas

Political participation is the engine that drives the representative form of government in the United States. Individuals who wish to take part in government, whether in an official capacity or to simply voice their discontent, have endless ways of doing so.

Traditionally, participation is seen to encompass three types of activities (Salisbury 1975). The most traditional participation type is a legitimizing act, which affords citizens the ability to offer consent to individuals or representatives who provide support for their activity and make decisions about the roles they play. This is integral to a society based on a representative democracy in which elected officials act as proxies. Second, participation is seen as instrumental to political power. In this sense, gaining the support of the public is important for obtaining political power and making decisions. The extension of this would be that conflict would arise concerning resource allocation intended to cull public support. Third, participation is seen as a public solution to the issues facing the society. The public would come to a consensus through discourse and debate to determine the best course of action.

These three traditional conceptions of participation hinge on public activity and not cohesion. In fact, participation in all three forms promotes divergent viewpoints. Whether through voting (the most traditional form), grass roots movements, or civic discourse, individuals are free to voice their opinions in modern US and Texas democracy. In short, this participation is the cornerstone of public influence in democracy. The ability of the public to build opinion and work together often determines the success of their influence on the system.

With so much freedom to participate—freedom granted by the First Amendment—why do many Texans stay silent?

Texas is a state known for low or coerced types of political participation. The state's history suggests that political participation is not welcomed, as much of it was spent stifling the voices of many in the population. While the traditional view of political participation is seen as all-encompassing, the history of Texas has been to keep those freedoms away from large segments of its population.

In this chapter, we'll discuss participation, public opinion, and how the individual can become more impactful and capitalize on political participation, both in Texas and theoretically. To do that, we must look at examples of political participation and the factors that affect it as well as the process through which the individual develops his or her own ideology.

Reading 10.1

Selection from "The Current State of Political Ideology in the United States"[1]
from *The American Politics Project*
Darrell Lovell

POLITICAL IDEOLOGY AND DEVELOPING PUBLIC OPINION

Political ideology is the grounds for much debate. On popular, and unpopular, issues; the political landscape has become one where lines are drawn and trenches dug. In the age of polarization, political rancor, commercial pandering along political lines, and understanding the origins of those debates is important. While Republican, Democrat, Tea Party supporter, and countless other groups have attempted to unify individuals, it is political ideology that guides decision-making. A political ideology transcends the common political party moniker and provides support for it. Understanding how individuals develop and relate to political ideology requires the examination of how they develop their views on government and politics and how we classify those concepts.

In its basic form, political ideology is defined by Erikson and Tedin (2003) as "beliefs about the proper order of society and how it can be achieved." Developing an understanding of society and the path it should take to reach the optimal structure is the goal. Ideology allows individuals to define their environment and develop their optimal opinion of how it should be structured. (Parsons, 1951) Creating these expectations can unify groups of individuals and eventually leads to the creation of societal and political practices. Developing these concepts and sharing them allows a group to come together as the structure of a society and the decisions made within it has the ability to bring individuals, with otherwise few common characteristics, together. (Freeden, 2001) It stands to reason that competing concepts would draw lines between ideologies. The acceptance and discussion of those ideologies are a part of the society's structure.

Political Socialization

The development of these political values and attitudes happens over time. Political socialization suggests that this process is life-long and involves a number of political agents that contribute to the development of a person's outlook on political activity and the developing of their values. (Hyman, 1959, Beck, 1977) What agents have the most impact is determined on a case-by-case basis. The range of socialization agents or influencers can include parents, the media, and social class influencers among others. The following five agents are predominant in the political socialization process (Asher, 2001, Campbell, 2006, Mayer, 1993, Page & Shapiro, 1992):

1. Family. The foundation for a person's political ideology is developed at an early age and the biggest influence on this process is the nuclear family. Parents are a driving influence on young people and are often the template for their actions. Politically active parents have a significant influence on developing the presets of ideology and participation. As those around the child or individual are or are not politically engaged they are teaching their child, sibling, or family member habits. Political conversations around the dinner table can have a significant effect on the development of ideology and opinion.

2. Environment. The influences around a person can have a significant impact on ideology. The affluence of the physical area, the social and ethnic make-up, and the general political views of those around can have an impact on development. The debate between urbanization versus suburban or rural areas is a by-product of this debate. Political make-up is directly affected by the environmental parameters that a person is exposed too. Being exposed to extreme poverty or affluence can be a strong political driver. Living in a diverse community versus a homogenous community can have the same effect.

3. Political persuasion/information. As people age the type of information they seek out and the avenues for education have a significant impact on their socialization. Whether the person seeks divergent or complimentary viewpoints, the political allegiance from the source of information can weigh on political ideology creation and maturation. Much of this is viewed in the realm of susceptibility to messaging. That messaging can come from a political party or outside influence such the media or influential figures. The ideology of the conveyor of the information is transferred in some degree to the

individual. While it is most productive to seek out divergent information, the most common use of persuasion or information is used to seek out positions and influences that reaffirm ideology and ideals.

4. Education. The environment of learning and the type of information provided can have an impact on political ideology and socialization. Teachers who use conscious or unconscious examples or influences can have an impact on young people. The acceptance or willingness to challenge that authority has an impact on how individuals view society.

5. Personal experience. The previous four influences are learned. They are behaviors from others experience or information gathered. Experience takes place later in life as individuals develop favorable opinions or prejudices based on what has happened to them rather than something learned.

These five factors provide a view into how our predispositions for ideology are developed. If these influences consistently trend towards one side of the political spectrum then that person is likely to have a predilection to that ideology. The importance of factors is weighed different from person to person as well. A person living in a home without politically active or engaged parents will not have as big an influence from them.

DIRECTIONAL NATURE OF POLITICAL IDEOLOGY

As ideology is developed, categorizing it allows people to join larger political agents. Ideology is traditionally conceptualized in a directional sense dating back to the French Revolution. Left or right, it's a question many people ask and helps provide a general understanding of a person's views. Historically the right is for tradition and the maintenance of the status quo while the left pushes for societal change. (Erikson & Tedin, 2003) This view provides a basic idea of how ideology is conceptualized. To gain a more intricate knowledge of American political ideology we have to break down the subsets that exists on this directional continuum.

Conservative Right

The right is most closely connected to the term conservative today. Conservative ideology follows the status quo mandate pushing for many of the traditional views and policies seen after the American Revolution. Conservative policy focuses on several important aspects of society. Most notably is the intention to deregulate the economy. Conservative ideology is individualistic in nature, seeking to reduce the impact government has on business practices to allow individuals to seek out and attain singular wealth. (Elazar, 1970, 1972) Many of the concepts draw from Milton

Friedman's free market capitalism theory that advocates for little to no role for the government in economic practice, most notably advocating for free trade practices. Along these lines, the reduction of regulatory agencies and their ability to levy fines on corporations is frowned upon. Environmental restrictions and regulations are an example of policy that conservatives work against to open avenues to economic prosperity. Antiabortion claims are closely identified with the conservative ideology as well as several religion-driven platforms that advocate against issues such as same-sex marriage and advocates for activities such as prayer in school.

This view is characterized as low taxation, low services. Not just regarding economic practices, the reduction of taxes on individuals feeds into the individualistic nature of conservative theory. While paths to attainment and advancing individual wealth drives policy-making, conservatives believe the role of government revolves around protecting a specific set of rights and moral activity. While this ideology frowns on government services such as welfare or state sponsored healthcare, it is believed that resources should be allocated to preserve certain aspects of government.

Left is for Liberals

As the system suggests, the left represents much of the opposite viewpoint. Liberal is the term most commonly used to identify a person with a leftist ideology. Liberals push for social change as the driving force. Individual attainment or wealth is pushed to the background if there is a societal gain to be achieved under the liberal idea, Elazar (1970, 1972) would categorize this as a moralistic viewpoint. While conservatives align with an individualistic ideology, which focuses on personal well-being and attainment, liberals are believed to take a more holistic view of society. That is not saying that liberals do not have self-interest, they certainly do, but their ideology is geared to evolve society and policy to a point where progress towards a set of policies that benefits social change to a more idealistic society.

The liberal agenda has several components that revolve around that idealistic approach. First, advocacy for social progress through government activity. Employing a government that uses positive rights (rights that prompt government activity) to affect change. Support of social programs is at the forefront of this movement. Allocating resources and administering services, while understandably costly, are justified and encouraged by those with a liberal ideology based on the potential gains for the society as a whole. These programs include healthcare aid, economic aid in the form of unemployment insurance and welfare, housing aid, as well as education. To offset these costs, liberals are in favor of a higher tax structure that is progressive in nature, meaning it taxes the higher income individuals and corporations more than the poor. Another aspect of advancing or progressing society involves regulation.

The government is expected to regulate markets and areas of society that affect individuals. The economy is a prime target as liberals practice a Keynesian view, economy with regulation from government agencies, on fiscal policy. Taxation is the primary attempt at regulation but also there is assurance regulation. In this case government is responsible for ensuring that corporations are fair and equitable to the consumer as well as protecting worker's rights and standards. Last, liberals are in favor of rights to freedom of speech and individual activity. Part of the liberal platform advocates a pro-abortion and same-sex marriage stance as well ensuring that freedom of expression is preserved and protected.

Additional Directions: Hybrid Ideology of Libertarians and Populists

Liberals and conservatives are the traditionally dominant powers in U.S. ideology. Historically one of the two sides has dominated in the two-party system. Fifty-eight percent country identifies as Republican or Democrat in a 2014 Gallup poll. That is a majority but is at an all-time low for the two-party system. Independent or third parties have risen to prominence in the political landscape due to disconnection with primary ideologies, expanse of access to information, or a lack of activity from the two sides.

In 2014 Gallup reported that 23 percent of people identified as a libertarian, a group that is seen as a conservative/liberal option. Libertarians advocate for economic conservatism and social liberalism. People that practice this ideology advocate for the protection of civil rights and liberties. In fact, the main role of government under the libertarian ideology is focused on protecting such things. With that, the constitution is a staunch starting point by which those with this ideology mandate government activity. Protection of rights and freedoms outlined in the constitution are placed with the highest priority. This could mean the advocacy of action by the government or a mandate of inaction. Libertarians are staunch supporters of freedom of speech and promote government activity to protect it. Conversely, on matters such as the legalization of marijuana, abortion, state assisted suicide, and flag burning libertarians would rather government remove itself from the process and allow individuals to govern their actions. This starts a desired reduction of government influence advocated by libertarians.

This spills over into a conservative view of economics. Following advocacy of reduced government, under the libertarian ideology, economics should be free from government regulation. Eliminating environmental and regulatory practices are encouraged to allow freedom in economics as well as to the individuals. The elimination of income tax and support for social programs is a high agenda idea as well. Placing libertarianism on the scale is extremely low services and low taxes, but high individual rights. The later qualification is where social value is applied to the ideology.

The final major ideology currently on the U.S. political landscape is populism. As an ideology populism is considered to be economically liberal but socially conservative. Populism advocates for the advancement of rights and powers for common people rather than policies or activities that benefit economic or political elites. Its roots in the U.S. lie in the agricultural or agrarian era. Many famers in the late 1800's and early 1900's followed these views as it protected their social views and economic interest. Populist advocate for heavy government regulation. From restricting and overseeing the free trade market to restricting international trade, and competition for the local economy, populists pushed for a heavy hand from the government to ensure the interests and well-being of domestic economics. Populist in Texas, for example, date back to the creation of the state and worked against the expansion on the transcontinental railroad because it would reduce sales and the economic value of local farmers and businesses. The focus economically is placed on building a domestic economy that is not dependent on foreign interest.

Going along with their rural or agricultural economic views, the ideology takes its social cues from a conservative outlook. Social issues such as the institution of prayer in school and religion in government is advocated; placing populist on the side against social progression where it comes to moral issues such as abortion or same-sex marriages. Stiff penalties for criminals are advocated. In cases such as drug possession populist advocate for stiff penalties as a deterrent. Finally, freedom of speech is to be limited. Unlike its liberal counter-parts libertarians and liberals, populist look to restrict freedom of speech once in crosses a line. It strives to maintain the status quo.

Some of these concepts overlap. How they are employed and used make up the differences of these four ideologies. Uni-or-bi-directional thinking, left versus right, leaves out other striving ideologies in the U.S. political landscape. Liberals and conservatives are still the predominant political ideologies, but as research shows, the progression of political socialization and persuasion has expanded our views on ideology and created a number of additional arch-types that can be expanded and acted upon on election-day or through civic engagement.

History of Voting in Texas

Traditionally, political participation is seen in the form of elections and, from the individual side, voting. Voting is seen as the predominant form of political participation, and it offers a consistent, tangible reward. That reward has not always been available to or meant for everyone in Texas. Because the state has power over the voting process—from registration to election oversight—Texas has wielded significant power in this arena. As time has passed, voting has become a dying art in the state, and Texas's voting trends routinely fall below those at the national level. Much of that is attributed to the state's checkered history, particularly its propensity to restrict the voting rights of certain segments of its population.

Tradition of Exclusion

Texas began as a state intent on limiting the vote to a very small segment of the population. Under the state's early constitutions, only men who were white or Hispanic had the right to vote (if they met age, residency, and citizenship requirements). Those laws were very loose, both before and after the Civil War. Still, the fact that early Texas suffrage was relegated to men of those ethnicities was a sign of things to come. By constitutional law, all other minorities and women were restricted from the vote in pre-Civil War Texas. While the state had few other restrictions, the ban on minority voting was staunch and strict. After the Civil War, the state was forced to comply with the Thirteenth, Fourteenth, and Fifteenth Amendments (which substantiated the right of all men to vote), but the state continued to keep and exploit their traditions that excluded minority voting.

As stated before, the state had little in the way of restrictions. The state did not require citizenship to vote. As was common amongst Western expansion states, the state allowed immigrants to vote, with the only requirement that they declare their intent to become US citizens. Also, the state did not require voting registration, and elections were overseen by local officials. That opened the floodgates for minorities to be targeted and used. Most notably, voters were brought over the border in south Texas and offered food and money to vote. The "new voters" would be housed overnight, and in the morning, they'd be handed ballots to cast when needed. African Americans were organized through "owl meetings," where they were offered copious amounts of food, housed overnight, and hustled to the voting booths the next day.

This was a costly but effective practice. The participation rates amongst those communities were high until the early 1900s. Those numbers dropped significantly when these practices were outlawed by voter registration laws in 1891. While the state had no secret ballots (instead, they were controlled and color-coded by the parties), the laws applied to cities with more than ten thousand people and were geared toward helping the white elites stay in power. This is clear in the requirement of a four-month window of registration, which brought down the participation in minority communities.

As Texas tightened its laws, the state's elites sought to take steps that restricted the access to the vote even more.

White Primaries and White-Only Political Parties

One of the earliest attempts to subvert the system of open voting was the use of white primaries. These primaries are self-explanatory. Terrell Election Law, written by Alexander Terrell in 1903, shifted control of the election process from conventions to the primary structure. As discussed in previous chapters, the primary system selects which candidates will get delegate shares of votes to represent the party in the general election. Under the new law, the control of these primaries was shifted to the party leadership. The Texas Democratic Party, the dominant party at the time, employed the law in 1906 and restricted access to its primary to white males only. This was allowed because at that time, the Texas Democratic Party was a white-only party, meaning that its membership was restricted to white males. The action was a blatant violation of the Fifteenth Amendment, a fact that prompted a repeal attempt in 1910 (which was unsuccessful) and prompted further legal action in 1924, when black political leaders sued the state, attesting that the law violated the Constitution. Nixon v. Herndon

The original case (*Nixon v. Herndon*) was heard and decided in 1927, when the Supreme Court found that the state of Texas could not prohibit access to the primary vote, as it would exclude voters from a state-sponsored election. The decision temporarily removed the restrictions and opened the process to all voters.

> That political parties today perform a state function seems clear. They conduct the entire process of nomination. And since nomination by the Democratic Party in Texas is normally equivalent to election, the party primary is the decisive election. To this extent, then, the party administers the business of the government (*Harvard Law Review* 1933, 815).

The issue with the Texas statute, however, was that it invested the power over the primary election in the parties and not the state. As private entities, Texas's political parties were free to restrict membership as they saw fit; they could not violate political or constitutional rights because they were not agents of the government. This was the basis of the state's argument in 1935 in *Grovey v. Townsend*; the state asserted that, because political parties were not a part of the government and were, in fact, private, they could restrict participation as they saw fit. The court agreed and briefly reinstated the use of restrictive primaries.

The battle over white-only primaries waged in Texas for another decade. While Hispanics could vote (and continued to fall prey to the same type of manipulation seen at the turn of the twentieth century), African Americans still fought to gain the right to reenter the playing field.

Poll Taxes

While minorities were kept from the booth in droves, they were not the main population targeted. Poverty-stricken citizens in the state have been kept from the vote as the traditionalistic structure has played out. Historically, the weapon of choice in this case has been the poll tax. In 1902, Texas was a system in which many people still bartered for services—something that was prevalent in rural communities—and money was in short supply. As Texas farmers struggled (making little more than $25 per month on average), the state instituted a $1.50 poll tax, later raised to $1.75, to register and participate in the voting process.

The tax functioned as a deterrent in two ways. First, poor farmers and other individuals had a choice to make. With a of nearly $2 fee, was it worth nearly 10 percent of their wages to participate in the election process? Many simply chose not to participate and keep the money. The poll tax was an effective deterrent because it forced poor citizens to make that difficult choice and effectively suppressed their ability to mobilize. Second, the election officers and state legislature mandated that those who paid the tax attach their receipt to the ballot. The receipt would have a designation confirming they had paid the tax. It was also a way to manipulate the vote and dispel any attempt at a secret ballot. Finally, in 1949, under pressure from interest groups and advocates for voting rights, the government did away with the receipt to secure a truly secret ballot.

Response and the Lead-up to Major Change with the Voting Rights Act of 1965

Texas's freewheeling ways would start to come to an end in the mid-1940s, when it attracted the attention of the federal government. The state had played fast and loose with the voting laws, classifications regarding voting, and its constitutional power over the voting system. As the federal government started to take notice, it acted to displace Texas's activity and systematically reduce Texas's abuse, leading up to a major shake-up in 1965.

The reaction started in 1944, when the NAACP brought a case to outlaw the use of white primaries and parties in *Smith v. Allwright*. The argument was that political parties are agents of the government and, dating back to *Nixon v. Condon* (1933), their activity classified them as agents of the government that carry out government business. The Supreme Court found in favor of the NAACP, declared parties to be agencies of the state, forced compliance with the Fifteenth Amendment, and removed the loophole Texas political parties had exploited.

Another landmark case took place in 1966 due to Texas's continued use of the poll tax in state elections. Two years after the Twenty-Fourth Amendment (which was not ratified by the state until 2009) outlawed poll taxes, the law was challenged. The dual-ballot system that enabled the use of poll taxes for state elections was overturned in *US v. Texas* (1966), which declared its use at the state level unconstitutional.

Texas continued to attempt voter restriction: it declared that voters must register each year and that youths must vote where their parents lived, therefore nullifying the absentee ballot and adding unfair residency requirements. These attempts were shot down by the federal government. The authority for this came in large part from the Voting Rights Act of 1965.

Reading 10.2

Selection from "The Return of Immigrant Voting: Demographic Change and Political Mobilization"[2]
from *Democracy for All*
Ron Hayduk

Reading Introduction: Connecting Voting History to the Practices of Today

Ron Hayduk (2006) examines the state of the immigrant in today's political system. While we look at voting as both a civic virtue and a duty, there are barriers for those living in the United States who do not have a history here. Understanding these changes in voting, both historically and then connecting them to the current landscape, is important. As will be discussed, the changes in access to voting have been cleared in many cases, but there are still lingering effects that minimize voter impact within certain communities. This impact is outlined well by Hayduk as he seeks to frame the current situation of immigrants, including those in Texas.

Immigrants are dispersing, making their way into every part of the country. Nearly every census tract in the U.S. now contains foreign-born residents. In many states, they constitute a significant and growing proportion of the total adult population. Over twenty-one states have adult noncitizen populations that comprise more than 5 percent of the state's total adult population (see table 10.1). Seven states and the District of Columbia have an adult noncitizen population that is over 10 percent of the total.

TABLE 10.1 States with High Percentage of Noncitizens

State	Percent of Adult Population Who Are:			
	Native-born Citizens (%)	Naturalized Citizens (%)	Noncitizens (%)	Citizenship Rate of Foreign-born Adults (%)
California	67.6	13.6	18.8	42.0
New York	75.3	12.0	12.8	48.4
Nevada	81.1	7.5	11.5	39.5
Texas	83.0	5.8	11.2	34.2
New Jersey	78.8	10.3	10.8	48.8
Florida	80.2	9.5	10.3	48.1
Arizona	85.0	4.9	10.1	32.7

Source: U.S. Census Bureau.

2   Ron Hayduk, Selection from "The Return of Immigrant Voting: Demographic Change and Political Mobilization," *Democracy for All*, pp. 43-55, 220-221. Copyright © 2006 by Taylor & Francis Group. Reprinted with permission.

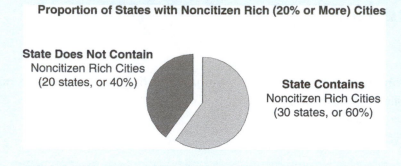

FIGURE 10.1
Source: U.S. Census Bureau.

Most states have cities with large populations of noncitizens. Thirty states (60 percent) contain cities with populations that are 20 percent or more non-citizens (see figure 10.1).

Even the states with a relatively low percentage of noncitizens overall often contain cities that do have large noncitizen populations. Of the forty-two states with noncitizen populations below 10 percent, twenty-nine states contain cities with noncitizen populations above 10 percent of the voting-age population. In immigrant-rich states, the proportion of noncitizen residents is significantly larger, particularly at the local level. In California, for example, where nearly 19 percent of the state's total population is composed of noncitizens, over 25 percent of the adult population in California is noncitizens in at least eighty-five cities; eighteen municipalities have noncitizen adult populations of between 40 and 49 percent; and noncitizens comprise a majority of the adult population (50 to 63 percent) of another twelve municipalities. The noncitizen population in Los Angeles is approximately one-third of the total.[1]

Eight hundred and seventy-four cities across the country have an adult noncitizen population of more than 10 percent of the city's total adult population. The city having the most noncitizens is Chamblee City, Georgia, with 64.5 percent. There, close to seven out of every ten adult persons in Chamblee City cannot vote because of citizenship restrictions. Similar disparities can be found across the country. One hundred and ninety-three cities have a noncitizen population of more than 25 percent of the city's total adult population (one out of four), and twenty-one cities have an adult noncitizen population of 50 percent or more (one out of two). (See table 10.2).

The ten most populated cities in the United States have a large percentage of adult noncitizens. Los Angeles has close to a 33 percent adult noncitizen population, followed by San Jose at 25 percent and New York, Houston, and Dallas at 23 percent (see table 10.3).

TABLE 10.2 Selected Cities with High Proportion of Noncitizens

	Selected Cities	State	% Noncitizen Eighteen Years Old and Over
1	Chamblee, DeKalb County	Georgia	64.5
2	Cactus, Moore County	Texas	63.7
6	Bell Gardens, Los Angeles County	California	56.5
7	Royal City, Grant County	Washington	56.3
14	Wendover, Tooele County	Utah	52.2
15	Santa Ana, Orange County	California	51.9
18	El Cenizo, Webb County	Texas	51.3
19	Somerton, Yuma County	Arizona	50.9
22	Greenfield, Monterey County	California	49.8
24	Sweetwater, Miami-Dade County	Florida	48.5
25	Bridgeport, Douglas County	Washington	47.9
26	Hialeah Gardens, Miami-Dade County	Florida	47.6
27	Coachella, Riverside County	California	47.5
29	Parlier, Fresno County	California	47.2
31	Cockrell Hill, Dallas County	Texas	46.3
33	Hialeah, Miami-Dade County	Florida	45.7
34	Lynwood, Los Angeles County	California	45.6
38	Roberts, Jefferson County	Idaho	43.8
39	Union City, Hudson County	New Jersey	43.7
41	Gervais, Marion County	Oregon	43.1
44	Hidalgo, Hidalgo County	Texas	42.9
46	Doraville, DeKalb County	Georgia	42.5
47	Brewster, Okanogan County	Washington	42.2
48	Rio Bravo, Webb County	Texas	42.1
49	Passaic, Passaic County	New Jersey	42.0
50	Wilder, Canyon County	Idaho	41.9
51	Paramount, Los Angeles County	California	41.5
52	Mesa, Franklin County	Washington	41.3
53	San Fernando, Los Angeles County	California	41.1
54	Norcross, Gwinnett County	Georgia	41.1
56	Fellsmere, Indian River County	Florida	40.8
58	Sullivan, Hidalgo County	Texas	40.6
59	Firebaugh, Fresno County	California	40.3
60	Sunland Park, Dona Ana County	New Mexico	40.3

Source: U.S. Census Bureau.

TABLE 10.3 Large Cities with High Proportion of Noncitizens

Top Ten Most Populous Cities	% of VAP Who Are Noncitizens
Average	22.5
New York City	22.9
Los Angeles	32.5
Chicago	16.4
Houston	22.9
Phoenix	17.5
San Diego	16.6
Dallas	22.7
San Francisco	16.7
San Jose	24.9
Austin	13.8

Source: U.S. Census Bureau.

Similar patterns appear in towns, townships, and villages. There are 250 towns and townships nationwide where the adult noncitizen population constitutes 10 percent or more of the total adult population. In the most disparate, Mattawa, Washington, the adult noncitizen population constitutes 77.7 percent of the town's total adult population. (See table 10.4 for other examples).

TABLE 10.4 Selected Towns

Town	Number of Noncitizen Adults	% of Noncitizens	Total Adult Population
West New York, New Jersey	16,601	46.6	35,644
Cicero, Illinois	23,051	41.2	55,998
Addison, Texas	2,521	21.5	11,738
Madison, Wisconsin	1,155	19.2	6,030
Pembroke Park, Florida	1,392	30.5	4,565
Herndon, Virginia	5,400	34.1	15,827
Rye, New York	8,905	26.5	33,601
Center Town, Colorado	430	28.3	1,520
Stillmore, Georgia	137	25.6	535

Villages also follow this pattern of distribution and concentration. There are 129 villages throughout the country that cross the 10 percent adult noncitizen threshold, with the highest being Stone Park Village in Illinois at 47.4 percent.

There is another category, "census designated places" (CDPs), which refers to unincorporated areas that contain significant concentrations of noncitizens. Over 700 CDPs nationwide contain 10 percent adult noncitizens. The highest CDP adult noncitizen population concentration is in Muniz CDP, Texas, at 76.4 percent. Most significantly, there are thirty-five CDPs at a 50 percent or greater adult noncitizen population threshold.

IMPACT ON RACIAL COMPOSITION OF THE U.S. AND FUTURE TRENDS

Since 1965, most immigrants have come from Latin America, Asia, and the Caribbean, changing the ethnic and racial composition of the U.S. population. The U.S. Census reports that several states and locales now have a majority minority population—such as California—led by Hispanics who have surpassed African Americans as the single largest "minority" group in the U.S. Moreover, the Census Bureau projects that the U.S. will become a country of "minorities" in the next forty-some years. Latino and Asian populations in particular will grow rapidly. Latinos are expected to reach 25 percent of the population by 2050, and Asians are expected to reach 10 percent of the population by 2050. African Americans are projected to grow slightly, to about 15 percent. By 2025, close to 50 percent of Latinos and Asians will be eligible to vote.

NATURALIZATION AND IMMIGRANT VOTER PARTICIPATION

Despite increases in the number of immigrants who have naturalized in recent years, the average time it takes to obtain citizenship is nearly ten years. According to the United States Citizenship and Immigrant Services (USCIS, formerly the Immigration and Naturalization Service, or INS), the time it takes all immigrants to naturalize has increased over the past 30 years. In 1965, for example, it took seven years for immigrants to become citizens but by 2000 it took ten years. In addition, not all immigrants naturalize at the same rates: in 2000, immigrants Europe, Africa, Asia obtained citizenship fastest (8 years), followed immigrants from South America (9 years), and North America (11 years).[2] The time it takes to become a "permanent resident," a prerequisite to apply for citizenship, can take even longer. Backlogs in processing applications and increased requirements—largely due to a host of anti-immigrant legislation, among other things—produce a cumbersome naturalization process that is significantly more difficult, time consuming, and costly than it was in earlier times in the U.S. In some parts of the country, the processing time for citizenship applications is over two years, and in twenty-nine of the thirty-three district offices of the USCIS the processing time is over one year.[3] In addition, the number of naturalization applications that are denied has risen, and many others are deterred from applying altogether.[4]

Still, the number of immigrants who naturalized rose from 6.5 million in 1995 to 11 million in 2002.[5] Several factors have driven up the number of immigrants who have naturalized and/or applied for citizenship. For example, one of the consequences of the Immigration Reform and Control Act of 1986 (IRCA) was that more immigrants became eligible for citizenship. About 2.7 million undocumented immigrants were legalized by this federal law and became eligible for citizenship by 1994. In addition, a host of anti-immigrant legislation at the federal and state levels led to an unprecedented number of applications for citizenship, because the legislation denied immigrants a range of public benefits from education and health care to public assistance. Sparked by Proposition 187 in California in 1994, several federal anti-immigrant measures ensued, including the Personal Responsibility and Work Opportunity Reconciliation Act of 1996 (the federal welfare reform law) and the Illegal Immigration Reform and Immigrant Responsibility Act of 1996. The latter allowed the federal government to deport legal immigrants for minor offenses, even if they were committed decades ago. By naturalizing, immigrants could retain access to social programs and be safer to respond to anti-immigrant sentiments and policy.[6] Over a four-year period—between 1996 and 2000—the number of new adult citizens rose by 30 percent.[7] The post–September 11 antiterrorist legislation—such as the USA PATRIOT Act—further stripped immigrants of due process and led to the detainment and deportation of tens of thousands of immigrants. Since 1996, a million immigrants have been deported. Taken together, they drove up naturalization applications and the number of new citizens.

As the foreign-born naturalize and the native-born children of immigrants come of age, their growing numbers increasingly make them potentially decisive players in politics. In 2000, 6.2 million new citizens were registered to vote and 5.4 million of them actually cast ballots. In fact, new citizens accounted for more than half the net increase in registered voters in 2000. In several immigrant-rich states, including California, Florida, New York, and New Jersey, new citizens comprised more than 10 percent of all voters.[8] In 2004, the number of new citizen registrants and voters was even greater. Although immigrant influence in electoral politics is growing, immigrant political power lags far behind their numbers. Even when immigrants do naturalize, they tend to vote at lower rates than native-born citizens. Variation exists, however, among different immigrant groups.[9]

The overall proportion of Latinos and Asians in the voting population is sharply lower than that of whites. In 2000, Latinos represented 12.6 percent of the total U.S. population but only 5.3 percent of all votes cast. Similarly, Asians were 4.2 percent of the population but cast only 1.9 percent of the votes. Whites, on the other hand, were 70 percent of the total population but cast over 81 percent of all votes.[10] Latino immigrants generally take longer to naturalize than Asian immigrants, but register and vote at higher rates than Asians. Foreign-born whites and Asians vote at lower rates than their native-stock counterparts, but foreign-born naturalized black and Latino citizens vote at higher rates than their native-born counterparts.[11]

THE REPRESENTATION GAP

Equally important, the number of Latino and Asian elected officials lags far behind that of other groups (particularly whites and African Americans). The largest group, Latinos, has a significant representation gap. Latino elected officials almost never exceed the percentage of Latinos who can vote. Although gerrymandering, racial bloc voting, and single-member districts may contribute to the representation gap, lack of voting rights for noncitizens is a significant factor. Figure 10.2 shows the gap between the proportion of Latinos and the total number of Latino elected officials in selected states, which are representative of other states as well.

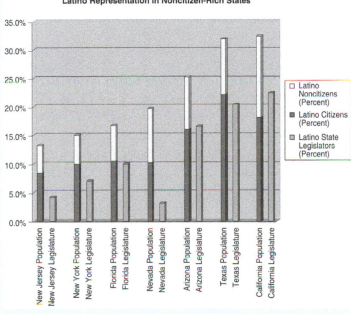

Latino Representation in Noncitizen-Rich States

FIGURE 10.2

Source: Census 2000 Summary File 1, Table GCT-P6, Race or Hispanic or Latino – 2000; The Council of State Governments, The Book of the States, 2004 Edition, Vol. 36, at 82 (2004); National Association of Latin Elected Officials, 2004 National Directory of Latino Elected Officials (2004). Data provided by Joaquin Avila and Chart produced by Ari Weisbard.

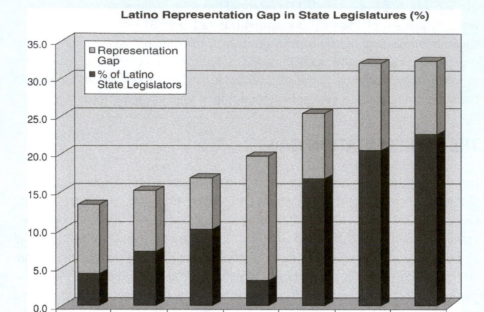

FIGURE 10.3

Source: Census 2000 Summary File 1, Table GCT-P6, Race or Hispanic or Latino - 2000; The Council of State Governments, The Book of the States, 2004 Edition, Vol. 36, at 82 (2004); National Association of Latin Elected Officials, 2004 National Directory of Latino Elected Officials (2004). Data provided by Joaquin Avila and Chart produced by Ari Weisbard.

This gap is also apparent in state legislatures. In these seven immigrant-rich states, on average 8.4 percent of Latinos are noncitizens, while only 5.6 percent of all non-Latinos are noncitizens. This might explain, in part, why Latinos only get 12 percent of the legislative seats on average (see figure 10.3), even though they are 22.1 percent of the total voting-age population.

But the representation gap is nowhere more apparent than in the nation's largest metropolitan areas, the very places where new immigrant groups comprise significant and increasing proportions of the population (see figure 10.4). For example, as Mollenkopf and Logan point out, "Whites hold political office in both Los Angeles and New York City at far higher rates than their population share and blacks hold offices at about parity with their population or a little more, but Latinos and Asians hold much less representation than their population share. Indeed, their current level of representation matches their much smaller population share twenty years ago."[12]

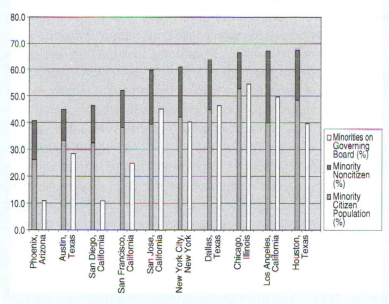

FIGURE 10.4

Source: Census 2000 Summary File 1, Table GCT-P6, Race or Hispanic or Latino–2000; Major City Websites; National Association of Latin Elected Officials, 2004 National Directory of Latino Elected Officials, Passim (2004); UCLA Asian American Studies Center, National Asian Pacific American Political Almanac, 2003–2004; Telephone Survey (Week of September 5–10, 2004) for Black Elected Officials (Includes Office of Mayor for Some Cities). Data provided by Joaquin Avila and figure produced by Ari Weisbard.

The cumulative lack of political power—from few votes to few representatives—translates into fewer immigrant pathways to opportunity, worse socioeconomic conditions, and government policies that slight them.

Striking parallels exist for two additional large disenfranchised groups: the 4.5 million mostly black and Latino ex-offenders who are denied voting rights by state felony disenfranchisement laws; and the approximately 4.5 million residents in U.S. Territories who cannot vote in U.S. federal elections.

THE SOCIOECONOMIC STATUS OF IMMIGRANTS

Immigrants are disproportionately relegated to the lower socioeconomic order. One in four low-wage workers is foreign-born, and one in four low-income children is the child of an immigrant.[13] Despite the fact that immigrants work more than most other Americans—for more hours and often at two or more jobs—large numbers of immigrants and their families have low incomes, lack health insurance, and are food insecure.[14] "Immigrants compose an increasingly large share of the U.S. labor force and a growing share of low-wage workers."[15] Hourly wages of immigrants are lower on average than native-born citizens' wages by a significant margin; nearly one-half of immigrants earn less than 200 percent of the minimum wage as opposed to one-third of low-wage, native-born workers. In 2002, 22 percent—over one out of five—children of mixed-status families lacked health insurance, compared with 12 percent of children with citizen parents.[16]

Yet, immigrants play a vital role in the economy and public revenues. The Cato Institute, for example, reported that in 1997, immigrant households in the United States paid an estimated $133 billion in taxes to federal, state, and local governments—from property, sales, and income taxes. The National Research Council of the National Academy of Sciences reported that typical immigrants pay an estimated $80,000 more in taxes than they receive in federal, state, and local benefits over their lifetimes.[17]

Contrary to popular belief, the majority of immigrants are documented, or "legal." As of 2002, approximately 12.2 million immigrants were "legal permanent residents" (35 percent) of all 34 million immigrants residing in the U.S.; about 9 million were undocumented immigrants (27 percent). The remaining 11.3 million foreign-born were naturalized citizens (32 percent).[18] Thus, of the 34 million foreign-born people that currently live in the U.S., over 12 million legal permanent residents are noncitizens and are barred from voting—more than one-third. If we include "undocumented" or "illegal" immigrants, the number of noncitizens rises to 18 million, or nearly 60 percent of all immigrants.

POLITICAL MOBILIZATION: RENEWED NATIVISM AND EFFORTS TO BUILD PROGRESSIVE POLITICS

The demographic changes have significant political implications, especially in the states and metropolitan areas where immigrants are concentrated. Six states are the home for the overwhelming majority of new immigrants—California, New York, Florida, Texas, Illinois, and New Jersey (in that order)—and within these states immigrants are concentrated in eight metropolitan regions: Los Angeles; New York City; Miami; Anaheim; Chicago; Washington, D.C.; Houston; and San Francisco. These immigrant-receiving states and locales, several of which now have majority minority populations, play an important role in choosing representatives for Congress—affecting the apportionment of seats in the House of Representatives—and hold critical electoral votes for the presidency. At the state and local level, where they make up a larger proportion of the potential electorate, immigrants can have an even greater impact. Emerging patterns of immigration are creating new political fault lines with the potential to alter the balance of social and political power. Immigration is changing the political arithmetic, propelling parties and politicians who jockey for advantage to adjust campaign strategies to reflect evolving electoral conditions. As immigrants naturalize and native-born children of immigrants come of age, their growing numbers increasingly make them potentially decisive players in politics. Yet a sizeable number of adult noncitizens remain locked out of formal political processes.

Demographic changes have prompted cross-cutting currents. On the one hand, there is intensified debate about the newcomers and a rising nativism, particularly after September 11 and the beginning of the War in Iraq. Consequently, conflict over U.S. immigration and immigrant policy has intensified, heightening tensions between contending social and political groups. Nativistic responses have led to legislation that restricts immigration and tightens border control as well as increases domestic surveillance, including rounding up immigrants suspected of criminal activity and a sharp increase in deportations. Legislation has been passed and/or proposed that limits illegal immigrants' access to drivers' licenses and a wide variety of social services such as education, health care, and welfare.[19]

On the other hand, we see a growing immigrant rights movement that has forged alliances with a broad range of social justice activists. Even while anti-immigrant sentiments have reigned in public discourse and policy, a mobilization among immigrant groups and their political allies is evident. Witness the proliferation of immigrant rights organizations that engage in a broad range of advocacy and activism and who build alliances with other groups on a range of issues, including labor, housing, education, health, welfare, and foreign policy. Immigrants lobby legislators and engage in protest politics with greater frequency and force. Indeed, labor unions, housing organizations, and welfare rights groups have reached out to immigrants where they have common ground and shared interests. For example, many such groups—spearheaded by labor unions—mounted an Immigrant Workers Freedom Ride in 2003 that sent busloads of immigrants from nine cities, then converged on Washington, D.C., and ended up with 100,000 marching in New York City. Inspired by the "freedom rides" during the civil rights movement, the planners hoped to focus public attention on immigrants' rights—particularly as workers—and show immigrant strength. Immigrant groups have also mobilized voter registration and get-out-the-vote efforts. In 2002, for example, Arab American groups registered 250,000 new voters and ran forty candidates (twenty-six of whom won).[20] In 2004, immigrant political mobilization reached new heights. Such activity reveals a growing sense among new immigrants that they possess legitimate claims on the American polity, and they are commanding greater attention. Yet, immigrant political power lags behind their numbers. Initiatives for immigrant voting rights flow from these trends. Essentially, they are seen as a pathway to political power.

As we shall see, several key characteristics are present in these campaigns to expand the vote to all residents of communities: demographic shifts propelled immigrant mobilization; proponents of noncitizen voting engaged in effective grassroots organizing, coalition building, and lobbying; and sympathetic politicians, mostly liberal Democrats, enacted or supported legislation. Opponents of noncitizen voting have been more conservative Democrats and Republicans, representatives of all political stripes who view noncitizen voters as a potential threat to their incumbency, community residents and groups that feel threatened by the influx of newcomers, and those who object on many other grounds, which will be described in the next chapter. In every case, immigrant voting rights campaigns have been highly contentious.

[...]

NOTES

1   James P. Smith and Barry Edmonston, eds., *The New Americans: Economic, Demographic, and Fiscal Effects of Immigration* (Washington, D.C.: National Academy Press, 1997).

2   Moore, Stephen, 1998.

3   Passel, Jeffrey and Clark, Rebecca, 1998.

4   The terms "immigrants," "foreign born," "aliens," "émigrés," "refugees," "asylees," "newcomers," and "noncitizens" refer to the same persons and are used interchangeably. Persons who are not naturalized citizens of the United States are specified as such. Similarly, "non-citizen voting," "alien suffrage," "immigrant voting," "resident voting," and "local citizenship" refer to the same practice.

5   There is a discrepancy in the scholarship about how many states, which states, and at what times these states allowed noncitizens to vote. Tallies that calculate this figure using the date when noncitizen voting rights ended state that "at least twenty two states and territories allowed noncitizens to vote and hold office." See Leon Aylsworth, "*The Passing of Alien Suffrage,*" *American Political Science Review* 25, no. 1 (February 1931): 114–16; and Virginia Harper-Ho, "Noncitizen Voting Rights: The History, the Law and Current Prospects for Change," *Law and Inequality Journal,* no. 18 (2000). Raskin rightly questioned the accuracy of this figure (Jamin B. Raskin, "Legal Aliens, Local Citizens: The Historical, Constitutional, and Theoretical Meanings of Alien Suffrage," *University of Pennsylvania Law Review* 141 [1993]: 1401). More recent scholarship shows "an upper limit of 35" states and territories that "ever permitted noncitizens to vote" (Marta Tienda, "Demography and the Social Contract," *Demography* 39, no. 4 [2002]: 602). My research, with the assistance of law students at New York University, shows that as

many as forty states and federal territories at one point or another allowed noncitizens to vote [...].

6 Franklin, however, was not a proponent of alien suffrage later in his life.

7 Raskin, "Legal Aliens, Local Citizens," 1401; Christopher Collier, "The American People as Christian White Men of Property: Suffrage and Elections in Colonial and Early National America," in *Voting and the Spirit of American Democracy*, ed. Donald W. Rogers. (Urbana: University of Illinois Press, 1992).

8 Raskin, "Legal Aliens, Local Citizens," 238–39.

9 Noel Ignatiev, *How the Irish Became White* (New York: Routledge, 1995); Rogers Smith, *Civic Ideals: Conflicting Visions of Citizenship in U.S. History* (New Haven, Conn.: Yale University Press, 1997); Josh DeWind and Philip Kasinitz, "Everything Old Is New Again? Process and Theories of Immigrant Incorporation," in Immigrant Adaptation and Native-born Responses in the Making of Americans: A Special Issue. International Migration Review 31 (Winter, 1997): 1096–111; E. Bonilla-Silva, "Rethinking Racism: Towards a Structural Interpretation," American Sociological Review 63, no. 3 (1997): 465–80; David Roediger, *The Wages of Whiteness* (London: Verso, 1991); and Alexander Keyssar, *The Right to Vote: The Contested History of Democracy in the United States* (New York: Basic Books, 2000).

10 Robert F. Worth, "Push Is On to Give Legal Immigrants Vote in New York," *New York Times*, April 8, 2004; Alexandra Marks, "Should Noncitizens Vote?" *Christian Science Monitor*, April 27, 2004; Teresa Borden, "What Does Citizenship Mean: Cities Debate Whether Noncitizens Should Vote," *Atlanta Journal-Constitution*, July 2, 2004; Miriam Jordan, "Noncitizen Parents Seek Voting Rights in School Elections," *Wall Street Journal*, September 14, 2004; and Katia Hetter, "Right to Vote Sought for Noncitizen Parents: Measure Would Apply to Elections for School Board," *San Francisco Chronicle*, July 9, 2004.

11 These countries include Barbados, Belize, Canada, Chile, Israel, Uruguay, and Venezuela. For information on policies and practices in Europe and elsewhere, see T. Alexander Aleinikoff and Douglas Klusmeyer, *Citizenship Policies for an Age of Migration* (Washington, D.C.: Carnegie Endowment for International Peace, 2002); David Earnest, "Noncitizen Voting Rights: A Survey of an Emerging Democratic Norm" (paper prepared for the 2003 annual convention of the American Political Science Association, August 28–31, Philadelphia); Jan Rath, "Voting Rights," in The Political Rights of Migrant Workers in Western Europe, ed. Henry Zig Layton (Newbury Park, Calif.: Sage, 1990); Raskin, "Legal Aliens, Local Citizens," 1401; Harper-Ho, "Noncitizen Voting Rights"; and the Immigrant Voting Project, "Immigrant Voting Project: Democracy for All," http://

www.immigrantvoting.org. Day, Stephen and Jo Shaw. "European Union Electoral Rights and the Political Participation of Migrants in Host Polities." *International Journal of Population Geography*. 8, 183–199. 2002; Baubock, Rainer. "Expansive Citizenship – Voting Beyond Territorial and Membership." *PS: Political Science and Politics*. Washington, D.C.: American Political Science Association. Vol. 38, No. 4. October, 2005; Waldrauch, Harald. "Electoral rights for foreign nationals: a comparative overview." Paper prepared for Exploratory Workshop: "Citizens, non-citizens and voting rights in Europe," sponsored by the European Science Foundation, the Europa Institute and the School of Law, University of Edinburgh. University of Edinburgh, UK. June 2–4, 2005.

12 Today, there are distinct categories of immigrants, the main distinction being "documented" or "legal" versus "undocumented" or "illegal" immigrants. Legal permanent residents are those who obtain immigrant visas or "green cards" because they (1) are related to a U.S. citizen or permanent resident, (2) possess a needed or desirable job skill or ability, or (3) are spouses or children of green card holders. Other categories of legal immigrants include asylees, refugees, and "nonimmigrant" foreigners (such as students, tourists, diplomats, and temporary workers).

13 Unless otherwise noted, all data on immigrants are from the U.S. Bureau of the Census and the U.S. Citizenship and Immigration Services (USCIS, formerly the Immigration and Naturalization Service [INS]).

14 A useful distinction can be made between "immigration policy" and "immigrant policy," which analysts sometimes employ. "Immigration policy" determines which immigrant groups are permitted to enter the U.S. and in what proportions and numbers. A distinct but related set of "immigrant policies" refers to federal, state, and local laws and policies that influence the integration and the treatment of immigrants after they have arrived. The federal government sets U.S. immigration policy. U.S. immigrant policy is composed primarily of various state and local provisions and programs, which are less consistent and coherent than federal policy. Immigrant voting rights, for the most part, fall into the latter category of immigrant policy. Of course, both immigration policy and immigrant policy flow from the larger formal and informal rules and processes that shape governance and operate in economic and social life more generally.

15 Jeffrey S. Passel, "Election 2004: The Latino and Asian Vote," Urban Institute Immigration Studies Program, July 27, 2004, http://www.urban.org/UploadedPDF/900723.pdf.

16 Such political exclusion is also evident for the 4.5 million residents in U.S. territories and the over 4 million ex-offenders who lack voting rights.

17 Chilton Williamson, *American Suffrage From Property to Democracy, 1760–1860* (Princeton, N.J.: Princeton University Press, 1960).

18 *Minor v. Happersett*, U.S. Supreme Court, 88 U.S. 162, October term, 1874.

19 Louise Renne, former San Francisco city attorney, asked, "If non-citizens can vote, can Osama bin Laden vote in a school election?" *San Francisco Chronicle*, July 10, 2004; see also *Sing Tao Daily*, July 13, 2004.

20 Of course, other electoral reforms are crucial to rectify the bias of the electorate and the nature of the political parties, such as Election Day voter registration, effective campaign finance reform, ballot access reform, and the inauguration of alternative representational schemes (such as proportional representation or instant runoff voting), if more democratic electoral politics and outcomes are to be achieved; Ronald Hayduk and Kevin Mattson, eds., *Democracy's Moment: Reforming the American Political System for the 21st Century* (Lanham, Md.: Rowman & Littlefield, 2002).

As Texas proved repeatedly to be a chronic violator of voting rights and privileges, the federal government took action. After the passage of the Civil Rights Acts of 1964 and 1965, the federal government attempted to eliminate racial segregation at the voting booth by declaring that nine southern states that were routinely inhibiting access to voting for minorities were subject to the Voting Rights Act. The act attempted to protect citizens by restricting states' ability to pass legislation that violated the constitutional rights of any citizen or group. It restricted Texas's ability of Texas to make its own voting laws. Instead, any state law that attempted to alter the voting system would have to undergo a process called preclearance, in which the US Justice Department could can block any change it declared to be a constitutional violation, whether it was intentional or not. The provisions in the VRA were meant to permanently confirm the rights of minorities and provide fair access to the political system. Since its passage, the VRA and preclearance have signaled debate over the lack of bilingual ballots in states with large bilingual populations, and they have been used to fight unfair redistricting laws and to challenge the voter ID laws in Texas (in 2011).

The preclearance clause has since been removed from law by the Supreme Court. A 2013 decision (in the case of *Shelby County v. Holder*) struck down the formula used in Section 5 that outlined preclearance. The reasoning of the court was that the formula to determine if a state would stand to be reviewed under the section was outdated and placed an undue burden on states and local governments. The high court's decision was met with disapproval from then-president Barack Obama and leaders of voting and civil rights organizations. As a response, Texas revisited its voter ID law and put it into action following the decision. That law's saga continues. In July 2016, the law was struck down by a federal district court, which ruled the law to be discriminatory (although the majority opinion did acknowledge that the law's intent was not discriminatory). The case is currently being appealed to the Supreme Court.

Voter Requirements

While voters are struggling to get to the polls in Texas, the days of the state restricting the vote are in the past. Many voter requirements and qualifications comply with federal law. They are as follows:

- You must be eighteen years of age (you can register at the age of seventeen years and ten months to be able to participate)

- You must be a US citizen

- A resident in the state and district for thirty days prior to an election

- There is no party registration

Voter registration is permanent. While a district may change, voters can update their addresses and districts online today, as the secretary of state's office oversees and conducts the process. If you move between districts or counties, you must reregister. Through federal law (the Help America Vote Act passed in 2002), the federal government has implemented procedures to help states register and track voters. The state must develop an accessible system that offers transparency to voters regarding their registration status, and the state must keep track of voter rolls, which are to be purged and tracked to ensure there is no criminal activity or foul play in the voting booth.

Reading 10.3

Selection from "Texas House District"[3]
from *Campaigns from the Ground Up: State House Elections in a National Context*
John Klemanski and David Dulio

Reading Introduction: Looking at the Restrictions and Effect on Voting

John Klemanski and David Dulio (2014) outline an examination and simulation of Texas voting and campaign practices. The theory is that we can simulate the actions in a vote and how the political process will play out. To do that, as with any election, you must be able to understand and predict what the restrictions are on voting and participation. The authors take an extended look at that in the

3   John Klemanski and David Dulio, Selection from "Texas House District," *Campaigns from the Ground Up: State House Elections in a National Context*, pp. 98-104, 159-160. Copyright © 2014 by Taylor & Francis Group. Reprinted with permission.

state of Texas and in House District 144, providing the reader with a valuable look at the current voting landscape and what factors can contribute to low turnout.

TEXAS'S POLITICAL CONTEST

Much of contemporary Texas politics is informed by the state's economy, culture, diverse population, and rich history. While the economy in Texas is diversified and varied today, in the past it was based on producing, processing, and shipping goods to external markets. For much of its history, "the Texas economy was dependent on external demand and the prices paid for three products: cotton, cattle, and petroleum" (Haag, Keith, and Pebbles 2003, 33). For instance, "King Cotton" was grown across Texas and barged down Texas rivers to the Gulf of Mexico, where it was shipped throughout the United States and Europe. Cotton was the "economic heart" of Texas during its early years as a state (Keith et al. 2012, 24). Even today, Texas produces more cotton than any other state in the United States.

Cattle is another commodity that has been, and continues to be, important to the economy of Texas. Early on, the cattle business consisted of rounding up stray cattle found across the state. By the late nineteenth century, however, Texas had taken advantage of a growing demand for beef and turned it into an economic boom. In the early 1900s, the largest ranch in the state, XIT, had so much land devoted to cattle that it was using over 1,500 miles of fencing (Keith et al. 2012).

Cotton and cattle have remained important to the Texas economy. Today, the average cotton harvest yields roughly 5 million bales of lint and 2 million tons of cottonseed, and Texas remains the number one cattle state with about 11 million head. Even so, the biggest economic impact comes from the petroleum and petro-chemical industry. "For much of the twentieth century, petroleum was the basis for the Texas economy. From the first major oil discovery in 1901 at Spindletop, near Beaumont, … Texas and the production of crude oil have been synonymous" (Keith et al. 2012, 25). While the United States looked for less expensive oil elsewhere in the world, the 1970s oil embargo put in place by the Organization of Petroleum Exporting Countries (OPEC) led to an economic expansion in the state. This was followed by a downturn in the oil markets in the late 1980s.

The modern Texas economy is more diverse, global, and tech-heavy and includes biotech corporations, computer software and hardware companies, and aerospace industries, among many others. Texas had a gross state product (GSP) of nearly $1.4 trillion in 2013. This puts Texas at thirteenth in the world among nations, behind Australia and in front of Spain. The most economically diverse areas of Texas are the urban areas, such as the Dallas-Fort Worth metroplex, but even those areas most dependent on the historic economic drivers have altered and diversified their economies (Keith et al. 2012).

Texas is divided into nine regions that have different cultural, economic, and political tendencies—Panhandle (which includes Amarillo), West (Lubbock, Midland, and San Angelo), North (Dallas and Fort Worth), East (Tyler and Lufkin), Central (Austin), Gulf Coast (Port Arthur and Corpus Christi), South (Laredo and Brownsville), Southwest (El Paso), and German Hill Country. (See Maxwell, Crain, and Santos 2014 for a detailed description of these regions.) While regional definitions are useful, it should be noted that "cultural divisions are often blurred and transitional," meaning there is not always a large divide between the regions. For example, the state's largest city, Houston, is located at the intersection of the East, Central, and Gulf Coast regions (Maxwell, Crain, and Santos 2014, 8).

Why are there so many regions in Texas? In part it is because Texas is so vast—nearly 270,000 square miles—and because so many different races and ethnicities have contributed to Texas's makeup. These groups include Native Americans, Hispanics, African Americans, Anglos (defined as non- Hispanic whites), and Asian Americans. Today, Texas is one of the most diverse states in the United States. Indeed, it is one of four states—Hawaii, New Mexico, and California are the others—whose population is majority-minority, or where the majority of the population is from underrepresented minority groups. According to 2012 US Census Bureau estimates, the Texas population is about 44 percent non-Hispanic white, 38 percent Hispanic, 12 percent African American, and 4 percent Asian.

As noted above, Texas has voted for the Republican presidential candidate since 1980. After the 2012 elections, both US senators from Texas were Republicans, and Republicans held a strong advantage in the state's congressional delegation, with twenty-four members to the Democrats' twelve. In 2014, the vast majority of statewide elective officials—including governor, lieutenant governor, attorney general, and various commissioners and judges—were Republicans. In the state legislature, Republicans also had majority control, holding 95 of 150 seats in the State House and 19 of 31 in the State Senate during 2014. The Texas legislature is considered part time; the Texas Constitution limits the meeting of the legislature to 140 days every two years (see Table 10.5). The governor, however, can call the legislature into special session, which has happened more often in recent years (Maxwell, Crain, and Santos 2014). This creates a true citizen legislator model in Texas, since members of the legislature receive only limited compensation for their service and have a career outside of government.

While Republicans dominate the state's elective offices, the citizens of Texas do demonstrate some variability in both party identification and ideology. In a recent survey of registered voters in Texas, 46 percent reported that they considered themselves Republicans, while 44 percent said they thought of themselves as Democrats. At the same time, more respondents said they considered themselves "conservative" (45 percent) than said "liberal" (21 percent), while the rest, 34 percent, said they thought of themselves as "moderate" (Ramsey 2013). Another

TABLE 10.5 Texas at a Glance

2012 state population (est.)	26,060,796
2012 number of US congressional seats	36
Number of state senate seats	31
Number of state house seats	150
2011 state senate district population (target)	811,147
2011 state house district population (target)	167,637
2010 House District 144 population	161,859
Voter registration by party	No
Full-time legislature	No
Legislative term limits	No
Independent redistricting commission	No

dynamic in Texas is the Tea Party. While this anti-government, anti-tax movement did not begin in Texas, it does have strong roots there. Indeed, one of the most popular public figures among Tea Party faithful is US Senator Ted Cruz, and many other Republican members of the Texas congressional delegation are sympathetic to the group's goals. Residents of Texas are also supportive of the Tea Party. In a survey at the end of 2013, 19 percent of respondents said they would vote for a Tea Party candidate and 22 percent said they would vote for a GOP candidate.

The conservative tendencies of many Texans should not come as a surprise. Much of what drives Texas's political culture is linked to modern conservative principles. Indeed, "the ideological context for Texas politics and government centers on a Texan Creed. The Texan Creed incorporates many of the same ideas that were influential for other Americans: individualism, liberty, constitutionalism, democracy, and equality. ... Among the five ideas, individualism holds a special place for most Texans" (Keith et al. 2012, 13).

Election Day in Texas tends to see lower voter turnout compared to the United States generally. Indeed, Texas usually ranks near the bottom in turnout among the fifty states. In the 2012 and 2008 presidential elections, Texans voted at a rate that was double digits lower than the national rate. The 1988 election was the only time turnout in Texas came within 5 percent of the national figure, yet the state still ranked forty-sixth in turnout. Similar patterns emerge in midterm election years; turnout has been more than 10 percent lower than the nation in three of the last four midterms and has not ranked higher than 42nd since 1990.

There are few legal restrictions related to voting in Texas. Those who have been declared by a judge to be mentally incompetent may not vote, nor can those convicted of a felony who have not completed their sentence (i.e., currently incarcerated or on parole, supervision, or probation). In 2012, the total population of felons who could not vote was nearly 475,000. Texans must register to vote before casting a ballot in either a primary, general, or special election; anyone wishing to register must do so 30 days prior to an election. Because of Texas's large Hispanic population, registration materials are available in Spanish as well as English.

Two other aspects of casting a ballot in Texas deserve mention, as they can impact a campaign plan. First, in 1987 Texas adopted early in-person voting. Between seventeen and four days before Election Day, Texans can cast a ballot in person at a variety of locations, including grocery stores, churches, and schools. This can have a big impact on a campaign's GOTV efforts. The reform's impact on turnout has been small, however. Also, there is not a relaxed absentee ballot law in Texas. The few groups that may vote by mail via absentee ballot include those who plan to be away from their precinct, those who are sick or disabled, and those who are over 65 years of age.

A more controversial change in Texas is the adoption of a voter identification law, which requires anyone wishing to cast a ballot to show an approved form of state identification. If someone wishes to cast a ballot but has no acceptable identification, they may cast a provisional ballot, which also allows someone to cast a ballot if their name does not appear on the voting rolls. An individual who has identification, and whose name does not exactly match but is "significantly similar" to how it appears on official voter rolls, may sign an affidavit and then cast a ballot. This law, and others like it across the United States, has a clear division of proponents and opponents. Proponents, typically Republicans, argue that it helps control voter fraud. Opponents argue that it dampens turnout, especially among groups who tend to vote Democratic—African Americans, the poor, and young people. The first year the law was in effect was 2013. "Officials said that statewide, 2,354 provisional ballots were cast this election, which is about 0.2 percent of voters. In the last off-year election, in 2011, there were 738, or 0.1 percent of the ballots cast that year" (Lyman 2013). The impact this law has on voter turnout will be monitored by many in the coming election years, both in Texas and across the nation.

Some states have very strict campaign finance laws, including low limits on contributions to candidates, while others have much looser campaign finance laws. Texas falls into the latter category. As Keith et al. (2012) note, much of what exists in Texas campaign finance law has come about as a reaction to scandal. Candidates in Texas were not required to disclose their contributions and expenditures until 1973, and even then only candidates who faced opposition had to do so. In 1991 the state Ethics Commission was created and now serves as the entity that receives state campaign finance reports. Candidates for many offices in Texas are required to file their reports electronically. There are no limits on how much individuals or PACs can give to candidates for office, except in the case of judges.

As with voter registration materials, the Election Day ballot is printed in Spanish in many counties in Texas. Since the passage of the Voting Rights Act in 1965 and amendments to the Act in 1992, the US Justice Department has required "political subdivisions"—these tend to be counties—to print ballots in a language other than English whenever a single-language minority group reaches 5 percent of the voting age population or 10,000 in number. After the 2010 Census, Harris County, which includes Houston, was required to print ballots in Vietnamese in addition to English and Spanish.

CHARACTERISTICS OF THE 144TH DISTRICT

There are 150 seats in the Texas State House. It is one of the largest lower chambers in state legislatures across the nation; Connecticut, Georgia, Missouri, New Hampshire, and Pennsylvania are states that have larger lower chambers. The target number of residents for each district in the State House after the last round of redistricting was 167,637. The total 2010 population in the 144th District was 161,859 (about 3.5 percent less than the target population); the voting age population of the district was 108,509.

Only after a long and protracted redistricting battle were the characteristics of the new 144th District known. The plan originally passed by the legislature created a district that was more heavily Republican than the district that had been in effect until 2010, as was the case with several other districts due to the GOP's control of the redistricting process in Texas in 2012 (Ramsey and Murphy 2011). In fact, in the originally designed new 144th District, statewide Republicans would have beat statewide Democrats by an average of 26 points in 2008 and 2010. The district also contained fewer Hispanic voters than it did previously. As noted in the lawsuit challenging the legislature's original maps, the originally proposed 144th District would have been significantly less Hispanic than the district that was in effect previously. A federal district court threw out the original plan and imposed an interim plan for the Texas House, but it was ultimately vacated by the US Supreme Court. The Supreme Court ordered the district court to create another plan. In this map, the new 144th District was labeled a "Hispanic opportunity district" by the district court. This was due in part to the fact that the minority population in Harris County increased by over 700,000 while the Anglo population decreased by 82,000; at the time of the district court's revision, Hispanics made up 23 percent of the voting age population in Harris County.

The entire 144th is located in Harris County, which includes Houston and many of its suburbs. As noted above, this is an area of Texas that has seen tremendous growth in its Hispanic population. In fact, the 144th's population is 70 percent Hispanic (Batheja 2012). The district stretches from the city of Houston, a small portion of which is included within the district borders, across Upper San Jacinto Bay and Duck Bay into Baytown. It also includes parts of South Houston in the southwestern corner of the district, Pasadena, and Deer Park. The district includes a sizable industrial area along the northern tier of the district north of the Pasadena Freeway. This part of the district "is in the heart of the region's blue-collar petrochemical/ refinery area" (Houston Chronicle 2012). The Houston Shipping Channel is a major border for much of the district in the north, except where the district extends across the channel toward Cloverleaf. A large park honoring the Battle of San Jacinto, the decisive battle in Texas's war with Mexico in 1836, is also in the district.

Even though the 144th is in an area that might signal strong Democratic leanings, the politics of this district exhibit many tendencies of a swing district. The district voted for John McCain over Barack Obama in 2008 by about 3 percent, but it supported Obama by about 2 percent over Mitt Romney in 2012. The district voted for Democrat Bill White over Rick Perry in the 2010 governor's race by nearly 8 points. However, in what might be used as a proxy for party identification given the lack of party registration figures, the district on average supported the Democratic candidate for the Texas Supreme Court over the Republican candidate by nearly 10 points in 2008 but supported the GOP candidate over the Democrat by nearly 4 points in 2010 (Haenschen 2012). In 2012, the 144th was an open-seat contest; the previous office holder, Republican Ken Legler, had passed away unexpectedly in June 2012. However, he had already decided not to run, at least in part because of the district's newly drawn lines. At the time of his decision, Legler noted: "Those that know me know I do not back down from a fight. … I seem to always enter a contest as the underdog and exit the victor. I have no reason to believe that 2012 would be any different. However, the sad fact is that the Federal Court has seen fit to give me a district that will be a constant electoral struggle every two years throughout the decade. That is a political distraction from legislative responsibilities that I choose not to accept" (Holley 2012). The fact that two campaign newcomers were competing in the general election made this toss-up district all the more competitive. It ended up being the closest race in Harris County.

Summary: Why Has Voting Waned?

Texas's history with voting rights is checkered, and voting has been spotty in recent years. Voting ebbs and flows on a national basis, and Texas is no different. Texas is one of the states that lags behind the national average regarding voter participation. Per the United States Elections Project, Texas was forty-ninth in the nation in 2010 (with only 32 percent of eligible voters exercising their right) and forty-seventh in 2012 with 47 percent participation—well behind the national average of 58 percent. Texans do not turn out to vote. The question is: Why? Why are Texans staying away from the polls? Why aren't residents of one of the nation's most populous states voicing their opinions in the voting booth?

One reason is the state's one-party nature. As the state is predominantly conservative and Republican, a case can be made that Democrats have little incentive to cast votes in candidate elections. In midterm election years, the state is one of the worst, if not *the* worst, when it comes to numbers of people going to the polls. In the 2014 midterms, only 201,008 voters participated in the Democratic primary. While the options are slim on that side of the ballot in the state, that is a significantly low number. When it comes to general elections, however, the race is usually already decided; the Republican Party typically has a lock on the race by the time polls open.

Another issue is redistricting. As explained in the chapter on campaigns and elections, redistricting is the process of creating congressional and senatorial districts. Texas's lines are drawn by its senate, a largely Republican body, to favor their party members. This plays into the one-sided nature of the ballot. It is not just Republican dominance, either. Of thirty-six congressional races in 2014, thirteen were uncontested. With no choice to be made, Texans have little incentive to get out and vote.

While Texas's politics are largely culpable for low voter turnout, there are several other reasons. Primarily, is there an incentive to get to the polls? In this, we ask: Does the cost equal the potential benefit of casting a vote? When examining whether to vote, several factors can come into play. Money, time, knowledge, issue saliency, familiarity with candidates, and many other personal factors could weigh into the action of voting. If casting a ballot will cost too much or cause too much of an inconvenience, voters may choose to abstain. There must be a tangible benefit to voting. Some of these benefits may include seeing quick action, voting for a candidate who has a reasonable chance to win, voting for laws or issues that hit home, voting to make a point, or showing disdain through the ballot box. The second part of the equation must outweigh the first for people to visit the voting booth.

There is also the case of voter burnout. As Texas leaves many of its referendum, initiatives, and amendments up to public vote, it can be argued that there are simply too many choices to make, especially when candidate elections are factored in. Without a presidential election to draw voters to the polls, it can be difficult to get them to act on midterm elections or for local (county and municipal) elections. Again, there must be a personal connection to draw members out to the polls.

References

Asher, H. *Polling and the Public: What Every Citizen Should Know.* Washington, D.C.: SAGE, 2011.

Beck, P. A. "The Role of Agents in Political Socialization." In *Handbook of Political Socialization*, 115–141. New York, NY: Free Press, 1977.

Bouillon, H. *Libertarians and Liberalism: Essays in Honour of Gerard Radnitzky*. Aldershot, UK: Avebury, 1996.

Bowler, S., D. Brockington, and T. Donovan. "Election Systems and Voter Turnout: Experiments in the United States." *Journal of Politics* 63, no. 3 (2001): 902–915.

Campbell, D. E. *Why We Vote: How Schools and Communities Shape Our Civic Life*. Princeton, NJ: Princeton University Press, 2006.

Cohen, G. L. "Party over Policy: The Dominating Impact of Group Influence on Political Beliefs." *Journal of Personality and Social Psychology* 85, (2003): 808–22.

Cotrell, C. L., and J. Polinard. "Effects of the Voting Rights Act in Texas: Perceptions of County Election Administrators." *Publius: The Journal of Federalism* 16, no. 4 (1986): 67–80.

Elazar, Daniel J. *Cities of the Prairie: The Metropolitan Frontier and American Politics*. New York: Basic, 1970.

Elazar, Daniel J. *American Federalism: A View from the States*. 2nd ed. New York: Thomas Y. Crowell, 1972.

Erikson, R. S., and K. L. Tedin. *American Public Opinion*. 6th ed. New York: Longman, 2003.

Freeden, M., ed. *Reassessing Political Ideologies*. London: Routledge, 2001.

Jones, J. " Record-High 42% of Americans Identify as Independents." Gallup.com. January 8, 2014. http://www.gallup.com/poll/166763/record-high-americans-identify-independents.aspx?utm_source=40%%20independents%202012&utm_medium=search&utm_campaign=tiles.

Gitlin, T. *The Bulldozer and the Big Tent: Blind Republicans, Lame Democrats, and the Recovery of American Ideals*. Hoboken, NJ: John Wiley & Sons, 2007.

Holsti, O. R., and J. N. Rosenau. "Liberals, Populists, Libertarians, and Conservatives: The Link between Domestic and International Affairs." *International Political Science Review* 17, no. 1 (1996): 29–54.

Hyman, H. *Political Socialization*. New York, NY: Free Press, 1959.

Jost, J. T., C. M. Federico, and J. L. Napier. "Political Ideology: Its Structure, Functions, and Elective Affinities."*Annual Review of Psychology* 60, (2009): 307–337.

Jost, J. T., J. Glaser, A. W. Kruglanski, and F. J. Sulloway. "Political Conservatism as Motivated Social Cognition." *Psychological Bulletin* 129, no. 3 (2003): 339.

Kerlinger, F. N. *Liberalism and Conservatism: The Nature and Structure of Social Attitudes*. 1. New York, NY: Lawrence Erlbaum Assoc. Incorporated, 1984.

Mayer, A. K. "Does Education Increase Political Participation?" *Journal of Politics* 73, no. 3 (2011): 633–645.

Mayer, W. G. *The Changing American Mind: How and Why American Public Opinion Changed Between 1960 and 1988*. Ann Arbor, MI: University of Michigan Press, 1992.

Page, Benjamin, and R. Shapiro. *The Rational Public: Fifty Years of Trends in Americans Policy Preferences*. Chicago: University of Chicago Press, 1992.

Parsons T. *The Social System*. New York: Free Press, 1951.

Pew Research Center (2012). "Changing Face of America Helps Assure Obama Victory." http://www.people-press.org/2012/11/07/changing-face-of-america-helps-assure-obama-victory/.

Pew Research Center (2014). Ibid. http://www.people-press.org/2014/10/17/political-polarization-in-action-insights-into-the-2014-election-from-the-american-trends-panel/.

Rahn, W. M. "The Role of Partisan Stereotypes in Information Processing about Political Candidates." 37, no. 2 *American Journal of Political Science* (1993): 472–496.

Rivers, C. "'Conquered Provinces'? The Voting Rights Act and State Power." *Publius: The Journal of Federalism* 36, no. 3 (2006): 421–442.

Salisbury, R. H. "Research on Political Participation." *American Journal of Political Science* 19, no. 2 (1975): 323–341.

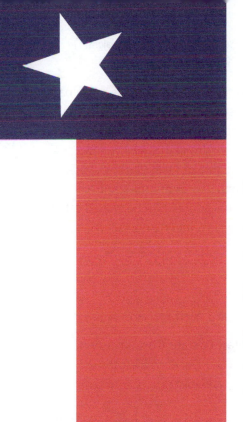

CHAPTER 11

The Structure and Process of Elections and Successful— and Sometimes Harmful—Campaigns

"**F**riends and neighbors." For years, Texas has operated on this system; which counts on name recognition to bolster support and win elections. Campaign finance, voting decisions, and participation were predicated on the ideas of who you know and whose name you can recognize.

Without more information, voters will look for something familiar or to people whose opinions they value and consider viable during an election campaign rather than investigate the candidate's actual merit. Texas has functioned on this theory for quite some time. Whether it's a state or federal election or a vote for the legislature, executive, or judiciary, in the absence of information, resonance takes over and drives political decision making.

This idea can be scary. After all, the value of elections and democracy is that an informed public takes part in a decision to determine who and what is best for them. In the absence of an informed public, other influences, such as opinion makers and those with special interests, will direct the flow of action in a democracy. In Texas, the system survives on the latter and has created a culture that has learned how to benefit from it.

As discussed in the previous chapter, participation rates among Texans, especially minorities, lag behind the national average. In short, Texans are not interested in the labor pains—they just want the baby. In this case, it could lead to a system of restrictive representation that is devoid of accuracy. With campaign finance regulation in the state a nonstarter and unopposed incumbents becoming the norm, in a one-party state, we must evaluate the effect of democracy and whether it is carried out in the fashion intended.

As Madison pointed to in his theory of active citizenship, power attainment is not a bad thing. It is what drives public officials to seek office in the first place. It also drives the public to participate in the process and substantiate the system as conceived and intended in order to obtain adequate representation.

In this chapter, we'll address that issue and examine the structure of Texas elections and the effects of campaigns. While the types of elections the state conducts are important, the manner in which voters relate to candidates and how the candidates function within the system often drive the view, perception, and effectiveness of the elections system and democracy itself.

Governing the Elections

Elections in Texas start with an appointed position: the secretary of state. This office, which is appointed and confirmed, governs elections and ensures that the elections are certified. The secretary of state is responsible for carrying out all elections by administering the system used to carry out the vote.

Chief among the office's responsibilities is making sure the vote is tabulated correctly. With high- and low-profile issues (for an example of the former, consider the 2000 presidential election counts in Florida), throughout history, ensuring that voter tabulations are accurate and posted on time is a fundamental part of the responsibility of governing elections. In Texas, the counting team is responsible for tallying the vote and ensuring that ballots are certified and do not violate the rules, which include no overvoting (choosing more than one candidate) and no ineligible voters.

This task has been turned over in 157 counties to direct-recording electronic systems (DREs), which are electronic voting systems that not only provide electronic balloting but also tabulate results. The choice of these voting systems is left to the counties in Texas if they do not violate the rules set forth by the state and secretary of state's office. Electronic voting systems have the advantage of being quick, manageable, and familiar to many people. However, these systems could scare off voters in certain populations that are not tech savvy, including the elderly (traditionally a large voting bloc), minorities, and the impoverished. All three of these communities are susceptible to not having access to information based on a lack of available resources or a limited understanding of technology. Decisions made by the state regarding systems need to take these concerns into consideration.

The secretary of state is also in charge of carrying out the entire election code. This includes the guidelines for what system can be used, the method for tabulating election results, and the local personnel who will carry out the vote. Each district and poll must have a captain and chair to oversee the election. These positions are tasked with ensuring that elections at polls around the state are carried out within the rules of the Texas Election Code.

Part of the election system is designing the ballot. As mentioned before, the "friends and neighbors" method is front and center in Texas and certainly extends into the voting booth. How the ballot is presented provides an important topic for discussion. One of those discussions is about long versus short ballots. Long ballots include all elections on one ballot. From the presidential election to local referendums and initiatives, these choices are placed on the same ballot in an attempt to present them to people while they vote in predominant elections. Short ballots break up choices into separate elections to avoid voter burnout—a result of inundating voters with too many choices, which can force them to stop voting or choose not to finish the ballot.

Another choice is to conduct a partisan or nonpartisan election. Partisan elections have the party affiliation attached to candidates, while nonpartisan elections do not. Texas conducts partisan elections. Concerns over partisan elections revolve around diminishing the importance of personal or character choice. As will be discussed, elections are designed to provide an accurate representative for a district. A partisan election allows for a choice to be made without knowledge about the individual candidate. Proponents of this election type suggest that party identification is an integral part of a candidate's makeup and allows for common understanding and connection to ideologies and platforms.

Ballot access[1] is also under the control of the secretary of state. Ballot access is one of the major challenges facing third parties. As discussed in the chapter on political parties, getting on the ballot is a major battle in Texas. Currently, the Green and Libertarian parties, along with the Republicans and Democrats, have access to the ballot. Candidates from other parties would have to meet petition and fee requirements to gain access to the ballot or run as write-in candidates. These ballot requirements differ based on the office being sought but are consistent in one aspect: receiving two percent of the vote in the previous election is factored in. For a race for US representative, access to the ballot requires five hundred signatures and a fee of $3,125. For a high court justice position in Texas, the fee for access is $3,750, and five thousand signatures are required. Local government offices require a fee ranging from $375 (for constable in a county of less than two hundred thousand people) to $2,500 (district judge). Obtaining this support and raising these funds is a tough battle for many.

Lastly, there is the issue of voter registration. Texans can register to vote when they are eighteen years old, and they must vote in their home counties. There is an exception for college students who live away from home for an extended period, but usually a person must vote in the county that he or she registered and resides in. Military personnel and those living overseas (including in Mexico or Canada) can cast absentee ballots; applications for absentee ballots must be filed at least eleven days before the election, and the ballot must be postmarked within five days after the election. These ballots are cast physically outside the district but are included as part of the district count.

---

1   The structure and requirements reviewed in this chapter can be found in the Texas Election Code, http://www. statutes.legis.state.tx.us/?link=EL. The code provides statutes and limitations on all specifics regarding the structure of elections, the requirements placed on voters, and how elections are carried out by detailing the standard usage and processes that have been approved by the state of Texas.

Requirements to vote are that you are at least eighteen years old, not mentally incapacitated, and not a felon carrying out punishment. If you are a felon who has completed a sentence, you can reregister to vote. Other requirements have come under more fire.

Voter ID laws have become a staple of dissent in Texas. As discussed in the chapter on public opinion and participation, voter ID laws are a roadblock to voting for minorities and those new to the state. Former Governor Rick Perry argued the laws would ensure that voting was carried out properly and provide the state with a stable way to guarantee an absence of voter fraud. Acceptable forms of ID are as follows:

- Texas driver's license issued by the Texas Department of Public Safety (DPS)
- Texas Election Identification Certificate issued by DPS
- Texas personal identification card issued by DPS
- Texas license to carry a handgun issued by DPS
- United States military identification card containing the person's photograph
- United States citizenship certificate containing the person's photograph
- United States passport

Types of Elections

Texas sets itself apart from other states in how elections are carried out. From the presidential election to votes for local offices and referendums, Texas has a unique way of handling the election process. Texas practices the direct representative system, which means that a district or constituency selects a single member to serve as its proxy. These winner-take-all elections comprise the candidate election system in Texas. The focus is on selecting a representative who is an accurate proxy for those in their district; hence, the residency and participation requirements outlined in the legislative chapter. The single-member-district concept is the grounding for American democracy and the purpose of candidate elections both nationally and in Texas. This concept is designed to ensure accurate representation based on proximity to elected representatives and shared interests.

Primaries

The first step in the system in Texas is the primary election. This election determines who the political parties will select to run in the general election. Parties can employ one of two methods to carry out this stage: a traditional primary or a caucus. Texas is in the majority of the states that use the latter. Primaries are emblematic of general elections: candidates campaign within the voting area, and constituents turn out on a specific date to cast a ballot awarding the primary votes, based on population, to determine the winner of the primary. Primaries can be conducted according to one of two types of rules:

1   Open rules allow anyone in the area to participate in the election. Regardless of party affiliation, any registered voter can vote in any party's primary. This allows for voters from the opposing party to take part in the opposite party's election.

2   Closed rules restrict access to the primary to only those who are registered members of the party in question. This restricts the voter base and lowers the ability of opposing party members to "sandbag" the primary. It also restricts the access of any moderates or independents seeking to participate.

Primaries in Texas are conducted under open rules, meaning anyone can participate. This allows all voters access. However, until 2015, Texas Democratic primaries were carried out in a unique fashion that has been coined the "Texas two-step." Under this system, during the day of the primary, voters turned out to the polls to determine the winner of the primary, who was then allocated seventy-five percent of the delegates. After the polls closed, registered voters who had participated in the primary that day could return in a closed-rules setting to participate in a caucus, or town-hall type meeting, to vote under closed rules on party business and to allocate the remaining 25 percent of the primary delegates. Caucuses were held by precinct and doubled as meetings to decide local party business. The two-step process was designed to 1) pick a winner and 2) meet the party business requirements set forth by the Texas Election Code.

Texas Democrats ditched this confusing process in 2015 in favor of a traditional primary that allocated delegates to any candidate who received 15 percent or more of the vote. In 2016, the Democratic Party switched to a formal primary election that allocates primary delegates through a statewide election. The reasoning for the move was simple: the party was worried its process was confusing to voters and left some people out of fully participating in the primary election.

Since Texas is a winner-take-all state, there must be a victor by majority vote in all primaries except those for the presidential election. In state elections, a candidate must receive a majority (one more than half) of the vote to be declared the victor. If no candidate wins a majority, the top two vote getters enter a runoff primary to decide who will take the election. Runoff primaries, which usually garner a low turnout, are closed to anyone who voted in the opposing party's primary during the first round of the election and are held two months after the general primary.

Texas's presidential primary, along with the primaries of thirteen other states, is held on what is now known as "Super Tuesday" (in 2016, Super Tuesday was on the first of March).

This winner-take-all race is part of a large number of elections that have come to be predictors of primary success: in 2008 and 2012,[2] all four parties' presidential nominees emerged victorious on Super Tuesday. While the presidential race takes precedence, races for the governor and other state and federal offices take center stage, by design, in midterm years, when the president is not up for election.

General Elections

General elections happen at every level in Texas. Once the primaries have been decided, general elections for federal offices (such as the presidency and congressional seats) as well as state and local offices are held. General elections take place between the primary winners from the parties on the ballot. Usually, the race is between Republican and Democratic candidates; however, third-party candidates can participate in the race if they receive enough support in previous elections or through a write-in campaign.

In a general election, a plurality is all that is needed to win, unlike the majority required in the primary election. Among the candidates, the one who receives the most votes claims the office. General state and federal elections are conducted on the first Tuesday after the first Monday in November of even-numbered years. Local elections, like those for mayor, will often happen on this schedule as well.

General elections are where the concept of straight-ticket voting comes into play; this is the concept of voters simply choosing to vote for everyone on the ticket who belongs to one party. This applies in elections for the presidency all the way down to local elections. The case for straight-ticket voting is that it helps voters identify candidates whose platforms agree with their ideology. The downside is that it often removes the need for voters to investigate candidates. Even if a voter selects straight-ticket candidates, they can alter their individual selections if they choose to.

Special Elections

Special elections in Texas decide a number of different issues, from legislative matters to policy to settling candidate and policy-based elections. Participation in special elections in Texas is not nearly as high as in other contests. While the presidential election of 2012 got 49 percent[3] of the state's registered voters to the polls and midterm elections routinely draw between

---

2   Ballotpedia.org, https://ballotpedia.org/Main_Page.

3   Ballotpedia.org, https://ballotpedia.org/Main_Page.

25 and 35 percent,[4] special elections can draw as few as two to four percent due to their low profiles and often very specific topics.

Popular referendums—where legislation is initiated within the public, sent for legislative approval, and returned to the public for a vote—are a staple of special elections. These are specified elections to pass laws with public approval. Legislative referendums—which start in the legislature and are passed to the public—and constitutional amendments (outlined in the corresponding chapter) are other types that call for popular approval. These elections can involve state law, local ordinances, or amendments to documents. The important factor is that they need popular approval. Each special policy election must be published and the public given notice of when the election will take place (this is decided by the legislature). Low-profile issues largely fall by the wayside, as only those people who are hyperinvolved pay attention. Higher-profile issues, such as the vote on Houston's Equal Rights Opportunity law, gain much more attention due to their greater resonance.

Candidate elections can be the subject of special elections as well. These elections occur when no one candidate receives a majority of the votes. The requirement for a plurality of the vote mandates a runoff election between the two top vote getters. This can happen in the primary or general election process with any state or local election. Candidate elections have a much higher profile than topic-oriented special elections, as they involve two people who have sought office for a long period of time. One caveat: the person who wins the general election may not necessarily be the favorite in a runoff election, as he or she is tasked with fighting for the support of those whose chosen candidate is no longer an option.

Indicators of Success: Incumbency, Running Unopposed, and Redistricting

A number of factors affect how elections will turn out. Visibility and access to information are chief across all elections, be they candidate or policy elections. Visibility and saliency of the issue dominate the latter. If the issue has a high level of relevance amongst groups that will spend money to publicize it, the election will receive higher participation. The expansive field of literature dealing with election success on the candidate side is too enormous to address here. However, we can point to a few effective predictive and election-impacting factors, including the roles of incumbent success, running unopposed, and redistricting.

In Texas, the past three elections have seen a spike, in relative terms, in the amount of incumbent turnover (when an incumbent retires or does not seek reelection). Per election filing data, Texas had the second-lowest incumbent turnover in the nation, with only six out of

---

4   Office of the Texas Secretary of State, http://www.sos.state.tx.us/elections/historical/70-92.shtml.

165 seats at the state and federal levels lacking an incumbent. That number rose to nineteen in 2012 and then to 26[5] in 2014. Despite the rise in numbers, running as an incumbent is a clear path to success in the state. In 2014, only eleven of the 150 incumbents were defeated in state or federal elections in the state.

Why is running as an incumbent so effective? There are several reasons, but none is more significant than the familiarity factor. When discussing state elections, much of the decision-making process for voters is based on who they know and what the candidates have done for them. In a single-member district state where there can be only one winner for a seat, name recognition provides a significant leg up. Also, in smaller counties or elections where the incumbent can provide tangible benefits, running as the incumbent offers a substantial advantage. As will be discussed later in this chapter, money is usually provided in the form of campaign donations to viable and familiar candidates as well.

While running as an incumbent is one key to victory, running unopposed is much easier. State elections have historically fallen prey to the unopposed election at a rate much higher than federal elections (Squire 2000). The reason is that state elections, unlike federal elections, have become more significant, especially in Texas, as the state government and officials – both state and federal representatives - accrue more power over policy. While the profiles of these seats have risen, questions have been raised about the effect of money and campaign access and whether the elections are truly open to all comers. In addition, the hybrid nature of the Texas legislature favors individuals who have jobs that allow time for legislative activity, since it is not a full-time position. These factors lead to cases in Texas where incumbents or those seeking state office often running without opposition. While democracy is founded on challenged elections (Dahl 1963, 1967), there is often no challenger to be faced. In 2013, Texas approved Proposition 8, which amended the constitution to allow someone running unopposed for state or local office to take office without winning the election if the person is the only qualified candidate running for the office. In 2014, forty-three[6] representatives in the Texas House were "elected" under Proposition 8 due to the absence of qualified competitors.

Last on the list is redistricting. The view of redistricting can be muddy. At its core, it is the action of redrawing district lines to accommodate changing states. Following the release of new census data every year, Texas has the option to revisit the way the state's districts are designed (as is allowed by the US Constitution). This process is carried out by the state senate and, without specific guidance from the US Constitution, it is open to political manipulation. Scheduling becomes an issue in the process, as the census data is collected in even-numbered years but not produced until well into the spring and early summer of odd-numbered years, when session is almost out. In 1950, the constitution was amended to give control of redistricting to the Legislative Redistricting Board, which is made up of the lieutenant governor, the speaker of the house, the comptroller, the land commissioner, and the attorney general—all

---

5   Ballotpedia.org, https://ballotpedia.org/Main_Page.

6   Electproject.org, http://www.electproject.org/.

elected positions. The board has 150 days from the end of session to present a plan for redistricting.

If done in an ethical and bipartisan way, the process can give a state a proper picture of its political districts, which in turn helps in deciding representation. When those virtues are left by the wayside, redistricting is referred to as gerrymandering or creative redistricting. This is the process by which a state senate committee takes advantage of political affiliation to draw the district lines in a way that benefits the party in control. Redistricting has crossed so far over into gerrymandering that, even though it is an illegal practice, the state legislature is expected to exploit the process, and Texas history confirms this expectation. The process can break up districts and cause battles not only between ideologies and political parties but also over the makeup of the districts in regard to economics, the ratio of large and small cities, and ethnicity.

The practice was popular as states looked to redefine an emerging nation and, in the case of Texas, was used until the 1960s. At that time, the Supreme Court attempted to settle these disputes by mandating, with its decision in *Baker v. Carr* (1962), that districts have equal population. This reinforced the "one person, one vote" nature of elections.

Since the adoption of the Legislative Redistricting Board, the dominant party in Texas has benefitted, but not without challenge. *White v. Regester* (1973) contested the use of at-large, multimember districts in Dallas, contending that it was an attempt to reduce the impact of minority voting. The challenge was upheld in 1976, and the county was forced to switch to single-member districts. Since 1970, the Republican Party has gained more control over the process. Democrats have challenged their decisions, and the federal court has seen fit to intervene. In 2000, when two seats were added due to population growth, a point of contention arose as the Democrats accused the all-Republican LRB of manipulating the lines. A panel made up of three federal judges redrew the lines to fit in with the Voting Rights Act of 1965. Still, the Republicans benefitted from the process.

A significant verdict was handed down in 2006, when the Supreme Court heard a challenge from interest groups and Texas Democrats regarding an attempt to redistrict mid-decade. The reasoning behind the redistricting effort was that it was intended to draw a state that was politically representative. The dissent said that the lines were drawn in order to create a political disadvantage for certain groups and Democratic candidates. In *Davis v. Bandemer* (1986), the US Supreme Court found that, although the process of redistricting is inherently political, if it does not unduly subjugate the people, there is no constitutional prohibition on mid-decade redistricting.

With a spike in population (mainly in the Hispanic community), redistricting was a hot topic in 2011. With the Republicans increasing their control, the call came to redraw the lines to represent the emerging population. While the demographics were changing, the feeling was that the process would be overtly political, so dissenters initiated the challenge process, delaying the Texas primary that year. Looking to avoid a battle of preclearance, Texas attempted to avoid the US Justice Department, which joined the suit against the redrawn map. The challenge was upheld, and the redistricting effort was overturned by a federal appeals court;

the redrawn map did not receive clearance due to its attempt to limit the minority vote in districts. In 2013, Texas challenged the decision in the Supreme Court, which struck down the ability of the federal court to make the decision, and Texas Republicans were granted victory as their ability to implement their districts was upheld.

At its best, redistricting is a progressive step taken by government to maintain a positive connection with an emerging population. However, redrawing lines can create problems. Per Hayes and McKee (2009), redistricting or gerrymandering can cause disenfranchisement amongst communities if the lines are moved. Voter roll-off (abstaining from voting in a new district) doubles in districts that have been redrawn and can have a negative effect on voter turnout, especially in a community commonly affected by overtly political redistricting.

Campaign Finance in Texas: The Real Wild West

Since 2010, campaign finance has been a source of significant debate. At the federal level, the government, before 2010, had attempted to limit the effect of money in the election world. Stipulations on reporting requirements, restrictions on allowable sources and types of donations, and even failed attempts at capping contributions were indicative of a culture that saw money in politics as something to be monitored at the federal level. In 2010, this changed with the *Citizen's United v. FEC* (2010) case. In that decision, the Supreme Court found that Super PACs (political organizations that are not characterized as part of the government or political system), share the same rights and privileges regarding political activities that individuals do. This decision pushed campaign finance into overdrive and, in a sense, has contributed to a rise in its impact: "developments before and after *Citizens United* affected political advertising and, perhaps ironically, the opposition advertising with which political campaigns are often most concerned" (Garrett 2013, 83). Political actors are now free to take actions based on their beliefs without the consent of anyone. They are also free to provide money outside the realm of what is considered to fall under the restrictions on political or government entities. R. Sam Garrett further examines the ramifications of *Citizens United* in Reading 11.1.

Reading 11.1

"Money, Politics, and Policy: Campaign Finance Before and After Citizens United"[7]
from *Campaigns and Elections American Style*
R. Sam Garrett

CITIZENS UNITED: A MAJOR CHANGE IN CAMPAIGN FINANCE LAW FOR THE 2010 ELECTION CYCLE

Immediately following the 2008 elections, when Barack Obama was elected president and Democratic majorities won House and Senate contests, the next election cycle began. Although the 2010 congressional elections were expected to be competitive, observers did not anticipate that, in the midst of those elections, a major change would occur in campaign finance law. These developments were substantial not only for the policy boundaries they created, but also because they directly affected which groups could advocate for or against candidates.

Citizens United is notable for a variety of legal, policy, and practical political reasons. Like *Buckley* before it, *Citizens United* also is important for reasons that extend far beyond the case itself. Indeed, especially as it was first presented, *Citizens United* addressed a relatively narrow question about applicability of the electioneering communication provision. The implications of the case, however, were far broader. By the time the Supreme Court issued its five-to-four decision on January 21, 2010, advocates had come before the justices not the standard single time, but twice, and the Court had expanded the issues in play. Essentially, the attorneys were asked to address the questions they had initially presented and whether those questions also had implications for other Supreme Court precedents which, in turn, had major implications for the nation's campaign finance law—and, thereby, policy questions for Congress and federal agencies.

This section presents an overview of those developments and why they are important for understanding *Citizens United* and its aftermath. Before proceeding, it is important to note that discussion here is intended to be a general academic and policy-oriented overview. Some important constitutional and legal issues are mentioned in passing, but those interested in a detailed legal discussion should also consult other sources.[1]

In *Citizens United,* an incorporated, tax-exempt 501(c)(4) organization called Citizens United challenged the electioneering communication provision. The

7   R. Sam Garrett, "Money, Politics, and Policy: Campaign Finance Before and After Citizens United," *Campaigns and Elections American Style*, ed. James A. Thurber and Candice J. Nelson, pp. 86-88, 93-99. Copyright © 2013 by Taylor & Francis Group. Reprinted with permission.

group presented itself not as an interest group, as the organization was generally perceived, but as a media company that made documentary films. Citizens United contended that its film about then-presidential candidate Hillary Clinton (*Hillary: The Movie*) did not qualify as an electioneering communication and, therefore, that the group should not be required to form a PAC to air the film in theaters and through video-on-demand cable, as it planned to do ahead of the 2012 elections. The FEC disagreed and Citizens United sued.

After a district court sided with the FEC, Citizens United appealed to the Supreme Court, which heard initial oral arguments on the electioneering communication questions in March 2009. In an unusual move, instead of issuing a decision, the Court ordered the parties to file additional briefs and appear again for a second round of oral arguments. Among other questions, the Court asked whether, in order to rule on whether Citizens United's film qualified as an electioneering communication and, as such, had to be paid for with hard money (i.e., by a PAC rather than Citizens United itself), the Court should reconsider its 1990 opinion in *Austin v. Michigan Chamber of Commerce.* In *Austin,* the Court determined that political speech could be restricted based on the speaker's corporate status. *Austin* essentially confirmed that corporations could not spend funds to influence federal elections.

Once the Court broadened *Citizens United* to include not only the status of the electioneering communication provision, but also the broader question of corporate-funded independent expenditures, the case transformed from addressing the relatively narrow question of whether the electioneering communication provision applied to limited-distribution films, to considering the much broader question of corporate independent expenditures in general. The case, therefore, now had the potential to alter the decades-old ban on corporate spending in elections, in addition to, or maybe even regardless of, the electioneering communication issue. The legal and policy communities immediately took notice both because of the substantive questions involved and because the second round of oral arguments were scheduled for September 2009. Even if an expedited decision was issued as expected, most observers expected that the best-case scenario would be a ruling in the mid- or late fall of 2009—setting the stage for a potentially major change in campaign finance law and practice halfway through the 2010 election cycle.

Super PACs and Other Groups in the Policy and Political Environments

Super PACs are significant in federal elections because they provide a new mechanism for people and groups to aggregate unlimited funds calling for election or defeat of federal candidates. But where do they fit in the policy and campaign environments? What can they do that other groups cannot, or vice versa? The answer is important because how a group is regulated determines what it can do—and where policymakers are typically engaged in debate over whether the activities of people or groups should be condoned as protected political speech or regulated as a perceived loophole that could facilitate corruption.

The name "Super PAC" suggests that these groups are both similar to and different from traditional PACs. Traditional PACs (e.g., those that have been on the scene since the 1970s) also allow their donors to pool resources to support or oppose candidates and, like Super PACs, are primarily regulated by the FEC. Super PACs are unique, however, because of their ability to amass unlimited contributions. Traditional PACs and Super PACs also differ in their ability to make contributions: traditional PACs can do so; Super PACs cannot.

Perhaps most importantly, Super PACs and traditional PACs are both political committees. [...] [B]eing a political committee means the entity is regulated primarily by FECA. Among other important points, political committees must regularly file financial reports with the FEC and can make only limited contributions. Super PACs, however, essentially are a different kind of political committee, because although they report to the FEC they can accept unlimited funds but cannot make contributions.

Understanding Super PACs also raises the important distinction between political committees and other entities this chapter calls "politically active organizations." While political committees are party committees, candidate committees, and PACs, and are regulated primarily by FECA and the FEC, politically active organizations are regulated primary by the Internal Revenue Code (IRC, i.e., federal tax law) and the Internal Revenue Service (IRS). Politically active organizations include two major kinds of entities designated by their placement in the IRC—527s and 501(c)s. Sometimes colloquially referred to as "nonprofits," both kinds of groups are tax-exempt entities.

Best known for the relatively brief period in the early 2000s—particularly the 2004 presidential election—two prominent 527 groups, Swift Boat Veterans for Truth on the Republican side and the Democratic group America Coming Together, battled over Democrat John Kerry's presidential campaign. Although all political committees are 527s for tax purposes (e.g., reporting investment income to the IRS), not all 527s are political committees. The small subset of groups claiming to be 527s, but not political committees, generated controversy before and after the 2004 election cycle. The FEC eventually levied substantial fines on some 527s for failing to register as political committees.[2] In some ways, Super PACs appear to have assumed the role that 527 organizations played in previous elections. Like Super PACs, 527s, too, can accept unlimited funds and may make unlimited expenditures, but the extent to which the groups should be regulated by FECA and the FEC has been hotly debated. Because Super PACs are widely understood to be political committees—in this case, with clear permission to accept unlimited contributions and make unlimited independent expenditures—they appear to offer more regulatory certainty than the case-by-case assessment employed with 527s.

Three kinds of 501(c) organizations—501(c)(4) social welfare groups, 501(c)(5) unions, and 501(c)(6) trade associations—were particularly important in 2010 and 2012, both independently and when interacting with Super PACs.[3] These entities engaged in political activities before *Citizens United,* but some observers viewed the decision as giving (c)(4)–(5), and (6) organizations more freedom to engage in independent expenditures because typically the groups are incorporated (and, hence, can use corporate treasuries to make independent expenditures). The degree to which these 501(c)s can engage in independent expenditures versus other activities (e.g., conducting more general "social welfare") while maintaining their tax-exempt status remains open to debate.[4] Nonetheless, particularly in 2010 and 2012, many 501(c)(4)s, (5)s, and (6)s made substantial independent expenditures on their own and funneled funds to Super PACs.

Using these 501(c) entities to route funds to Super PACs has important implications for transparency. Unlike political committees, some politically active organizations—including 501(c)s—do not typically report their donors to the FEC. Although any entity making an independent expenditure or electioneering communication must report that activity to the FEC, donors are only identified if they contributed specially for the "purpose of furthering" independent expenditures or electioneering communications.[5] Therefore, routing contributions through 501(c) organizations permitted Super PACs—at least in 2010 and 2012—to avoid disclosing the original source of funds used for independent expenditures as long as those funds were given to the 501(c) for general purposes and not specifically for independent expenditures.

POLICY AND POLITICS: THE AFTERMATH OF 2010

The monumental changes in campaign finance law in 2010 did not necessarily spur public policy changes. In fact, as of this writing, Congress has not amended campaign finance law to respond to *Citizens United,* the development of Super PACs, or the other post-2010 topics discussed above. Dozens of bills—mostly sponsored by Democrats—proposed various options, ranging from disclosure to constitutional amendments—but none became law. During the 111th Congress (2009–2011), the House narrowly passed the DISCLOSE Act (H.R. 5175), a bill that would have required additional reporting about the original sources of contributions and additional documentation throughout political transactions. Amid criticisms about the bill's applicability and proposed spending restrictions, however, the measure died in the Senate.

The FEC also has not issued new regulations on the topic—partially due to a partisan split among the agency's six commissioners. The agency did issue advisory opinions providing guidance to campaigns and other players in some circumstances. The first wave of AO activity occurred in the summer of 2010, when the FEC approved two related AOs in response to questions from the Club for Growth[6] and Commonsense Ten.[7] In these instances, the commission determined that the organizations could solicit unlimited contributions for use in independent expenditures.[8] In both AOs, the FEC also advised that, while post–*Citizens United* rules were being drafted to amend agency reporting forms, would-be Super PACs could file letters with the commission indicating their status. Hence, the FEC had recognized—albeit not through regulation—the concept of Super PACs. AOs also permitted federal candidates and party officials to solicit contributions for Super PACs. The commission advised, however, that contributions solicited by federal candidates and national party officials must be within the PAC contribution limits established in FECA (for example, $5,000 annually for individual contributions).

Given the monumental changes in campaign finance law post-2010, it might seem surprising that more than a full election cycle later so few concrete policy changes have occurred. Indeed, proregulatory campaign finance groups sharply criticized President Obama, Congress, and the FEC for not responding to limit the decision's effects—just as others have cheered *Citizens United* as a restoration of corporate and union speech that requires no response. As this [...] has shown, finding policy options that are constitutionally viable, that would have the desired effect, and that are politically viable is easier said than done.

This [...] has introduced the rules of campaign finance and tried to demystify how various contribution limits and reporting requirements apply to various people and groups. As the discussion has shown, 2010 ushered in substantial changes in permissible campaign spending. [...]

NOTES

1   In addition to the case itself, several amicus curiae ("friend of the court") briefs were filed and are available on the FEC website at http://www.fec.gov/law/litigation_related.shtml#-cu_sc08. See also, for example, Lowenstein, Hasen, and Tokaji (2012) and Youn (2011).

2   For historical background, see, for example, Garrett, Lunder, and Whitaker (2008). Joseph E. Cantor served as an original coauthor of earlier versions of the report.

3   Importantly, the 501(c)s discussed here do *not* include 501(c)(3)s. These public charity organizations (e.g., schools and houses of worship) only may engage in limited political activity.

4   On tax issues, which are beyond the scope of this [...], see, for example, Lunder and Whitaker (2011).

5 This distinction takes root in litigation surrounding FEC disclosure regulations and FECA reporting requirements. For additional discussion, see Garrett (2012b).

6 AO 2010–09.

7 AO 2010–11.

8 Ibid.

REFERENCES

Austin v. Michigan Chamber of Commerce. 1990. 494 U.S. 652.

Biersack, Robert, Paul S. Herrnson, and Clyde Wilcox, eds. 1994. *Risky Business? PAC Decisionmaking in Congressional Elections.* Armonk, NY: M. E. Sharpe.

Buckley v. Valeo. 1976. 424 U.S. 1.

Burton, John Michael, and Daniel M Shea. 2003. *Campaign Mode: Strategic Vision in Congressional Elections.* Lanham, MD: Rowman & Littlefield.

Citizens United v. Federal Election Commission. 2010. 130 S. Ct. (slip opinion).

Corrado, Anthony. 2005. "Money and Politics: A History of Federal Campaign Finance Law." In Anthony Corrado, Thomas E. Mann, Daniel R. Ortiz, and Trevor Potter, *The New Campaign Finance Sourcebook,* 7–47. Washington: Brookings Institution Press.

Dulio, David A. 2004. *For Better or Worse? How Political Consultants Are Changing Elections in the United States.* Albany: SUNY Press.

Garrett, R. Sam. 2010. *Campaign Crises: Detours on the Road to Congress.* Boulder, CO: Lynne Rienner Publishers.

———. 2012a. "Seriously Funny: Understanding Campaign Finance Policy Through the Colbert Super PAC." *Saint Louis University Law Journal* 56 (3): 711–723.

———. 2012b. "The State of Campaign Finance Policy: Recent Developments and Issues for Congress." Congressional Research Service report.

———. 2012c. "Super PACs in Federal Elections: Overview and Issues for Congress." Congressional Research Service report.

Garrett, R. Sam, Paul S. Herrnson, and James A. Thurber. 2006. "Perspectives on Campaign Ethics." In *The Electoral Challenge: Theory Meets Practice,* edited by Stephen C. Craig, 203–224. Washington: CQ Press.

Garrett, R. Sam, Erika Lunder, and L. Paige Whitaker. 2008. "Section 527 Political Organizations: Background and Issues for Federal Election and Tax Laws." Congressional Research Service report.

Hohnenstein, Kurt. 2007. *Coining Corruption: The Making of the American Campaign Finance System.* DeKalb, IL: Northern Illinois University Press.

La Raja, Raymond J. 2008. *Small Change: Money, Political Parties, and Campaign Finance Reform.* Ann Arbor: University of Michigan Press.

Lowenstein, Daniel Hays, Richard L. Hasen, and Daniel P. Tokaji. 2012. *Election Law: Cases and Materials,* 5th ed. Durham, NC: Carolina Academic Press.

Lunder, Erika, and L. Paige Whitaker. 2011. "501(c)(4) Organizations and Campaign Activity: Analysis Under Tax and Campaign Finance Laws." Congressional Research Service report.

McConnell v. Federal Election Commission. 2003. 540 U.S. 93.

Medvic, Stephen K. 2001. *Political Consultants in U.S. Congressional Elections.* Columbus: Ohio State University Press.

Mutch, Robert E. 1988. *Campaigns, Congress, and the Courts: The Making of Federal Campaign Finance Law.* New York: Praeger.

Nelson, Candice J., Stephen K. Medvic, and David A. Dulio, eds. 2002. *Shades of Gray: Perspectives on Campaign Ethics.* Washington: Brookings Institution Press.

Ortiz, Daniel R. 2005. "The First Amendment and the Limits of Campaign Finance Reform." In Anthony Corrado, et al. *The New Campaign Finance Sourcebook*, 91–122. Washington: Brookings Institution Press.

Pfau, Michael, and Henry Kenski. 1990. *Attack Politics: Strategy and Defense.* New York: Praeger.

SpeechNow.org v. FEC. 2010. 599 F.3d 686 (D.C. Cir.).

Thurber, James A., and Candice J. Nelson, eds. 2000. *Campaign Warriors: Political Consultants in Elections.* Washington: Brookings Institution Press.

Whitaker, L. Paige. 2010. "The Constitutionality of Campaign Finance Regulation: *Buckley v. Valeo* and Its Supreme Court Progeny." Congressional Research Service report.

Wisconsin Right to Life v. FEC (WRTL II). 2007. 551 U.S. 449.

Youn, Monica, ed. 2011. *Money, Politics, and the Constitution: Beyond* Citizens United. New York: The Century Foundation Press.

Texas has not shared the federal government's apprehension about campaign finance's influence on elections and the political system. Texas has been an open-contribution state, allowing money and politics to not only mix but also become married in a sense. Money allows candidates access to voters and voter groups. The ability to extend a brand and build relationships helps candidates, especially those in low-profile state elections, gain the necessary connections to claim voters' support, which is essential in all elections. With voters seeking out candidates they are familiar or comfortable with, the ability to "buy" a connection has become integral to success, specifically in state activities. This is where campaign finance and money come into play.

Texas has sparse limits on campaign finance in the state. While the state has followed suit with reporting laws from the federal level, Texas's Ethics Commission oversees campaign spending and contributions in the state. Any contribution that is deemed a political expenditure—which is classified by the commission as money contributing to a political act—must be reported. Candidates and elected officials must have a treasurer and provide detailed reports to the TEC twice a year[8] (on January 1 and July 15) or incur a $500 fine. Lobbies and contributors must file a report for any contribution over $500 as well. These reports are a step in the right direction, as they attempt to increase transparency. There is no cap on spending by those considered to be from outside the government—not a government employee, elected official, or political actor. Table 11.1 shows the levels of contributions that a candidate in Texas is allowed to receive.

Violations of TEC rules can be met with fines. The commission can oversee activity and fine those who do not comply with their statutes; however, the fines are minimal. The effect of the fine for breaking these statutes does not act as a significant deterrent.

As campaign finance rolls on, the effect of money is significant. Personal wealth has become a prime indicator of election success. As the state and federal elections in Texas have

---

8   Texas Ethics Commission, "Research Advisory Opinions, Statutes, and Rules." https://www.ethics.state.tx.us/main/research.htm.

Table 11.1 Federal and Texas Campaign Contribution Limits

Donors	US—Presidential and Congressional Elections					Texas—Statewide and Legislative Elections	Texas Judicial Elections
	Recipients				Special Limits	Recipients	
	Candidate Committee	PAC[1]	State, District, and Local Party Committee[2]	National Party Committee[3]		Candidate Committees, PACs, Party Committees	Candidate Committees
Individual	$2,700* per election	$5,000 per year	$10,000 per year combined limit	$33,400* per year	Biennial limit of $95,000* ($37,500 to all candidates and $57,500[5] to all PACs and parties)	Unlimited	$1,000–5,000 per election, depending on judicial district population[8]
State, District and Local Party Committee[2]	$5,000 per election combined limit	$5,000 per year combined limit	Unlimited transfers to other party committees			Unlimited	
National Party Committee[3]	$5,000 per election	$5,000 per year	Unlimited transfers to other party committees		$35,000* to Senate candidate per campaign[6]	Unlimited	$5,000–25,000 per election[9]
PAC, Multicandidate[7]	$5,000 per election	$5,000 per year	$5,000 per year combined limit	$15,000 per year		Unlimited	
PAC, not Multicandidate[7]	$2,700* per election	$5,000 per year	$10,000 per year combined limit	$33,400* per year		Unlimited	

Sources: https://texaspolitics.utexas.edu/archive/html/vce/features/0702_01/cfrules.html, http://www.fec.gov/info/contrib-limitschart1516.pdf

Full Source: Federal Election Commission. Record. 29(1). Jan. 2003. Accessed at http://www.fec.gov/pdf/record/2003/jan03.pdf, July 19, 2004; Texas Ethics Commission at http://www.tec.state.tx.us and its Acting Executive Director, Sarah Woelk (telephone call, July 19, 2004); Armstrong, G., and K. Strama. "Texas." In Lobbying, PACs, and Campaign Finance: 50 State Handbook. P. Christianson, et al., eds. Eagan, MN: Thomson West, 2002.

Full Footnotes:

These limits are indexed for inflation. "Per election" means each (in Texas, each contested) election in which the candidate appears on the ballot; hence, limits apply separately to primary, general, and any runoff elections.

1. These limits apply to both separate segregated funds (SSFs) and political action committees (PACs). Affiliated committees share the same set of limits on contributions made and received.
2. A state party committee shares its limits with local and district party committees in that state unless a local or district committee's independence can be demonstrated. These limits apply to multicandidate committees only.

3. A party's national committee, Senate campaign committee, and House campaign committee are each considered national party committees, and each has separate limits, except with respect to Senate candidates (see Special Limits column).

4. Each of the following is considered a separate election with a separate limit: primary election, caucus or convention with the authority to nominate, general election, runoff election and special election.

5. No more than $37,500 of this amount may be contributed to state and local parties and PACs.

6. This limit is shared by the national committee and the Senate campaign committee.

7. A multicandidate committee is a political committee that has been registered for at least six months, has received contributions from more than fifty contributors, and—with the exception of a state party committee—has made contributions to at least five federal candidates.

8. Total contributions from an individual may not exceed $5,000 for candidates for statewide judicial office and for judicial candidates in judicial districts with a population of more than one million; $2,500 for candidates in districts where the population is between 250,000 and one million; and $1,000 for candidates in smaller judicial districts. Current judicial district population figures are available from the Texas Secretary of State at http://www.sos.state.txt.us/elections/laws/populations.html.

9. The Judicial Campaign Fairness Act (Texas Election Code 253.151–176) on third-party contribution limits restricts PAC contributions to a statewide judicial candidate to $25,000 and contributions to any other judicial candidate to $5,000 unless the contributor (individual or PAC) files a written declaration of intent to exceed these limits. These limits do not apply to the principal political committee of a state party or county party organization. However, all judicial candidates are also subject to aggregate limits on the total cash and in-kind contributions received from all PACs, including party committees. The aggregate limits are $300,000 for candidates for statewide judicial office; $75,000 for candidates in appeals court districts with more than one million people or $52,500 for candidates in smaller appeals court districts; $52,500 for candidates for district courts or statutory county or probate courts where the population of the judicial district exceeds one million, $30,000 in districts with 250,000 to one million, and $15,000 in smaller districts. Law firms and affiliated PACs and individuals face more stringent limits. Candidates may not accept a contribution of more than $50 from a law firm or its affiliates if the total a candidate has already accepted exceeds $30,000 for candidates for statewide judicial office or candidates for office where the population of the judicial district exceeds one million; $15,000 for candidates in districts with a population between 250,000 and one million; and $6,000 for candidates in smaller districts.

become akin to an arms race, many are shut out of the election process if they do not have personal wealth to invest or a vast campaign treasure chest to put into action. This had led to the increased impact of donor fundraising and pandering to voters and contributors to increase a candidate's abilities to seek office. The ability to amass a political war chest has become a necessary art form for those running in Texas. Former governor Rick Perry routinely outraised his opponents on his way to victory. In 2010, he raised nearly $40 million, dwarfing the $26 million his opponent, Bill White, had raised. David Dewhurst, whose fortune reached its height at $200 million, was formidable. In an unsuccessful bid for Senate in 2012, he outraised future presidential candidate Ted Cruz $33 million to $10 million. Still, Cruz used his base to work past the longtime US representative. It takes a minimum of $10 million to win a US Senate race in Texas today, while a state election would take as much as $2 to 3 million.

The lax campaign finance laws have turned Texas politics into a race to the bank. Texas contributors gave over $300 million in political contributions in 2012, and that number will continue to rise in coming federal elections. Republicans benefit from their wealthy economic bases, while Democrats benefit from major contributions from the legal system.

Campaigning Beyond Money

Running a successful campaign takes more than simply raising a war chest. Using the funds in an effective way is extremely important. Campaign tactics and plans are essential to a candidate's success on the election trail. Being able to resonate with voters by building congruency between the candidate's platform and public opinion has become a path to election success. Simply being knowledgeable is no longer acceptable when it comes to earning a seat at the elected officials' table. Candidates must be able to convey their message in a way that connects with their audience. They must also be able to withstand what has become a near-twenty-four-hour cycle of campaigning, complete with appearances, speeches, policy papers, and, yes, the occasional assault on character or ideology.

Traditionally, canvassing has been an effective campaign tool. "Beating the streets" was a clear way to gain awareness and the ever-important name recognition. If a person remembers your face, he or she is likely to vote for you; that is the traditional mantra of many campaigners. Facial and name recognition have a large impact when it comes to campaigning. Being able to place a name with a face or shaking someone's hand before and after a ten-minute conversation is often a high priority for those seeking office. "'Traditional' forms of voter contact still make up a large percentage of campaign budgets and may be used even more frequently than radio and television advertising" (Hogan 1997, 552). In a local race or a small town, the need for these types of ads is not as significant.

Today, things have changed. While the "friends and neighbors" tactics work at the local level, they have lost their effectiveness when it comes to larger elections for statewide or federal offices. Even in large cities, campaigning has left familiarity behind for the high-tech world of mass messaging. How you formulate that message is extremely important.

A large part of that involves the staff that is hired. Professional campaigners are hired to guide candidates as managers or strategists. These positions are reserved for seasoned staffers who know how to develop a strategy and reach the public. The larger your financial coffers, the more experience you will be able to buy. In state or federal elections, these positions are necessary, as they not only direct the message and advise the candidate but also manage the campaign staff and the tactics they use.

The tasks of these staffs are largely functional. Staffer responsibilities can range from strategy to making phone calls to soliciting donations. While candidates rarely walk the streets, staffers will be seen passing out information on behalf of their "boss." Staffers are also tasked with research regarding issues and, most importantly, opponents. Understanding the public opinion of the area and what a candidate faces are large parts of the staff's function. If they do their jobs properly, they can make the election easier for the one who's running. If a staff can identify the base voters as well as those likely to flip, they can provide that information to target messages. While campaign leadership positions are paid, staffers are mostly amateurs—individuals who believe in the candidate and would like to take part in the process.

Their work can often be temporary in the primary process as the candidates sweep through the state or area. Street-level staffers are usually unpaid volunteers—often college students looking for experience or a way to boost their profiles or earn school credit. Either way, a candidate must find a way to embolden their ranks if they want to succeed.

Staffers are often given a direction to work in; many times, this is what determines the style of the campaign. The candidate will formulate the plan of attack (or whether there will be an attack at all). Once the staff is compiled, their job is to craft a message that will resonate with Texas voters. That can be affected by several factors, none more important that the tack the candidate will use. Whether it is TV ads, radio appearances, billboards, or written information, the candidate and their staff must set a tone for their campaign. Will the campaign focus on their platform or the character of the candidate? Will the campaign engage in aggressive politics and look to expose the opponent, and if so, to what level? The venom of a campaign can drive the types of decisions that are made within it. Whatever they are, they must resonate with the voters.

Nearly two-thirds of campaign funds go to TV commercials. A well-done advertisement in a prime time slot on local TV can cost a candidate up to $10,000. Because ads need to be seen between three and five times to be most effective, the cost of those ads can add up quickly. To run in a state legislative or federal election, for example, the candidate could have a budget that tips the seven-figure scale.

The types of ads that are run can determine the tone of a campaign. An attack ad is exactly what it sounds like. In this type of ad, the campaign focuses on the opponent's flaws and tries to expand on them. Attack ads are usually shrouded in gloomy colors and use ominous tones when discussing the opposition. Attacks can be carried out on policy backgrounds, character, or a specific event.

Attack ads are at the core of mudslinging. Mudslinging, which is the practice of assailing someone's character, is a tried-and-true tradition in Texas that dates back to the state's inception. Mudslinging campaigns focus on the negatives of an opponent instead of his or her positions on the issues.

Overall, attack ads have a high level of resonance but walk a fine line as to which candidate they benefit. A poorly executed attack ad can elicit sympathy for an opponent or show a candidate's nasty side. In 2014, gubernatorial candidate Wendy Davis was chastised for an attack ad that showed an empty wheelchair in a dark room; her opponent, Greg Abbott (who is paralyzed) eventually won the election. The nature of the ad shed a negative light on Davis due to the negative perception of the tactic.

Biographical ads are designed to establish a basic connection. Candidates use these ads to explain what they believe in and who they are. New candidates use them to explain their stances and introduce themselves to the public. Comparison ads focus on the differences between candidates. Usually issue based, comparison ads strike a middle ground between attack and biographical ads; they provide information but can also point out the flaws in an opponent.

While TV is still the predominant tool of campaign advertising, local and state elections are seeing the impact of the digital age. Digital campaigning started to take hold in 1997. Many people did not use the Internet before then (Herrnson, Brown, and Hindman 2007), but by the year 2000, most candidates in larger races were using digital media in their campaigns. Today it is a must-have because the voters many candidates are chasing rely more on digital information in their day-to-day lives. According to Herrnson, Brown, and Hindman, 41 percent of candidates in state elections use the Internet in some fashion. This study was conducted three election cycles ago but lays the groundwork for understanding the impact of the Internet on campaigns. The decision on how to use it is affected by the candidates themselves and the make-up of their constituencies.

Many candidates have websites that provide information about the issues, the candidate, and how to donate. This tool is great for disseminating information, but that is not sufficient. A website is a static presence with limited interaction capability. Social media has solved that problem. According to a study conducted by the Pew Research Center in 2016, 39 percent of millennials report getting their political information from Facebook. A digital platform that has more users than any cable company has subscribers, Facebook is the new wave of campaigning. In the past, campaign staffers had to worry about keeping a message fresh and in the public eye, but Facebook's immediacy and ability to populate the information landscape have allayed those worries.

Gone are the days when candidates and traditional media outlets formed the "information elites." Instead of controlling the information, social media (Facebook, as well as platforms such as Instagram and Twitter) has opened access to the masses, especially the young. To address this, candidates have been forced to alter their tactics. Now they campaign over the Internet around the clock, scheduling messages to keep the issues and candidates fresh in the public's mind. In a Pew Research study that examined three weeks of activity in three candidates' campaigns—Hillary Clinton's, Donald Trump's, and Bernie Sanders's—the average number of individual social media posts (between Facebook and Twitter) was 367. The fewest came from Sanders with 357 and the most from Clinton (381). Trump posted 365 times.[9]

Social media is inexpensive and could eventually diminish the need for a large TV budget. It has become a viable tool, not only for campaigning but for fundraising as well. However, the digital age is not for everyone. Candidates running in districts with younger and more tech-savvy or educated individuals are relying more on social media today, but the community as a whole has not caught up. Areas that have older demographics or that are less educated are still addressed in the traditional ways.

---

9   Pew Research Center. "Candidates differ in their use of social media to connect with the public." July 18, 2016. http://www.journalism.org/2016/07/18/candidates-differ-in-their-use-of-social-media-to-connect-with-the-public/.

Texas and the 2016 Election

Heading into the 2016 election, the analysis from pundits and predictors was that Texas was, for the first time in recent memory, up for grabs. With a nontraditional presidential candidate and changing demographics in the state, it was thought that the red dot was ready to turn blue. That did not happen on the whole. Texas still leaned to the right, and the dot stayed red. However, the shade changed.

One area in which the state seemed to improve on its tradition was in voter turnout, but "improvement" is in the eye of the beholder. Texas has traditionally been an underperformer when it comes to voter turnout, falling below the national average in presidential elections. In 2016, the turnout was record setting. Of its 15.1 million registered voters, Texas turned out 8,969,226 voters (59.39 percent of registered voters). That beat the previous record set in 2008, when 8,077,795 (59.5 percent of registered voters) participated. While that number did not outstretch the percentage, it did show a high level of participation.

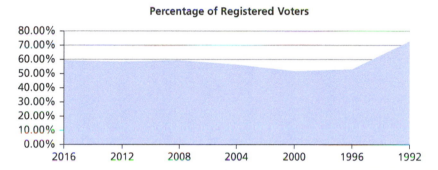

Percentage of Registered Voters

Source: Texas Secretary of State. https://www.sos.state.tx.us/elections/historical/70-92.shtml.

Year	Registered Voters	Voters	Percentage
2016	15,101,087	8,969,226	59.39%
2012	13,646,226	7,993,851	58.58%
2008	13,575,062	8,077,795	59.50%
2004	13,098,329	7,410,765	56.57%
2000	12,365,235	6,407,637	51.81%
1996	10,540,678	5,611,644	53.24%
1992	8,439,874	6,154,018	72.92%

Source: Texas Secretary of State. https://www.sos.state.tx.us/elections/historical/70-92.shtml.

While the number of registered voters is on an uptick in Texas, the percentage of the state's voting-age population (VAP) that participates still lags behind the national average. Texas has traditionally fallen behind the national average in VAP and did so this year. According to

United States Election Project, the state ranked forty-ninth in voter turnout among those who were age eligible. As seen in the accompanying charts, it is a trend for the state.

Year	Voting Age Population	Registered	Percent Registered	Voters	Percent of VAP	National Average
2016	19,307,355	15,101,087	78.21%	8,969,226	46.45%	54.70%
2012	18,279,737	13,646,226	74.65%	7,993,851	43.73%	53.60%
2008	17,735,442	13,575,062	76.54%	8,077,795	45.55%	56.90%
2004	16,071,153	13,098,329	81.50%	7,410,765	46.11%	55.40%
2000	14,479,609	12,365,235	85.40%	6,407,637	44.25%	50%
1996	13,698,284	10,540,678	76.95%	5,611,644	40.97%	No data
1992	12,916,937	8,439,874	65.34%	6,154,018	47.64%	No data

Sources: Texas Secretary of State, https://www.sos.state.tx.us/elections/historical/70-92.shtml; US Elections Project, http://www.electproject.org/2016g.

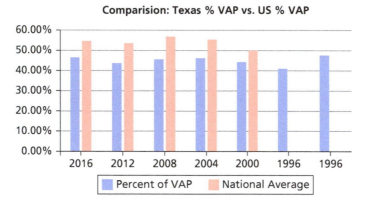

Sources: Texas Secretary of State, https://www.sos.state.tx.us/elections/historical/70-92.shtml; US Elections Project, http://www.electproject.org/2016g.

As Texas decides what type of state it will be moving forward, there are further areas to explore. This section recaps the primary takeaways from the 2016 cycle and attempts to provide analysis that aids in understanding how these trends could affect the political landscape in Texas.

Measured Backing of Trump

Texans were faced with a tough decision in the 2016 presidential election. In this ruby-red state, the primaries started with a Republican Party that seemed to have more candidates (seventeen) than coherent ideas and a Democratic Party whose candidate was seemingly already anointed. What shook out was a divisive Republican figure (Donald Trump) and a Democratic candidate with a standout resume but tough-to-get-behind personality.

Trump won a rough election that caused a lot of high-level and personal discussions. While the left accuses him of dividing the country, his right-wing base champions him as the man who will bring America back to prominence. In Texas, his victory was less than stellar. While he won by a comfortable margin with 304 Electoral College votes (including thirty-eight from Texas), his margin of victory was one of the slimmest for a Republican in recent memory. He beat Clinton by 9.1 percent in the final tally; that was the first time since 1996 (when Bob Dole narrowly beat Bill Clinton) that the Republican candidate's margin of victory was lower than double digits. As this section examines, several factors led to this small margin of victory.

Seemingly anointed the nominee from a very small primary field, Clinton won out over progressive Democratic challenger Bernie Sanders nationally despite protest at the Democratic National Convention. Clinton presented a standard liberal agenda, while Sanders attempted to connect to the far left, advocating for less spending, standing up to special interests, and higher subsidies. In Texas, those calls fell on deaf ears. While losing to Trump on the national level, Clinton helped the Democrats wedge into the political landscape in Texas, coasting to the primary victory with 65.2 percent of the vote versus Sanders' 33.1 percent. It yielded her 147 of the state's delegates.

Ultimately, Clinton lost the election in the Electoral College despite what turned out to be a popular-vote advantage that was the largest in history for a candidate who lost the race. Overall, Clinton gained 48.2 percent of the popular vote (65,844,954) to Trump's 46.1 percent (62,979,879). It is just the fifth time in US history that the popular-vote winner failed to win the election.

Year	Candidates	Popular Vote	Percent of Popular Vote	Electoral College
2016	Donald Trump	62,985,106	45.9%	304
	Hilary Clinton	65,853,625	48.0%	227
	Differential	*2,868,519*		
2000	George Bush	50,462,412	47.8%	271
	Al Gore	51,009,810	48.3%	266
	Differential	*547,398*		
1888	Benjamin Harrison	5,443,633	47.8%	233
	Grover Cleveland	5,538,163	48.6%	168
	Differential	*94,530*		
1876	Rutherford Hayes	4,034,142	47.9%	185
	Samuel Tilden	4,286,808	50.9%	184

Continued

Year	Candidates	Popular Vote	Percent of Popular Vote	Electoral College
	Differential	*252,666*		
*1824	John Q. Adams	113,142	30.9%	84
	Andrew Jackson	151,363	41.3%	99
	Differential	*38,221*		

* Jackson was denied the presidency by a 13–7 vote in the House of Representatives.
Source: Atlas of US Presidential Elections.

Clinton's popularity translated to Texas and led to some wins within the state, which are outlined in this section. Overall, Clinton was able to gain 560,000 more votes than Barack Obama had in 2012.

Republican Primary Fight

Two Texans were part of the seventeen-person scrum. Former governor Rick Perry and Senator Ted Cruz were considered legitimate primary candidates in the Republican Party. Both had government experience and were popular in the state. Perry had a successful track record as governor, and Cruz straddled the line between fiscal conservative and perceived outsider that Texans gravitate towards.

Perry's run in the primary was short-lived. A popular governor, he was on his second run for the White House. He struggled in the 2012 primary to show his readiness for the presidency. The missteps were more financial, as money was tough to come by in the crowded Republican field (Schleifer, 2015). Cruz, however, was in the fight for the long haul. He was the first to jump into the race and was able to gain the financial power to compete with the eventual president. As he outlasted other strong contenders, Cruz gained momentum, which was helped by a Super Tuesday win in Texas; he took 104 of the 155 delegates, beating Trump soundly with 43.8 percent of the vote versus Trump's 26.8 percent.

As Cruz progressed, he and Trump went from being friends to foes. During early debates, Trump and Cruz aligned on issues such as fiscal conservativism. The race ended when Trump started to pull away from the field as he gained more overall primary delegates and finished on a sour note, with the two candidates trading personal attacks ranging from Trump going after Cruz's father and wife to Cruz's calling Trump a liar.

This left Texas Republicans with a choice to make: back Trump, who was not a straight-line Republican, or cast in with Democrats. While Trump is not what Texas Republicans would traditionally vote for and he "played dirty" against their choice, they aligned with the New York businessman on Election Day.

Trump's victory, while slimmer than most (as noted above), had coattails in some areas of Texas. As is noted in this section, the Republican Party only lost four seats in the Texas House and held firm in the state senate and highest appeals courts. Down the ballot, in large metropolitan areas that saw an uptick in straight-ticket voting, Democrats benefitted. But in rural and suburban areas, Trump's solid lead at the top of the ticket helped keep Republicans in power in the state.

Presidential Voting Analysis

Coming out of the 2016 election, there has been a rising debate about the validity of exit polling.[10] Heading into election night, predictions were that Clinton was in the lead. Of course, the results were quite different, and Trump ended up winning a solid victory at the national level. How that victory has been characterized and understood has fallen under the same debates in Texas as those across the nation.

While Texas was solidly in Trump's corner, the victory was not as significant as those of most Republicans in the state's recent history. The narrow win highlights the need to understand which segments of the population voted for the Republican candidate in order to understand why his margin of victory was slimmer. Official exit polling, which has taken a hit in the perception of its credibility in the United States, paints a picture of a state that is on the verge of change in several areas. The validity of that change and where it happened is up for debate.

Official polling shows that Trump carried the traditionally conservative voting blocs in Texas. Male voters (57 percent), particularly white males (71 percent), voted en masse for Trump, as did those above the age of thirty; this swung more to the right as the age progressed. White voters came out for the right at a rate of 69 percent, while 66 percent of nonwhites voted for Clinton. While Clinton did well in the state among her core demographics, the win was not solid. She failed to reach the national average in the overall female vote, gaining just 49 percent of that demographic overall, compared to 54 percent nationally.

According to exit polling, African Americans voted 84 percent for Clinton, slightly lower than the national average of 88 percent (Tyson and Maniam, 2016). African American males in Texas supported the Democrat with 78 percent of their vote, and 91 percent of African American females cast their vote for Clinton.

Evangelicals in Texas voted for Trump at an 85 percent rate, while those who do not report as evangelicals supported Clinton at 55 percent. The debate becomes interesting as you break the information down into subcategories. Texans who made more money (51 percent among those earning over $50,000) and college graduates (51 percent) put their weight behind the Republican candidate. Those numbers outstretch the national averages, which saw only 42 percent of college graduates and 48 percent of those earning over $50,000 voting for the Republican candidate.

---

10   http://www.cnn.com/election/results/exit-polls/texas/president. Exit polling results surveyed 24,558 respondents nationally and 2,827 in Texas.

Rural voters were seen as the backbone to Trump's win. Stumping on a populist message that promised jobs and open access to economic attainment to the flyover states, people in rural areas came out in droves for the future president, providing 61 percent support for the Republican. While the rural areas get most of the notoriety, Trump also did well in the suburbs, beating Clinton 49 to 45 percent. In Texas, those numbers grow in every direction: Trump landed 58 percent of the suburban vote and 70 percent of the rural vote. Looking at the geography, Trump won handily in East, South Central, and West Texas. All those areas share the rural moniker; manufacturing or blue-collar populist economics are the focus. In the large metro areas of Dallas and Houston, Clinton pulled the advantage with 49 and 50 percent of the vote, respectively. Her biggest victory came in the southwest, where she beat Trump 54 to 41 percent.

Exit polling is flawed, however. This particular data set includes just 2,827 respondents and is a snapshot from election night of what the data on participation showed. According to these results, Texas fell in line, with a few surprises. The number of African American females that are represented here who voted for Trump (9 percent), is considered a high number among that demographic, which turned out only 4 percent nationally for the Republican. Also, the pull of Trump's populist platform was alluring for those in the suburbs and rural areas and was enough to silence a rise in urban support for the Democrats.

How did Hispanics Vote?

One demographic statistic that has been hotly contested and shows the flaws in exit polling deals with how Hispanics in Texas voted. According to the same exit polling, the state's largest minority voted for Trump at a 34 percent rate. That number has since fluctuated, when talking about exit polls, to 28 percent (Krogstad and Lopez, 2016). That gain was astounding in the days after the election, as it was higher than anyone thought the Republican would obtain; it outdid Mitt Romney (27 percent) and got close to John McCain (31 percent)—or beat him, depending on what data you believe. Data and analysis have since disputed the claim.

Further analysis has the Hispanic vote in Texas all over the map. Despite a significant amount of national heat regarding the tone of his message towards Hispanics, Trump's platform, which was tough on immigration and supported deportation, did not have a significant effect on participation. According to the Secretary of State's office, the number of Hispanic voters rose from 3,340,878 in 2012 to 3,696,414. Considering the rise in the Hispanic population in those four years, that is not a significant bump.

There are exit polls that suggest that Hispanics in Texas are not as blue as many believed. A more in-depth poll has the numbers quite smaller than the exit polls. Latino Vote[11] conducted a 5,600-person study of Latinos in eleven states and the District of Columbia; included in that sample were three hundred Texans. Within that sample, the percentage who voted for

---

11   Latinovote2016.com, "Latino Decisions 2016 Election Eve Poll." http://www.latinovote2016.com/app/#all-tx-all.

Trump was 16 percent—a stark contrast to the exit polling numbers for Texas reported above. Drilling down, Hispanics supported Republican candidates for Congress at only a 12 percent rate. Among this group, support for the Deferred Action for Childhood Arrivals program (80 percent) and the importance of immigration laws (80 percent) were high on the list of issues that influenced their vote. Further polling shows that, in counties that are considered large, Hispanics supported Clinton with 80 percent of the vote. In small counties, the number drops slightly to 77 percent (Pedraza and Wilcox-Archuleta, 2016).

These are all estimates. That is the nature of polling. But the results here, depending on which are accurate, shows a unique view of a demographic that is projected to be leading in Texas soon. Accessing that demographic as one that is viewed as being open to Republican candidates will be important moving forward.

Dollars Equal Votes

The path to a win on Election Day in Texas is still about the amount of money candidates spend. Coming into the 2016 election, candidates could spend anywhere from $80,000 to $10 million to ensure a seat. With Texas holding true to its tradition of keeping important state races off the ballot in presidential election years, the number of high-profile races was small. However, that did not stop candidates in these races from bringing the big bucks. As a frame of reference, in 2014, the Texas Senate ranked fifth in the nation in average contributions at $415,247 per candidate. The Texas House ranked third in the same metric at $188,419 per candidate.[12]

Election	Candidates	Party	Campaign Contributions	Incumbent (I)	Winner (W)	Margin of Victory
US House of Representatives						
USH 23	Hurd	R	$3,197,957	I	W	3,767
	Gallego	D	$1,670,051			
USH 5	Hensarling	R	$1,188,686	I	W	117,838
	Ashby	L	$0			
USH 34	Vela	D	$666,778	I	W	42,273
	Gonzalez	R	$0			
USH 33	Veasey	D	$318,711	I	W	59,758
	Mitchell	R	$47,506			
USH 32	Sessions	R	$541,375	I	W	139,520

Continued

12 2014 numbers provided by Ballotpedia, https://ballotpedia.org/Texas_House_of_Representatives_elections,_2016.

Election	Candidates	Party	Campaign Contributions	Incumbent (I)	Winner (W)	Margin of Victory
	Stuard	L	$3,188			
Texas Supreme Court						
SC 3	Lehrmann	R	$149,213	I	W	1,436,934
	Westergren	D	$9,143			
SC9	Guzman	R	$110,402	I	W	1,444,241
	Robinson	D	$0			
SC 5	*Green*	*R*	*$109,915*	*I*	*W*	1,158,030
	Garza	*D*	*$64,354*			
Texas Criminal Court of Appeals						
CC 6	Keasler	R	$5,002	I	W	1,234,007
	Burns	D	$0			
CC 2	Keel	R	$4,516		W	1,302,004
	Meyers	L	$0	I		
CC 5	Walker	R	$2,116		W	1,278,562
	Johnson	D	$0			
Texas Board of Education						
BOE 5	**Bell-Metereau**	**D**	**$85,745**		**L**	
	Mercer	**R**	**$11,737**	**I**	**W**	30,817
Texas State Senate						
TSEN 20	Hinojosa	D	$435,471	I	W	49,975
	Arellano	R	$10,704			
TSEN 19	Uresti	D	$243,160	I	W	36,792
	Flores	R	$21,773			
TSEN 12	Nelson	R	$348,065	I	W	Unopp
TSEN 24	Buckingham	R	$294,607		W	132,444
	Leeder	D	$9,745	I		
TSEN 22	Birdwell	R	$230,278	I	W	122,474
	Collins	D	$1,942			

Continued

Election	Candidates	Party	Campaign Contributions	Incumbent (I)	Winner (W)	Margin of Victory
TSEN 13	Miles	D	$192,389		W	163,656
	Rohn	L	$0			
Texas House of Representatives						
THR 107	Sheets	R	$548,844	I		
	Neave	D	$288,794		W	828
THR 41	Guerra	D	$450,556	I	W	5,938
	De Shazo	R	$52,434			
THR 105	Anderson	R	$403,687	I	W	120
	Meza	D	$106,211			
THR 113	Burkett	R	$311,419	I	W	5,707
	Bowers	D	$30,669			
THR 43	Lozano	R	$264,057	I	W	11,306
	Garcia-Utley	D	$14,305			
THR 144	Perez	D	$142,245		W	5,522
	Pena	R	$31,686	I		

* Elections were selected based on campaign finance and disparity of spending. Those in bold are races in which the candidate who spent less won.

Source: *Texas Tribune*, "Here's how much Texas candidates spent per vote in the November elections." March 1, 2017. https://www.texastribune.org/2017/03/01/heres-how-much-texas-candidates-spent-vote-general-election/. To view all campaign funding, visit this website.

The marquee race in Texas was between Republican incumbent Will Hurd and Democratic challenger Pete Gallego for US House District 23. This heated race was a return bout of the 2014 election, when Hurd initially took the seat from Gallego (Livingston and Lutz, 2016). Between the two candidates, they raised and spent $4,868,008, with the incumbent Hurd raising a state-high $3,197,957, which was double Gallego's numbers. The district, which spans twenty-eight counties from El Paso to San Antonio, has changed political allegiance in the previous three elections, but Hurd was able to break the cycle and win reelection.

Of the races noted in the table,[13] only one race had a winner who spent less than her opponent. Rebecca Bell-Metereau spent nearly $74,000 less than her opponent, Ken Mercer, for Board of Education seat five. The incumbent did not invest much in the way of fiscal

13   For a full report on campaign spending, see the table cited in the *Texas Tribune* at https://www.texastribune.org/2017/03/01/heres-how-much-texas-candidates-spent-vote-general-election/.

resources in the race and still managed a comfortable 30,817-vote win. It is also the only race shown in the table in which the incumbent was outspent by the challenger. This provides justification for the idea that a significant advantage is enjoyed by incumbents in Texas in regard to campaigning and access to resources.

Incumbents Reign Supreme

The incumbency advantage has long been a staple of Texas politics. In 2016, the advantage remained in Texas, as incumbents won races at an extremely high rate. In 2016 legislative races, Texas incumbents faced few challenges. Seventy percent faced no opposition in the primary, and 66.3 percent ran a general race against an opponent who was not from the other major party.[14] Overall, in 41.8 percent of Texas state elections, the incumbent faced no major-party opposition. In the Texas Senate, only three incumbents—Republicans Kevin Eltife and Troy Fraser and Democrat Rodney Ellis—chose not to run. In each of the remaining thirteen elections, the incumbent won every race. Each of their party replacements won as well, keeping the Senate balance between Democrats and Republicans at 11–20. This offers proof that incumbency is not only individual but party based as well.

Of 209 total state races, 176 were won by incumbents.[15] Of the thirty-three races with alternate outcomes, twenty-eight had no incumbent. Only five races saw the incumbent replaced: four the Texas House of Representatives and one on the Texas Criminal Court of Appeals. Overall, Democrats in Texas took five seats in the Texas House (four where the incumbent was beaten)—a coup for their party, but the gap between the two parties (95–55) is still significantly in favor of Republicans.

Texas House District	Incumbent	Winning Challenger	Margin of victory
107	Kenneth Sheets – R	Victoria Neave – D	836
117	Rick Galindo – R	Philip Cortez – D	1,536
118	John Lujan – R	Tomas Uresti – D	4,801
144	Gilbert Pena – R	Mary Perez – D	5,542

Source: Texas Secretary of State. http://elections.sos.state.tx.us/elchist319_state.htm.

In thirty-six races for the US House of Representatives, there was no changeover. Of those seats, twenty-five were won by Republicans and eleven by Democrats, consistent with the number heading into the election.

---

14   Ballotpedia.org, "Texas State Senate Elections." https://ballotpedia.org/Texas_State_Senate_elections,_2016.

15   Texas Secretary of State, "Voter turnout report." http://elections.sos.state.tx.us/elchist319_state.htm.

Incumbent success was still very high in the Texas state elections. Name recognition and the ability to raise funds have been significant advantages for incumbents in Texas and remained so in 2016.

Counties Changing Colors

While Republicans reigned supreme in the state, there was hope for the Democrats, as the blue on the map in Texas is growing. Major metropolitan areas went with the Democrats, as usual. Counties such as Harris, Bexar, Dallas, Travis, and El Paso all stuck to the Democratic ways in the 2016 election.

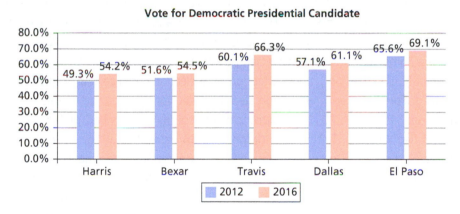

Source: County clerks' offices.

Those counties remained the Democratic candidate's base. The gains made in those counties show that Clinton made a bigger impression on metropolitan voters than Barack Obama did in 2012, as she added to the traditional level of support in those areas.

A bigger surprise came in smaller counties such as Fort Bend and Kenedy. Fort Bend, a suburban county on the outskirts of Houston, saw Clinton score a five-point gain over the 2012 numbers. Democratic support in the suburban county was 48 percent in 2008 and 46 percent in 2012, when Obama was the candidate. That number jumped to 51 percent for Clinton—a large rise in support and a surprise, considering how well Trump did with suburban voters in Texas.

Kenedy County is a rural county that flipped from red to blue for the second consecutive time. Located in South Texas, the county is 79 percent Hispanic or Latino and has a younger demographic[16] with a median income of roughly $26,000. Those numbers aligned with the Democratic Party and moved the needle back in their direction. In 2008, Kenedy County went

---

16   U.S. Census Bureau. "American Fact Finder."

for Barack Obama with 53.5 percent of the vote; that support fell to 49.4 percent in 2012. Clinton was able to recapture the county, with 53.2 percent of the county voting for her.

County capture was not all headed in the Democrats' direction. Jefferson County is located in Southeast Texas, with industrial Golden Triangle cities such as Beaumont and Port Arthur making up most of its population. The county's shift toward Republicans was notable, as the mainly industrial county has a growing minority population of African Americans (estimated at 34.3 percent) and Hispanics (18.9 percent),[17] a voting bloc that has traditionally been in the Democrats' corner. Despite the demographics, the county went red, voting 48.9 to 48.4 percent in favor of the Republican candidate. The last time the county went red was in 1972, but it has been trending red since 1996.

Despite the results in Jefferson County, the shifts overall align with a general vote that had the Democrats bringing Texas back into play for the first time in recent memory. A big reason for this is the use of straight-ticket voting. The option to pick a partisan side for every election on the ballot has been a strong source of temptation in Texas. In 2016, it had a big effect in Harris County, where 35 percent of voters cast a Democratic straight-ticket vote, versus 30 percent for the Republican Party. That had a ripple effect on local elections, and several Republican judges were displaced. Fort Bend also had a high straight-ticket voting rate, and in this case, it also swung from right to left. In 2012, 39 percent of the county's voters had pulled the lever for straight-ticket Republicans. That number dropped to 36 percent in 2016, while 38.8 percent voted the straight ticket for Democrats. Straight-ticket voting is an increasingly big issue; current Texas Speaker of the House Joe Straus is leading a charge in the current legislative session to outlaw the practice, arguing that low levels of voter engagement are in part due to the ability to vote by straight ticket and not engage with candidates down the ballot in local elections. The numbers show that straight-ticket voting had a significant impact on the 2016 election.

What's it All Mean?

Texas is still red; in fact, the power in the state is still ruby red. The Republican Party controls each branch of government and has a stronghold on the state's representation in the US Congress, although that margin of victory narrowed in 2016. While the Republican Party is in control, there are glimmers of hope that Texas could be up for grabs.

There was a flip in several counties that are traditionally Republican, and the Democrats are holding strong in metropolitan areas; in the case of Houston, that control is spreading to the suburbs with the flip of Fort Bend County. Those small moves, coupled with Clinton's relative success in keeping the vote close, means that there could be light at the end of the tunnel for Democrats. The changing demographics of the state (especially where Hispanics and young

---

17   U.S. Census Bureau. "2015 census population estimates." https://factfinder.census.gov/faces/tableservices/jsf/pages/productview.xhtml?src=bkmk.

people are concerned) could mean that, for the first time in recent memory, the talk that Texas is up for grabs could be substantiated. This could all change, as the Republicans control both the state and the federal government.

All this means that the next four years will be interesting where trend analysis and election results are concerned.

Summary

When examining campaigns and elections, there are various aspects to consider. The state has specific types of elections and campaign tactics that fit its unique culture. From the "friends and neighbors" ideology to the high-tech tactics we see emerging in the state today, there are significant avenues by which to examine the processes that come with campaigning and elections as well as their traits. Chief among these is the idea that Texas is a state in which unique factors in each area determine how elections and campaigns are run. The styles and types of elections that we see in Texas are driven by the public and what they will accept. Texas's constituents dictate the style and tone that is acceptable for candidates running for office. They are also responsible for making key decisions in special elections and are tasked with turning out to vote often. The willingness of the public to get out and vote and to be aggressive in the election process (as is also discussed in the previous chapter) plays a significant role in this process. While Texas looks to capitalize on its makeup, the tactics that go with voting access, along with the effects of the status-quo nature in the state regarding gerrymandering and campaign styles, will be something to watch as new factors emerge in the digital age.

References

Ansolabehere, S., and J. M. Snyder Jr. "The Incumbency Advantage in US Elections: An Analysis of State and Federal Offices, 1942–2000." *Election Law Journal* 1, no. 3 (2002): 315–338.

Baker v. Carr, 369 US 186 (1962).

Bonneau, C. W. "The Effects of Campaign Spending in State Supreme Court Elections." *Political Research Quarterly* 60, no. 3 (2007): 489–499.

Collins, G. *As Texas Goes. .. : How the Lone Star State Hijacked the American Agenda.* New York, NY: WW Norton & Company, 2012.

Cox, G. W., and S. Morgenstern. "The Increasing Advantage of Incumbency in the US States." *Legislative Studies Quarterly* 18, no. 4 (1993): 495–514.

Cox, G. W., & Morgenstern, S. "The Incumbency Advantage in Multimember Districts: Evidence from the US States." *Legislative Studies Quarterly* 20, no.3 (1995): 329–349.

Dahl, R. A. *A Preface to Democratic Theory: How does popular sovereignty function in America?* Chicago, IL: University of Chicago Press,1963.

Dahl, R. A. "The City in the Future of Democracy." *American Political Science Review* 61, no. 4 (1967): 953–970.

Dahl, R. A. *Democracy and its Critics*. New Haven, CT: Yale University Press, 1989.

Davis v. Bandemer, 478 US 109 (1986).

Erikson, R. S. "The Advantage of Incumbency in Congressional Elections." *Polity* 3, no. 3 (1971): 395–405.

Essig, C., Bhandari, A., and McCullough, J. *Texas Tribune*, "Here's how much Texas candidates spent per vote in the November elections." March 1, 2017. https://www.texastribune.org/2017/03/01/heres-how-much-texas-candidates-spent-vote-general-election/.

Hayes, D., and S. C. McKee. "The Participatory Effects of Redistricting." *American Journal of Political Science* 53, no. 4 (2009): 1006–1023.

Hogan, R. E. "Voter Contact Techniques in State Legislative Campaigns: The Prevalence of Mass Media Advertising." *Legislative Studies Quarterly* 22, no.4 (1997): 551–571.

Holbrook, T. M., and A. C. Weinschenk. "Campaigns, Mobilization, and Turnout in Mayoral Elections." *Political Research Quarterly* 67, no.1 (2013): 42–55.

Hoppe, Christy. "Texas Democrats Dropping Confusing Caucus System." *Dallas Morning News*, June 2015.

Key, V.O. *Southern Politics in State and Nation*. Knoxville, TN: University of Tennessee Press, 1949.

Krogstad, J.M., Lopez, M.H. "Hillary Clinton won Latino vote but fell below 2012 support for Obama." *Pew Research Center*. November 29, 2016. Accessed February 13, 2017.

Livingston, A., Lutz, E. "U.S. Rep Will Hurd victorious in rematch with Pete Gallego." *Texas Tribune*. November 8, 2016.

Pedraza, F., Wilcox-Archuleta, B. "Donald Trump did not win 34% of Latino vote in Texas. He won much less." *Washington Post*. December 2, 2016. Accessed February 13, 2017.

Pew Research Center. "Among Millennials Engaged in Primaries, Dems More Likely to Learn about Election from Social Media." Accessed February 9, 2016. http://www.pewresearch.org/fact-tank/2016/02/09/among-millennials-engaged-in-primaries-dems-more-likely-to-learn-about-the-election-from-social-media/.

Pew Research Center. "Candidates Differ in Their Use of Social Media to Connect with the Public." Accessed July 18, 2016. http://www.journalism.org/2016/07/18/candidates-differ-in-their-use-of-social-media-to-connect-with-the-public/.

Schleifer, T. "Rick Perry drops out of presidential race." *CNN*. September 15, 2015. Accessed February 14, 2017.

Schwab, Nikki. "Explaining the Texas Two-Step." *US News and World Report*, March 4, 2008.

Squire, P. "Uncontested Seats in State Legislative Elections." *Legislative Studies Quarterly* 25, no. 1 (2000): 131–146.

Thielemann, G. S. "Local Advantage in Campaign Financing: Friends, Neighbors, and Their Money in Texas Supreme Court Elections." *Journal of Politics* 55, no. 2 (1993): 472–478.

Thielemann, G. S., and D. R. Dixon. "Explaining Contributions: Rational Contributors and the Elections for the 71st Texas House." *Legislative Studies Quarterly* 19, no.4 (1994): 495–506.

Tyson, A., Maniam, S. "Behind Trump's victory: Divisions by race, gender, education." *Pew Research Center.* November 9, 2016. Accessed February 13, 2017.

Weeks, O. D. "The Texas-Mexican and the Politics of South Texas." *American Political Science Review* 24, no. 3 (1930): 606–627.

White v. Regester, 412 US 755 (1973).

Williamson, A., and F. Fallon. *Behind the Digital Campaign: An Exploration of the Use, Impact and Regulation of Digital Campaigning*. London: Hansard Society, 2010.

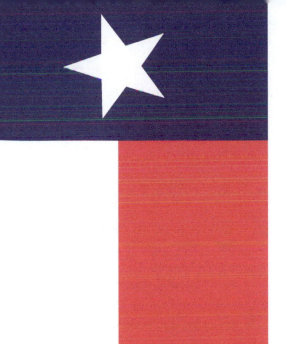

CHAPTER 12

Parties and Their Role in the Political Evolution of Texas

The idea of ensuring a republican government is wrapped up in the idea of a two-party system. In order to have a productive discussion about politics, at least two sides of the issue need to be heard. That concept has been tested in Texas.

The value of the two-party system is in providing diverging viewpoints in an effort to reach quality policy outcomes. Presenting citizens with at least two different outlooks attempts to ensure a choice. It also benefits a citizenry that has grown less politically and civically active over time. Framing issues as a choice between A or B makes them digestible for those looking to participate in the election process.

In Texas, the two-party system has been pared down. Texas has been, in effect, a one-party state for a majority of its history. Whether the reigning party was Democrat or Republican, the state has tested the idea that policy discussion need two divergent viewpoints. With its prevalent conservative ideology, Texas quite often works from the same side of the coin as the Republican Party (which traditionally represents the conservative view), while liberal ideologies are promoted by the state's Democrats, who are attempting to increase their influence and mount a stronger challenge.

That one-party setup has made for an interesting dynamic: the choice for voters in Texas centers on valuing their vote in a system under which a number of elections are predetermined based on party identification. Evaluating the impact of the system and its evolution is important for understanding party politics in Texas. This chapter examines those ideologies as well as how the party process has developed over time and currently works today. Also, can third parties (or the Democratic Party) make headway in a bright red state?

Basics of Political Parties

Political parties are complex entities. The goal of a political party is to work to get its candidates elected to office in order to implement a platform of issues into government. Parties have transcended that idea and become a way for individuals to identify themselves. In an age of polarization and party identification, being a Republican, Democrat, Libertarian, Tea Party supporter, or a member of any party has come to be a considerable identifier for individuals. In this chapter, we'll discuss how these parties have evolved in Texas and how the system impacts its government.

Function of a Political Party

The United States operates what is largely considered a two-party system. As discussed in the chapter on campaigns and elections, the system of selecting elected officials is geared to function in the single-representative system, which is known as an election-by-lot structure. In this system, constituents seek to elect an accurate representative from within their community. How the public or individuals define an accurate representative is personal. It can be by demographics, ideology, or policy preferences. Identifying that choice is the basis of voting dynamics. Candidates are chosen from within the predominant political parties operating in the nation.

As political parties form and provide services, one of their major impacts is fostering debate. The basis for the two-party system that currently operates in the US and Texas is that it provides at least two opposing sides on issues. As deliberation and debate are the important steps to creating quality policy in legislatures, having two identifiable viewpoints to prompt policy deliberation is essential. That debate is designed to use opposing viewpoints to engage and force a process that creates well-thought-out policy options that serve the public interest.

As political debate has become a yes-or-no question, figuring out how to vote or what to argue for is important. Party alignment (as discussed in the political participation chapter), participation, and capitalizing on ideology can be fleeting. Accommodating and aggregating ideology and people with similar views is an important step in the political process. Parties, as they provide divergent viewpoints, have become the manifestation of that need. Those with similar ideologies and issue prioritization are provided a beacon to rally around. Having an ideological base for people to be attracted to is an important function of political parties.

Figuring out where to align can be as simple as choosing the left or the right. As discussed in the section on political ideology, the US political system is based on a "side of the aisle" framework. For many, the question is "Do I sit on the left or the right side of the aisle?" Deciding that seating placement can be done by choosing positions on issues or by aligning with demographics.

Political Party Theories

Classical liberalism is a melding of individual liberties and economic freedom. With roots in the work of John Locke, Thomas Hobbs, and Adam Smith (among others), classical liberalism advocates for limited government guiding areas where the people empower it. That guidance is intended to focus on ensuring civil liberties. Government interaction with the people is intended to center on granting equality amongst citizens and establishing a fair structure based on liberties and civil rights. Economically, Smith's "invisible hand" concept is meant to work in place of government interaction: instead of counting on government intervention, the natural flow of market forces and an attention to self-interest and well-being will protect the economic interests of the citizens.

Today, classical liberalism in Texas centers on economic and personal freedom blended with progress and a level of religious activism. While the theory tends towards a conservative view, classical liberalism in Texas has incorporated what social progress advocates have argued for in terms of individual liberties. Not to be confused with advocates for social policy or government services, advocates for economic freedom (such as Ross Perot) or equality along racial lines (such as Barbara Jordan) are front and center in classical liberal culture.

Social conservatism has a close connection to both conservative ideology and classical liberalism on the economic side. Primarily, social conservatism shares many of classical liberalism's ideas about deregulation and economic freedom. In regard to government activity, the less government intervention in economic matters. the better. as the system is believed to be designed to work within itself. The two theories diverge when it comes to the role of government and the view of civil liberties. While liberalism can trend toward social freedoms, social conservatism pushes for government assurance of traditional social values. In this role, the government has the responsibility to set the standards of society where they are necessary. Those standards are to be enforced in order to preserve the status quo, even if that preservation comes at the risk of social stagnation.

In Texas, this push towards those social values has manifested in a connection to religious viewpoints. Instead of allowing for progress on liberties such as legalizing marijuana, the values are kept closer to a conservative or religious viewpoint. That viewpoint is expected to be upheld and preserved by the government. Today, that tradition is alive and well. The state has pushed policy in the direction of religious and social conservatism: a prime example is the state's constitutional amendment (passed by popular vote in 2005) defining marriage as a union between a man and a woman.

Another example is the 2013 law that placed healthcare restrictions on abortion clinics. In what women's rights advocates saw as an attack on a female's right to choose, the state passed restrictive laws on abortion clinics that outlawed the procedure at or beyond twenty weeks of pregnancy, required clinics to meet stringent surgical requirements, and required doctors to have the ability to admit patients at a hospital within thirty miles. The final two requirements were appealed: the surgical requirements (which closed a large number of clinics) and the restrictions dealing with admitting privileges were struck down by the Supreme Court, while the other tenets were upheld. The law was seen as a push in the direction of religiously charged social conservatism.

These two theories (classical liberalism and social conservatism) are alive and well in Texas. A social conservative nature has been a constant throughout Texas's political history. It was a major part of the Democratic Party, which controlled Texas for nearly a century, and has transferred to the conservative Republican Party. The real debate is on social progress, as Texas has trended toward being socially conservative while remaining classically liberal when it comes to economics.

Traditionally, Texas has blended in a connection to middle-class economic and social rights. Populism centered on the state's agricultural industry has been a consistent part of Texas's political history. As explained in the chapter on public opinion, populism has roots in middle-class advocacy. Over the years, populists have advocated for government intervention in both social and economic affairs to protect the interests of "regular people." Populists have pushed for low taxes on the middle class and farmers while also advocating for social intervention. Protecting both conservative social interests and economic well-being, populism has connections to the other two predominant theories. The move for government intervention departs from those conservative views.

From the traditional views of the two dominant parties to the trend towards social conservatism, Texas's political outlook is rooted in these three theories.

Issue Identification in Texas

Texas politics has its own culture. Theoretically, Texas has its roots in conservatism, regardless of which theory is practiced or dominant in the landscape. Understanding how those theories are translated and acted upon is how we go from political ideology or theories such as social conservatism and classical liberalism to what we know as political parties. The most reliable path of identification with political parties revolves around positions on separate issues. Issue identifiers guide party choice based on where an individual aligns on specific issues. Feelings on healthcare, same-sex marriage, or the economy drive a person left or right on the ideological spectrum. As discussed in the chapter on public opinion, that spectrum has multiple directions. In Texas, however, the arrow points right (and often far right) for most individuals.

The issues that drive Texas political culture and choice begin with economics. Whether it is making the state amenable to corporations or passing pro-business policies, business drives much of Texas's political culture. Also, there is a push in Texas to reduce or minimize economic debt and resist accepting federal funds. Those in favor of the populist viewpoint, which advocates for government intervention in the economy, would fall closer to the middle of the political spectrum.

Another issue, or issue set, that drives issue identification in Texas revolves around religious or "traditional" social policy. Those who advocate for a hard-line or more religious standpoint on issues such as same-sex marriage or abortion indicate an alignment with the conservative ideology, or the right. Those who advocate staunchly for civil liberties or against government intervention that protects religiously charged or traditional morals would align with the liberal ideology, or the left. Other issues, including healthcare, education, and the view of foreign policy, can indicate issue identification and help determine political leanings and where an individual should align.

While issue identifiers are the most reliable measure of political allegiance, they are dependent on several variables. The first is that individuals must understand the factors involved with the issues. If there is a gap in information or understanding, that dilutes the ability to use issue identifiers. Also, there is a value in issue saliency. As individuals consider a certain issue, some will place a higher value on it than others. A person could identify with the conservative viewpoint on several issues, but a smaller subset of issues on which they align with the liberal viewpoint could carry more weight and drive the otherwise conservative voter to the Democratic Party. Having political parties that drive the political conversation is an essential step to allowing the system to function properly.

Reading 12.1

Selection from "Democratic Texas"[1]
from *Big, Hot, Cheap, and Right: What America Can Learn from the Strange Genius of Texas*
Erica Grieder

Reading Introduction: History of Political Parties in Texas—Democrat to Republican

Keeping track of how Republicans and Democrats trend and work has taken time. The two parties have traded tenets of their ideologies over the centuries, and that is especially true in Texas. Historically, Texas has been a blue state. The Democratic Party was dominant in the state until the late 1960s. However, economic issues and a national question regarding social policies and progress caused a seismic shift. Erica Grieder tracks the changes in both predominant parties in the state and examines how Texas traded blue for red.

The state has helped provided the intellectual underpinnings for the religious right. In the small town of Aledo, outside Fort Worth, self-proclaimed historian David Barton publishes scores of books and tracts arguing that America has always been conceived of as a Christian nation. The Tea Party also has a connection to Texas. That movement's avuncular godfather, Ron Paul, was the longtime congressman from Lake Jackson, a leafy exurb of Houston.

Within the state, Republican hegemony is unquestioned. The GOP controls every statewide office in Texas and both houses of the legislature. In the state House of Representatives, Republicans have a supermajority. Democrats have not won a statewide election since 1994. In 2010, they didn't even come up with a candidate for the Comptroller's Office—a noticeable gap in a state with only seven statewide executive offices.

Given the sheer redness of Texas, it's easy to lose sight of the fact that fifty years ago Democrats were just as dominant in Texas as Republicans are today. For decades, Texas was one of the most influential Democratic states in the country. Dozens of congressmen have their offices in a building named for Sam Rayburn, the Texan who spent about half a century in Congress, including seventeen years as Speaker of the House, longer than anyone else in that chamber's history. The first American president from Texas, Lyndon Johnson, made civil rights his first priority,

---

1   Erica Grieder, Selection from "Democratic Texas," *Big, Hot, Cheap, and Right: What America Can Learn from the Strange Genius of Texas*, pp. 132-134, 136-139, 144-147, 250-252. Copyright © 2013 by Perseus Books Group. Reprinted with permission.

and when today's Democrats go to battle over the proper role of government, many of the programs they're defending were created by Johnson as part of his Great Society.

In other words, Texas used to be plenty Democratic. So before we ask when the state will turn blue, we should ask another question: How did it get so red?

Texas, like the other former Confederate states, was Democratic before the Civil War, and it stayed that way for almost a century once it expelled the carpet-bagging Republicans of the Reconstruction era. Between 1883 and 1960, Texas sent only five Republicans to the US House of Representatives and none to the Senate.[1] During the same period, all of its governors were Democrats, every one of its lieutenant governors was a Democrat, and the Democratic Party continuously controlled both houses of the state legislature.

The Republicans could usually manage to field a candidate, at least for state-wide offices, but their candidates weren't seriously competitive. When historians focused on that period refer to winning "the election," the referent is typically the Democratic primary—the general election was a foregone conclusion. Only during presidential election years did more voters turn out for the general election than for the biennial primaries, and it wasn't uncommon for a Democratic runner-up to net more votes in the primary than the Republican nominee in the general. In 1912 and 1914, even the Socialist candidates got more votes than the Republicans.

The 1952 elections dramatized the state of play with unusual clarity.

Allan Shivers, the sitting Democratic governor, was up for reelection. He had ascended to the office in 1949 after the incumbent, Beauford Jester, died of a heart attack while traveling via train to Galveston with his girlfriend. Shivers's succession presented the party with a problem. Jester had been part of the party establishment, and in Texas terms he was a moderate. He favored spending more on public schools, made no move to stop the University of Texas (UT) as it inched toward integration, and even toyed with the idea of repealing the poll tax.[2] But like most Texas Democrats, he kept his liberal impulses in check.

On integration, for example, it had been Jester's position that the University of Texas's medical branch was obligated to admit black students as long as they were qualified. The Supreme Court had already ruled, in 1950's *Sweatt v. Painter*, that the University of Texas Law School had to admit black students. The state had tried to skirt the Fourteenth Amendment by announcing plans for a second, blacks-only law school—its constitution already called for a separate-but-equal system of public schools—but the Court was unimpressed, given that UT was bound to be the better of the two. In the words of the Court, "It is difficult to believe that one who had a free choice between these law schools would consider the question close." Jester, accordingly, argued that the only alternative to integrating the medical school would be to provide a second, equally good one for black students, but because building a second medical school was clearly out of the state's price range, UT would have to be integrated. Once Jester put the matter that way, the legislature grudgingly acquiesced.

Shivers, his successor, was less diplomatic, and he didn't hesitate to wade into the biggest fight available, which was with the federal government.

When Texas joined the Union in 1845, among its terms was that the state's rights should extend into the Gulf of Mexico for nine nautical miles. Other states got only three. Texas's reasoning was that it was, at the time of the annexation agreement, a sovereign country. The United States had already set a precedent by recognizing Mexico's ownership over its near-shore waters for nine nautical miles. For the better part of a century the issue rarely came up, and when it did, the country was happy to humor Texas on this point. It was just another piece of pointless Texas vanity. "Nobody cared. Who cares? [You] want to keep the muddy, sandy bottom in the Gulf of Mexico, set your hair on fire," explained Jerry Patterson, the Republican land commissioner, in 2008. "But then when offshore production of oil and gas became a reality, all of a sudden, the federal government cared."[3]

Even as it remained Democratic, Texas was emerging as one of America's more conservative states. John Nance Garner, for example, served two terms as Franklin Roosevelt's vice president. Once he came back to Texas, he denounced New Deal spending at every opportunity. In 1944, conservative Democrats formed a group, the Texas Regulars, that meant to block FDR's reelection. If they could get to the nominating convention, they figured, they could throw a wrench in the gears and maybe send the nominating process to the US House, where the conservative wing of the party was more influential. "The Texas type of conservatism seems more virulent and entrenched than most other strains," wrote George Norris Green in his 1979 study of the state's political establishment at midcentury—a period he dubbed "the primitive years."[4]

Most Southern Democrats, of course, were conservative, and Texas was Southern then—or, at least, more Southern than it is now, politically speaking. (Today, when asked which region Texas belongs to, some Americans would say the South, some would say the West, and some would say the Southwest; the best answer is all of the above or none of the above.) During the first half of the twentieth century, though, the question was simpler. Texas was clearly more affiliated with the South than with any other region, even though Texas's politics had never fully mapped onto that of its former Confederates, and over the years, the state occasionally broke with the region.[5] (In 1928, for example, Texas supported Herbert Hoover for president, even though six southern states backed the Democrat, Al Smith.)

A hundred years after the annexation, however, Texas politics in many respects matched what would be expected from a southern state. Like the rest of the former Confederate states, Texas was still working through the ruination of the Civil War and Reconstruction. The state's alternative regional identities were as yet inchoate, and the nation as a whole was already uneasy about Texas, reasons already mentioned. The state was considered part of the South, and relations between the South and the rest of the country were somewhat strained; in addition to the resentments that persisted in the wake of the nineteenth century, the South was still segregating African Americans and abusing them. Beyond that, there were idiosyncrasies particular to Texas, such as the fact that the state's oil industry had emerged as a force in American politics, and outsiders were wary of that lobby. Texan politicians couldn't get very far on their own; it was by affiliating with the southern bloc in Congress that they had their best shot at power.

Texas's southern side helps explain its conservative attitude toward labor. America's organized labor movement had taken shape at the beginning of the twentieth century in response to grim working conditions in plants and factories at the time. The movement got less traction in the South. The region was not heavily industrialized then, and a cheap workforce was one of the South's competitive advantages, as it is today. Accordingly, the prospect of reform didn't hold quite the same urgency. This is why most southern politicians were opposed to initiatives such as Franklin Roosevelt's 1938 Fair Labor Standards Act, which outlawed most child labor, established a minimum wage, and set a standard forty-five-hour work-week, among other things.

Texas, with its populist tradition, was surprisingly friendly to organized labor at the beginning of the century. In 1920, according to historians George Norris Green and Michael R. Botson Jr., "Texas workers were protected by laws that rivaled or surpassed those in more industrialized states"—including provisions for a minimum wage and workers' comp, and regulations on child labor.[6] But support for organized labor was offset by the broader support for business, even among relatively progressive Democrats. Lyndon Johnson, for example, came from a cotton and cattle family, rode to school on a donkey, and never forgot how it felt to be poor. "I know that as a farm boy I did not feel secure," he would say later, looking back on those early years.[7] Classmates have recalled how the young Johnson thought it was outrageous that a man could lose his farm when the price of cotton lurched from forty cents a bale to four.[8] He was one of a handful of southern congressmen who had supported the Fair Labor Standards Act (Sam Rayburn, his great mentor, was another). However, in spite of these progressive leanings, Johnson shared in the broader Texan suspicion of unions. In 1945, electrical workers with the Lower Colorado River Authority walked off the job, warning that they would interrupt power and electricity if the bosses refused to think about letting them bargain collectively. Johnson was livid. "The sick in hospitals are endangered. Farm products will spoil," he scolded. "Texans will not tolerate this stoppage or sabotage."

The Anglo majority also opposed civil rights. In the 1920s, Texas had barred African Americans from voting in the Democratic primary, which was tantamount to barring them from voting at all, given that the winner of the Democratic primary invariably won the election. (This "white primary" statute was overturned by the

Supreme Court in 1944's *Smith v. Allwright*; Thurgood Marshall, later appointed by Johnson as the Supreme Court's first black justice, successfully argued the case.)[9] Texas was also the last state to get rid of the poll tax, which it did in 1962. While the tax was in effect, politicians had taken the opportunity to secure the minority vote by offering to pay people's poll taxes for them. Voters took the usual opportunities to resist civil rights; in the 1950s they backed referendums calling for segregated schools and against intermarriage.

At the same time, the issue of civil rights wasn't quite as polarizing in Texas as in other southern states. Plenty of Texas Democrats were Dixiecrats, particularly in east Texas, which has witnessed the worst racial abuses and is still the only place in Texas that could be mistaken for Louisiana. But the Dixiecrats never dominated the party, and it was rare for statewide elections to hinge on civil rights. In 1948, South Carolina's Strom Thurmond won four southern states as a third-party candidate for president. Revealingly, he pulled only about 9 percent of the vote in Texas, which went for Harry Truman.[10]

It's not particularly surprising that Texas voted for Lyndon Johnson in 1964. He was a Texan. No matter that he had already begun his push for civil rights. But in 1968, even with Johnson out of the running, Texas went Democratic again. It was one of only thirteen states to support Democratic nominee Hubert Humphrey, while five southern states, including neighboring Louisiana and Arkansas, went for George Wallace, the former governor of Alabama running as an independent on behalf of segregation.

There were, it seemed, issues much more important to Texas than race. Texans may have been bigots, but they weren't completely stupid, and, characteristically, they rarely lost sight of their self-interest. As in most matters, they were pragmatic rather than ideological. This had already become clear in 1952, the Shivers (D) versus Shivers (R) year. At the beginning of that year's presidential race, Democratic nominee Adlai Stevenson had been polling comfortably ahead of Republican nominee Dwight Eisenhower in Texas. But Shivers had resolved to make Texas's ownership of offshore oil a defining issue. He had pressed the point with both candidates. Stevenson told Shivers that he wouldn't restore Texas's claim to the tidelands. Eisenhower said that he would. So Shivers endorsed Eisenhower, and plenty of Texas Democrats followed his lead, giving Ike the win.

Texas's electoral votes didn't end up making much difference, considering the landslide victory Eisenhower ended up winning. Even so, he kept his promise to Shivers and signed a law giving Texas its nine nautical miles in 1953—a law that has since contributed several billion dollars to Texas coffers. "All because of the guy who was governor, who decided that his state was more important than his party," reflected Jerry Patterson. Texas also backed Eisenhower's reelection in 1956.

More important, perhaps, was that by 1958 Yarborough happened to have help in the right places, which he hadn't before. In a 1992 obituary of Ed Clark, a longtime political fixer, *Texas Monthly*'s Robert Draper recalled a chance encounter between Clark and Yarborough in the 1980s. Having run across Yarborough on Congress Avenue in downtown Austin, Clark couldn't resist a taunt: "You know how you used to always say that the '56 election got stolen away from you? Well guess what. So was the '54 election."[11]

In 1958, by contrast, Yarborough had picked up some crucial support from popular leaders. The special Senate election was an open, winner-takes-all affair, and among the declared candidates was a Republican, Thad Hutcheson. Rayburn and Johnson thought Hutcheson had a chance at winning because he was closer to the Texas mainstream than Yarborough was. Not a big chance, maybe, but it would have been a problem given the R after Hutcheson's name. Johnson had just become the Senate majority leader, and neither he nor Rayburn, then Speaker of the House, could afford to lose a Democratic senator. They threw their support behind Yarborough, who won with a plurality after Hutcheson and another Democrat, Martin Dies, split the conservative vote. If there had been only one conservative in the race, that person would likely have won. But once Yarborough got into the Senate, he managed to stay there for a while, since he wasn't impinging on anybody's private life or anything; he was elected for a full term in 1958.

Given all of that, it's not surprising that Texas Democrats kept their hold on power for so many years even after it was clear that they weren't fully aligned with the national party. Most of the state's politicians were Democrats, so the party had cornered the market on talent. In addition, the Democratic Party infrastructure was strong enough to support vulnerable Democrats like Yarborough. At the presidential level, however, those factors didn't apply, which is why Republicans had an opening there.

That was one of the reasons John Kennedy wanted Lyndon Johnson as his running mate. Having him on the ticket might help shore up support in the southern states, where Democrats were wary of a Catholic liberal from Massachusetts, and it would definitely get him Texas. This was sound thinking. Kennedy did carry Texas in 1960, and it's safe to say that with a different running mate, he might not have. Johnson hadn't wanted to risk losing his powerful post in the Senate, and the state had tweaked its election rules to allow Johnson to run for both senator and vice president; he won the Senate reelection with a wider margin than the Kennedy-Johnson ticket mustered. Texas's loyalty to Johnson, that is, didn't extend to a more general embrace of Kennedy's vision for America. In 1961, after a special election to fill the Senate seat Johnson had vacated by becoming vice president, John Tower became Texas's first Republican senator since Reconstruction.

But the party identity of the state hadn't switched over yet. The Democrats were still conservative, and they were still the default party of Texas. The 1970 Senate election made both of those facts clear. Yarborough may have been the incumbent, but he was still vulnerable. He had been one of the few southern

Democrats to vote for the Civil Rights Act and the Voting Rights Act, and he had vocally opposed the war in Vietnam. He was, in other words, still out of line with majority opinion. He had won reelection in 1964 against a fairly well-liked Republican, George H. W. Bush, but that had been a landslide year for Democrats, not least in Texas. This time around, LBJ wasn't going to be at the top of the ticket. Bush, who had been elected to Congress in 1966, decided to try again.

Bush's chances were scuttled, however, by another Democrat. Lloyd Bentsen, a moderate congressman from the Rio Grande Valley, defeated Yarborough in the primary. In the general election, pundits observed that the two candidates, Bush and Bentsen, were eerily similar. "The only evident difference between them, judging from their own TV spots, seemed to be that Bush loosened his tie a little more and kept one hand in his pocket while strolling," recalled Al Reinert for *Texas Monthly* in 1974.[12] It was like Shivers versus Shivers all over again, and as in 1952, the tie went to the Democrat, Bentsen.

But the Democratic establishment was in decline, and 1972 proved to be a critical inflection point. Connally, the popular former governor, had returned to politics as the head of Democrats for Nixon, a national organization. Texans, who had voted against Nixon in 1968, chose him over George McGovern the second time around. Tower won reelection to the Senate; Yarborough had tried to stage a comeback, but he didn't even win the Democratic primary. Democrats managed to win the gubernatorial election, but it was messy. They had started the race with two heavy-hitting candidates, both of whom were part of the Democratic estab-lishment—Preston Smith, the incumbent governor, and Ben Barnes, the incumbent lieutenant governor. In 1970, the suggestion that neither would win would have been unthinkable. In 1971, a scandal changed everything. Frank Sharp, a Houston banker and developer, had arrived at an understanding with various legislators. He would loan them hundreds of thousands of dollars, which they would use to buy stock in one of his companies and they could then sell for a profit, so long as they dealt with some legislation that would benefit the company in question in the interim. Even by Texas's standards, it was blatant fraud. Federal regulators noticed and intervened. Although neither Smith nor Barnes was among the high-ranking officials who ended up facing charges, they did end up so covered in mud that when the primary rolled around, neither of them even made the runoff.

The Democrats' choice came down to Sissy Farenthold, a fairly liberal state representative, and Dolph Briscoe, the former state representative and rancher from Uvalde. Both had campaigned as outsiders, a message that proved effective against Smith and Barnes, both consummate insiders, although it didn't work so well against each other. Briscoe, the more conservative of the two, won the runoff. His victory in the general election was relatively narrow, all things considered. The Republican candidate, Henry Grover, came within 100,000 votes of winning. He might have won altogether if not for the fact that Tower, by then a popular and influential senator, clearly preferred Briscoe.

It would be one of the last times that a Texas Republican crossed party lines to help a Democrat get elected. Texas's political realignment was afoot. And when the Republicans got power, they would prove to be partisans of a different stripe than the Democrats had been.

NOTES

1 http://en.wikipedia.org/wiki/United_States_congressional_delegations_from_Texas#United_States_House_of_Representatives.

2 George Norris Green, *The Establishment in Texas Politics: The Primitive Years, 1938–1957* (Westport, CT: Greenwood Press, 1979), 120.

3 http://www.laits.utexas.edu/txp_media/pr/speaker_series_files/transcripts/200810_patterson.html.

4 Green, *The Establishment*, 3.

5 To take an early example: most antebellum southerners were Jacksonian Democrats who had wanted to annex Texas, but there were also southern Whigs who thought expansion wasn't worth the trouble. Very few Texans, by contrast, would have agreed that the republic's fate wasn't a paramount concern for the United States.

6 George Norris Green with Michael R. Botson Jr., "Looking for Lefty: Liberal/Left Activism and Texas Labor, 1920s–1960s," in *The Texas Left: The Radical Roots of Lone Star Liberalism*, ed. by David O'Donald Cullen and Kyle G. Wilkison (College Station: Texas A&M University Press, 2010), 113.

7 http://millercenter.org/president/lbjohnson/essays/biography/2.

8 Mark K. Updegrove, *Indomitable Will: LBJ in the Presidency* (New York: Crown, 2012).

9 http://www.law.cornell.edu/supct/html/historics/USSC_CR_0321_0649_ZO.html.

10 http://www.texasalmanac.com/topics/elections/presidential-elections-and-primaries-texas-1848–2012.

11 Robert Draper, "Death of a Fixer," *Texas Monthly*, November 1992, 12.

12 Al Reinert, "Should These Men Be Smiling?," *Texas Monthly*, April 1974, 59.

Reading 12.2

Selection from "The Rise of the Right"[2]
from *Big, Hot, Cheap, and Right: What America Can Learn from the Strange Genius of Texas*
Erica Grieder

Texas wasn't quite part of the Deep South bloc. The state had broken with Dixie on a couple of occasions before the civil rights era. It naturally went for Johnson in 1964 and stayed Democratic, voting for Hubert Humphrey, in 1968. Carter carried the state in 1976, but narrowly, and since then Texas has given its electoral votes to the Republicans in every presidential election. It would have done so even if four of those elections hadn't had Texans (George H. W. Bush and George W. Bush) at the top of the ticket.

So Texas turned red after Johnson signed the Civil Rights Act, but not simply because of it. A number of other factors were at work. The first was that Texas Democrats were running out of steam. After they had dominated state politics for about a century, the bench was running thin, and the leadership was losing its way; the Sharpstown scandal had showed as much. Democrats started losing elections and Republicans started winning them.

Texan Democrats increasingly felt, too, that their contributions to the national party had been underappreciated. At the time of his death in 1973, Johnson considered himself a failure, as did most Americans, largely due to the trauma of Vietnam. In Texas, however, he retained his loyalists, who were bitterly disappointed when subsequent Democrats tried to distance themselves from Johnson. They saw civil rights, the Great Society, and the war on poverty as part of Johnson's record, not just JFK's. The fact that outsiders saw it differently made some Texans irritable.

Things came to a head in 1976 when Jimmy Carter, the Democratic presidential candidate, sat for an interview with *Playboy* magazine. Nationally, the interview was notorious because it made Carter seem odd. "I've committed adultery in my heart many times," he revealed. Texans, however, were more shocked by a comment Carter made at the end of the interview, bundling Johnson with the post-Watergate Nixon and dismissing them both as liars and crooks.

Newspapers reported that Lady Bird Johnson, the president's beloved widow, was surprised (which everyone took to mean that she was furious, but too gracious, as usual, to say so). Former governor John Connally was more vocal in his disapproval. He had been an inconstant ally over the years, a protégé of Johnson's who turned against the older man as his own political fortunes rose and Johnson's seemed to recede. On that 1963 day in Dallas, Connally had barely even bothered to acknowledge the vice president. In 1972, he had become the head of Democrats for Nixon, a national organization. But when the *Playboy* interview hit the newsstands, Connally wheeled around and thundered that Texas Democrats should vote for Gerald Ford. Carter did carry Texas's electoral votes, but by a narrow, 3-point margin.

Texas's realignment also had an ideological dimension. At the national level, both parties were changing: the Republicans emerged as the conservative party, the Democrats as the liberal one. Texas Democrats, as discussed, tended to be conservative. By the 1970s, the disjunct between Texas Democrats and the national party was becoming harder to ignore, especially because as the southern states turned Republican, the southern bloc in Congress, with which Texan politicians had been affiliated, was losing its influence. Northern Democrats had less reason to compromise with their counterparts elsewhere. It became clear that Texas Democrats were, in national terms, more like Republicans than Democrats. It was no surprise that Texas would back Ronald Reagan over Jimmy Carter. His socially moderate supply-side conservatism resonated with Texans, as did his running mate, George H. W. Bush. Republicans were about to retake the state.

As Texas Democrats started to lose their grip, Republicans were working to win. They had started to organize at the grassroots level, specifically in the churches. The religious right, a national phenomenon, arose largely in response to the social changes of the 1960s and 1970s—"social changes" being a euphemism for feminism. In 1960, the pill debuted. In 1973, *Roe v. Wade* established the legal right to abortion. In 1975, South Dakota became the first state to outlaw marital rape. These kinds of radical changes were eroding the historical role of women as the long-suffering stewards of national morality, and religious conservatives soon organized to fight back. Focus on the Family was founded in 1977, followed by the Moral Majority in 1979.

Despite being conservative, Texas hadn't been a particularly moralistic state. Sloth was the source of its classically liberal virtue: the government wasn't disposed to exert itself. The legislature had been socially moderate in the 1960s, when such issues arose, but by the 1980s the religious right had emerged as a force in Texas politics.

Such a quick transformation was odd. To get an explanation, I went to see Kathy Miller, the head of the Texas Freedom Network, an Austin-based nonprofit that works to keep the church and the state separate, as both God and Texas had intended. She argues that it was precisely because of Texas's slightly schizoid nature that the theocrats were able to muscle in. On the one hand, Texas is kind of southern, so it has a long tradition of action-oriented Protestantism. Similarly, Texas isn't northern. Those states have historically led the nation on church-state separation, because, among other reasons, they're the states that got most of America's Catholic immigrants.

New England Protestants, as broad-minded as they were, didn't necessarily want their kids going to the parochial schools that were popping up.

At the same time, Miller continues, Texas has this western, libertarian, antigovernment side. The government itself is small and undernourished, and Texans don't pay much attention to it. The religious right figured that if it could get access to the levers of power, it could push its agenda without much interference. And the religious right wanted to test its ideas in Texas. For today's ideological crusaders, Texas is usually worth the trouble. The state is so big, and so diverse, that if you can get something done in Texas, you can probably scale it elsewhere.

All the elements for a takeover, in other words, were in place: means, motive, and opportunity. It would have been the perfect crime, except for one problem: Texans themselves. The voters had historically favored fiscal conservatives over social ones. The two aren't mutually exclusive, of course, but neither are they intrinsically connected. Miller, who spends much of her time trying to track what the far right is up to, is clear on this point: even if the religious right is getting stronger, it doesn't speak for a majority of the state. "I do feel, and I know, that Texans believe the separation of church and state is a foundational principle for our country," she says. "We've polled on that."

The leaders of the religious right probably knew that too. That's why targeting party infrastructure, rather than voters themselves, was a key factor in the religious right's rise to power. If Texas was becoming a one-party state, then the movement wouldn't need to compete at the polls anymore. It could compete at the precinct caucuses instead. If it won influence within the Republican Party, that was tantamount to getting influence in the state. It's also, surely, one of the reasons that strategists set their sights on the State Board of Education. Texans, like everyone else, believe in evolution and don't think abstinence-only sex education is effective. Minors, however, don't vote, and if they talked to their parents about sex, America wouldn't have such fraught debates about sex-ed curricula in the first place. Any concrete gains the religious right could achieve with regard to public education, then, would be less likely to elicit a backlash at the polls next time an election came around.

Migration to Texas may also have played a role in the state's partisan switch. During the 1970s, the population of Texas swelled by nearly 30 percent. It was a hard decade for most of the United States. Things were pretty good in Texas, though. Oil and agriculture were so dominant that the state's economy was countercyclical. Jobs were plentiful, and about 3 million people moved to Texas from other states. Many of the newcomers were northern and lacked the knee-jerk anti-Republicanism of the Old South. Even among Texas Democratic officials, party identification wasn't such a fiercely tribal matter. A number of legislators, including Rick Perry and Phil Gramm, joined the voters in switching sides.

In 1978, Texas elected a Republican, Bill Clements, as governor. It was the first time the state had sent a Republican to that office since Reconstruction. Democrats have taken back the governor's mansion twice since then—in 1982, with Mark White, and in 1990, with Ann Richards—but neither victory was resounding, and neither politician was reelected.

In 1999, Rick Perry became the first Republican ever to serve as lieutenant governor. The legislature was soon to follow. In 1997, the Texas Senate got a Republican majority for the first time ever. The Texas House of Representatives didn't get its first post-Reconstruction Republican majority until 2003.[1] Since then, however, there have been few moments of weakness for Republicans in Texas. In 2009, it looked like the House might become bipartisan again; the Republicans controlled it by the narrowest possible majority, 76–74. But the Democrats' hopes were quickly quashed; after the 2010 elections, Republicans returned with 101 state representatives to the Democrats' 49.

The Voting Rights Act would have blocked either party from any redistricting effort that was aimed at reducing minority representation, but it didn't prohibit discrimination for partisan reasons. Democrats were perfectly aware of that, having drawn the maps according to their own preferences back when they had control. As of 2003, the House delegation included 10 Anglo Democrats. All of them could be targeted without too much legal trouble. It was even possible, Republicans thought, to redraw the districts so that the Texas delegation could lose Democrats but gain a couple of minorities.

The Democrats in Austin were upset, but outnumbered. On the other hand, there were enough of them that if they left en masse, they could deny the Republicans the quorum they needed to hold the vote. In May of that year, 51 state representatives snuck away under the cover of night. They turned up in Oklahoma, outside the reach of the Texas authorities. It was almost the end of the regular session, so the idea was to stay in Oklahoma long enough to run out the clock, which they did. Then Perry (who had become governor) called a special session to force them to take up the issue. This attempt also failed, this time thanks to the Democratic senators who bolted to New Mexico.

The tactic was effective, but there was no sustainable strategy. "There were several possible scenarios that could have ended with a Democratic victory," noted Steve Bickerstaff, a professor of law at the University of Texas, in a 2007 study. "By the summer of 2003, however, none was realistic."[2] The Republicans had too much power, both in Texas and in Washington.

Significantly, too, the Democrats were losing on the public relations front. Their plight had brought them acclaim from national progressive groups such as MoveOn.org, but Texans were getting tired of the drama. The scheme hadn't been popular initially among Texas's moderate voters. Some of the Anglo Democrats targeted were fairly senior in Congress, and most of them were moderate; none of them were hugely controversial. But by the same token, Texans weren't rushing to man the barricades; a limited government tends to keep a low profile.

And the Democratic leaders in Texas were getting tired too. John Whitmire, a state senator from Houston, was the first to leave New Mexico. He told reporters he was homesick. Eventually, the Republicans were able to corral the requisite number of Democrats. They sat there stewing while Republicans tore up the old maps and then kept stewing through 2004 as Republicans picked up seven of the ten targeted districts. In 2002, Texas had 17 Democrats and 15 Republicans in the US House. In 2004, it had just 11 Democrats and 21 Republicans.

Not only that, the new maps took measures to ensure that the Republican gains would be resilient. Texas's demographics were changing more rapidly than anyone, even the demographers, had anticipated.[3] This motivated Texas Republicans to be less invidious about certain racially sensitive issues than some of their national counterparts were; it was in 2001 that Perry signed the Texas version of the DREAM Act, the measure that allows certain unauthorized immigrants to pay in-state tuition rates at Texas's public colleges and universities. But the expectation was still that African Americans and Hispanics would favor Democrats, and so in some cases Republicans drew Democratic districts in areas that were getting more Democratic anyway. "What can I say?" wrote Bickerstaff. "The partisan design was masterful." Ten years later, the Republican dominance is so thorough that Democrats sometimes look like a third party, after the right and the far right.

This brings us to the other interesting aspect of the situation. Despite the fact that Texas's government has become more conservative, Texans themselves haven't really changed. Neither has state policy, broadly defined.

In other words: an unstable equilibrium. Its political leadership is more conservative than its electorate, and if anything, the gap is growing. The Republicans are moving farther to the right, even as the people of Texas look less and less like the affluent, older Anglo men who are running the place.

And yet Texans haven't stopped electing Republicans. This point tends to cause national observers to conclude that Texas has gone crazy. But there's a much more compelling explanation. Forty years ago, for the reasons described, Texas voters started to give Republicans a chance, and thus far, they haven't been disappointed—or, at least, they haven't been disappointed enough to do anything about it. For decades, Republicans have had the edge in structure, in organization, in money, and in candidates, whereas Democrats are still trying to recover their footing.

Texans are, ultimately, a pragmatic people. Politicians and their excesses can be justified by the economy alone. And that's one area where no one's been disappointed. So maybe it doesn't matter if the state's leaders breathe fire, pray for rain, turn up at Tea Party rallies, and spend all day suing the federal government.

How crazy is that, really? Texas is a pretty good place to live; that's why several million people have moved here since the beginning of this century. There are plenty of areas where Texas lags behind the nation as a whole, but none of them are new, and in most of them—schools, criminal justice, poverty, quality of life—Texas is showing some improvement. What's new is that outsiders have started focusing on the state's shortcomings. That's a sign of progress, in a way, if it means the United States has higher expectations for Texas in this century than it did in the last one. Rightfully so. Twenty-first-century Texas is a better place than people expect and getting better all the time, even if it has its work cut out for it.

NOTES

1 http://www.laits.utexas.edu/txp_media/html/leg/features/0303_01/slide1.html.

2 Steve Bickerstaff, *Lines in the Sand: Congressional Redistricting in Texas and the Downfall of Tom DeLay* (Austin: University of Texas Press, 2007), 221.

3 See author interview with Steve Murdock.

The Major Player and the Foil: Republicans and Democrats Today

That political party landscape has become a two-party system in which a duo of major parties—Republicans and Democrats—drives public debate. These two parties have dominated the political landscape in the United States in large part due to the "big tent" model. This model applies to a small group of parties that offer a soft landing spot for a wide range of individuals to join. Under the big tent model, the platform of the group is varied and wide, opening the party and alignment with it to as many individuals as possible. Republican and Democratic leaders have played off this model to strengthen their parties' hold as the two major parties in the nation. Basing their platforms on their home-base ideologies, the two have worked to expand their issues and attention across the board to open the party to potential members. This could include assimilating aligning ideologies to grow numbers and, at times, minimize threats.

This took place most recently in the South (including Texas) when the Tea Party, a conservative populist movement, burst onto the scene. The Tea Party proved a threat to Republicans and Democrats alike, and the former have altered their stance to align more with the fiscally conservative nature of the Tea Party. Incorporating their views has allowed their supporters to join, or rejoin, the Republican Party. As we will see in a selection from Erica Grieder later in this chapter, the opposite happened in the mid-1900s when Texas Democrats were unable to retain the populist vote; this helped to split their power block in state government.

Republicans align with conservative ideology. With the driving forces behind their party being low taxes, low services, Republicans have provided a large meeting place for conservatives, especially in Texas. Traditionally, Republicans align with fiscal conservativism, with policies and advocacy that push for economically friendly policies. In Texas, Republicans push for a lack of regulation on the environment and economic activity. Socially, Republicans, both in and out of Texas, align with religious points of view and push for alignment with a platform that advocates for the preservation of conservative views. Most Republicans in Texas are against same-sex marriage and abortion. Going along with their fiscally conservative nature, they argue against heavy spending on social programs.

The Republican platform in Texas has become extreme over the years. Limiting government, along with preserving individual and religious freedoms, are current priorities. The state's predominant party has pushed for so-called Religious Freedom acts that allow businesses to deny service based on religious objections, and it has pushed for "reparative therapy" for LGBTQ people as part of their platform. In education, Texas Republicans have worked to eradicate evolution from the curriculum; they have included a plank in their platform that restricts the teaching of evolution and maintains a connection to creationism. They used similar conservative principles to institute pay-for-performance policies for teachers in 2006. Touting the impact of bonuses based on quality performance, Texas education saw an increase in graduation rates and test scores in districts where bonuses were high. That program was cut due to a budget crisis in 2013.

Texas is a bright red state. As we will see, the Republican Party has become the truly dominant party in Texas. Of the 181 legislators in Texas, 117[3] are Republican (twenty of thirty-one state senators and ninety-seven of 150 representatives in the House); both US senators and twenty-five of the thirty-six representatives[4] to the US House are from the party as well.

As Republicans have slowly taken over the state in the past forty-five years, Democrats have looked for ways to work their way back into the process. At the risk of becoming bystanders in state politics, Texas Democrats have taken a page from their Republican Party counterparts' playbook and worked to appeal to the extreme factions of their party base. As this has transpired, officials in the Texas Democratic Party have pushed for platforms and taken stances on issues that have pulled them away from the state's conservative base.

Among those issues that the Democrats have pushed for has been the decriminalization of marijuana in the state, which they added to their 2012 platform. In a stark departure from the state's traditionalistic views on drugs, Democrats advocated for the regulation of the drug and its sales. Later that year, Colorado initiated the policy that would later lead to the legalization of the drug in their state. Texas Democrats currently tout Colorado's $134

---

3   Legislative Reference Library of Texas, "Membership Statistics for the 85th Legislature." http://www.lrl.state. tx.us/legeLeaders/members/memberStatistics.cfm.

4   Ballotpedia.org, "Texas Representative Districts." https://ballotpedia.org/United_States_congressional_delegations_ from_Texas.

million increase in tax revenue[5] from the sale of marijuana as an incentive to take a step in that direction.

Democrats in Texas have picked other fights—namely, against limiting women's rights regarding abortion. Gubernatorial candidate Wendy Davis led the charge in 2013, staging a filibuster to stall out a policy that would severely hamper access to legal abortion in the state. The filibuster was later ended due to Davis's violation of the rules of the Senate, but it was a landmark moment when Texas Democrats showed a willingness to fight against the one-party system.

As Texas Democrats push towards a more aggressive platform that also centers on empowering the national healthcare and education laws with supporting state law, a back-and-forth battle with the Republicans has begun. As the party has built support among young voters—who crashed the 2008 primaries to select Barack Obama over Hillary Clinton—it has started to gain numbers in the Texas Legislature (Keeter, 2006). While still at a severe disadvantage in both chambers, Democrats are closing the gap in the legislature. Shifts in popularity and voting patterns prompted a strict redistricting effort in 2003; this led to the notorious "Texas Eleven" conflict, when eleven Democratic state senators left the state to stall out a special session that would have led to redistricting efforts favorable to Republicans. The group, aptly named "the Texas Eleven," eventually returned to the legislature after forty-six days in New Mexico. This political move showed that Republicans regard the growth of the Texas Democrats as an increasing threat. Currently, there are fifty-five Democratic representatives in the House but only eleven state senators. That will have to change before Texas Democrats become a force in Texas policy again, but their numbers are growing.

Party Organization in Texas

While elected officials are the faces of political parties, the structures of the organizations run much deeper. As both Republicans and Democrats tout well-thought-out platforms, their base and their ideas are generated from a defined party structure that attempts to build from the ground up. Party organization is guided by the Texas Election Code, which states that both of the dominant parties in Texas must have similar party structures. There are two sides to the structure: temporary (which deals with the selection of elected officials and delegates) and permanent (which decides on party platforms, issues, recruitment of candidates, and fundraising).[6]

---

5   State of Colorado, https://www.colorado.gov/pacific/revenue/colorado-marijuana-tax-data.

6   The structure of Texas parties can be found in the Texas Election Code at: http://www.statutes.legis.state. tx.us/?link=EL.

Temporary Structure

As discussed in the chapter on campaigns and elections in Texas, the Democratic and Republican Parties work through a convention system to elect representatives, or delegates, to the state party structure. Both parties work from the national level down to the precinct level in a four-tiered system: national, state, county, and precinct. The purpose of this system is to ensure cohesion and guarantee that the parties represent the party membership from the ground up. At the state level, that means building a group of elected representatives and delegates from stage to stage to send to the national convention.

The hierarchal structure begins at the precinct level. The main goal of a precinct convention is to nominate delegates from the area to participate in the county convention. At this level, the precinct will suggest platform ideas regarding issues and focus of the party as well as delegates to participate in the discussion at the next level. Precinct conventions happen on the second Tuesday in March of even-numbered years after elections close.

Those delegates attend county/district conventions and repeat the process, which takes place on the third Saturday after precinct conventions. If the district or county has multiple senatorial districts, it will have a corresponding number of meetings. Here, the counties/districts will select delegates to move onto the state level and will adopt resolutions and platform ideas to send for consideration at the state level. There are currently thirty-two districts in Texas.

Biennial state conventions are held in June of even-numbered years. As party delegates progress further up the ladder, they reach the state level, where primaries are held for Republicans and the two-step primary process is held for the Democrats. These processes, which are outlined in the elections and campaigns chapter, determine the delegates who will travel to vote on behalf of the state in the presidential nomination process and nominate candidates for the Electoral College. Party leaders, including a chair, vice chair, and executive committee, are elected at the convention and are tasked with producing the party's platform for the coming election year.

Permanent Structure

While the temporary structure is tasked with electing leadership and outlining platform ideology, the permanent part of the party organization is tasked with ensuring that the organization functions. The structure is made up of elected precinct chairs, county/district executive committees, and the state executive committee and leadership. These officials have five specific tasks that rule their operations:

1   Strategy. Elected officials run their campaigns; party officials organize how the organization's message will be carried out and explained. With involvement from leadership at every level, party and election strategy to increase membership is decided upon to ensure that the message from every level is consistent and functional.

2   Recruitment of candidates. While it would be interesting for candidates to nominate themselves or volunteer, there is a process that goes into selecting candidates to run for office. Part of the permanent structure's job is to identify potentially influential or successful community members who would be successful at running for office and who also share their party's ideology and would be willing to promote it. Candidates can range from community leaders on the left to business or economic leaders on the conservative, or right, side.

3   Fundraising. Candidate fundraising gets much of the attention in contemporary politics, but the task of filling the party's coffers falls to the organization. While high-level elected officials and candidates are tasked with raising millions, the party will provide stipends and funds to smaller races or local candidates and will fund activities that the party may carry out.

4   Information. As these levels and structures suggest, managing information and the consistency of a message can be difficult from rung to rung. Part of the permanent party leadership's challenge is to ensure that the control of information and methods for conveying the party platform stays in one place and is managed in a way that benefits the party.

5   Voter mobilization. As Texas becomes more diverse, this is quickly becoming the party leadership's greatest task. Organizing voter drives and participation, which can be low in Texas (especially on the Democratic side), falls to this level of the organization. Invigorating the voter base and addressing its needs is part of the permanent structure's job. Also, as Texas grows, the party leadership will build strategies to address and recruit citizens who may be moderate or looking to examine their party allegiance. As this push continues, the use of Spanish-language signs will start to increase, as will the willingness to promote the party's agenda to varying communities.

Combining these aspects, you have a structure that is one part elected and one part private. The elected, or temporary side, is tasked with organizing the platform and assigning power to delegates, who represent the party's platform. The permanent structure has two responsibilities: ensuring that there is a cohesive group that works towards specific goals and providing the needed resources. As this structure bears out, the two predominant parties operate in a similar fashion; this could help them resist opposition and continue to be the dominant political forces in the state.

Third Parties

If Texas is a one-party state in practice—with Democrats fighting an uphill battle—then third parties are left to work their way into relevance on the political landscape. Third parties can have a significant impact, but the roles they play are different in the big tent model of Texas and US politics. Conservative third parties have played a role (albeit a minor one) in Texas politics throughout its history. These parties have benefitted from periods of dealignment. This is the process in which individuals become disenfranchised by their current (or the dominant) party, prompting them to cease being active in that party and become free agents.

With the two-party system not offering a major alternative, third parties have had their moments—specifically, the Populist Party in the late nineteenth and early twentieth centuries and, most recently, the Tea Party and Libertarian Party. These parties have taken advantage of periods between realignment—when individuals reintegrate into the major parties—to build numbers and grow their influence on the political landscape.

As they are on the periphery, third parties play specific roles. The first of these is that of spoiler. In Texas, third parties have played this role extensively. The Populist movement broke away from the conservative Democratic Party at the turn of the twentieth century as it sought to blend ideas from social conservatism with economic protection for the working class and farmers. This party pushed policies that would have traditionally been touted by the conservative party but moved it into an area that targeted a different population.

Another role these parties can play is to drive the political discussion into specific areas. The Tea Party movement, considered an extreme conservative movement, has taken control of a share of the Republican platform in Texas. The caucus had a major influence on the platform and agenda of the state legislature and then-governor Rick Perry in 2011 and has continued to work its way into the platform of the Republican Party in Texas. Tea Party supporters and officials have managed to take offices, although their victories have been over moderate Republicans as much as over liberal Democrats. A number of influential state and legislative officials in Texas are considered Tea Party members, including former US Representative (and 2012 presidential candidate) Ron Paul and Senator Ted Cruz, a 2016 presidential candidate. There is a debate over whether the Tea Party is in fact a party or simply a subsection of the Republican Party; some also wonder if the caucus's impact is waning.

Third parties also provide divergent viewpoints. The Green Party, which is not strong in Texas, provides a consistent focus on environmental policy. While the party has not been successful at gaining office, they have pushed for policies through advocacy and member messages that have had some effect. They have not taken hold in Texas, but the party offers a good example of the issue impact of third parties.

While they serve a role, third parties face serious barriers to success. The first of these is simply getting on the ballot. Gaining access to the ballot is dependent on the Texas Election Code, and there are different requirements for each elections. Getting on the primary ballot for the presidential election in Texas costs $5,000 and requires five thousand signatures. State senate races require $1,250 and five hundred signatures. County election costs can range between $375 and $2,500, and they require five hundred signatures or 2 percent of the electorate.[7] For many third parties, funding ballot access can be an insurmountable hurdle. If a party receives 5 percent of the vote in a statewide election, the party retains its place on the ballot in the following election.

Once third parties are on the ballot, the single-representative system plays against them. One representative to one district means that it is winner-take-all. That style means that third-party candidates must overcome the two-party (and in Texas, one-party-dominant) system, which is a significant barrier. Factors include both finances and press attention. With a smaller membership base, the coffers for third parties are significantly lower. Without wide-spread appeal and attention, either from the media or generated internally, third-party success is extremely difficult in Texas.

Examples of Third Parties in Texas

While Republicans (with a large faction of Tea Party supporters mixed in) are the dominant party in the state, third-party options lean conservative as well. Libertarians are the most active group but have been dealt a membership blow with the rise of the Tea Party. Until the upstart movement emerged, Libertarians were the preferred alternative in Texas for conservatives. However, their perception as being socially liberal and economically conservative plays towards the middle.

Libertarians are straight out of the classical liberalism theory school, advocating for government protection of civil liberties and social rights while removing it from economic activities. That line of thinking has kept their numbers down. While they appeal to the conservatives in the state, advocating for social progress and civil liberties protections has driven hard-line conservatives to the Tea Party and Republicans. On the other hand, the party's conservative economic views alienate moderate liberals. The ramification is low numbers. At the party's last convention in 2014, only 219 delegates attended: that number is smaller than the attendance at most Republican rallies. Still, the party consistently places candidates on various ballots in Texas and has managed to stay afloat.

Traditionally liberal parties struggle in Texas. The Green Party developed a base in the state in the 1990s, buoyed by the run of Ralph Nader for the presidency. The party, concentrated in the state's large population centers, developed its platform around an environmentally conscious approach. Their platform is traditionally pluralist, pushing for a singular focus. Advocating for government attention to this stance moves the needle far to the left, making it a challenge to gain traction in Texas. The Green Party has gained automatic ballot access just twice, in the

---

7   Texas constitution and statutes, http://www.statutes.legis.state.tx.us/?link=EL.

2000–2002 and 2010–2012 election cycles. While the Democratic Party has gained traction in small increments over the past two years, the Green Party has failed to keep up.

References

Baddour, D. "Texas Lawmaker Files Bill to Legalize Marijuana." *Houston Chronicle*, March 4, 2015.

Buchanan, J. *On Classical Liberalism and Libertarianism*. United Kingdom: Palgrave Macmillan, 1986.

Cotton, A. "Colorado Marijuana Tax Revenues Total $3.2 million in February." *Denver Post*, April 9, 2014.

Davidson, H. "Wendy Davis Abortion Filibuster Ends in Chaotic Dispute over Midnight Vote." *The Guardian*, June 26, 2013.

Hall, J. A. "Classical Liberalism and the Modern State." *Daedalus* 116, no. 3 (1987): 95–118.

Himmelstein, J. L., and J. A. McRae. "Social Conservatism, New Republicans, and the 1980 Election." *Public Opinion Quarterly* 48, no. 3 (1984): 592–605.

Jacoby, W. G. "The Impact of Party Identification on Issue Attitudes." *American Journal of Political Science* 32, no. 3 (1988): 643–661.

Jost, J. T., J. Glaser, A. W. Kruglanski, and F. J. Sulloway. "Political Conservatism as Motivated Social Cognition." *Psychological Bulletin* 129, no. 3 (2003): 339.

Klein, Stephen P., Laura S. Hamilton, Daniel F. McCaffrey, and Brian M. Stecher. "What Do Test Scores in Texas Tell Us?" Santa Monica, CA: RAND Corporation, 2000. https://www.rand.org/pubs/issue_papers/IP202.html.

Keeter, S. "Young Voters in the 2008 Presidential Primaries." *Pew Research Center.* February 11, 2008.

Kliff, S. "Wait, How Did Texas Republicans Pause Wendy Davis' Filibuster?" *Washington Post*, June 25, 2013.

Niemi, R. G., S. Wright, and L. W. Powell. "Multiple Party Identifiers and the Measurement of Party Identification." *Journal of Politics* 49, no. 4 (1987): 1093–1103.

Olson, M. *The Logic of Collective Action*. 124, *Harvard Economic Studies*. Cambridge, MA: Harvard University Press, 2009.

RePass, D. E. "Issue Salience and Party Choice." *American Political Science Review* 65, no. 2 (1971): 389–400.

Taggart, P. A. *Populism*. 3, *Concepts in the Social Sciences*. Buckingham: Open University Press, 2000.

Walsh, E. "'Texas 11' Call on Bush to Stop Republicans." *Washington Post*, August 11, 2003.

CHAPTER **13**

Outside Advocates: The Role of Interest Groups in Texas's Political System

G auging the influence of interest groups in Texas has come to the forefront of political analysis regarding the state, and the perception of interest group politics is as bipolar as they come. Read one study on the transparency and influence of Texas interest groups, and you will find the state lauded for its reporting; read another, and the level of legislator captures and the influence of these groups is vilified. Like it is on other hot-button topics, Texas is open about its spending and practices regarding politics. For most, reading that would send interested parties on their way with positive feelings about the major influences on Texas's legislators. However, the opposition pulls the rug out from under the transparency argument, saying it is laudable but ultimately toothless in a state whose ethics commission operates with little to no punitive power. The system's absence of a cap on donations to campaigns and politicians is seen by some as feeding into the individualistic aspect of its political culture; to others, it is an example of little institutional control over the influence game being played in the capital. Add in the fact that legislators perform what is in essence a full-time job on a part-time schedule, and opponents of interest group influence have enough ammunition to bury the practice.

With lobbies and interest groups representing minority groups, economic interests, public interests, and almost any other interest imaginable, this system is susceptible to influence, and the study of interest group activity can stretch for pages. Whether one argues the virtues of a system that is open to contribution and voice or decries a system ripe for capture and takeover, interest groups are a mainstay in the Texas political system.

The number of interest groups operating in the state today is in the thousands and covers the gamut when it comes to categories and types. For this survey of the field of interest groups in Texas, I chose to focus on the theory that underlies the activity while providing outside typology regarding these groups.

Interest groups, at their core, are responses to social and/or pluralist problems. They form because of a gap in the system that needs to be filled by policy or government activity. How each gap is filled and who exerts influence on policy will be a focus of this chapter.

To survey these actions, I will examine the basic theories that coalesce around these questions by covering the reasons these groups form and why individuals choose to join them. I will then move on to the types and tactics that are prevalent in Texas. Along the way, I will incorporate analysis from standard-bearers in the field to provide insight into the role interest groups play and the way they have become such an integral part of the Texas political process.

Why We Join Interest Groups

Individuals function as actors in the policy process (Birkland 1998). According to Birkland, individuals are the targets of both policy makers and advocacy groups, and the number of actors in the policy process creates a logjam or cluster of opinions. If the opinions of individuals were addressed all one at a time, this would confuse or hinder the process further. The remedy for this is the creation of localized groups, such as the issue or advocacy organizations involved in this study, to advocate for and deliver a centralized opinion.

The number of actors in the policy-making process is often seen as a detriment because a large number of influencers have many different interests that would need to be addressed in order to form policy. This is where advocacy and interest groups come into the process. Interest groups are important—perhaps central—to the policy process because the power of individuals or popular control is greatly magnified when they form groups (Birkland 1998). Concentrating their individual power into one group provides individuals with a way to be heard, which addresses a concern that prevents many people from participating in the policy process. This is one of the main reasons people join interest groups: to increase the power of their political voice. Thus, interest groups are attractive because individuals can combine their ideas with those who hold similar ideological viewpoints in order to have a greater influence on policy.

While the allure of an improved, concentrated stake in the policy process is important, it is not the only reason, or even the primary reason, that individuals join advocacy groups. Rather, they join such groups because the groups address issues that affect them personally, building a personal connection between the person and the group (Marsh 1971). As personal connection is essential to an individual's joining a group, it is important to examine how the connection is forged.

Three theories, while differing in ideology, provide explanations of the reasons why individuals join advocacy groups and take part in the policy process. First, Truman (1951) presented disturbance theory to explain why people engage with interest groups. This theory suggests that individuals decide to participate in group activity when a disturbance alters the status quo. Once this happens, individuals are apt to join groups of like-minded people or those facing similar issues in order to act against the disturbance and restore their personal equilibria. This is an appealing and easily accepted theory because its essential reasoning is grounded in a logical formula: there is a cause-and-effect relationship between external forces (disturbances) and the formation of new interest group organizations (Berry 1978, 382).

Another theoretical basis for joining advocacy groups is exchange theory (Salisbury 1969). Salisbury suggests that individuals join groups because they receive a benefit for doing so, and this drives individuals to become more civically engaged. Exchange theory is similar to disturbance theory in that it suggests a cause-and-effect relationship, but it is not expressly reliant on a signaling or focusing event.

Both theories suggest that, to become involved, individuals must realize what is important to them. Problem definition can be measured using a threshold model to determine when individuals will act (Doan and Wood 2003). This theory conceptualizes how the public identifies issues and starts to push for new policy based on the rational choice perspective, which suggests that issues exist on a spatial plane that has a tipping point—namely, the balance between cost and benefit. When the cost outweighs the benefit for an individual, the threshold is crossed and the individual starts to mobilize. Once this happens to a group of individuals, momentum is created in the community and issues are brought to the attention of decision makers regarding the balance between the public's need and the lack of current policy.

Salisbury (1969) and Truman (1951) suggest that individuals act in groups only when they are prodded to by outside influences. Another view on participation in groups is that individuals feel the groups serve a civic or altruistic purpose. While materialistic and reward-based models provide an obvious reason for advocacy-group identification, there is a segment of the population that joins advocacy groups for a simple reason: they believe their civic duty includes influencing public policy. The desired result of the activity is a collective benefit and not an individual one (Forsythe & Welch 1983; Moe 1980).

Types of Interest Groups and those Operating in Texas

There are multiple ways to classify advocacy groups. Groups can be studied as national or local, public interest or special interest, or institutional or membership-based. This section examines the differences between these types of groups and what each can offer to the policy process. There are groups that serve economic interests versus public interests and groups that look to achieve change on a large or broad scale. When identifying groups, we have to take into consideration the reasoning for their formation and the people who contribute to them with time and money.

Reading 13.1

Selection from "Interest Groups in Texas"[1]
from *Texas Politics: Governing the Lone Star State*
Cal Jillson

Reading Introduction

Cal Jillson examines the current landscape of interest groups in Texas to add definition regarding activity and typology. Jillson breaks these groups down by characteristics and functions. These help to understand how these groups operate and the role they play in Texas today.

Interest groups
Organizations that attempt to influence society and government to act in ways consonant with their interests.

Both the United States and Texas Constitutions protect the right of citizens to join together, discuss their views, and press their interests on government. The 1st Amendment to the U.S. Constitution declares that, "congress shall make no law … abridging … the right of the people peaceably to assemble, and to petition the Government for a redress of grievances." Similarly, Article 1, section 27, of the Texas Constitution declares that, "citizens shall have the right, in a peaceable manner, to assemble together for their common good and to apply to those invested with the powers of government for redress of grievances or other purposes, by petition, address, or remonstrance."

The most prominent contemporary definition of **interest groups** comes from David B. Truman's classic study of the governmental process. In terms similar to Madison's, Truman defined an interest group as "any group that, on the basis of one or more shared attitudes, makes certain claims upon other groups in society."[1] Others highlight the interplay of interest groups and government. Graham Wilson noted that "interest groups are generally defined as organizations, separate from government though often in close partnership with government, which attempt to influence public policy."[2]

---

1   Cal Jillson, Selectin from "Interest Groups in Texas," *Texas Politics: Governing the Lone Star State*, pp. 56-63, 184-185. Copyright © 2011 by Taylor & Francis Group. Reprinted with permission.

Despite the prominence of modern interest groups, politicians and scholars continue to ask whether they strengthen or weaken democracy. Two general answers have been offered. **Pluralism** suggests that groups arise to represent most interests in society and that the struggle between groups produces a reasonable policy balance. In this view, interest groups play a positive, even necessary, role in democratic politics. **Elitism** contends that effective, well-funded interest groups are much more likely to form, win access, and exercise influence on behalf of the wealthy and prominent than the poor and humble. In this view, the playing field is tilted in favor of the wealthy and powerful and, hence, democracy is at risk.

In this [...] we evaluate the organization, activities, and effectiveness of interest groups in Texas. We describe the kinds of interest groups active in Texas and how they seek to influence the political process. We ask what legal restraints are in place to regulate and control their activities and what additional reforms might be advisable. As we shall see, interest groups and their lobbyists play an influential, even dominant, role in Texas government and politics.

INTEREST GROUPS IN TEXAS

Both nationally and in Texas, the interest group world is tilted toward occupational or economic groups that represent corporate, business, and professional interests. In the traditional political culture of Texas, these interests tend to be especially well-organized, well-funded, and influential.

They play offense. Labor, public interest groups, and social equity groups tend to be less well-organized, less well-funded, and much less influential. They play defense.[3] As we explore the world of Texas interest groups, we will find that elitism is a better guide than pluralism.

Business Interests

Groups that represent business come in many shapes and sizes, but together they are the dominant force in Texas politics. They work to promote a strong business environment—which usually means protecting the competitive position of the state's largest businesses, encouraging support for new and expanding businesses, and discouraging business taxation and regulation. A few very prominent groups

Pluralism The belief that the interest group system produces a reasonable policy balance.

Elitism The belief that the interest group system is skewed toward the interests of the wealthy.

Q2

Which Texas interest groups tend to be best organized?

Peak associations Peak associations, such as the U.S. Chamber of Commerce, represent the general interests of business.

Trade associations Associations formed by businesses and related interests involved in the same commercial, trade, or industrial sector.

represent business in general, while most represent narrower sectors or types of businesses.

Peak associations, such as the Chamber of Commerce, which in Texas is known as the Texas Association of Business (TAB), represent the interests of business throughout the state. The TAB was established in 1922 and is a force in Texas politics. Its website unabashedly says, "our business is business, and TAB has been on the forefront of each legislative initiative that has made Texas the best business climate in America."

Trade associations, such as the Texas Oil and Gas Association, Texas Hotel and Lodging Association, and the Texas Good Roads and Transportation Association, represent particular business sectors. Finally, most major corporations, including ExxonMobil, Texas Instruments (TI), and Electronic Data Systems (EDS), lobby the Texas state government. These companies and their employees pay taxes into the state's coffers, support or oppose candidates and officeholders, and have information that state officials need to do their jobs. The associations and their representatives have never had much trouble getting the attention of Texas officials.

Since business lobbyists are sure public officials are listening, they can afford to speak softly. One famous story from mid-century, told by Robert Caro, a well-known biographer of LBJ, concerned a Johnson protégé named Alvin Wirtz. Wirtz was a former state senator, a named partner in a top Austin law firm, and the top business lobbyist of the 1940s and 1950s. Caro says that, "As a lobbyist ... the most he might say to a legislator was, 'I just want you to know that I have been employed by a group to help pass this bill. There is a great deal of interest in seeing that it is passed. I hope you'll vote the courage of your convictions.'"[4] Legislators generally assured Senator Wirtz that they would surely vote their convictions and then proceeded to do precisely what he expected of them.

Professional Interests

Professional associations Organizations formed to represent the interests of professionals in occupations like medicine, law, accounting, and cosmetology.

Like business, Texas professions are well-organized and influential. While there are no Peak associations representing all of the professions, the most prominent **professional associations**, including the Texas Medical Association, the Texas Bar Association, the Texas Association of Realtors, and the Texas Federation of Teachers, are well represented in Austin. Only occasionally, as in the case of medical malpractice reform, do the professional associations—in this case, the associations representing doctors and lawyers—go toe-to-toe.

Usually, each quietly and effectively works its own side of the street.

In addition to the prominent and well-funded associations representing the doctors, lawyers, realtors, and teachers, there are dozens of other professional associations. They represent the accountants, architects, engineers, dentists, nurses and pharmacists, barbers, hair dressers and cosmetologists, surveyors, plumbers, and many more. The goal of interest groups representing professions is to keep incomes up by limiting entry into the profession, usually through some sort of licensing procedure, in exchange for modest state regulation and oversight. These groups generally dominate state policy that affects them because they care more than anyone else, they know the issues better than anyone else, and they are eager to serve on the state boards that regulate their professional activities.[5]

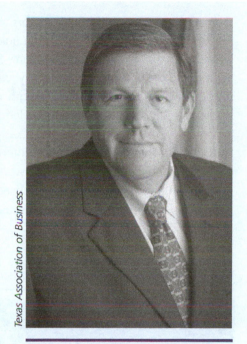

Texas Association of Business

Bill Hammond was named President and Chief Executive Officer of Texas Association of Business & Chambers of Commerce (TABCC) on April 1, 1998.

Agricultural Interests

Farming and ranching are still important parts of the Texas economy, but not nearly as important as they once were. While they have to fight harder for attention, when issues that matter to rural Texans come before state government, the Texas Farm Bureau speaks for the bigger producers and the Texas Farmers Union speaks for the smaller family farms and ranches. Commodity producers, including cattle, cotton, grain, poultry, sheep, and timber, have their own associations ready to act when their interests come into play.

Organized Labor

In states like Michigan, Pennsylvania, and New York, organized labor shapes state policy on workplace safety, employment security, and workers' rights. Not so in Texas. In Texas, business shapes labor policy. Texas is one of twenty-two mostly southern and southwestern **right-to-work** states. These states prohibit the closed or union shop, in which a majority vote of a business' workers to join a union requires every worker in the business to join the union, pay dues, and abide by union rules. Right-to-work laws weaken unions in relation to management and owners. They allow individual workers to decide whether to join the union. Some do, and some—wanting to save the union dues—do not, and the union is weakened as a bargaining unit. In 2009, only 5.4 percent of Texas's 10.6 million workers (compared to 12.4 percent nationally) were members of a labor union.

There are pockets of union strength in Texas. The Texas chapter of the American Federation of Labor and Congress of Industrial Organizations (AFL-CIO) and the Oil, Chemical, and Atomic Workers of Texas are strong in the Houston-Beaumont-Port Arthur area. The Service Employees International Union (SEIU) had some success in organizing janitors and health care workers in Houston in 2006 and 2007. Texas unions can affect local and regional issues and elections, but they usually struggle when they attempt to operate in Austin. They lose most direct confrontations with business interests.

TABLE 13.1 Texas 2009 Lobby Contracts by Interest Represented

Interest Group	Max. Value of Contracts	Min. Value of Contracts	No. of Contracts	Percentage of Max. Value
Energy/Natural Resources	$62,315,000	$32,230,000	1,228	18%
Ideological/Single Issue	$55,221,570	$23,516,570	1,768	16%
Health	S41,770,000	$19,910,000	986	12%
Miscellaneous Business	$37,600,000	$18,425,000	830	11%
Communications	$20,380,000	$10,180,000	378	6%
Lawyers & Lobbyists	$19,365,000	$11,490,000	341	6%
Real Estate	$18,735,000	$9,220,000	461	5%
Finance	$16,177,000	$8,012,000	413	5%
Construction	$13,341,000	$6,826,000	293	4%
Insurance	$12,495,000	$6,350,000	260	4%
Computers & Electronics	$12,485,000	$6,035,000	283	4%
Transportation	$12,385,000	$5,475,000	349	4%
Other	$6,640,000	$3,045,000	176	2%
Agriculture	$6,335,000	$3,015,000	142	2%
Labor	$5,760,000	$2,700,000	123	2%
Unknown	$2,635,000	$1,030,000	94	1%
TOTAL	**$343,639,570**	**$167,459,570**	**8,125**	**100%**

Source: Texans for Public Justice. *"Austin's Oldest Profession: Texas's Top Lobby Clients and Those Who Serve Them,"* 2010 edition, III, Lobbyists, *http://www.tpj.org/reports/austinsoldest09/clients. html.*

Ethnic Groups

Texas is a majority-minority state, but the state's interest group structure is still very much dominated by Anglo interests. While prominent minority interest groups have operated in Texas for nearly a century, they have generally not prevailed in the Texas legislature and courts. Their successes usually came when Congress and the federal courts weighed in. The National Association for the Advancement of Colored People (NAACP) and the League of United Latin American Citizens (LULAC) have operated in Texas since 1915 and 1929, respectively. The NAACP initially focused on voting and political access while LULAC focused on equal educational opportunity.

The period of greatest success for the NAACP, LULAC, and related groups came from the mid-1940s through the mid-1960s. The national NAACP and its Texas chapter won a series of voting rights victories, including *Smith v. Allwright* (1944), which opened up the Democratic party primary to blacks. LULAC and the newly formed G.I. Forum (composed of Mexican American G.I.s who had recently returned from World War II and were insisting upon equality) prevailed in a case, *Delgado v. Bastrop ISD* (1948), which declared that Mexicans could not be segregated in public schools. LULAC prevailed again in *Edgewood ISD v. Kirby* (1989), which mandated equalization of school funding between rich and poor districts.

Larry Kolvoord, Austin American-Statesman

Angie Garcia, state senior adviser to Texas League of Latin American Citizens, and Gary Bledsoe, president of the Texas NAACP, worked closely together to see that minorities were well represented in the state's new social studies curriculum.

Neither the NAACP nor LULAC have been particularly effective in recent years. In fact, LULAC has been challenged by two newer and more aggressive organizations, La Rasa and the Mexican American Legal Defense and Education Fund

(MALDEF). Like the unions, interest groups representing minorities have been most effective in areas where their numbers are concentrated. The NAACP has been most effective in the state's urban centers, especially Houston and Dallas, while LULAC, La Rasa, and MALDEF have been most effective in South Texas, especially San Antonio and the Rio Grande Valley. At the capitol, they strain to be heard over the louder voices of business and the professions.

Religious Groups

For most of the 20th century, religion was important to many Americans, but it was not an organized political force. A series of Supreme Court rulings prohibiting state-sanctioned prayer and religious symbolism in the public schools seemed to many religious people to threaten the complete exclusion of religion from public life. By the late 1970s, Christian conservatives had begun to organize and push back.

Religious groups have been strongest in the Midwest and South and very strong in Texas. Since 1994, Christian conservatives have controlled the state's Republican Party and are central to Governor Rick Perry's support coalition. Governor Perry has held several "policy briefings" with a group of conservative Texas ministers called the Texas Restoration Project. Christian conservatives, often represented in court by the Liberty Legal Institute, campaign for prayer in the public schools, faith-based social policy initiatives, abstinence-based sex education, strict limits on access to abortion services, home schooling, charter schools, private school vouchers, and defense of traditional marriage.

Religious conservatives are not unchallenged in Texas. The moderate Baptist General Convention of Texas elected an Hispanic president in 2004, a black president in 2005, and a female president in 2007. The Catholic Church and the Interfaith Alliance have worked extensively in local communities to improve education, alleviate poverty, act as a liaison between those in need and social service agencies, and help with employment, language training, and health care. The Texas Freedom Network stands for separation of Church and state and worries about prayer in the schools and faith-based social programs. But in Texas, religious conservatives are close to power, whispering in the governor's ear, while religious moderates and secularists whisper earnestly to the Democrats about the dangers of mixing religion and politics.[6]

Single Issue Groups

Some groups are tightly focused on one or a few related issues. The best example of a prominent single issue group is the National Rifle Association (NRA). While a national group, the NRA is powerful in Texas. The NRA favors a broad understanding of the gun owner's rights and opposes government restrictions on those rights. The Texas Constitution protects the right to bear arms but allows the legislature to regulate the right to prevent crime. In Texas, this means arming honest citizens so they can better resist the criminals.

Texas's strong support for the right to bear arms came under close scrutiny in the 2000 presidential campaign. In 1995, Governor George W. Bush signed a bill that gave Texans the right to carry concealed weapons. In 1997, he signed an amendment to the concealed-carry law that stripped out provisions forbidding concealed weapons in churches. The amendment required churches to post signs if they wanted to exclude guns. On September 16, 1999, seven people were shot and killed in a Fort Worth church. Vice President Al Gore, soon to be the Democratic nominee for president, criticized George W. Bush, soon to be the Republican nominee for president, for supporting the 1995 law and the 1997 amendments.[7]

The most recent debate over guns in public places came in the wake of 24-year-old Fausto Cardenas's January 21, 2010 visit to the Texas state capitol. Cardenas entered the capitol to seek a meeting with Senator Dan Patrick (R-Houston). When his request to meet Senator Patrick was denied, Cardenas walked out of the capitol, took out a gun, and fired several shots into the air before he was subdued by state troopers. Under the 1995 law described above, anyone with a valid concealed-carry permit can bring a gun into the capitol. The *Wall Street Journal* reported the story by observing that, "Lawmakers in firearm-friendly Texas are embroiled in a debate over how to make the state Capitol safer: get rid of guns or encourage even more."[8] Will lawmakers who were willing to let guns be carried in churches now be unwilling to allow them in the capitol? Probably not – several lawmakers regularly go to work armed.

Abortion is another highly contentious issue that has spawned single issue groups on both sides. The Texas chapter of the National Abortion Rights Action League favors "a woman's right to choose," or simply "choice." Supporters of the pro-choice position envision a situation in which abortion is legal and women and their doctors decide when it is appropriate. The Texas Right to Life Committee lobbies the Texas legislature to regulate the timing and circumstances under which abortions are available. Pro-life interest groups play an influential role in Texas politics while pro-choice groups have a very rough time. In 2005, Texas passed a law requiring written parental approval for unmarried women under 18 to secure an abortion.

Public Interest Groups

Many groups claim to pursue the public interest, rather than partisan, ideological, or economic interests. Like the single issue groups, the most prominent public interest groups are national groups with Texas chapters. The best example of a non-partisan public interest group is the Texas League of Women Voters. The League of Women Voters works to enhance voter awareness and participation. Despite their claims to the contrary, most public interest groups lean to the right or the left. Examples on the left, in the sense that they support an activist government, are the Center for

Public Policy Priorities, Texans for Public Justice, Common Cause, and Public Citizen. These and similar groups work for the rights of children and the poor, consumer safety, environmental protection, and open government. The "good government" groups are often patronized and, more often, ignored by the powers that be in Texas politics.

On the right are the Texas Public Policy Foundation and the Texas Eagle Forum. The Texas Eagle Forum works for traditional values, law and order, small government, and low taxes. Conservative leaders are more likely to growl than to plead if they feel public officials are drifting from the approved path. In the summer of 2006, Lt. Governor David Dewhurst and Senator Kay Bailey Hutchison both suggested the need for a guest worker program as part of their re-election campaigns. Cathie Adams of the Texas Eagle Forum told Gardiner Selby of the *Austin American-Statesman* that "Dewhurst and Hutchison seem to speak for corporations. 'What we are up against [Adams said] is the taxpaying citizen versus the elites who are only looking out for the cost of doing their own business . ... This is hurting. I'm sorry that maybe our voices haven't been loud or clear enough.'"[9]

INTEREST GROUP ACTIVITIES AND RESOURCES

Q3

How do interest groups try to influence the political process?

Texas state governments, with the singular exception of the strong state government created by the post-Civil War Reconstruction Constitution of 1869, were designed to be weak and diffuse so that they could not dictate to private individuals and interests. This is particularly true of the Texas Constitution of 1876, the current constitution, with its weak governor, part-time legislature, elected judges, and diffuse and under-funded bureaucracy. Interest groups wield great influence in Texas because, oftentimes, they are better organized, better informed, and better funded than Texas state government.

Interest groups use a variety of tools in their attempts to influence the elected and appointed officials of state government. Most groups have knowledge and expertise that the public officials need. Some groups have deep pockets, some have many members, and some have a small number of influential and well-connected members. Other groups have influential leaders or well-established ties to important economic and ideological networks. Interest groups and their lobbyists deploy their resources to influence the making and implementation of public policy in Texas.

NOTES

1 David B. Truman, *The Governmental Process: Political Interests and Public Opinion* (New York: Knopf, 1958), p. 33.

2 Graham Wilson, *Interest Groups* (Cambridge, MA: Blackwell, 1990), p. 1.

3 L. M. Sixel, "Unions Vie for Health Care Workers," *Houston Chronicle*, July 18, 2007, A1.

4 Robert A. Caro, *The Path to Power: The Years of Lyndon Johnson* (New York: Alfred A. Knopf, 1982), p. 375.

5 Robert T. Garrett, "Lobbyists Revision Would Help Client," *Dallas Morning News*, April 30, 2007, A1, A8.

6 See Texas Lyceum poll on religion, ethics, and public morality. http://www.texaslyceum.org/pollpage.aspx.

7 Adam Clymer, "Gore Assails Bush on Texas Law that Permits Guns in Church," *New York Times*, September 18, 1999.

8 Ana Campoy, "Texas Duels Over Guns," *Wall Street Journal*, February 8, 2010, A8.

9 W. Gardiner Selby, "Dewhurst, Hutchison Speak Out on Immigration," *Austin American-Statesman*, July 26, 2006.

The Role of Interest Groups

There is a place in the policy science/democracy dynamic for public input (DeLeon 1995). An informed public can make a valuable contribution to effective policy if its members, or their groups, are given the opportunity to take part in the policy process. Providing the public with access to quality information and opportunity to act on it can increase civic engagement, especially in a decentralized or subfederal government. Yet ensuring that these groups have a coherent and understandable voice is an issue that needs to be addressed. One potential solution is the identification and inclusion of advocacy groups in Texas policy discussion.

Policy makers work with the community, often via community groups or public advocates, to determine the facts and aspects of issues that establish the criteria for future policy (DeLeon 1995). Questions that policy makers might ask of community representatives deal with who will be affected by a proposed policy and to what extent. This collaboration helps to determine what is possible—which often is not an optimal or perfect solution—and it is vital to the success of the policy process.

While public advocates take part in all aspects of policymaking, they can be especially useful in identifying environmental parameters and time constraints. They work within the community to educate people and mobilize efforts to identify issues and put them into a policy context. These advocates, most notably advocacy groups and community leaders, work for specific causes and usually on behalf of specific population groups. Especially at the local level, they serve as a bridge between public opinion and policy (Andrews and Edwards 2004). In many cases, these groups are more knowledgeable about the needs of the community than any other participant in the policy innovation process.

The value of public advocates lies in their ability to speak in a unified voice to analysts and decision makers on behalf of their constituencies. Putting issues into context is vital to the success of the public in the policy process. If decision makers receive thousands of letters, this demonstrates interest in a problem but does not provide a concise view of how the community would like to see the issue resolved. In mobilizing together, often under the umbrella of an advocacy organization, the public can address decision makers with a clear voice and vision.

The fact that these advocates act in congruence with the public interest gives them increased value, as opposed to a corporation that has a lobbyist or a special interest group that is not dedicated to addressing public need (Herrington 2005). Without input from the public, getting a realistic idea of the urgency of the situation or the desired activity would be difficult. This work adds to the process by which analysts and those in government define the scope of the problem to aid in developing policy, which is the goal of both decision makers and advocacy groups.

Reading 13.2

Selection from "Theory of Emergent and Changing Interest Group Tactics"[2]
from *Choices and Changes: Interest Groups in the Electoral Process*
Michael M. Franz

Reading Introduction: Interest Groups and Elections

Michael Franz presents evidence that interest groups, namely PACs, are most active in the election process. As we have discussed previously, interest groups can be seen as policy centric, but Franz presents a case where interest groups—more precisely, their influence and power—are measured by the impact of campaign

2   Michael M. Franz, Selection from "A Theory of Emergent and Changing Interest Group Tactics," *Choices and Changes: Interest Groups in the Electoral Process*, pp. 54-57, 197-198. Copyright © 2008 by Temple University Press. Reprinted with permission.

donations and election activity. The excerpt below highlights this role and canvasses this activity as a major function of interest groups in the current political landscape.

THE RELATIONSHIP BETWEEN GOALS AND TACTICS

The interest group literature focuses predominantly on two electoral goals, which are most often applied to the allocation of PAC money: access or replacement (Sabato 1984). These are alternatively called pragmatic or ideological goals (Evans 1988).[1] Access goals are derived from the monetary needs of candidates running for office. Many interest groups, in recognizing these needs, seek access by alleviating the fund-raising requirements of relevant office seekers, thus demonstrating loyalty through campaign contributions (Austen-Smith 1995). It is hoped that this loyalty will result in some ability to influence how members of Congress design policies.[2]

Elections, however, are more than symbolic moments during which organized interests can attempt to form bonds with politicians. Elections can be used to create more directly a policymaking environment that reflects the desires of participating interests. That is, while one use of elections is the formation of closer bonds, another is the direct election of more favorable candidates (or the defense of vulnerable ones). In this sense, contributions or other electioneering efforts are designed to move votes at the ballot box.[3]

Consider the following example of a conscious shift from the goal of access to that of replacement. In 1981 the National Association of Retired Federal Employees (NARFE) asked the Federal Election Commission for advice on a planned strategy to contribute to members of Congress. NARFE had spent considerable time and energy seeking access to sympathetic legislators. According to one solicitation from the group to its members, "NARFE's national office is working very hard on establishing a good working relationship with all the members of Congress." The group was frustrated in its efforts, however, and sought to alter its tactics. As such, NARFE "now believes that an essential element of protecting its interests in maintaining the Federal Retirement System separate and apart from the Social Security System is by electing individuals whose views are sympathetic to [the group]." NARFE sought advice from the FEC on how to use already existing funds to that effect (Advisory Opinion 1981–34).

For the most part, however, we rarely know the explicit goal of interest group electoral participation; we usually infer it from their observed activity. For example, we know interest groups consider voting record and institutional position (relevant committee, party leadership role, for example) in deciding whom to support, and we assume contributions in this context are most likely designed to secure policymaking access (Gopoian 1984, Grenzke 1989, Poole, Romer and Rosenthal 1987, Romer and Snyder 1994). There is also evidence that interest groups consider district-level characteristics (percent unionized, per capita income, for example) when seeking access to members representing relevant constituencies (Davis 1992, Wright 1985). For example, labor surely wants access to legislators who represent constituencies with a high number of union workers.

On the other hand, we know that a member's party, ideology, and electoral vulnerability often predict the receipt of hard money contributions (Endersby and Munger 1992, Evans 1988, Herndon 1982, Malbin 1980, Nelson 1998). We often assume to that effect that interest groups contribute to competitive candidates because the marginal impact of those dollars on the electoral outcome is greatest. Replacement-inspired contributions only make sense in such races.

One should be cautious, however, in dichotomizing access and replacement. Evans (1988, p. 1050) makes this point: "Just as ideological, electoral change-oriented PACs are likely to target close races, seeking to protect ideologically compatible and defeat incompatible members, pragmatic, access-oriented PACs might believe that the more the members need the contributions, the more likely they are to respond gratefully later on. Thus, both types of PACs may contribute in close races and marginality may not differentiate between them."

Therefore, it might be better to understand groups as on a tactical continuum, from favoring pure access to pure replacement, in contrast to treating each contribution decision as the dependent variable. When we look at electoral activity at the interest group level, we should see that groups tending toward access will, on balance, contribute more to safe seat incumbents, to members on important committees, and to legislative friends and ideological allies. In contrast, groups tending toward replacement will, on balance, contribute more to competitive candidates or to candidates in open seats.

This conceptualization does not preclude interest groups from engaging in both access and replacement politics, however, or from making candidate-to-candidate assessments and supporting friends and allies for even idiosyncratic reasons—what Gopoian (1984) refers to as "parochial issue concerns." As groups tend to favor one goal over the other, however, we should see disparities in spending at the aggregate group level, and as that preference changes, so too should the pattern of spending.

What drives a group to favor access over replacement, however? Or vice versa? The standard approach is to examine differences across group types. Labor groups and nonconnected PACs are considered more ideological and therefore more likely to invest in open seats, competitive races, and so forth. Corporations are seen as more pragmatic and therefore more likely to give to both parties in hopes of gaining access.

This approach may be too static, however. What about labor makes them more ideological, and what makes corporations more pragmatic? Are these orientations always true? Further still, are there not important differences within group types (i.e., not all labor unions have the same viewpoints)? Indeed, one of the most undeveloped questions in the literature on interest groups electoral politics concerns the origin of these goals.

One answer is to assume that groups have different viewpoints on the persuadability of candidates. More specifically, replacement groups view legislator preferences as fixed (hence the need to elect new ones), while access groups do not (Apollonio and La Raja 2004). But this argument also suffers; what drives an interest group to make this very different judgment about policymakers?

Alternatively, I assert that all interest groups have some orientation to both the *ideological* and *partisan* make-up of Congress. On balance, while corporations may be more conservative and favor the Republican Party, and labor may be more liberal and pro-Democratic, it is certainly possible for some corporations to be more liberal than some conservative unions, and for unions and corporations to vary their participation on the basis of who is in power and the likelihood that one party or ideology will retain or gain control of the policymaking environment. As ideological and partisan conditions change, then so too should the group's evaluation of how to participate in elections.

The idea that larger contextual factors drive the political participation of interest groups is not new. Indeed, one consistent story of American political development is the manner in which organized interests have historically responded to dominant power dynamics, both by conforming to the manner in which policy is created at the time or by moving beyond (and challenging) constraining institutional relationships (i.e., strong parties; Archer 1998, Coleman 1996, Harvey 1996, Parker and Coleman 2004). For example, both Clemens (1997) and Hansen (1991) investigate the relationship between interest groups and parties in the early and mid-20th century.

Do interest groups only react to existing political contexts, however? Do not groups play some independent role in shaping this context? For example, when we note that politics in America is more polarized in recent years and that interest groups respond to that characteristic, are we precluding the likelihood that interest groups had some role in bringing to life such polarization? Indeed, we should not deny this possibility; prior behavior may make the current political context for interest groups more favorable (or even ideal). Because each new election is in a sense an independent game, however, interest groups must defend that context or work harder to change it. In other words, as a new election season dawns, interest groups respond to the current conditions—regardless of previous behavior.[4]

NOTES

1 Wright (1985) distinguishes them as type I and type II strategies. See also Jacobson and Kernell (1983). I could also add the goal of issue salience. Certainly, the goal of some electoral behavior (issue advocacy campaigns, for example) might be to put issues or policy proposals on the agenda. I'm less interested in this goal, in that it is more easily classified as a lobbying tactic and not one necessarily directed at one candidate (Kollman 1998). Indeed, most evidence indicates that if an advertisement mentions or pictures a politician, it is usually interpreted by viewers as designed to affect election outcomes.

2 There is no consensus, however, on whether access strategies are successful. There is an extensive literature on the relationship between roll call votes and PAC contributions, with some finding effects and others finding null results. Smith (1995) reviews this literature and argues that contributions are likely to affect roll calls under certain circumstances; when the issue is not salient with the national electorate, for example. See Baumgartner and Leech (1998) for a critique of the literature. Alternatively, there has been more empirical success in showing that contributions affect levels of member of Congress participation (Hall and Wayman 1990) and committee voting (Wright 1990). I am not concerned in this research with testing the effectiveness of tactical choices.

3 To be sure, this second goal of elections can be pursued in a variety of ways, but it is harder and less likely to succeed. Election outcomes are no easy thing to affect (Goldstein and Freedman 2000, Green and Krasno 1988, Jacob-son 2004), and interest groups have scarce resources.

4 Sorauf (1975, pp. 22–23) asks a similar question for political parties: should we understand them as independent or dependent variables in party systems? He argues the latter: "Probably the most nearly precise way to summarize the relationship between political parties and the course of political development in general during the last hundred years and more is to say that the role of parties and party systems has changed to one of adaptation and adjustment rather than one of innovation."

Interest Group Tactics

To understand the success of interest groups, we must examine the way they capitalize on their roles and membership. As we have discussed, interest groups are only as powerful as their support makes them. Being able to obtain and grow that support is only part of the equation. Determining the proper course of action that will achieve policy and election benefits is something that all interest groups, regardless of classification or type, must go through.

Developing tactics that achieve the group's motives and goals requires detailed planning and execution. What follows is an examination of insider and outsider tactics. Insider tactics are those that have a direct impact: the tactic is delivered directly to the person or entity that is being addressed. Outsider tactics are those that take place outside that relationship and are meant to have a residual effect without a direct connection. Insider tactics are more effective, but outsider tactics are more common because most groups lack connections and access to decision makers.

Reading 13.3

Selection from "Interests and Interest Groups"[3]
from *Interest Groups and Lobbying: Pursuing Political Interests in America*
Thomas Holyoke

Reading Introduction: Insider Tactics—the Art of Lobbying

Insider tactics are predicated on cultivating relationships. These tactics involve face-to-face or intimate interactions that build a dynamic between the interest group and the person or population being addressed. Traditional way to do this involve lobbying (which is discussed in the text), but these tactics can include any activity that develops a bond between the two sides.

Lobbying is the activity most commonly associated with insider tactics. A seemingly seedy perception accompanies the term, but under the most technical definition, it is characterized by arguing a point of view and trying to convince someone to agree with it. As Thomas Holyoke suggests, lobbying is a skill that feeds into the most basic definition of insider tactic. The ability to build a relationship through trust or the favor system is an integral tool used by interest groups—one that can be expanded upon and exploited when needed.

DEFINING INTERESTS AND INTEREST GROUPS

It is easy to identify members of Congress because the process of becoming one is clearly laid out in the Constitution. Regulatory agencies are also pretty easy to distinguish from other organizations because they are created by acts of Congress. Even political parties can be identified without too much trouble. Interest groups, though, are harder. In fact, scholars cannot even agree on what to call them. Is an

---

3   Thomas Holyoke, "Selection from 'Interests and Interest Groups'," *Interest Groups and Lobbying: Pursuing Political Interests in America*, pp. 10-13, 33. Copyright © 2014 by Taylor & Francis Group. Reprinted with permission.

"interest group" the same as an "organized interest," "social movement organization," "special interest group," "private interest," "pressure group," "lobby," "nongovernmental organization," or "political organization"? Perhaps it would be easier to start by thinking about why some entities are not interest groups. Presidents and executive branch officials often pressure Congress to pass (or to not pass) legislation, and members of Congress try to pressure them in return, and they all try to influence the decisions of Supreme Court justices. These policy makers lobby in that they try to persuade each other to enact policies they desire, but they are not working for interest groups. They serve in institutions created by public law to formally make policies benefitting all citizens within their jurisdictions. They wield powers that flow directly or indirectly from the nation's most fundamental law, the Constitution. So while government officials and lawmakers lobby each other, no government institution is an interest group. Apologies to the Metropolitan Water District.

Political parties are not interest groups either. Apologies to Democrats, Republicans, and all of America's small third parties. Parties gain political power by trying to get enough of their members elected to office to command a majority and thus directly control lawmaking institutions. To do that, they need the support of a majority of voting citizens, which means trying to represent many different groups of people at once, often bitterly realizing that trying to represent everyone usually results in failing to represent anyone well. When we talk about an **interest group**, we refer to a singular **interest**. Each group represents one need or desire, or at most a few very closely related needs or desires, held by only a small number of people. Consequently, most interest groups cannot gain formal political power by electing their members to public office. They represent too few people. Whatever influence interest groups have in government, it is *informal* rather than formal.

Corporations are not interest groups either. They exist first and foremost to make a profit in the marketplace and return that profit to their shareholders, not lobby for government largesse and favorable policy. Nor do they represent any definable group of people with a common interest. Their shareholders might be considered constituents, but most of them are involved with the company to make money, not influence policy. Corporations often do wade into the political arena, usually because a change in policy (or lack of policy change) will have a direct impact on their financial bottom lines. Moreover, some corporate executives have tried to claim they actually represent the interests of their employees and customers, sometimes even persuading them to contact lawmakers on the company's behalf, as Allstate Insurance did with its forty-five thousand employees in the 2011 fight over whether to raise the nation's debt ceiling (Dash and Schwartz 2011) and as Caterpillar did when the fight happened again in 2013 (Yang and Hamburger 2013). CEOs, however, are not accountable to their employees and customers and thus cannot be said to represent them in the political process. The same is true of universities, hospitals, and similar nonprofit organizations. They are not interest groups. Apologies to Citibank and the

United Way. Corporations and nonprofits do collectively employ more lobbyists in Washington, DC, than true interest groups (Salisbury 1984), but they tend to only lobby sporadically (Brasher and Lowery 2006). Real interest groups represent some portion of the public, not just their own leaders and CEOs.

Interest groups, then, are private organizations, not formal parts of the government. This is why they are sometimes called nongovernmental organizations. They primarily exist to provide informal political representation to citizens, usually by persuading lawmakers that it would be valuable to enact policies that help these citizens pursue strongly felt interests. A person's interest is fundamental to their character and is often grounded in economic need, aspects of personal identity (e.g., profession, ethnicity, sexual orientation), perceptions of fairness and justice, desires to acquire or achieve, and even metaphysical beliefs and values including religion. More broadly, interests define a person's perception of who they are and what they believe so strongly, so intensely, that its absence would change that person's identity. They would be a different person without that interest. Interest groups are thus formal aggregations of people sharing the same interest.

American society is extremely diverse, and so the number of different interests that are felt intensely enough to motivate people to form an interest group is probably unknowable. Not every individual interest leads to a mobilized interest group, often only because there are not enough other people who share the same interest to form a group, or because people with similar interests are too geographically dispersed (though today this is not the barrier it used to be). Those who do find enough soul mates who share their interest, who believe the interest should be embedded in the nation's laws (and thus also apply to everyone else), and who are willing to dedicate enough time and money might then form an interest group. This is the beginning of a workable definition of "interest group," but further development requires exploring the concept of self-interest.

A CULTURE OF SELF-INTEREST

Interest groups only exist to represent their members' self-interests. People join or otherwise support an interest group because they want it to advocate for policies that make it easier for them to pursue their personal interests, even though public policy is supposed to treat everyone equally. While some interest groups do claim to advocate for the *public* interest or *common* good rather than just the good of their members, that is still simply their point of view. Ask coal miners and users of energy from coal-fired plants in West Virginia whether the common interest is served when environmental laws force their mines to shut down, putting them out of work. Ask Louisiana's shrimping industry if it is well served by offshore oil drilling that is supposed to make the United States energy independent even though oil spills kill marine life. Coal miners and shrimpers benefit from cleaner air and cheaper oil but are hurt by lack of income. Policy that serves one person's idea of what ought to be true for everyone benefits only that person's self-interest, often at the expense of somebody else's self-interest.

Simply put, we create interest groups to help us further our personal interests through the nation's lawmaking process. This should not be surprising. Our political and economic systems are based on the fundamental belief that everyone has a right to pursue his or her own self-interest, and that no one's interest is more or less legitimate than anybody else's. We expect our government to protect this right to pursue our self-interest, and we often look to public officials to help us out by enacting policy prioritizing our self-interest, even when it is harmful to a majority of other citizens. We may talk about the virtues of compromise and the public interest, but then we denounce our leaders as incompetent or corrupt when new policy in any way threatens our self-interest. Compromises are only "obvious" and "sensible" when they give us what we want. In other words, we recognize no public interest in our political system, only many individual interests that sometimes aggregate into interest groups. Could it be any other way?

Outsider Tactics: Gaining Attention through Mobilization

While lobbying and election results are the best way to measure success and activity for interest groups, those with smaller budgets—and even some with big budgets—create success in other areas. Connecting with a decision maker is the quickest route to results, but changing information and perception can be helpful. To do that, outsider tactics, or tactics that do not involve directly interacting with decision makers, can create a path to success.

Outsider tactics vary depending on the needs of an organization, but they are designed to leverage public opinion through appeals, normally without money. While direct impacts associated with lobbying are not as common, affecting the agenda and impacting issue saliency or recognition are key areas in which interest groups can be effective.

Mobilization movements are at the top of the list of outsider tactics. The ability to galvanize support for participation is Interest Group Activity 101 for most organizations. To make mobilization movements work, groups will rely on or rally around an event.

Focusing events serve as important opportunities for politically disadvantaged groups to champion messages that had been effectively suppressed by dominant groups and advocacy coalitions. Such events can therefore be an important tool for groups seeking policy change.... Focusing events gain attention more suddenly and rapidly than problems such as crime or disease that longer-term analysis of statistical evidence seeks to understand (Birkland 1998, 54).

These events are important for galvanizing support. While it may seem sadistic or shameful to capitalize on these events, they provide what many movements need: provocation. Focusing, or rallying, events can range in type. Many are associated with tragedy (hence, the sadistic nature of some tactics) or with something that resonates with the public.

One example of a focusing event is the terrorist attacks on September 11, 2001, after which charity and policy capitalization increased. Attention and willingness to restore security was at an all-time high, and groups from the Red Cross to those in the White House and Congress took advantage by mobilizing support to raise both relief and operational funds as well as to pass bills.

A less traumatic focusing event happened in the 2008 presidential election. A race between an African American male, Barack Obama, and a woman, Hilary Clinton, sparked increased attention and willingness to participate. When the Texas Democratic caucus (the now defunct two-step process outlined in Chapter 11) took place, the evening caucus was busting at the seams with young Texas Democrats and participants looking to take part in a historic election. Focusing events and the mobilization movements they spur can create political collateral in the form of membership and activity if they are leveraged properly.

Mobilization efforts are intended to expand the relevance of an issue. Bringing the issues into focus or expanding their scope to appeal to a wider audience can be useful and serve as an indicator of success. That success is important for interest groups because their relevance and longevity is closely tied to showing they can be effective in the political and policy land-scape. "Group efforts to expand issues are important because they increase the likelihood of more influential and powerful actors entering the conflict on the side of policy change (Schattschneider 1960/1975). This increased attention can further tilt the balance of debate in favor of pro-change groups" (Birkland 1998, 57).

Summary

Should Texas citizens fear the role of interest groups in the state's politics? Coming out of this literature, that is a question that must be considered when discussing these groups. Regardless of the type of group or their tactics, interest groups are the manifestation of a need that the public wants addressed. The abilities of advocacy groups, the necessity for their creation, and their role in the process is not only allowed for in the state governing documents; it has become a staple in the way that the state's political system works.

The optimistic view of these groups is that they provide information and an outlet for individuals and even coordinated industries to take part in the government. The most genuine among us believe that interest groups exist to serve the interests of the public. Their ability to increase the size of an individual voice or provide information is needed in the current political landscape. The line between interest groups being advocates for the community and those with anti-communal agendas, for some in Texas, is growing blurry. There has been a noticeable increase in the amount of money being poured into the political arena from these groups. While social interest groups that serve civil, minority, or social rights attempt to regain the public's trust, the increased dependency on these groups and the state's political leaders openness to them have created a system that is ripe for being taken over by those with considerable financial backing, with little or no influence from the public itself. In Texas, interest groups—an arena long seen as a source of civic participation—have morphed into an activist culture dominated by money (specifically, the lobbies and PACs that have it). Groups with powerful business, economic, or political ties have, in growing instances, captured the system by using that influence to swing the balance of power from a public to private focus. That backing, along with an individualistic–traditionalistic political culture, can create a system that gains a perception as being corrupt.

While it is easy to view political activity by interest groups as being much less social and much more pluralistic today, do not lose sight of the groundings of the activity. While big-money groups exist, social interest groups are alive in Texas. When lobbying and election contributions dominate headlines, public outsider tactics are still being used, especially with the advent of social media and technology, which have made these activities and gaining support for them a realistic goal that was not available to social groups as little as fifteen years ago.

While there are reform calls to limit campaign and financial contributions and to empower an ethics commission, interest/advocacy group activity is pervasive in the state today.

References

Andrews, K. T., and B. Edwards. "Advocacy Organizations in the US Political Process." *Annual Review of Sociology* 30, (2004): 479–506.

Berry, J. "On the Origins of Public Interest Groups: A Test of Two Theories." *Polity* 10, no. 3 (1978): 379–397.

Birkland, T. A. "Focusing Events, Mobilization, and Agenda Setting." *Journal of Public Policy* 18, no. 1 (1998): 53–74.

DeLeon, P. "Democratic Values and the Policy Sciences." *American Journal of Political Science* 39, no. 4(1995): 886–905.

DeLeon, P., and K. Kaufmanis. "Public Policy Theory: Will it Play in Peoria?" *Policy Currents* 10, no. 4 (2001): 90–104.

Doan, A., and D. B. Wood. "The Politics of Problem Definition: Applying and Testing Threshold Models." *American Journal of Political Science* 47, no. 4 (2003): 640–653.

Embry, J. "The Most Powerful Group in Texas Politics Has Wentworth in Its Sights." *Austin American-Statesman*, December 7, 2011.

Forsythe, D., and S. Welch. "Joining and Supporting Public Interest Groups: A Note on Some Empirical Findings." *Western Political Quarterly* 36, no. 3 (1983): 386–399.

Grieder, Erica. "The Private Sector's Influence on the Public's Interests of Texas." *Texas Monthly*, January 14, 2013.

Gray, V., and D. Lowery. "Interest Representation and Democratic Gridlock." *Legislative Studies Quarterly* 20, no. 4 (1995): 531–552.

Herrington, B. J. *Players in the Public Policy Process: Nonprofits as Social Capital and Agents*. New York, NY: Palgrave Macmillen, 2005.

Kriesi, H. "The Political Opportunity Structure of Social Movements: Its Impact on Their Mobilization." In Jenkins, J., and B. Klandermans. *The Politics of Social Protest: Comparative Perspectives on States and Social Movements*, 167–172. Minneapolis, MN: University of Minnesota Press, 1995.

Marsh, D. "On Joining Interest Groups: An Empirical Consideration of the Work of Mancur Olson Jr." *British Journal of Political Science* 6, no. 3 (1976): 257–271.

Meyer, D.S. *Social Movements and Public Policy: Eggs, Chicken, and Theory*. Center for the Study of Democracy, 2003. www.democ.uci.edu.

Moe, T. M. "A Calculus of Group Membership." *American Journal of Political Science* 24 no. 4 (1980): 593–632.

Naoi, M., and E. Krauss. "Who Lobbies Whom? Special Interest Politics under Alternative Electoral Systems." *American Journal of Political Science* 53, no. 4 (2009): 874–892.

Nownes, A. J., and G. Neeley. (1996). "Public Interest Group Entrepreneurship and Theories of Group Mobilization." *Political Research Quarterly* 49, no. 1 (1996): 119–146.

Public Integrity Group. *Texas: Legislative Financial Disclosure Ranking*. 2011. https://www.publicintegrity.org/2009/06/25/9058/texas-legislative-financial-disclosure-ranking.

Ramshaw, Emily. "A Part-time Legislature, but in Whose Interest?" *The Texas Tribune*, January 13, 2013.

Salisbury, R. H. "An Exchange Theory of Interest Groups." *Midwest Journal of Political Science* 13, no. 1 (1969): 1–32.

CPSIA information can be obtained
at www.ICGtesting.com
Printed in the USA
LVHW062032141118
597140LV00002B/4/P